*Studies in Modern History*

General Editor: **J. C. D. Clark**, Joyce and Elizabeth H
British History, University of Kansas

*Titles include:*

Marc Baer
THE RISE AND FALL OF RADICAL WESTMINSTER, 1780–1890

James B. Bell
EMPIRE, RELIGION AND REVOLUTION IN EARLY VIRGINIA, 1607–1786

James B. Bell
A WAR ON RELIGION
Dissenters, Anglicans and the American Revolution

James B. Bell
The Imperial Origins of the King's Church in Early America
1607–1783

Joe Bord
SCIENCE AND WHIG MANNERS
Science and Political Style in Britain, c.1790–1850

Jonathan Clark and Howard Erskine-Hill (*editors*)
SAMUEL JOHNSON IN HISTORICAL CONTEXT

Jonathan Clark and Howard Erskine-Hill (*editors*)
THE INTERPRETATION OF SAMUEL JOHNSON

Jonathan Clark and Howard Erskine-Hill (*editors*)
THE POLITICS OF SAMUEL JOHNSON

Edward Corp
THE JACOBITES AT URBINO
An Exiled Court in Transition

Eveline Cruickshanks and Howard Erskine-Hill
The Atterbury Plot

Diana Donald and Frank O'Gorman (*editors*)
ordering the world in the eighteenth century

Richard D.Floyd
CHURCH, CHAPEL AND PARTY
Religious Dissent and Political Modernization in Nineteenth-Century England

Richard R. Follett
EVANGELICALISM, PENAL THEORY AND THE POLITICS OF CRIMINAL LAW REFORM
IN ENGLAND, 1808–30

Andrew Godley
JEWISH IMMIGRANT ENTREPRENEURSHIP IN NEW YORK AND LONDON 1880–1914

William Anthony Hay
The Whig Revival 1808–1830

Mark Keay
WILLIAM WORDSWORTH'S GOLDEN AGE THEORIES DURING THE
INDUSTRIAL REVOLUTION IN ENGLAND, 1750–1850

Kim Lawes
PATERNALISM AND POLITICS
The Revival of Paternalism in Early Nineteenth-Century Britain

Marisa Linton
THE POLITICS OF VIRTUE IN ENLIGHTENMENT FRANCE

Karin J. MacHardy
WAR, RELIGION AND COURT PATRONAGE IN HABSBURG AUSTRIA
The Social and Cultural Dimensions of Political Interaction, 1521–1622

James Mackintosh
VINDICIÆ GALLICÆ
Defence of the French Revolution: A Critical Edition

Robert J. Mayhew
LANDSCAPE, LITERATURE AND ENGLISH RELIGIOUS CULTURE, 1660–1800
Samuel Johnson and Languages of Natural Description

Jeremy C. Mitchell
THE ORGANIZATION OF OPINION
Open Voting in England, 1832–68

Paul Monod, Murray Pittock and Daniel Szechi (*editors*)
LOYALTY AND IDENTITY
Jacobites at Home and Abroad

Marjorie Morgan
NATIONAL IDENTITIES AND TRAVEL IN VICTORIAN BRITAIN

James Muldoon
EMPIRE AND ORDER
The Concept of Empire, 800–1800

F. D. Parsons
THOMAS HARE AND POLITICAL REPRESENTATION IN VICTORIAN BRITAIN

Julia Rudolph
WHIG POLITICAL THOUGHT AND THE GLORIOUS REVOLUTION
James Tyrrell and the Theory of Resistance

Lisa Steffen
TREASON AND NATIONAL IDENTITY
Defining a British State, 1608–1820

Lynne Taylor
BETWEEN RESISTANCE AND COLLABORATION
Popular Protest in Northern France, 1940–45

Joseph Tendler
OPPONENTS OF THE ANNALES SCHOOL

Anthony Waterman
POLITICAL ECONOMY AND CHRISTIAN THEOLOGY SINCE THE ENLIGHTENMENT
Essays in Intellectual History

Doron Zimmerman
THE JACOBITE MOVEMENT IN SCOTLAND AND IN EXILE, 1746–1759

Stephen Burley
HAZLITT THE DISSENTER
Religion, Philosophy, and Politics, 1766–1816

---

**Studies in Modern History**
**Series Standing Order ISBN 978–0–333–79328–2 (Hardback) 978–0–333–80346–2 (Paperback)**
(*outside North America only*)

You can receive future titles in this series as they are published by placing a standing order. Please contact your bookseller or, in case of difficulty, write to us at the address below with your name and address, the title of the series and the ISBN quoted above.

Customer Services Department, Macmillan Distribution Ltd, Houndmills, Basingstoke, Hampshire RG21 6XS, England

# Law and Government in England during the Long Eighteenth Century

## From Consent to Command

David Lemmings
*Head of the School of History and Politics, University of Adelaide*

© David Lemmings 2011, 2015

All rights reserved. No reproduction, copy or transmission of this publication may be made without written permission.

No portion of this publication may be reproduced, copied or transmitted save with written permission or in accordance with the provisions of the Copyright, Designs and Patents Act 1988, or under the terms of any licence permitting limited copying issued by the Copyright Licensing Agency, Saffron House, 6–10 Kirby Street, London EC1N 8TS.

Any person who does any unauthorized act in relation to this publication may be liable to criminal prosecution and civil claims for damages.

The author has asserted his right to be identified as the author of this work in accordance with the Copyright, Designs and Patents Act 1988.

First published 2011 by
Published in paperback 2015 by
PALGRAVE MACMILLAN

Palgrave Macmillan in the UK is an imprint of Macmillan Publishers Limited, registered in England, company number 785998, of Houndmills, Basingstoke, Hampshire RG21 6XS.

Palgrave Macmillan in the US is a division of St Martin's Press LLC, 175 Fifth Avenue, New York, NY 10010.

Palgrave Macmillan is the global academic imprint of the above companies and has companies and representatives throughout the world.

Palgrave® and Macmillan® are registered trademarks in the United States, the United Kingdom, Europe and other countries.

ISBN-13: 978-1-137-50695-5   paperback
ISBN-13: 978-0-230-29301-4   hardback

A catalogue record for this book is available from the British Library.

A catalogue record for this book is available from the Library of Congress.

# Contents

| | | |
|---|---|---|
| *List of Tables* | | vii |
| *Preface and Acknowledgements* | | viii |
| *Note on Works Cited in Endnotes* | | x |

| 1 | **Introduction: Law, Consent and Command** | 1 |
|---|---|---|
| | English society and the rule of law: 'Legitimate expectations' | 3 |
| | An imperial state at law? Legislation and the common law | 7 |
| | An age of enlightenment? Politeness, professionalism and the imperatives of eighteenth-century government | 11 |

| 2 | **The Local Experience of Law and Authority: Quarter Sessions, JPs and the People** | 17 |
|---|---|---|
| | JPs and quarter sessions before 1680: Medieval ideas and seventeenth-century practice | 19 |
| | Eighteenth-century justice work | 26 |
| | Local administration: Statutory authority and oligarchy | 41 |

| 3 | **Going to Law: The Rise and Fall of Civil Litigation** | 56 |
|---|---|---|
| | Patterns of litigation | 57 |
| | Motives and meanings: The experience of litigation | 64 |
| | The law world we have lost: Complaints, explanations and consequences | 72 |

| 4 | **Crime and the Administration of Criminal Law: Problems, Solutions and Participation** | 81 |
|---|---|---|
| | Crime as a 'social problem': Public opinion and the degeneracy of the common people | 83 |
| | Punishment solutions: Middle-class consciousness, the bloody code and the penitentiary | 94 |
| | Policing and prosecution solutions: Professional law enforcement | 106 |

| 5 | **Parliament, Legislation and the People: The Idea and Experience of Leviathan** | 126 |
|---|---|---|
| | The politics of legislation: Parliament, sovereignty and the law | 128 |
| | 14,000 acts: The substance of legislation | 142 |
| | Making legislation: Representation, procedure and participation | 159 |

| 6 | Conclusion: An Imperial State? Governance, People and Law in the Eighteenth Century | 172 |
|---|---|---|
| | Summary: From consent to command | 173 |
| | The new 'empire of laws'? Law, state and society in an age of empire and opinion | 180 |

| *Notes* | 186 |
|---|---|
| *Appendix: List of Statutes Cited* | 235 |
| *Bibliography* | 239 |
| *Index* | 261 |

# List of Tables

2.1 Indictments, Presentments and Recognizances, Cheshire Quarter Sessions, 1678–1818    29

2.2 Administrative Business, Cheshire Quarter Sessions, 1678–1818    42

# Preface and Acknowledgements

This book was conceived after I had finished an earlier study of English lawyers and legal culture in the eighteenth century, and originated in my desire to write a more general book which discussed the common law tradition and its contribution to modern governance. It builds upon an essay that I wrote for *The Oxford Companion to the Romantic Age: British Culture 1776–1832* (1999), edited by Iain McCalman, and I am very grateful to Iain for providing me with the opportunity to think broadly about law and government. Serious research began in 2000 when I was awarded a Large Grant from the Australian Research Council for a project entitled 'An Imperial State at Law: the English and the Rule of Law, 1689–1832'. I hereby acknowledge the significant impetus that funding provided for my work, and apologize for the length of time it has taken to produce the principal outcome. My main excuse is my commitment to other research projects and books, which have been completed in the meantime.

The book has been so long in the pipeline that it is not possible to remember and properly acknowledge everyone who has contributed to it. However, I would like to thank all of my old colleagues at the University of Newcastle in New South Wales, where I was based until 2006, and my new colleagues at the University of Adelaide: both institutions have provided valuable research infrastructure support – especially library services – and indispensable human companionship and kindness. I would also like to thank the Lewis Walpole Library (Yale University), the Humanities Research Centre (Australian National University) and All Souls College, Oxford, all of whom elected me to visiting fellowships during the lifetime of the project: they all provided superb research materials and congenial settings for reflection and writing. In addition I am very grateful to the staffs of the British Library in London, the Bodleian Library in Oxford, the Cambridge University Library, and numerous local record offices for their courtesy and professionalism on my many research visits to the UK.

I have incurred many personal debts in the course of researching and writing this book. Over a long period of time, John Baker, Paul Brand, Joanna Innes, and Randy McGowen have provided invaluable criticism, support and encouragement. Chris Brooks and Alison Wall have kindly read parts of the text, and Wilf Prest has read and commented on the whole in draft. I much appreciate their patience and advice, a generous investment which has signally improved the final product. Indeed Wilf's own example as scholar and mentor has been an inspiration over the years. In addition, Jonathan

Clark has been a most patient editor. However my greatest debts are to my children Tom and Charlotte, who have both lived with this project for all their lives, and to my wife Claire, who has sustained me with encouragement beyond the call of duty when my enthusiasm waned. I thank you all most warmly.

# Note on Works Cited in Endnotes

All works cited were published in London, unless specified otherwise

# 1
# Introduction: Law, Consent and Command

> ... a man's first profession is to be a *good man*, in which he is miserably defective, if he be not a good citizen. ... *Statesmen* have no more claim to shut the general knowledge of *politics* from the people, than *priests* have of *religion*.
>
> Capel Lofft, *An Argument on the Nature of Party and Faction. In which is considered, the Duty of a Good and Peaceable Citizen at the Present Crisis* (1780), 6–7 (orig. emphasis).

> In his mind the law was no closed shop for lawyers. He held that the quality of the law depended not only upon the extent to which ordinary men and women participated in its administration as magistrates and jurors but also upon the existence of a public opinion sufficiently concerned to ensure a continuous review of the law in action. Here he saw a vital role not only for Parliament, the press, and the broadcasters, but [also] for members of the public.
>
> Lord Scarman, appreciation of Lord Devlin, *Guardian Weekly*, 23 Aug., 1992.

> Whenever Parliament is persuaded to assume the offices of executive Government, it will lose all the confidence, love, and veneration, which it has ever enjoyed whilst it was the *corrective and controul* of the acting powers of the State.
>
> Edmund Burke, *Thoughts on the Present Discontents* (1770), in P. Langford (ed.), *The Writings and Speeches of Edmund Burke* (Oxford, 1981), 294.

The experience of law and government shifted in the course of the eighteenth century with large adjustments to the legal instruments and processes of power. There were significant modifications in the structures and procedures of local authorities; a major decline in the reach of civil litigation; important developments in policing, the administration of justice and punishment; and generally, a massive increase in legislation, including many acts that overturned customary rights and cultures of government associated with common law proceedings. This book seeks to document and analyse these shifts, which amounted in the aggregate to a major change in the legal order, with an eye to how much 'ordinary people' participated in the processes of decision-making and consented to government. Its primary subject is the transforming relations between legal authority and the English people.

In the English context participation is important because medieval and early modern government traditionally involved many people as direct participants. As constables, jurors, witnesses, and litigants, or just as mere spectators in courts, they were active in the judicial institutions and processes typical of the common law. And the common law was the most visible agency of the royal administration. The Lord Chancellor was hardly exaggerating when he said (in 1747) 'I look upon the administration of justice, as the principal and essential part of all government. The people know and judge of it by little else'.[1] In a very literal sense, therefore, the distinctive feature of English government before 1750 was the rule of law.

It is important to understand that in this conception law was valued as much more than a popular check upon royal power and authority. Certainly direct experience of judicial processes, together with recent history about the constitutional struggles of the seventeenth century, helped to inform conservative ideas about law as the primary safeguard of individual liberty and property against arbitrary and oppressive government. However law also appeared in the form of a complex quasi-republican discourse. The longstanding elements of popular participation in the administration of justice were celebrated as the surviving guarantees of English freedom, in a positive, neo-classical sense. The jury, above all, represented 'the Original Majesty of the People of England': in modern parlance, when they served in that capacity individual Englishmen were citizens as well as subjects, because they shared in the decisions of government.[2] According to a succession of magistrates and judges who intoned messages like these at the opening of the local sessions or county assizes, sanctified as it was by time and struggle, the rule of law represented the basic historical principle of the constitution: that the community freely consented to major acts of power over life and possessions.[3]

After 1649 and 1689, when the prestige of church and king were weakened by revolution, regicide and religious dissent, ideas associated with the traditions of the common law were arguably the most important ideals which served to legitimate government by the elite of property owners.[4] It is therefore appropriate to begin this study of government in the long eighteenth century by inquiring more closely into the conditions of law at its beginning.

## English society and the rule of law: 'Legitimate expectations'

In recent years research on the governance of eighteenth-century Britain has moved away from previous preoccupations with parliamentary politics and refocused on the social contexts of power, national identity, and the state (especially in relation to warfare and empire). Given such a shift, legal-historical studies have naturally attracted considerable scholarly attention. There has been a great deal of excellent work on the history of crime, policing and punishment, a substantial body of published research on civil litigation and the legal professions, and several important studies of the eighteenth-century deluge of parliamentary legislation, some of which consider the connected issue of relations between the state and the localities.[5] But although most recent general surveys acknowledge the importance of 'the rule of law', especially for English (and colonial American) political identities, there has been little sustained discussion of *expectations* about law as expressed by contemporaries. By contrast the question I want to examine now is: what did people expect of law, on the basis of their previous experience and the promises made by their betters?[6]

The relative lack of scholarly attention to normal expectations of law is surprising because the English were remarkably law-minded, and said to be very sensitive to what they perceived as illegality, especially in government. The Suffolk magistrate Edmund Bohun, writing in the 1690s, observed:

> they must be *Governed Well*, that is, with Prudence, and Justice, as well as with Severity; for it may be there is no Nation under Heaven so impatient of *Injury*, and *Wrong*, as the *English*, and whatsoever is not precisely according to Law, they will esteem such, and when occasion serve, revenge it.[7]

The existence of widespread touchiness about rights under law would not be surprising, since Englishmen idealized their forms of government as a unique blessing which was denied to less fortunate peoples. As another magistrate put it pithily, English laws 'are the Best Framed, the Best Compacted Body of Laws now extant in the World'.[8] In what did their excellence consist? Certainly at a minimum English people were encouraged to believe their 'birthright' was to live in a society governed according to known laws: settled rules conferring liberty and protection of property, which could not be abrogated at the mere whim of kings or ministers. And in theory, the rules applied to everyone equally, in so far as they did not formally distinguish among individuals. Like most elements of the contemporary conception of law, this latter ideal was most clearly expressed in relation to the administration of justice: 'Justice is painted blind; a good Emblem to shew us, that in Judgment we are neither to pity the Poor, nor favour the Rich'.[9] Of course ideas of law and justice like these have resonated down the centuries. In the general sense of being intelligible, power-constraining and quasi-egalitarian the rule of law remains a major feature of modern Western ideals of government as one of the central ideologies (along with democracy) which legitimates authority; more particularly (and parochially) it is often regarded as an important inheritance of British constitutional history.[10] But these ideas about law had more concrete and affirmative meanings for Englishmen living in the early eighteenth century.

There are two good reasons for saying this. First, as suggested previously, there was the immediate historical context of seventeenth-century legal-constitutional disputes and their resolution in 1689. Not everyone accepted the displacement of James II, but for the politicians and propagandists tasked with defending the change of regime, the king's attempted manipulations of the law were given equal prominence with the threat of popery as legitimate justifications for revolution. They clearly believed that this was a popular tack:

> For as it is most evident that the Lives and Liberties of the *English* People are secur'd by Law; so there is Nothing so grievous to an *English* Commoner, as the breach of that Law.[11]

In longer historical perspective the 'Glorious Revolution' of 1688 was celebrated as the signal for the ultimate victory of law and liberty over abusive government by royal prerogative, with the antidote being the limiting provisions of the Bill of Rights and subsequent legislative advances. This story developed strongly after the accession of the Hanoverians in 1714, and became the prototype for the whiggish constitutional history expressed by Macaulay and Trevelyan, which lauds the progress of parliamentary government.[12] Its wide currency has had a slightly distorting effect, however. For parliament's self-conscious role was in a conservative tradition. Before the Revolution Members of Parliament did not explicitly regard themselves as constituting a positive element of government; and parliament's pretensions to power were normally represented as declarations of ancient fundamental law.[13] Certainly in 1688–9 parliament had made good its claim to an indispensable share in creating and abrogating law, and as we shall see, in the course of the eighteenth century most propertied people became accustomed to the absolute sovereignty of a legislating parliament.[14] Indeed the 'transcendent' power of parliamentary statutes had been acknowledged by lawyers and antiquarians from medieval times, most memorably in the words of Sir Edward Coke, while Tudor parliaments were famously ambitious and industrious in their legislative capacity.[15] But in the seventeenth century parliamentary sessions were relatively irregular, and did not produce a mass of particular laws, despite their central role in the constitutional struggle. Acts of parliament hardly constituted the regular business of government at the grass roots of society. To most contemporaries the triumph of law would have meant assuring the supremacy of common law, rather than parliamentary governance.[16]

The second reason for insisting on a vernacular meaning of the rule of law in the early eighteenth century is that English people's experience of authority was associated principally with the administration of justice.[17] In medieval and early modern society, local administration, like the regulation of interpersonal conduct, was most frequently encountered in 'juridical forms'. As mentioned previously, these processes typically required widespread participation among communities, especially among the village notables who served as parish officers and jurors, but also by many people of lesser property.[18] Naturally broad experience of this kind bred considerable cultural familiarity with law, as James Sharpe has remarked:

> Through frequent contacts with the legal machine, whether as litigants, local government officers, witnesses, jurors, sureties, or, indeed, as malefactors, the everyday culture of the English, the way in which they viewed the organization of social life, the way in which they acted and expected others to act, were informed by notions derived and at times adapted from the law.[19]

For example, as Garthine Walker has shown in relation to seventeenth-century Cheshire, many plebeian men and women had a relatively sophisticated knowledge of law which enabled them to negotiate among different agencies of authority, and sometimes even adapt judicial forms to legitimize their own actions. Moreover, the law was not simply a body of rules external to popular culture. In the context of the relatively unmediated communication of circumstances that was typical of contemporary courts it was naturally infused with a range of customary ideas and practices.[20] Thus in the case of Cheshire Walker demonstrates that arguments about natural right, fair dealing, and personal honesty and credit were articulated successfully in proceedings before the local bench of magistrates.[21] The implications of these dealings for contemporary ideas about the rule of law are important, and have not been fully appreciated by historians. As legal theorists have pointed out, consistent legal rulings are useful to individuals because they make for predictability and relative stability in interpersonal relations. To achieve these purposes they should also broadly respect conduct that communities already regard as legitimate. In these ways common law processes generate ideas about justice.[22] Certainly, it appears that in early modern England the rule of law had acquired an affirmative emphasis from its vernacular juridical idiom, even if the story was romanticized.[23] A culture of grass-roots participation in legal processes determining issues of life and property was taken for granted and valued explicitly because it betokened freedom, consent, and equity, virtues that respected the dignity and interests of ordinary people, as well as the imperatives of authority. Given such an inheritance of law, governments and particular laws were expected to conform to notions of substantive justice.

If they did not, then riot and other forms of direct popular action might well follow. It has been observed that in seventeenth and eighteenth-century England widespread participation in legal institutions licensed disorder; or to put it another way, people thought they had the right to enforce justice directly.[24] This was clearly evident in Georgian London, where street rioting was endemic until late in the century. Robert Shoemaker has noted that metropolitan 'mobs' demonstrated a strong sense of *legitimacy* by the common characteristics of their riots and demonstrations: they often took place on the dates of officially-sanctioned public commemorations; they were normally highly public and relatively disciplined; and they frequently followed traditional and quasi-official celebratory forms, such as the lighting of bonfires and the forced illumination or 'pulling down' of houses.[25] Even more tellingly, their actions sometimes explicitly mimicked 'official' legal punishments. For example in 1749 a newspaper recounted the following event:

> Yesterday a young Man was detected in picking the Pocket of a Person at the Pay-Office in Broad-Street, and deliver'd up to the Populace, who conducted him to a Horse-pond, and after ducking him well they stripp'd him quite naked and whipp'd him severely, making him run the Gauntlet before they permitted him to go off.[26]

London crowds regularly apprehended suspected pickpockets and other favourite victims and summarily ducked them in ponds, ditches or the River Thames, echoing the punishment courts had normally applied to scolds.[27] Summary whippings seem to have been less common, although in this case too there are obvious parallels with the 'official' practice, by which regularly convicted offenders were whipped through the streets near the scene of their crimes. The newspaper reports sarcastically described these kinds of spontaneous popular punishment as 'public justice', 'mob justice', or 'the Discipline of the Horse Pond', but these events – and the appropriation by crowds of symbols associated with lawful punishment such as the pillory, the gibbet and the halter – demonstrate the substantial continuities between early modern popular culture and the 'official' cultures of law.[28] These overlaps are not so surprising when one considers the social composition of some London riots, for despite the opprobrious terms used to describe them, riotous crowds were not uniformly made up of poor, unemployed and unsettled people. Rather they frequently included a sprinkling of independent tradesmen and craftsmen, in addition to a solid majority of journeymen, apprentices, petty tradesmen, servants and labourers, who together have been described as the 'respectable' element of the metropolitan labouring classes.[29] Moreover, there are many examples of local authorities tolerating popular demonstrations, thereby tacitly acknowledging the people's right to negotiate what they believed were proper social and moral norms; especially if they had some 'colour' of legality.[30] So although they certainly constituted rough justice for those on the receiving end, rather than demonstrating that plebeians were 'ungovernable', or contemptuous of law, the study of eighteenth-century riots and rioters reveals the lineaments of a citizenry conscious of its claims to a legitimate role in government.

## An imperial state at law? Legislation and the common law

These reflections have important implications for the relations between English society and the state. Recent historians of the Elizabethan and Stuart periods have identified the contemporary development of society and its concomitant demands for order and justice as the primary driver for the growth of the early modern state. In this formulation, the state is regarded as a 'reservoir of authority', providing the institutional resources necessary for the promotion of peace, rather than as a central bureaucracy imposing its will upon the community. Of course authority was expressed as royally-sanctioned law, but since everyday government was largely executed through legal instruments, parish officers and courts, institutions and processes which involved voluntary commitment and interactive communication, the English people effectively 'invited the state in'.[31] According to these interpretations, law therefore 'proved to be an incorporative force in early modern England, creating and intensifying links not only between individuals, but also between the communities of parish, country and realm'. Although this widespread legalism by no means necessarily promoted social harmony or justice in individual cases, it did mean that by the end of the seventeenth century the state was effectively 'embedded' within English society.[32]

However recent historical writing about the development of the British state over the course of the eighteenth century presents a very different picture. John Brewer has argued that in this period of semi-continuous global warfare 'civil society was put in harness to the juggernaut of state power'.[33] There is no doubt that the government raised more revenue from taxation than ever before, increasingly in the form of intrusive customs and excise regulations, and maintained unprecedented numbers of soldiers and sailors, including many Englishmen who were recruited against their will, sometimes under statutory powers.[34] Moreover the new 'army' of state servants required to organize this massive fiscal-military effort enjoyed unprecedented administrative powers which gave rise to considerable criticism, complaints clearly derived from the historically-informed expectations of good governance that were described previously. The officers of the excise were particularly resented because of their remarkable powers of search and surveillance and their direct dependence on the central government, administrative characteristics which offended against cherished traditions of personal freedom and local self-policing. Indeed, because they combined a ubiquitous national presence with unique statutory powers, and were answerable only to a central board of commissioners, for contemporaries the excisemen symbolized a radical and threatening departure in executive government under administrative law. More generally Brewer has noted the 'increased separation between government and public, between state and society' with the growth of an administrative culture that depended on professionals who acknowledged their first loyalty to the crown.[35]

In these circumstances it is arguable that eighteenth-century governance was becoming generally corrosive of the culture of law that had been the very essence of the early modern state. Certainly the long series of acts establishing and extending the excise was only the most notorious example of legislation that at least one critic believed to be out of step with 'the general Tenor of our *other Laws*, or even with *Magna Charta* itself, the Foundation and Bulwark of all our Liberties'.[36] The particular complaint in this instance was that the machinery established for prosecuting infractions of the excise regulations did not allow for a full trial by jury, but depended instead on private judgement by the excise commissioners hearing evidence from the revenue officers.[37] This kind of legal shortcut was hardly unique. As Sir William Blackstone pointed out in his *Commentaries*, similarly abbreviated arrangements for trial had been applied by statute to 'a vast variety' of minor criminal offences cognizable before JPs.[38] Summary conviction was also the defining characteristic of the courts of requests, or courts of conscience, statutory commissions established up and down the country for the recovery of small debts. By no means all the applications of summary jurisdiction were the result of modern statutes: for example the magistrates' responsibility for hearing prosecutions in master and servant cases dated from late medieval legislation. However it is clear that these forms of justice multiplied rapidly in the eighteenth century with fresh draughts of legislative power.[39] According to Peter King, by the later part of the century summary hearings before magistrates constituted the main forum in which English people encountered authority.[40]

Conservatives were deeply uneasy about this development because it deviated so markedly from the libertarian culture of common law. Blackstone warned that the widespread extension of these summary proceedings amounted to a major departure from the 'prudent foresight of our antient lawgivers': since they were unknown to the common law and its provisions for trial by jury, they were not conformable to 'the constitution and genius of our nation'.[41] From this midcentury lawyerly perspective, the legislative hyperactivity of parliament represented a threat, rather than a bulwark against royal tyranny. The problem had a particular salience for lawyers, but their concerns serve to illuminate general changes in the legal order. Certainly some leading eighteenth-century barristers and judges were alarmed about the condition of their culture and profession.[42] They recognized that around mid-century the common law was in danger of being marginalized by the 'multitude of legislators' in the House of Commons. Only a few years after he lauded the administration of justice as a primary point of contact between government and people, Lord Chancellor Hardwicke expressed concern that 'our statute books are increased to such an enormous size, that they confound every man who is obliged to look into them'. Hardwicke's specific complaint was neglect of the traditional practice by which public acts were always submitted to the House of Lords before being sent on to the Commons. He believed this had acted as a useful check on too much legislation, because the judges had been able to advise the Lords on the legal merits of the proposed measure, and thereby helped to stifle 'unnecessary, or ridiculous' enactments. Now most bills went to the Commons first, and MPs were much less restrained and not as well informed about the law. In these circumstances the Chancellor lamented the passing of 'old times' when 'very few laws were passed in parliament'.[43] Such a view was informed by the conservative idea of statute as supplementary to common law, an understanding of law and government that was fully shared by Blackstone, according to the evidence of his *Commentaries*. Indeed in his introductory lecture as Vinerian Professor of English law, given at Oxford in 1758, Blackstone had fulminated against the 'specious embellishments and fantastic novelties' introduced into the administration of justice by acts of parliament, a problem which had already been apparent in the sixteenth century, but was multiplied in modern times 'when the statute book is swelled to ten times a larger bulk'.[44]

Recent scholarship has confirmed that eighteenth-century parliaments produced a considerable volume of general laws, including several hundred acts relating to regulation of the poor and the creation or re-definition of criminal offences and punishments, in addition to the necessary measures for the raising and de-mobilizing the armed forces.[45] Historians have been more sanguine about the implications of parliamentary activism than contemporaries, however. Perhaps this is because they are accustomed to legislative absolutism, but it is also important to understand that eighteenth-century administration was not typically big government in the modern sense. In fact, despite the notoriety of the excise and other positive legislative interventions from the centre, the great bulk of acts originated locally, and were very specific or personal in their scope. Moreover, much of this new law was entrusted to local elites for execution, either in the form of special statutory commissions or those regular workhorses, the Justices of the Peace. Recognizing these peculiar characteristics, Paul Langford has described the growth of parliamentary law-making after 1689 as 'concessive' or 'empowering': it was governance that was highly localist in its orientation.[46]

It has been argued, however, that it is anachronistic to conceptualize eighteenth-century public life in terms that emphasize the importance of local interests over national affairs. In fact the ideas and practices which evolved out of parliamentary affairs suggest a more subtle relationship that accommodated the growing importance of national life and its chief political institution.[47] Edmund Burke, for example, insisted that MPs represented the nation and the general good; he famously argued that local interests were subordinate and individual constituencies should not expect to determine the conduct of their representatives by 'instructions'.[48] As David Eastwood has shown, for Burke and many other late Hanoverian political commentators the arrangements for government were expected to represent the nation's dominant social and economic interests, rather than the concerns of particular localities. So while they hardly conceived of a modernist role for the state as regulating affairs in the localities via centralized bureaucracies, parliamentarians had a 'centralized perspective' of the legislature's role, and adopted a high doctrine of sovereignty that recognized only limited accountability to the public.[49] In 1770 Burke admitted that since 1689 parliament had forsaken its traditional role of a check on executive power, and rather had adopted 'the constant habit of authority', as expressed in positive acts which clearly demonstrated it was an active part of the government. On this occasion he complained about the ongoing 'separation of the representatives from their constituents', which had come to a head in the House of Commons' recent refusals to accept the Middlesex electors' choice of Wilkes for their MP.[50] Indeed in the course of the eighteenth century the propertied elites who dominated parliament came to recognize that the sovereign authority of the legislature was not only able to protect their economic and social interests from the crown and the mass of the population; it could be usefully deployed in more positive ways via specific measures of local application.[51] Taken in the aggregate the growing stream of seemingly insignificant individual acts – typically authorizing turnpikes, enclosures, navigation schemes, and local corporations for poor relief or urban improvements – represented national 'policy', albeit of a piecemeal, reactive kind. As will be seen, although legislation like this did not usually empower central bureaucracies, it nevertheless conferred 'an astonishing array of legal powers' on the local commissioners and magistrates, often at the expense of common law rights and customs.[52] It was perhaps because these individuals were perceived to be at arm's length from government that there is little sign of general concern about the development of legislative government; but it is nevertheless true to say that the English 'became habituated, as the century passed, to multiple forms of centrally-directed governmental activity, at which their ancestors might have balked'.[53]

Writing about provincial government, Eastwood has argued that 'the Hanoverian political system embodied institutions the character of which might best be described as republican, participatory, and communitarian'.[54] Certainly there were institutions in the early nineteenth century which continued to include significant elements of popular participation – the administration of justice, parliament, and some organs of local government are the most obvious. As I hope to show, however, such a judgement ignores significant shifts in the workings and cultures of those institutions during the eighteenth century. The evidence of this study suggests that the dynamic and reciprocal, socially embedded state of the sixteenth and seventeenth centuries atrophied in the eighteenth, and the business of government became more linear and one-dimensional as parliamentary statute, rather than the culture of common law, became the principal instrument of government. English people who were accustomed to forms of government that involved widespread participation and consent would have been surprised by the relations of succeeding generations with law and the state.[55]

## An age of enlightenment? Politeness, professionalism and the imperatives of eighteenth-century government

It is important to emphasize that in the eighteenth century the structures of the domestic state remained relatively undeveloped, if the state is conceived simply as centralized government institutions staffed by professional bureaucrats. Indeed, although the power and reach of the central government increased in matters of revenue and military forces, some longstanding elements of administrative control from the centre declined in this period. After 1689 the privy council withdrew from the supervision and coercion of local authorities and the assize judges gradually gave up their role as a conduit of administrative advice and authority from the centre.[56] But this hardly meant stasis. Taking rather different perspectives on government, emphasizing popular engagement with local institutions and parliament, and considering the cultures and structures derived from the administration of justice and common law, it is the hypothesis of this book that there was a general decline of active and unmediated popular participation, and a corresponding increase in professionalization, or specialization, as paid officers and other specialists replaced lay people in important areas at the grass-roots and in key institutions.[57] They were not always strictly servants of the state, but their increasing presence and impact seems to represent a significant departure from the traditions of citizen service and popular representation enshrined in the culture of common law. Succeeding chapters will examine some of the principal dimensions of law and governance closely in order to address these issues. At this stage it is appropriate to consider more broadly how and why such a declension of popular participation might have occurred.

Obviously any full answer would be complex, and must ultimately take account of population growth and distribution, increasing economic opportunities and the difficulties of administering large urban centres. These important topics have been studied extensively, and are beyond the scope of this work. However opinion is important here too. Rather than being a conscious process of reform directed from above, the major changes that I think we can identify in the cultures and experience of government from the eighteenth century were clearly connected with increased social differentiation and the importance of 'politeness' for middling people. Claims have been made about social and cultural trends like these in relation to law and governance during earlier centuries. Writing about the Elizabethan and early Stuart period, Hindle has argued that in the provinces the 'middling sorts' associated themselves with the values of the state but also consciously limited its reach: for as vestrymen they were conscientiously intolerant of the 'disorder' associated with the poor, and deliberately excluded them from a role in parish governance.[58] However, it is doubtful how far middling people can be distinguished in their collective life experiences and values from those nominally below them in the social scale before 1700.[59] The large extent of upward and downward social mobility and the absence of a wide circulation newspaper and magazine press argue against strong middling social consciousness. Moreover there is plenty of evidence that the law's resources were accessed by relatively humble people, as well as the middling sort. In the eighteenth century, by contrast, self-conscious 'middle class' opinion can be identified with confidence, especially in correspondence with newspapers and periodicals, and contributions to other forms of polite association. And while suspicion of centralized administration is a general feature of eighteenth-century opinion, a more characteristic element of middling sentiment was intolerance of popular cultures and their representation in the administration of law and government. The new middle classes themselves probably had more influence over government than they had previously, but their influence was frequently mediated through the emerging organs of public opinion and exchange, agencies which could be reactionary, as well as progressive, even in the Age of Enlightenment.[60]

Together with the idea of enlightened progress, the concept of politeness is key here, especially as it relates to discrimination against popular cultures in the public sphere. In eighteenth-century English historiography 'the era of politeness' is usually distinguished from the development of the more exclusive professional ethos, which is seen as dominant in the nineteenth century. For example the earl of Shaftesbury, who was one of the principal advocates of Britain's cultural advancement in the wake of the Glorious Revolution, is said to have encouraged a social context which favoured the polite generalist, a cultured individual whose accomplishments allowed him to contribute positively across a range of public activities.[61] According to an emerging scholarly orthodoxy, the 'public sphere' of relatively open association, unprecedented press freedom and intellectual exchange first developed during the Georgian age; and alongside commercialism was one of the most creative characteristics of English society.[62] In its ideal form politeness was certainly meant to be socially inclusive, in so far as it encouraged freedom of expression and association, at least among those who were able to pass themselves off as gentlemen.[63] However in this book I shall draw attention to some trends which run counter to the usual scholarly complacency about the positive virtues of public exchange and active association. Paul Langford has previously pointed out that the corollary of relatively easy access to the status of politeness was an element of vulnerability on the part of those who identified themselves as respectable, and a corresponding repudiation of 'the supposedly brutish characteristics of the Englishman's character'. This kind of reactionary social impulse was evident in the wake of the resurgence of popular politics which occurred in the 1750s and 1760s, and Langford has associated it particularly with the new bourgeois elites who dominated rapidly developing towns and cities.[64] As we shall see, it can also be observed in the administration of justice, and the 'reform' of the penal code.[65]

Besides acting against perceived popular deviance and disorder, in its register of polite sensibility and secular reason enlightenment thinking might also entail the conscious detachment of government from its institutional exchanges with popular cultures. Certainly at least one sociologist of law has argued that enlightenment law re-defined itself by excluding what it saw as the savagery of lawless nature, while also conceptualizing its mission as confronting and ultimately taming 'wild and uncultivated regions'.[66] Admittedly contemporaries who wrote about law in these ways normally referred to America, or 'the Indies' for their negative exemplars. But supposedly rationalist and imperialist thinking like this had significant implications for the culture of English law and government generally as it stood around 1700. As Fitzpatrick has suggested, in addition to its impact in colonial settings it was often deployed to undermine existing systems of domestic ordering in Europe; and ultimately in England it tended towards Austinian positivism and the legal imperialism of property and improvement, as most famously expressed in Locke and Blackstone.[67] Moreover denigration and exclusion of the uncultivated in matters of law also naturally facilitated the elevation of the professional ideal, to the exclusion of lay involvement. For example in the early nineteenth-century common law courts it was the lawyers who were most active in excluding or at least severely limiting and controlling lay participation in the courtroom; and learned prejudice of this kind was also evident in the eighteenth century, being inspired by enlightenment ideas about knowledge, as well as middle-class social consciousness.[68] Indeed after mid-century a new consciousness of absolute sovereignty and the growth of progressive ideas about rational authority brought a heightened awareness of the need for the law to be respected: hence it had ultimately to be administered by professionals who had clear orders and were accountable to government for maladministration.[69] This study therefore attends closely to increasing specialization in the administration of justice, in addition to the administrative imperialism of the countless eighteenth-century statutes which empowered JPs, commissioners and other authorities in the name of improvement.

Associated as it frequently is with a conservative caricature of Blackstone's *Commentaries* and the common law, and judged by the hindsight of the Victorian Age, eighteenth-century jurisprudence is normally represented as being antithetical to reform. However the advanced contemporary thinkers on law and government who emphasized commercial development and the priority of national interests tended to aggrandize the particular kind of law associated with parliament and legislation, the instruments which became the effective motors of British imperial progress. It was a primary nostrum of the emerging eighteenth-century sociology of law that advancement to the stage of economic development which featured commerce went hand in hand with strong central authority and the infinite elaboration of law.[70] Statutory regulation was taken for granted as a necessary feature of this progress. Montesquieu, for example, thought of law as rules framed by legislators to suit the particular conditions of society, and Adam Smith believed that legislation was characteristic of 'more refined manners and improved government': for him a system of law based only on settled custom was typical of societies at a relatively primitive stage of development.[71] The writers of the Scottish Enlightenment in particular believed that law had to be flexible enough to evolve with the development of society, and the amount of legal regulation would necessarily increase with economic growth and sophistication.[72] In the hands of practical men, such flexibility placed a premium on enlightened reform: thus Smith's contemporary Lord Kames advocated the reform of the criminal law and the abolition of entails in Scotland along lines which he believed were appropriate to an enlightened and commercial people.[73] It is true that before the nineteenth century British jurists were usually rather conservative when it came to statutory reform of the law: as seen previously, Blackstone was certainly reluctant to countenance it and even Kames relied on the judiciary, rather than parliament, as the primary agency of law reform. But they distrusted the legal competence of MPs, rather than being against the very idea of legislating for the improvement of society. Indeed, Lieberman has shown that Bentham grossly exaggerated his differences with his predecessors in their attitude towards reform.[74] Moreover, the swelling extent of the eighteenth-century statute book shows that parliamentarians themselves were perfectly prepared to use their legislative powers, especially in specific cases, but also in some significant matters of general application. Although it is not correct to argue that they legislated carelessly, or thoughtlessly; given the dark side of enlightenment thinking sketched above, an important question for this book is how MPs and peers who inhabited the nation's most important agency of government took account of ordinary people when they passed new laws, especially when it came to the improvement projects beloved of propertied interests.

My primary subject in this book is the changing human conditions, contexts and experiences of eighteenth-century law, rather than the legal history of doctrine and substantive law. I am interested in who made law, who could or could not deploy it, who administered it, what formal processes applied, and (mainly by way of suggestions for further research) what was generally apprehended by *The Law*. In the course of discussing the social forms, structures, cultures and processes of law I will of course have recourse to examine the construction, content and application of particular *laws*, especially individual acts of parliament. Naturally the two are closely related, since the ways in which people interact with laws and their administration help to inform their ideas about the rule of law generally. But this book can hardly claim to be at all comprehensive in its scope: it is emphatically not a general history of the laws of England in the eighteenth century, along the lines of Holdsworth or his successors.[75] Rather I have attempted to take soundings at various levels and in several different areas: first 'local government', as experienced through quarter sessions; second private litigation, in several jurisdictions; thirdly crime and the administration of criminal law; and finally parliament and its legislative output. In discussing the findings I have concentrated on what I see as the principal issues arising out of the early modern inheritance of law and government: popular participation and citizenship, central-local-parochial relations, and the maintenance of common law traditions.

This broad approach requires us, following Dworkin, to discuss law as a type of social institution, or even a cultural formation, and especially to consider the issue of consent, since people share in government by law as participants, as well as subjects.[76] As suggested previously, around 1700 the rule of law was explicitly identified with substantive ideas about justice, equality of process and active consent derived from a legal regime which centred on the common law and the courts. I shall pay particular attention to the application of these ideals in the changing conditions of law which developed over the following decades. Perhaps some of the parliamentary legislation and its administrative regimes elicited no more than a 'habit of obedience' on the part of the English common people, and little substantive consent?[77] Certainly in mid-century one critic complained of 'a Crowd of Officers and Magistrates, chosen by the

Direction, and under the Influence, of the Crown, invested with absolute Power by a Cart-Load of Statutes'.[78] More particularly, can the new pre-eminence of parliamentary legislation be characterized as government by 'command', if active popular participation had largely withered away, and at a time when the electoral franchise was relatively narrow? This last question will be largely deferred to the conclusion, since it necessitates consideration of alternative forms of participation, and how far they can be characterized as consent. For the moment it is appropriate to turn to the local experience of law.

# 2
# The Local Experience of Law and Authority: Quarter Sessions, JPs and the People

> a history of the eighteenth century which does not place the justice of the peace in the very foreground of the picture, will be known for what it is – a caricature.
>
> F. Maitland, *Collected Papers*, ed. H.A.L. Fisher (Cambridge, 1911), i. 468–9.

> It would be hard to overemphasize the importance of the ceremonial ... on court day. In the cultural context of the time it served not only to make the community a witness to important decisions and transactions but also to teach men the very nature and forms of government. ... For most men the primary mode of comprehending the organization of authority was through participation in court-house proceedings.
>
> R. Isaac, *The Transformation of Virginia* (Chapel Hill, NC, 1982), 92–3.

> 'Tis hard to find a Man who has not sometime been call'd to bear Office in his Parish or Borough, or who has not served on the Coroner's Inquest, or on some Jury or Homage in Court-Baron or Court-Leet, if not at the Quarter Sessions or Assizes: Whereby the common people of *England* gain a greater experience in Justice than the practice of Law in foreign countries will allow to that sort of People.
>
> *The Claims of the People of England, Essayed. In a Letter from the Country* (1701), 15–16.

Many of 'the magistracy' have certainly been greatly deluded by the discretionary powers which, during extraordinary and critical times, they have been permitted to put forth. So strong is this delusion, that

some seem to think juries are a great inconvenience, subordinate officers dolts, and law and course of law perfect nonsense.
C.D. Brereton, *The Subordinate Magistracy and Parish System Considered in their Connexion with the Causes and Remedies of Modern Pauperism* (Norwich, n.d. [1827?]), 36.

In the villages, towns and cities of medieval and Tudor-Stuart England, men and women usually encountered law and authority in judicial forms. This was because governance was conceived primarily as obedience to the law, and the law was typically administered in courts: institutions whose authority consisted in the punishment of all kinds of infractions against law and custom, including what we would understand as the obligations of local administration. A veritable patchwork of courts had survived from medieval times: broadly speaking, there were the communal courts of the hundred and the county; the tenurial and franchise courts of the manor and the borough; and the ecclesiastical courts of the archdeacon and the bishop; as well as the 'assizes' – normally twice-yearly visitations of royal justices to the county towns and cities for hearing pleas of the crown and private suits. But by the end of the seventeenth century the most important institutions of government in the localities were the sessions of the Justices of the Peace: for the 'office' jurisdiction of the church courts was in decline, communal jurisdictions had generally been superseded by royal justice, and the assize judges were relinquishing their active role in county administration.[1] Indeed in many of the boroughs as well as all the counties, the JPs had been the pre-eminent symbols of 'the rule of law' since the sixteenth century.[2] In many ways they remained so until the early nineteenth century; although it is the argument of this chapter that the expressions of their authority, and the local experience of government generally, assumed a much less judicial character over the period covered by this book.

The present chapter focuses on the various judicial and administrative activities of the justices of the peace in quarter sessions: both in hearing and determining 'divers felonies, trespasses and other misdemeanours', and in their other public activities as governors of their local communities.[3] Where the survival of records permits, it also takes account of magistrates' proceedings as individual justices keeping the peace and exercising statutory authority, either in their own homes or with other JPs at what historians have come to call 'petty sessions'. But it is appropriate to take a general perspective from quarter sessions as a means of surveying the full gamut of the justices' activities, and illustrating the important changes in their work of governing the localities and enforcing the law. Two broad questions are addressed. First, to what extent was the experience of law and authority 'consensual', in the special sense of involving a broad cross-section of the communities as active and discretionary participants, as opposed to 'administrative', meaning here the imposition of rules and orders by magistrates on their own initiative as instruments of government, and frequently through paid dependants?[4] In this connection particular attention is directed to the undifferentiated application of judicial processes under ideas about communal obligation which were inherited from the Middle Ages, and their gradual abandonment in the eighteenth century. A second, closely-connected issue is the impact on the local experience of government of more and more administrative law in the form of the 'Cart-Load of Statutes' directed at the localities in unprecedented numbers after 1689.[5] In particular, how far were the new powers of JPs under statute accommodated to the processes, cultures and authority structures of the common law, as opposed to making them virtually absolute authorities in their own right, who were unaccountable for their decisions? This question is especially important in regard to the work of magistrates dispensing summary powers out of sessions. But before proceeding to examine the magistrates in action during the eighteenth century, it is important to understand a little about the origins and history of the justices of the peace.

## JPs and quarter sessions before 1680: Medieval ideas and seventeenth-century practice

As the office of justice of the peace had developed in England during the fourteenth century the justices' primary responsibility was to keep the peace and punish offenders within the counties and divisions for which they were assigned. Crucially, they became judicial officers rather than policemen, being commissioned 'to hear and Determine' offences; and statutes ordered all the justices for each county to hold four quarterly sessions for these purposes.[6] The office was introduced into Cheshire and Wales in 1536, and many incorporated boroughs acquired the privilege under their charters for their mayors, recorders and other principal officers to act as JPs.[7] As the public jurisdiction in medieval communal and franchise courts – the county court, the sheriff's tourn and the leet courts of the manor and the borough – gradually decayed with the rise of royal justice, the JPs also became the most important organs of local administration, being the authorities of choice to receive extra powers, responsibilities or instructions from crown and parliament.[8] But although they symbolized central authority in the form of their commissions and derived their powers from parliamentary statutes, there was considerable continuity between their proceedings and those of the older communal local authorities. This continuity took two main forms. First, in their general quarter sessions they were constituted as courts, with all the special characteristics of participation and publicity which were intrinsic to courts and the common law; and second, in carrying out their judicial responsibilities they necessarily continued to implement the basic principle of medieval governance: unpaid service and initiative on the part of the local communities. Both of these features were products of the cultural and practical constraints that characterized royal governance, rather than signalling any early tendencies towards quasi-democratic rule. But they endowed the administration of local authority with substantial representative characteristics nevertheless.

From a modern perspective it is somewhat ironic that although the great achievement of medieval administration was the growth and legitimacy of the king's courts, in the absence of a professional bureaucracy these institutions depended largely on the initiative and responsibility of ordinary people in the localities to make them work. However, this is to misunderstand the largely organic growth of law and governance in the middle ages. The commission of the peace is a case in point. Certainly from their inception in the fourteenth century the JPs were royal officials, invested with the power of the crown, and over the centuries individual magistrates and pairs of justices acquired considerable summary powers under statute. But they were hardly conceived as prefect-type administrators, who dispensed active authority delegated from above. Rather, in discharging their judicial responsibilities for the county or the borough, the justices naturally assumed the characteristics associated with virtually all long-standing forms of secular authority in England: they proceeded as courts, held public meetings on scheduled days, and assumed an institutional existence by maintaining a continuous record of their decisions. And by constituting courts they took on distinctive qualities of governance. Just like the other medieval courts which it had largely displaced by 1700, the court of quarter sessions required the presence of representative bodies or individuals from its constituent communities to give it life and legality. In theory the hundreds and the counties were 'present' in the forms of their juries, and from the sixteenth century when they became the basic units of local government the townships and parishes attended by their constables. The overseers of the poor were also frequently required to be present because of their involvement in relief or settlement cases.[9] Given the constraints imposed by the limited resources of central government and contemporary culture, this element of communal representation appears inevitable: the juries and the parish officers were perforce the primary means available to discover breaches of the law.[10] Indeed, the quarter sessions took over the common law procedure for administering criminal justice in the royal judges' eyres and the sheriffs' tourns, that of the jury of presentment stipulated by Henry II's assize of Clarendon. Thus in most counties juries summoned for each hundred presented offences from their particular localities, while the grand jury or 'grand inquest' of the county presented those which pertained to the county as a whole. And these 'offences' included communal administrative lapses, as well as what we would understand today as crime.[11]

In order to understand both the lack of procedural differentiation between administrative and criminal business, and the formally representative nature of quarter sessions, it is necessary to appreciate that medieval forms of local government depended on a theory of communal obligation under the law. According to this principle communities were held to be jointly responsible for all sorts of trespasses against the law, including administrative, military, and fiscal obligations, as well as the maintenance of the peace.[12] The idea, at least, survived into the eighteenth century.[13] Thus besides its responsibility to administer the criminal law, the grand jury of Middlesex was reminded, in May 1736 'Every Parish, *Gentlemen*, is by Law obliged to mend their own Roads; the Turn-pikes come in only in Aid; and if the High-way is not mended, the Parish ought to be Indicted'.[14] So if they defaulted on their statutory duties, such as those for labouring to maintain the highways and bridges, parishes, townships, hundreds or whole counties could be indicted or presented and subsequently convicted and fined, just as individuals could be indicted and convicted for theft or assault.[15] In theory this meant communal self-government under law: presentments originated from the grand jury's 'own knowledge and observation', while indictments were laid before them by others for the community's consideration as to whether there was a case to answer.[16] For example, at the quarter sessions for Cheshire in January 1769 'the inhabitants of the County of Chester' were the subject of ten separate grand jury presentments for not repairing bridges and roads, while the township of Helsby was indicted for not maintaining three-quarters of a mile of the king's highway leading to Chester, as they were obliged to under the law which flowed from the statute of 1555.[17] County indictments and presentments were never traversed, as those for felonies or misdemeanours might be, so there was no semblance of a trial in these cases. But townships and parishes might enter a traverse, as the township of Hoole did at the same Cheshire quarter sessions, when the highway surveyors for the parish entered into recognizances to appear at the midsummer quarter sessions and defend the issue.[18] And in the case of an indictment for petty larceny, or assault, which usually originated with the individual victim, if the grand jury found a 'true bill' and the defendant entered a plea of not guilty, a petty jury of the county would try the case.

Common law processes meant the community was formally involved as a party in all these quotidian exercises of governance, and at several levels. Indeed, the grand jury's role originated from the requirement in the justices' commissions that they 'inquire by the Oath of good and lawful Men'.[19] Thus if they were sufficiently qualified – in the seventeenth century quarter sessions grand jurors were usually freeholders on the margins of the gentry – local men served on the grand jury for the county, and the more humble might be summoned to the hundredal juries which in many places represented the county's constituent communities.[20] Moreover, the more 'substantial' householders were expected by custom to take their turns in serving the offices which executed the community's responsibilities in maintaining the peace and enforcing the law generally – the petty and high constables, the overseers of the poor, the surveyors of the highways, and of course the parish churchwardens. So, in theory at least, the idea of communal obligation which informed medieval local justice guaranteed representative governance. And although the law was ultimately dispensed by the justices, they were hardly expected to be Leviathans: as an MP pointed out in a House of Commons debate of 1777, when defending the magistrates of Birmingham against a charge that they had neglected to regulate the playhouses 'it was no part of a magistrate to act in the first instance, but officially on a complaint made or information given'.[21] But how far did these theories of communal participation and magisterial passivity under judicial processes of indictment and presentment inform local government in action?

The relations between communities and justices in quarter sessions have been most fully studied for the seventeenth century, so it is convenient to begin with some of that material, as a basis for comparison with the Georgian period. Of course the substance of relations between justices, officers, and juries depended on the individuals involved and the social context they inhabited, so historians have found considerable variations in the experience of English local government over time and place. But some tentative generalizations are possible. Certainly during the later sixteenth and seventeenth centuries, there were 'stacks of statutes' that had enlarged the JPs' powers.[22] Nevertheless Keith Wrightson has written persuasively of the justices' normal tendency to leave responsibility for enforcing the 'regulatory' legislation passed by the parliaments of the Tudors and Stuarts with the parochial constables and hundredal jurymen, thereby allowing them the discretion to soften the imperatives of government in the interests of maintaining harmony and prosperity in their villages and townships. Left to their own devices they were likely to present persistent trouble-makers, and local girls who bore illegitimate children liable to become chargeable to the parish; but they might well turn a blind eye to occasional drinking after hours or unlicensed ale-selling, especially if the offender was familiar and the infraction could be interpreted as good fellowship or a harmless attempt to supplement income.[23] The governance culture of these communities hardly made them rural arcadia, however; as Ingram has pointed out, any suggestion of a tendency to tolerance of neighbours did not extend to the wandering poor, who were subjected to the full rigour of the criminal law and the statutes against vagrancy; and even locals could be treated harshly at times of economic stress.[24]

It is well known that following Tudor precedents, early Stuart governments attempted to infuse a more active spirit into the local authorities, and the records of seventeenth-century quarter sessions which have come down to us frequently testify to campaigns for the reformation and regulation of the poor, especially in regard to issues like vagrancy, bastardy, apprenticeship, the regulation of alehouses, and attendance at church.[25] Although processed through the traditional forms, in the main the local initiative for these bursts of activity seems to have come from the magistrates, who were in turn often acting on the instructions of the Privy Council and ministers. For example in Lancashire and Essex between the 1620s and 1650s the JPs periodically harassed or persuaded the parish officers and jurors into co-operating by prosecutions for neglect and detailed articles of enquiry directing them to present more of these offences.[26] Building on the Tudor beginnings of petty sessions, special meetings convened by justices for their particular localities or 'divisions' and held between quarter sessions were also used to concentrate the officers' minds on specific concerns.[27] The impetus for reforming zeal was not always so one-sided, however. Indeed, in some parishes there is evidence that the initiative for some of these drives ultimately came from below, being the result of the 'slow assimilation of leading villagers to the concept of order proclaimed from the judicial bench'.[28] But whether willing or not, it appears that in most cases the village constables who were still the pivots of lawful authority at this level of English society were largely 'non-professionals', in the sense of being locally-appointed 'middling sorts' who served by turn and were enmeshed in the ordinary relations of the neighbourhood, rather than careerists who depended on the magistrates.[29] In this context of 'social' office-holding the continued use of the judicial machinery of presentment for regulation of this kind meant that many communities genuinely possessed the power to select particular miscreants and pass over others, to co-operate or not, even if the justices sometimes insisted on cracking down on certain categories of offences. So although they might be pushed with the combined authority of the Lord Keeper, the Council, and the justices in petty sessions, in the seventeenth century 'Acts of Parliament and Books of Orders were merely a dead letter without the cooperation and consent of parish officers'.[30] For example in July 1630 at the Chelmsford quarter sessions the constables of Little Coggeshall in Essex responded to the articles tendered to them by presenting one man for swearing profanely, one for tippling in an unlicensed alehouse and seven for non-attendance at church; but the high constables of the division reported that by contrast they had received no return at all from the constables of Hatfield Peveral, Ulting, Rivenhall and Kelvedon.[31] To this extent it can be argued that seventeenth-century communities continued to negotiate the experience of authority, even if they were targets of the early Stuarts' 'increase of governance'.

In addition to the officers and jurors who represented communities in the administration of the law, a broad range of people also interacted with quarter sessions as principals and witnesses in the prosecutions for the lesser felonies and misdemeanours which were the subject of indictments, rather than presentments. In a do-it-yourself legal regime which depended on largely private prosecution and an unlawyerized trial, individuals enjoyed considerable power in the administration of criminal justice, over and above the input from their communities via jury service and office-holding. Not the least element of this power consisted in making the decision of whether to prosecute in the first place. For the early seventeenth century the relative freedom of choice about going to law and the community's ultimate influence over the result appears from evidence previously cited about the frequent tendency to prosecute and secure the conviction of outsiders, rather than residents of the neighbourhood, who were probably more able to negotiate a settlement with their victims which avoided coming to court, and certainly less likely to be found guilty.[32] Moreover, the ability to use the criminal law seems to have been relatively widespread among the propertied. Admittedly, given the uneven distinction of wealth, and the fact that at this time there was no financial support for maintaining a prosecution, prosecutors were normally higher in the social scale than defendants. But they were hardly confined to the gentry and nobility: among a sample of prosecutors at the Wiltshire quarter sessions for 1616, 1619, and 1623 there was a fair proportion of people who were well below the level of the landed elite, including 'craftsmen or tradesmen who probably enjoyed only modest resources, a shepherd, and a widow who kept an alehouse'.[33]

An even better indication of the potential for grass-roots initiative in the administration of local government under the justices of the peace is the widespread use of binding over for the peace or good behaviour. This procedure was founded in the statutory powers of the commission, in so far as it consisted in every magistrate's power 'As a judge and by virtue of his office' to summon individuals who had threatened others with violence or who were of ill fame generally and order them to enter into penal bonds or 'recognizances', with sureties to guarantee they would keep the peace towards a named individual or be of good behaviour. The positive condition of the recognizance was that the offender had to appear at the next quarter sessions, where the court would listen to any further complaint as to his conduct in the meantime; he would then be released from the penalty or the bond would be proceeded upon at law for his default and he might be indicted for the offence.[34] Although this instrument invested every JP with very wide discretionary powers to act against individuals, the device was legally available to anyone who feared violence at the hands of another, and was prepared to take an oath to that effect. Indeed, it has been shown that it was widely used by private individuals in late Elizabethan and early Stuart times. The Cheshire quarter sessions records reveal that around 200–350 people a year were bound to the peace or good behaviour between 1590 and 1619, and the process seems to have been equally popular in Essex around the same time.[35] Moreover, like prosecuting criminal indictments, the instrument of binding over was by no means a preserve of the landed elite: in late Elizabethan Cheshire a sample of recognizances suggests the instigators of the action included significant numbers of husbandmen, as well as yeomen, while in seventeenth-century Wiltshire and Essex they included a cross-section of the 'middling ranks' and members of the 'popular classes'.[36] Unless the JP who issued the original warrant allowed a release on the complainant's advice of a settlement – a somewhat controversial procedure in the seventeenth century – the issue would proceed to quarter sessions.[37] There, although no jury was involved, the names of those people bound were called in open court, and the complainant had the opportunity to proceed with an indictment. Indeed there is evidence that on some occasions the complainants and defendants were given a brief hearing.[38] So as with the rest of their judicial business, although there was no guarantee of fair and equitable proceedings, the element of popular initiative and public participation in the work of the Tudor-Stuart quarter sessions is clear.[39]

At this point it is appropriate to summarize the analysis to date. Broadly, the business of local government under the JPs in early modern England can be divided into four areas. First, as the justices' titles and commissions emphasized, it was necessary to keep the peace and deal with interpersonal offences: principally petty thefts, riots, and assaults. Second, the JPs were charged with supervising the administration of the poor law and law of settlement, as well as execution of the various statutes which attempted to 'regulate' or 'reform' the habits, economic circumstances and morals of the population at large, and especially the poor. As seen, this regulatory work has been the focus of considerable research effort by historians of the sixteenth and seventeenth centuries.[40] Above all it involved supervision of alcohol consumption and sale, the attendance of individuals at church, and individuals' sexuality and mobility, as well as the prohibition of certain games and sports. Thirdly, the justices were responsible for the unexciting (and relatively understudied) administration and development of what would today be called the local 'infrastructure': the maintenance of roads and bridges, gaols, houses of correction, courthouses and shire halls, and other public property. Since all of these responsibilities required the expenditure of money and the action of subordinate officers, a fourth area of activity was the raising and administration of public funds, via rates, assessments and fines, and the appointment or supervision of the officers who collected the funds and carried out the duties, particularly the overseers of the poor, surveyors of the highways, and constables.[41] As the foregoing discussion has suggested, in the seventeenth century much of their work relating to the peace, interpersonal offences, social regulation, and the maintenance of local infrastructure was carried out at quarter sessions under judicial forms and in rough conformity with ideas about communal obligation and service. And these were conditions which gave considerable scope for community participation and individual agency 'from below', rather than facilitating full magisterial control. The question remains then, how far was this still true for the eighteenth century, and indeed, for the later seventeenth century?

## Eighteenth-century justice work

Perhaps the easiest way to approach the work of the JPs in the Georgian age, a period for which the experience of local authority is relatively understudied, is to take a detailed look at one locality and discuss it in the context of what we know about other areas.[42] For this purpose I have made a detailed study of the quarter sessions records for the county of Cheshire between the late seventeenth century and the beginning of the nineteenth. Cheshire has been chosen simply because of the continuous nature and high quality of its quarter session records. Although no claim is made here for any 'typical' status on the part of this county, its local government history is especially interesting because it was relatively remote from London and the prosperous lowlands of the south-east, by contrast with most of the other sessions which have been studied for the eighteenth century. Moreover, although most famous for its dairying and salt trade, Cheshire underwent partial industrialization at the end of the period, with the growth of mechanized textile manufacturing in the north of the county and the construction of the Chester and Bridgewater canals. Naturally this brought considerable population growth, with all its attendant problems for governance.[43]

In Cheshire, as in every other county and corporate borough in England, the justices met in quarter sessions in January (Epiphany), April (Easter), July (Midsummer) and October (Michaelmas), but they did not always assemble at the same place. Of course in the counties their location had some bearing on the degree of participation in the proceedings. In highly centralized counties such as Gloucestershire the castle or shire hall of the county town was the regular venue and a county-wide meeting occurred, with business from all parts of the shire.[44] But in counties divided by great distances or natural barriers, in a period when roads were poor and journeys were slow, meetings in a single location imposed hardships, and were likely to deter general attendance. For these reasons in several counties the sessions circulated among the principal towns, resulting in unofficial de-centralization of governance, by which the JPs and officers only attended their local sessions, although each meeting was still designated a general quarter sessions for the county.[45] Lincolnshire represented one of the extreme cases of such localism, for there were formally separate quarter sessions for the three parts of the county, and in each region every sessions was adjourned to all the principal towns in turn to deal with the local business.[46]

The Cheshire magistracy went some way to ensure all its communities had access to county government. In the late seventeenth century the bench always met at Chester in the east and Knutsford in the north every year, while the other two quarter sessions meetings alternated between the central and southerly towns of Nantwich, Northwich and Middlewich.[47] While the officers from every hundred were supposed to attend all the meetings, many justices only attended the sessions nearest their homes, and the selection of grand jurors who were mainly from the nearby settlements inevitably meant that the individual sessions concentrated on their local affairs.[48] It is interesting that this regime was amended in the eighteenth century, however, with the decay of public buildings in the lesser centres. Middlewich had been dropped from the calendar by 1730, and around that time Northwich was being visited less frequently.[49] Forty years later, only Chester and Knutsford were being visited, the first in January and April, and the second in July and October, and this was still the pattern in 1816–18.[50] Indeed, around 1770 sessions were frequently adjourned to Chester, where a couple of justices met to deal with minor administrative orders, and these private meetings multiplied further with increasing business in the early nineteenth century, when they were usually held in the office of the clerk of the peace. Such progressive centralization may be suggestive of a drive for administrative development and efficiency among the justices; a process which has been identified by several historians of local government.[51] But while some allowance must be made for improvements in communications, it also implies that the proceedings of the Cheshire quarter sessions were becoming more remote from the people of the county. This is a point which may be tested by close attention to the business of the sessions.

At the beginning of the eighteenth century it appears that quarter sessions around the country dealt with much of their business judicially, being 'still enmeshed in a procedure of presentment by juries, indictments, plaints and petitions'.[52] Certainly, like every other quarter sessions, when the Cheshire bench received the presentments of the officers or the grand jury, tried indictments by petty jury, or heard appeals from the decisions of individual magistrates, the justices sat in open court as a judicial tribunal, behind a raised table or bench.[53] Even their administrative orders were styled 'by this court'. But there is no doubt that in the course of the Georgian period the Cheshire sessions travelled a long way from the medieval ideal of self-government under the common law by establishing a clear shift towards magisterial initiative.

This shift is apparent from Table 2.1, which summarizes indictments, presentments and recognizances at the Cheshire quarter sessions for four triennial samples between 1680 and 1818. Following Wrightson, three broad categories have been used for analysis of the indictments and presentments. 'Criminal or interpersonal' offences consist principally of breaches of the peace involving violence or theft, together with assaults and occasional expressions of contempt for authority.[54] The second category of 'regulatory' offences relates to enforcement of the statutes intended to discipline the habits of the common people in their social and economic relations. The third category, 'obligation enforcement' means prosecutions brought against communities or individuals in regard to their duty of maintaining highways, bridges and watercourses. Offences committed by officers (and less frequently by potential jurors) consisting in failures of their duty to serve or other infractions have been counted separately. The statistics for the first category are difficult to interpret. The bare figures show that indictments were roughly constant between the later seventeenth century and the mid-eighteenth, during a period of demographic stability, before a major increase after 1800 with rapidly rising population in the textile areas.[55] The relatively straightforward statistical picture masks a considerable qualitative change, however. In 1678–80 the offences have a distinctive character: the grand jury found many indictments for poaching, riotous breaking and entering, and interpersonal assaults; on the other hand there were relatively few cases of petty larceny, by comparison with later samples, and they were often for trivial items, such as a cheese or a fustian waistcoat.[56] Obviously, the times were turbulent, and the characteristics of some prosecutions suggest the typical magisterial response to the popular hysteria generated by the Popish Plot and Exclusion crisis; there were certainly occasional indictments for seditious words, such as 'the papists did not need to feare the driveing on of their designes since popery was soe much practised in this Country of England'.[57] But in 1729–31 there was a similarly high proportion of assaults and other minor thefts and misdemeanours. By contrast, after the second half of the eighteenth century most of the prosecutions at Cheshire quarter sessions were for simple larceny, including some cases of non-capital grand larceny which were transferred from the assizes.[58]

What did this long-term change in the characteristics of criminal or interpersonal indictments represent? This was not a society which had abandoned spontaneous violence – the magistrates were still dealing with cases of assault in 1816–18 – but after the middle of the eighteenth century the overwhelming majority of offences tried at quarter sessions concerned property, and the signs suggest they were dealing with more serious cases of theft than their seventeenth-century predecessors. A similar transition from adjudicating relatively minor interpersonal disputes to a preoccupation with property theft has

Table 2.1  Indictments, Presentments and Recognizances, Cheshire Quarter Sessions, 1678–1818

| Category | 1678–80 | 1729–31 | 1769–71 | 1816–18 |
|---|---|---|---|---|
| **Indictments**[a] | | | | |
| Criminal/Interpersonal[b] | 65 | 72 | 59 | 347 |
| Regulatory[c] | 29 | 4 | 1 | 4 |
| Communal Obligation enforcement[d] | 3 | 3 | 14 | 16 |
| Individual Obligation Enforcement[e] | 7 | 2 | 12 | 3 |
| Officers[f] | 4 | 2 | 6 | 2 |
| **Presentments**[a] | | | | |
| Regulatory[c] | 89 | 3 | 6 | 1 |
| Communal Obligation enforcement[d] | 44 | 81 | 123 | 89 |
| Individual Obligation Enforcement[e] | 5 | 10 | 16 | 8 |
| Officers[f] | 6 | 31 | 7 | 32 |
| Recognizances[g] | 814 | 216 | 151 | 438 |
| Peace | 275 | 22 | 31 | 195 |
| Good behaviour | 162 | 59 | 2 | 6 |

*Sources:* Chester RO, QJB 3/3, 3/8, 3/13, 3/22, 3/23

[a] These items numerate indictments and presentments, not persons (note that many indictments and presentments relate to more than one person).
[b] Attempted rape and sodomy, seditious words, grand larceny (1816–18 only), petty larceny, slander (1678–80 only), fraud, receiving stolen goods, breaking and entering dwelling house, riot, assault, forcible entry, poaching (mainly 1678–80), contempt for magistrates or constables, perjury. Excluding any committed to the assizes.
[c] Swearing (all 1678–80), keeping inmates, erecting illegal cottage (all 1678–80), hedge breaking, enclosing the waste, absenteeism from church (all 1678–80) recusancy or Quakerism (all 1678–80), tippling in alehouse (all 1678–80), common drunkenness (all 1678–80), keeping disorderly house, possession of hunting animals/devices (all 1678–80), dangerous dog (1769–71, 1816–18), travelling with a false pass (1816–18), disobeying maintenance order (1816–18); causing common nuisances in highways; selling without a licence (e.g. on 9 April 1678 28 people were presented 'for Maltering, Swayleing and badgeing without a license' and on 8 Oct, 1771 nine people from Stockport were presented for selling grain without licences). Note in 1678–80 most of the regulatory presentments were for recusancy and non-attendance at church.
[d] Failure to repair bridges/roads, perform labour on highways, maintaining waterways, etc. Note presentments were either by the grand jury, by the relevant surveyor of the highway, or by justices 'of their own view'.
[e] As above, but for individuals obliged to perform these services because of tenure in land.
[f] Failure to serve, neglect of duties, or other offence on the part of officers or jurors. Note most of the presentments against constables in 1729–31 were against petty constables, by contrast with 1769–71.
[g] Total recognizances for bastardy, peace, good behaviour, to prosecute/testify, and to refrain from specific activities. (Excluding sureties for defaulting constables.) Note this item numerates orders, not persons (e.g. the person bound over and the sureties in each case). In 1678–80 the court was binding over large numbers of popish recusants from session to session.

been observed in the Lindsey district of Lincolnshire, and there it has been explained as a shift from 'vernacular justice' to 'a system of government from above'.[59] In other words, during the 1740s quarter sessions were adjudicating the people of Lindsey's problems of petty violence, quarrel and minor theft, whereas by the 1770s the magistrates appeared to be engaged in their own campaign against what they perceived as 'real crimes'.[60] Can we say the same for Cheshire? The statistics for recognizances may provide some clues here.

Certainly, the diminishing totals for recognizances in Table 2.1 are suggestive in regard to these issues, since frequent binding over has been regarded as an indication of widespread 'popular legalism' during the seventeenth century, and a similar decline has been noted in other parts of the country.[61] Caution is necessary, however. People were bound over for several different purposes, and long-term shifts in the totals might be misleading because of variations in the JPs' conscientiousness about returning recognizances to the clerk of the peace or releasing them without certification to quarter sessions.[62] Moreover, it is important to understand that recognizances could be 'discretionary' bonds, issued by magistrates for the suppression of conduct they regarded as undesirable, such as immorality and religious non-conformity, as well as originating in the complaints of private individuals. Indeed there is clear evidence that some early eighteenth-century Middlesex justices deployed them as instruments in the reformation of manners campaign designed to reform the morals of the poor.[63] Certainly, the total of all recognizances returned to Cheshire quarter sessions for 1678–80 is inflated because of the magistrates' fears about popery – in July 1679 they ordered the statute of 1597 relating to the imprisonment of rogues and vagabonds to be put in force, having heard rumours that Jesuits were travelling disguised as 'scotch pedlars' – and large numbers of popish recusants were presented and bound over from sessions to sessions, on the presentation of their names from the hundreds.[64] But even in metropolitan Middlesex the majority of recognizances were prosecuted by individuals, and the large shifts in the Cheshire sub-totals for recognizances to keep the peace or be of good behaviour do suggest that the late seventeenth-century JPs were dealing with far more interpersonal quarrels than their eighteenth-century successors.[65] Sure enough, where there is evidence, the substance of many cases around this time reveals people coming to the magistrates to control troublesome personal conflicts. Thus John Lowe of Stanthorne, husbandman, was summoned to appear at the Cheshire sessions on 15 July 1679 for abusive and threatening words towards Joseph Carter, he having called Carter 'a shabby rogue' and said 'hee would have a legg or an Arme of him'. Evidently Lowe did not give satisfaction as to his future conduct, for he was ordered to enter into further recognizances to appear before the Northwich JPs at their next monthly meeting. And at the same sessions George Barker of Over, tanner, was bound over in £40 and had to find sureties in £20 for calling William Spencer 'forsworne Rogue' and his wife a whore. Indeed, occasionally the JPs were asked to interpose the law between husband and wife, as in the case of James Massey of Warford, another husbandman who was bound over for his good behaviour in a penalty of £40, he 'being a common Drunkard abusinge his wife & followinge other women'.[66]

Given these stories of interpersonal quarrels taken to quarter sessions around 1680, the steep drop in the numbers of recognizances returned during the eighteenth century clearly shows diminishing popular engagement with the court. Indeed, noting a similar decline in Kent, Landau commented '[i]n the early eighteenth century, Quarter Sessions kept the peace through suasion, exhortation, and the power to awe. By mid-century Quarter Sessions no longer executed this office'.[67] But what was the cause of the change? Of course it is possible that with the progress of 'civility', or politeness, there were fewer interpersonal quarrels as restraint and modesty became established standards of good behaviour in English society, at least among people with pretensions. Certainly over the long term there is no doubt that in western society between the late middle ages and the twentieth century violence and personal incivility became increasingly unacceptable.[68] But in the eighteenth century there is little evidence for the growth of personal restraint among plebeian and lower middling men and women. One only has to turn to the evidence of individual JPs' notebooks for abundant examples of minor affrays and verbal abuse. The justice book of Dr. Edmund Tew, a JP of County Durham between 1750 and 1764, is filled with such disputes, mostly between the inhabitants of the parishes along the Tyne and the Wear who obtained a living from the local industrial and seafaring activities, but also from the people of the countryside nearby. For example on 1 June 1751 Tew issued a warrant against William Middleton, a maltmaker of Westo, upon the oath of Ann Bate for 'bruising in her secret parts and arm, disclosing them to several persons and threatening her life'. And on 4 July 1758 he granted a warrant against Nicholas Byars, a farmer of Bishop Wearmouth, 'for beating and bruising William Clark of Sunderland', a miller. The interesting point about these fights and arguments, which appear on almost every page of the notebook, is that few resulted in the issue of a recognizance, and even less led to the alleged malefactor making an appearance at quarter sessions. The reason for this is that Tew seems to have worked very hard to persuade the parties to settle their differences before him, to the extent that in more than a third of the cases where some outcome is recorded the result is annotated 'agreed', often with some monetary compensation. Dr. Tew was a wealthy clergyman with charitable and paternalist inclinations. He certainly disapproved of the fractiousness which typified the communities he governed (on one occasion he described a complainant as 'a quarrelsome foulmouthed fellow'), but he clearly believed it was his Christian duty to promote harmony, rather than impose the authority of the law.[69]

Moreover, it is important to understand that Tew's propensity to mediate rather than bind over to the sessions was not exceptional among rural magistrates, and that although judicial paternalism was hardly a new development, his practice represented an important departure from the common practice of their sixteenth and seventeenth-century predecessors.[70] William Hunt, a JP who sat in rural Wiltshire, kept a notebook recording his justice work, and this shows that he persuaded the parties to reach an agreement in over 70 per cent of assault cases that he heard in 1744–48. For example in July 1744 he granted a warrant against Richard Rutt of Market Lavington for beating Charles Laney of Bishop's Lavington. However he wrote 'upon hearing before me I advised the parties to agree it which was done'.[71] Like Hunt, the diaries of several justices serving rural Kent between 1700 and 1780 show they frequently reconciled complainants with their alleged persecutors, whereas JPs who were active in late Elizabethan and early Stuart times were much more likely to take recognizances. Indeed, parliament acknowledged and encouraged such mediating activities among justices in 1778 by passing a statute which granted individual JPs the right to award costs.[72]

Of course it is well known that parliament also legislated to increase the scope of summary conviction by individual JPs during the eighteenth century. Poaching is a case in point. By mid-century most offences under the game laws could be determined by one justice or by a pair of JPs in their occasional 'petty sessions' for the local district.[73] In this as in many other cases they might impose a fine or imprison the miscreant on the oath of one 'credible witness'. The change in process meant that game prosecutions largely disappeared from most quarter sessions, as they did in Cheshire.[74] However, the magistrates were hardly inattentive to the game laws: on the contrary, it has been suggested that a large proportion of the total population of Georgian gaols had been committed under their provisions.[75] Indeed, rather than being indicted and tried by a jury, men accused of poaching or keeping a gun and a dog normally found themselves at a 'hearing' in the front parlour of the local JP.[76] Thus on 27 February 1786 Edmund Waller of Hall Barn, Beaconsfield (in Buckinghamshire), JP, fined Edmund Rowls £5 for 'using a greyhound'. On the same day he convicted James Redding for 'wood stealing' and committed him to the house of correction, while he also summoned and tried Francis Sills and Elizabeth Burnham, who were accused of stealing cabbages by Charles Reeve. This last case went no further; Waller recorded it was 'settled'.[77]

Some contemporaries found such an extension of magisterial competence offensive, especially because summary justice appeared to undermine the constitutional protections provided by trial by jury and the common law.[78] After reviewing the Game Act of 1770, which gave JPs the power to order a poacher to be publicly whipped as well as imprisoned, William Eden complained 'the jurisdiction of individuals is aggrandized beyond measure', and condemned summary corporal punishment as 'inconsistent with every idea of English Liberty'.[79] Indeed, it has been argued by Bruce Smith that the further extension of summary proceedings by statute in the later eighteenth and early nineteenth centuries was a conscious and successful exercise which countered the contemporaneous development of the presumption of innocence in felony proceedings.[80] Having been legislated into their magisterial maw, gleaning, poaching, and the theft of vegetables were typical fare for the country magistrate dispensing justice in the later eighteenth century.[81] Richard Colt Hoare of Stourhead in Wiltshire was hearing very similar cases to Waller: in November 1787 he considered the case of Thomas Lapham of Stourton, who was found with two pheasants in his possession; while in April 1793 Rebecca Domine was convicted and ordered to pay 5s 'for culling wood out of a Hedge belonging to Thomas Ryall at Kilmington'. She was afterwards whipped on failing to pay. In 1794, at a joint petty sessions for Somerset and Wiltshire, Thomas and John Baimsden were convicted of poaching a hare on the oath of Robert Feltham and committed to gaol for several months.[82] Earlier in the century, the substance of summary justice in Wiltshire tended to take the form of convictions for swearing, keeping disorderly alehouses or selling liquor without licence. For example on 16 July 1700 Joseph Carter of Alderbury was convicted before Thomas Stringer JP and fined 10s for 'prophane swearing five severall oaths within the parish of Alderbury on the 18$^{th}$ day of Aprill last'. Nearly 70 years later, on 16 July 1766 Thomas Phipps, JP convicted Richard Munday on the oath of William Brown, excise-officer, for having sold beer in the parish of Allington without being licensed.[83] Certainly, there is change as well as continuity here. While the imposition of fines for swearing seems to have been another discretional strategy by which JPs arbitrated quarrels and avoided further proceedings at sessions, the involvement of the revenue officer represents the direct interest of the eighteenth-century fiscal state in maintaining a prosecution: according to one historian he was 'the symbol of a new form of government'.[84] Essentially, however, all these offences and magisterial strategies amounted to the same thing: like quarter sessions in the seventeenth century, although they were less concerned with the enforcement of religious worship, the magistrates were regulating the customary social and economic activities of the local population.[85] But there were at least two important differences. First, whether they convicted, dismissed, or 'settled' the case, the individual JPs were dispensing justice according to their own personal judgement on the merits of the evidence, with little legal accountability or community participation.[86] As one critic maintained 'Business is here disposed of ... without course of law, with hearing only one side, without a precedent, without oath of witnesses or the intervention of a jury, without a record or even a reporter, and on parole authority by "winks, frownings, and countenance"'.[87] And second, their proceedings suggest they were only seriously preoccupied with enforcing the law in cases of petty crimes against property, rather than in incidents of interpersonal quarrel, and in this they were largely focused on the supposed misdeeds of the poor. Indeed, the editor of one eighteenth-century JP's notebook has commented on the marked 'class bias' of eighteenth-century summary justice, and pointed out that the magistrates' propensity to settle interpersonal disputes severely limited popular access to the law.[88] Certainly, although they had far more discretion, like the excise officers they were acting as statutory instruments rather than creatures of the common law. And as Smith has shown, in dealing with petty theft it is easy to infer the intentions of parliament: legislators favoured summary proceedings because they made conviction more likely.[89]

Obviously this increase in their summary powers under statute represented a considerable accession of authority to individual magistrates, and for eighteenth-century novelists the corrupt and oppressive JP – Fielding's Justice Thrasher and Smollett's Justice Gobble – became a stock target for satire and moral reproach.[90] Of course these figures were grotesque caricatures; the literary sources also include some upright and honest magistrates, and the prevailing opinion is that the 'trading' justices who were able to live by fees and bribes in London and other heavily populated urban areas were largely absent from the country. Moreover derisory commentary about magistrates was hardly unique to the eighteenth century.[91] But the important point to understand is that eighteenth-century satirists and moralists gave special attention to JPs' tendency to imperious behaviour, as they believed it was encouraged by the multiplication of penal statutes, and they also noticed particularly their neglect of the common law.[92] Whether they were tyrants or Solomons, the unprecedented discretionary powers granted to eighteenth-century magistrates encouraged them to act on their own initiative, sanctioned by statute or not, and there were few checks and balances.[93] In these circumstances the JP could easily get carried away:

> His jurisdiction is extremely extensive, and comprises a multiplicity of persons and cases. The individuals who are brought before him are almost universally his inferiors; and commonly in the lowest ranks of society. The principal share of his business is transacted in his own house, before few spectators, and those in general indigent and illiterate. Hence he is liable to become dictatorial, brow-beating, consequential, and ill-humoured; domineering in his inclinations, dogmatical in his opinions, and arbitrary in his decisions.[94]

The author went on to suggest that justices knew they were relatively immune from regulation by the common law courts. Certainly the justices were left largely to interpret the statutory authorities for themselves: the subjects of their summary powers were normally too poor, ignorant and deferential to identify and act upon illegality or oppression, and despite Squire Western's experience of being the subject of two actions by criminal information in King's Bench, recent research suggests the judges of the common law courts were very reluctant to entertain such prosecutions.[95] Lord Mansfield narrowed the scope of criminal information for misdemeanour against magistrates by insisting on proof of pecuniary corruption, and it appears that few of their discretionary judgements or orders were reviewed by writ of *certiorari*. In fact the Westminster judiciary effectively discouraged reviews of this kind, especially in the exercise of their administrative discretion, where successive judges of King's Bench declared they would not interfere.[96] The judges' attitude on this issue seems to have been quite different from that of their seventeenth-century predecessors; and it is also clear that in the course of the eighteenth century lord chancellors raised the levels of proven misdemeanour required for them to remove justices from the commission.[97] Moreover, after 1700 it required more than usual wealth and courage for an individual to take a justice to court, for where *certiorari* was available there were often formal deterrents against such litigation, and parliament often made an unsuccessful prosecution subject to treble costs.[98] Several statutes even prohibited the action altogether; notably the act of 1746 which provided summary conviction for swearing, and all the proceedings under the excise legislation.[99] Parliament also passed statues in 1751 and 1804 that limited the ability of aggrieved individuals to prosecute JPs for damages in civil actions.[100] Here was a substantial check to the rule of law, since in many areas of their jurisdiction magistrates were effectively unrestrained by higher authorities.

Just as the courts tended to leave JPs alone, some contemporaries believed modern magistrates had detached themselves from the common law. Blackstone famously complained that the gentry were ignorant of the law, compared with their predecessors, despite their traditional responsibilities as JPs and MPs.[101] There was no longer any substantive provision for ensuring that the local bench of acting justices included a core or 'quorum' of men who were learned in the law.[102] Indeed, contemporary prints normally depict JPs in their justice rooms or in petty sessions as being solely dependent for their legal knowledge on one of the standard legal manuals, usually Burn's *Justice*, which is often open on the table, and perhaps with a set of the statutes at large in the background. In one print of 1794, significantly, a clerical justice has no law books, but a framed copy of the ten commandments is on the wall behind him.[103] Certainly it was popularly believed that clergy who became magistrates had no need for the common law to support their authority:

> Each raw Divine, that to the Bench aspires;
> Let him read this, and be what he desires
> ...

> Our Ancestors, queer Country Puts, we're told,
> Justice impartially dispens'd of old:
> Too scrupulously nice, they little knew
> What Sweets might thence to them and theirs accrue.
> T'oppress an Enemy, support a Friend,
> To serve some Interest, or some private End,
> Were rights to their dull stupid Souls unknown;
> Intent on Justice, and on that alone.
> They, for their Knowledge, por'd in paltry Books,
> The humdrum Works of *Littletons* and *Cookes*;
> But wiser Moderns scorn such antique Stuff,
> It is our Will and Pleasure is enough.
> ...
> See! now the Country views thee as some God,
> And anxious wait on thy decisive Nod'.[104]

It therefore appears that one possible explanation for the shifting patterns of interpersonal prosecutions and recognizances returned to the Cheshire sessions in the eighteenth century was a tendency for quarrels to be dealt with by individual magistrates, either by summary conviction or by settling cases themselves in an 'extra-legal' way, and this practice certainly implies a decline from the popular legalism of the seventeenth century. People were still bringing their petty disputes to magistrates, especially those living in the industrializing areas like the Tyne and Wear district, but in Cheshire at least they were less likely to be dealt with by a court, with the ultimate process of a trial in the face of the community.[105] Admittedly, prosecutions which resulted in indictments did not necessarily result in full quarter sessions trials. Research on sentencing patterns for common assaults in Essex and elsewhere suggests that in the mid-eighteenth century the justices in quarter sessions imposed nominal fines in large numbers of assault cases where the defendant pleaded guilty, thereby avoiding a complete hearing of the case, and most likely signifying their acceptance of an informal agreement between the parties. Blackstone deplored the practice because it apparently negated the possibility of making a public example of an offender.[106] However elements of public participation remained: indictments had to be found true by the grand jury before further prosecution, and confessions might be accompanied by oral statements from the prosecutor and defendant which helped to inform the bench's decision about sentence.[107] Interestingly, from the latter part of the century and into the 1800s quarter sessions in Essex, Cornwall and Surrey seem to have taken assaults more seriously, since there were fewer guilty pleas and a higher proportion of offenders was imprisoned.[108] The data for Essex implies that the court was becoming particularly concerned with assaults against officials or other forms of aggravated assault, and that for Cornwall shows the magistrates there were cracking down on men who worked in the tin mines, as well as other labourers and artisans. These sentencing characteristics suggest a clear change in the imperatives of the magistracy generally, whereby they were becoming preoccupied with correcting what they saw as potentially serious criminality among the labouring poor, rather than dealing with petty interpersonal quarrels.[109]

Indeed, despite the trouble taken by clerical justices like Edmund Tew, it has been argued persuasively that in the eighteenth century the greater gentry who were traditionally expected to serve as rural JPs and take the lead at quarter sessions were increasingly disinclined to trouble themselves with the 'drudgery' of dealing with the 'brutish and inhumane' interpersonal relations of the poor. 'Vernacular justice' was simply too insignificant.[110] Short of neglecting to act in the commission, the best way to discourage such grubby work was to take no action at all upon complaints grounded in the quarrels of the poor, while adopting a demeanour towards inferiors which emphasized 'the chasm separating rulers from ruled'.[111] It is true that in Cheshire the practice of binding over to the sessions seems to have undergone a partial revival around 1816–18, but more than half of the recognizances returned to quarter sessions in these years came from just one magistrate – another clergyman – and the increase is of limited significance in the context of the much larger population.[112] In these circumstances it is not only arguable that individual JPs were partially disconnected from the superior courts and the common law by the increased use of summary process; it also appears that the court of quarter sessions was increasingly detached from the culture and individual concerns of ordinary people. Moreover, the magistrates' processes of law enforcement were becoming professionalized.

Returning to the Cheshire quarter sessions and Table 2.1, and leaving aside the question of what it says about 'real' levels of theft, the peak of prosecutions in 1816–18 certainly shows the sessions were accessible to victims of property offences. Quarter sessions was facilitating more access to justice for propertied people, because by 1816 the justices frequently ordered payments partially to reimburse the costs of prosecutors on successful convictions, as they were authorized to do by legislation, and these incentives may have favoured the less well-off.[113] However, the early nineteenth-century increase in criminal indictments might also have been caused partly by the magistrates' established policy of appointing special constables for the apprehension of suspected thieves. There are occasional signs of special constables in the early eighteenth century – for example in 1729 three husbandmen were presented for allowing a man to escape out of their custody – but they only appear in force a century later.[114] In June 1817 thirteen constables were paid several sums for their per diem expenses in 'pursuing felons', having been appointed special constables 'to execute warrants in felony'.[115] The frequency of such appointments was a symptom of the general breakdown in the old traditions of office-holding by rotation in the context of eighteenth-century urbanization, but it also represented a modern approach to administration. Unlike the traditional constables of the townships, described by the Cheshire quarter sessions in 1828 as 'persons whose habits of life and occupations are incompatible with the duties of such as office', paid constables were dependants of the magistrates who were accountable for their performance.[116] Although we cannot be sure of their impact on the level of prosecutions, the introduction of semi-professional policemen provides evidence of the enhanced propensity for administrative intervention which typified the Cheshire quarter sessions in the early 1800s, by contrast with their predecessors of a century earlier. Their initiatives in policing culminated in 1829 with the successful solicitation of a pioneering act of parliament which introduced a force of paid officers under three high constables.[117]

Turning to the other indictments and presentments at quarter sessions, the statistics for Cheshire clearly show an enduring shift after 1678–80. As we have seen, in the seventeenth century, although they had their ups and downs, depending on the extent to which the parish officers co-operated in making presentments, there were frequent 'regulatory' prosecutions under the statutory prohibitions designed to facilitate official, rather than private, control of personal behaviour. But although the Cheshire quarter sessions received many presentments of this kind around 1680 – principally for recusancy and neglect to attend church, but also for a range of social and economic offences – they virtually disappear from the records in the eighteenth century. Henceforth, besides increasing indictments for property crime, a few presentments for nuisances and obstructions in the highways, and the supervision of officers, the indictments and presentments were principally matters of obligation enforcement: individual landowners were prosecuted for failing to maintain portions of roads contiguous to their property, and communities were presented or indicted for similar offences relating to highways, bridges and cawseys (i.e. causeways). Indeed, prosecutions of townships for not maintaining roads and bridges seem to have increased considerably in mid-eighteenth-century Cheshire, according to the statistics.

What does such a shift from regulation to obligation enforcement mean? Prima facie it might suggest that over the generations from around 1680 to 1770 the high constables and parish constables who were the normal source of the regulatory indictments and presentments in Cheshire had turned their attention from presenting unlicensed ale-selling, drunkenness, lodging strangers and non-attendance at church to drawing the justices' attention to the failures of local communities to maintain their thoroughfares. Certainly, in many parts of the country the drive for official regulation of personal behaviour tended to diminish after 1700, especially in regard to church attendance and extra-marital sex. Again, there are signs that some eighteenth-century magistrates believed quarter sessions should concentrate on more important business, and reduced the fines on conviction for petty offences in order to discourage prosecutions.[118] The other principal agency for controlling behaviour in these areas was the church courts, and they largely abandoned 'office' prosecutions for such offences in the eighteenth century.[119] As we have seen, however, this is not to say that JPs no longer concerned themselves with personal behaviour likely to threaten disorder or damage the community. But much of the remaining regulatory work was undertaken by individual JPs and by justices meeting in their petty sessions, where decisions were made without the encumbrance and expense of juries. Moreover, close attention to the records reveals a significant change in the characteristics of presentments.

In the late seventeenth century there were many presentments to quarter sessions from the constituent hundreds of the county. Unlike many other counties, Cheshire had no hundredal juries, and it is difficult to discern the process behind presentments. No doubt the mass presentations of popish recusants, quakers, and absentees from church originated in the JPs' enquiries, possibly at meetings in the divisions which were attended by the constables and other officers with power to make presentments.[120] But many of the other presentments from the hundreds of Cheshire at this time convey the sense that the local officials were reporting disorders born of grass-roots knowledge and on their own initiative, not as agents of the magistrates. For example in October 1677 the head constables of Stockport division in Macclesfield presented two men and two women (including a butcher, a hosier, and a dresser of flax) as common drunkards. And at the Nether Knutsford sessions in 1680 the Nantwich high constables presented Randle Gargreave of Nantwich for making an affray on Thomas Kirkham of Grosley and Kirkham for making an affray on Gargreave.[121] Clearly, they had broken up a fight. Contemporaneous presentments of individuals by the grand jury also frequently convey the sense that they must have originated from the local experience of the officers: thus Roger Davies, locksmith, also of Nantwich, was presented for abusive words to the constables, having said 'he cared not a turd or a fart for them'.[122] However from the end of the century presentments from the individual hundreds simply disappear, and by the early eighteenth century the Cheshire grand jury presentments largely relate to the civil defaults of communities, rather than individuals. Early Georgian quarter sessions proceedings for Hertfordshire continued to include occasional presentments of unlicensed or disorderly alehouses, scolds and harbourers of 'inmates' from parishes and hundreds, but communal presentments of this kind seem to disappear entirely after mid-century. Perhaps the last such return to the Hertford sessions was that made by the petty constables of Stortford at Easter 1751, when they presented the landlord of the Bell and Anchor Inn for being a 'disorderly and abusive man'.[123] In this context it is interesting that there is widespread evidence all over England and Wales for progressive neglect among constables of their duty to make 'true and genuine returns' about the state of their districts, rather than bland statements that all was well, a declension which led to the abolition of the constables' presentments by statute in 1827.[124] The change in the character of presentments surely implies that in Cheshire too the constables of the villages and townships were no longer reporting individuals for minor infractions of the social and economic order. Perhaps they were no longer expected to.[125]

By contrast with those for the late seventeenth century, the presentments for enforcing the obligations of the localities which are found in the Cheshire quarter sessions minutes 50 years later have the authentic character of governance from a greater distance, in so far as they relate mainly to the infrastructural problems which the minor gentlemen of the grand jury and the JPs themselves would have noticed in the course of their local travels. Moreover, the presentments of the county for repairing its bridges and roads functioned as simple devices for raising an additional rate from the propertied inhabitants: since quarter sessions itself represented the county, no defence would be forthcoming, and the problems were simply referred to justices to contract for the work, a fine being guaranteed. In the case of recalcitrant townships a heavy conditional fine would be levied until the justices were persuaded to grant a certificate that the repairs had been carried out.[126] Ultimately a further judicial short-circuit became available for dealing with the defaults of hundreds and townships through the procedure of justices themselves making the presentment 'on their own view', as they were encouraged to do by legislation of 1773; and it became a favourite of the Cheshire bench in the early nineteenth century.[127] The process had the double advantage that justices could present any community in the county, whereas high constables and surveyors of the highways were limited to their own localities; and the concurrence of the grand jury was unnecessary. Active justices with an interest in highway maintenance could therefore make occasional tours of the roads, using their power of presentment as an effective executive instrument for remedial action. Ultimately, if the township proved recalcitrant after indictment and conviction, quarter sessions could proceed to final judgement by issuing a writ of *levari facias* for the sum outstanding.[128]

So the changes in the characteristics of criminal indictments and recognizances, and the transition from frequent prosecution of regulatory offences to the preponderance of obligation enforcement depicted in Table 2.1 appear to represent three substantive changes in the work of the court. First, in Cheshire as in Lincolnshire, there does appear to have been a decisive distancing of the sessions from what has been called vernacular justice, as many interpersonal offences were dealt with summarily by individual JPs – often in an 'extra-legal' way – or simply ignored altogether; while quarter sessions concentrated on property crime, with the assistance of constables who made a trade of the business. Secondly, members of the village elites who seem to have co-operated with the justices in the enforcement of regulatory statutes during the seventeenth century were no longer participating in the process of governance at the level of quarter sessions. As we shall see, regulation of the poor had been largely devolved to petty sessions, where it was also dealt with summarily as matter for judicial administration. And third, in cases other than felony the machinery of presentment and indictment was becoming a rather empty instrument which disguised administrative intervention from the level of the magistracy and the grand jury, rather than the communities of villages and townships themselves. These shifts are important for a study which is concerned with engagement between the people and the law, and they did not go unnoticed among contemporaries. Blackstone, for example, cautioned against growing 'disuse' of trial by jury, and the corresponding increase in the power of the crown's servants in the determination of minor offences, especially the revenue officers. He was clearly concerned about departures from the processes of presentment and trial by jury, 'a two-fold barrier ... between the liberties of the people, and the prerogative of the crown'.[129] Moreover, he was also worried about diminishing understanding and appreciation of the common law's cardinal virtues as legal knowledge became the monopoly of lawyers.[130] He was right to worry, because both these trends – more 'extra-legal' executive governance and diminishing popular engagement with courts and legal processes – can also be observed in the JPs' general administration of the localities.

## Local administration: Statutory authority and oligarchy

The bulk of quarter sessions work which did not involve the use of juries and the procedures of the common law was derived from the magistrates' powers and responsibilities under the poor law and laws of settlement, and here too it is possible to discern some distancing of the court from people at the grass-roots of the localities. For instance in the seventeenth century the statute of 3, Charles I was interpreted as empowering quarter sessions to proceed originally in cases of bastardy, and there are many signs of the parties being heard in person.[131] Certainly Table 2.2 shows that in 1678–80 the Cheshire sessions were trying bastardy cases *ab initio*, in so far as the alleged father appeared on his recognizances and the court gave judgement of filiation with an order for maintenance or referred the issue to the divisional justices. Thus on 29 Apr. 1679 the sessions referred the case of Edward Astle of Hale,

Table 2.2  Administrative Business, Cheshire Quarter Sessions, 1678–1818

| Category | 1678–80 | 1729–31 | 1769–71 | 1816–18 |
|---|---|---|---|---|
| **Appeals** | | | | |
| Settlement[a] | 7 | 70 | 46 | 95 |
| Bastardy[b] | | 6 | 1 | 7 |
| Excise[b] | | 1 | | |
| Poor relief[c] | 1 | 6 | 3 | 3 |
| Rate[d] | 1 | 3 | | 1 |
| Other[e] | | | | |
| **Orders** | | | | |
| Apprentice (discharge) | | 2 | | |
| Bastardy[f] | 35 | | | 1 |
| Maintenance[g] | 2 | | | |
| Cottage[h] | 2 | | | |
| Commitment/punishment[i] | 14 | 5 | 14 | 223 |
| Pensioners[j] | 4 | | | |
| Officers (Appointments)[k] | 48 | 52 | 54 | 58 |
| Highway rates[l] | | 10 | 6 | 13 |
| Carriage rates[m] | | 3 | 3 | 2 |
| Vagrant rates[n] | | | | 11 |
| Collections/Assessments[o] | 29 | 78 | | |
| Turnpike[p] | | | 1 | |
| Price of grain[q] | | | 1 | |
| Certificates[r] | | | 2 | 7 |
| Payments on bills[s] | 1 | 91 | 223 | 926 |
| Debtors (discharge)[t] | 2 | 3 | 2 | 29 |
| References[u] | 8 | 12 | 8 | 17 |

*Sources*: Chester RO, QJB 3/3, 3/8, 3/13, 3/22, 3/23

[a] Appeals against removal orders, not including orders to hold over the hearing to a later meeting of the court.
[b] Appeals against fines for excise offences imposed by two justices.
[c] Appeals/confirmations of decisions made by two justices in: providing relief; rating individuals for chargeable relatives; seizures of goods to reimburse parishes.

**Table 2.2** Administrative Business, Cheshire Quarter Sessions, 1678–1818 – *continued*

[a] Appeal against poor rate assessment or distraint of goods for payment of rates or statutory assessments.

[b] Other appeals: appeal against summary conviction for unlicensed sale of goods.

[c] Hearings for proof of filiation and orders for charging the father for the maintenance of the child, and saving the parish harmless etc. Note these were not appeals.

[d] Original orders of the court rating persons for maintenance of relatives in distress.

[e] Order on petition to erect a cottage on waste.

[f] Order for arrest and commitment to the county gaol or house of correction (several in bastardy cases, 1678–80); orders for particular treatment or punishment of prisoners (including several orders for whipping in 1769–71 and 1816–18). In January 1679 five popish recusants were committed for refusing the oaths of supremacy and obedience.

[g] Orders for individuals to be admitted to the pension for maimed soldiers.

[h] Coroners and high constables appointed for the year at the Michaelmas sessions and occasional appointments of other officers (gaolers, keepers of houses of correction, surveyors, clerk of the indictments).

[i] Sixpenny rates on townships for repairing highways, and fines for not maintaining them.

[j] Orders for rates for carriage between London and Westminster and Cheshire, made annually. Also fixing of rates for carriage of soldiers' baggage (1816–18).

[k] Orders for setting rates for the conveyance and maintenance of vagrants.

[l] Individual collections or assessments, usually for repairing cawseys/bridges, as well as repairs to county buildings; also quarterly 'pay' for the county (£100 per year in 1729–31). Note that in 1678–80 and 1729–31 the JPs always proceeded by ordering separate collections or rates for particular repair or improvement projects, assessed by proportion on each hundred. By 1769 they were simply ordering payments from the treasurer's funds, having adopted a consolidated rate, in accordance with the legislation of 1739.

[m] Confirmation of orders made by turnpike trust.

[n] Order for return of the market prices of grain and quantity exported and imported (1770) under 10G3, c. 39.

[o] Certificates on petition: e.g. for loss of salt on which duty had been paid; for lord chancellor's brief to collect charitable contributions.

[p] Payments to officers (constables, surveyors, gaolers, overseers), tradesmen and victuallers on presentation of their bills and/or approval of their accounts. In 1769–71 largely payments to tradesmen for bridgework, but in 1816–18 many additional payments for special constables apprehending felons, and prosecutors claiming their charges.

[q] Release of insolvent debtors under periodic statutes. These orders were frequently accompanied by orders making over their effects to creditors.

[r] References to JPs and the clerk of the peace, including orders to view bridges etc (JPs), contract with workmen for repairs and improvements (JPs), to contract for transporting convicted prisoners overseas (JPs), to form a committee for the repair of bridges (JPs), to audit the treasurer's accounts (JPs), appointed commissioners to inspect the accounts of the Liverpool dock corporation (JPs), and to audit the accounts of the trustees for making the River Wear navigable (clerk of the peace, 1769-71, treasurer, 1816–18).

husbandman, to the JPs of the hundred of Buckloe at their next monthly meeting for the hundred, 'forasmuch as there is noe due proofe made to this Court touching the filiation thereof' (the proof was made out later at the same sessions). And on 13 July 1680 the Nantwich meeting of the court made a bastardy order on George Platt of Faddely after 'examinations taken upon Oath in open Court'.[132] In contrast, by 1729–31 the court was only hearing *appeals* in bastardy cases; original justice was dispensed wholly by the JPs in the relevant division. Men who appealed against their orders of maintenance would be granted a hearing in person before all the justices, but appeals of this kind were few and far between because of the prohibitively high costs – usually there were no more than two or three a year.

Indeed, whereas the quarter sessions minutes for the 1680s and 1690s include many orders on the petition of individuals for relief, or for building cottages on the waste, from the eighteenth century quarter sessions' proceedings relating to the administration of poor relief were almost entirely confined to the representations of the overseers, rather than the individual paupers or potential paupers themselves. Typically, the overseers of rival parishes argued as to which one was responsible for the legal settlement of poor persons and families, thereby making them responsible for relief. One parish would obtain an order from the divisional JPs for the removal to the parish of settlement of families who were liable to become a burden to their ratepayers, and the other would appeal against the order, denying the proof of settlement. The officers were able to support the costs of appeal because they could deploy the parish funds for the purpose, and the law of settlement generated a mass of work for the sessions as parishes attempted to protect their resources.[133] It was suggested in 1735 that 'half the Business of every Quarter-Sessions consists in deciding Appeals on Orders of Removal', and the records of the Cheshire sessions for the eighteenth century certainly bear that out, since long and complex orders take up much of the space in the records.[134] The JPs who heard these cases overturned the original orders of their fellow JPs relatively frequently, but a contemporary critic suggested they were generally inattentive to the relevant common law, and condemned their 'Carelessness' in examining the facts.[135] By the end of the century there seems to have been more concern about following legal forms and procedures. Nevertheless this was law work that was remote from its subjects: although their lives were decisively affected by the result, it was not business that the poor inspired or could even influence very much. They do not even seem to have been present at the hearing: the principals were the parish officers, and the main speakers were the counsel retained to argue the case.[136] Moreover, in quarter sessions as in other courts, the law was increasingly mediated by professionals, rather than experienced directly: in 1792 the JPs of Cheshire emphasized how far they had departed from the practice of widespread participation in their proceedings by ordering that no motion was to be received from any person who was not a barrister at law.[137]

Just as the bulk of petty crime and minor interpersonal disputes had been devolved to JPs in their parlours, much of the justices' face to face administration and regulatory responsibilities had been delegated to meetings of two or more JPs sitting together, often at a nearby inn. This was hardly a purely eighteenth-century development, but it went much further after 1700 as JPs were given more and more responsibilities by parliament.[138] Tudor-Stuart governments had prodded most counties into developing some form of local, 'private' or 'pettit' sessions for divisions, being either the hundreds or some other sub-unit of the county. In the seventeenth century their development was patchy and 'idiosyncratic', however.[139] During the eighteenth century they seem to have become more permanent and regular fixtures of local government, although they were often relatively informal in their proceedings, and there was considerable variation in organization and nomenclature.[140] In some places justices found it convenient to establish regular meetings of petty sessions, when they were available for all sorts of business, especially that which required the concurrence of two justices; such as hearing applications from overseers for the removal of immigrant families, and making orders of filiation on men who were the reputed fathers of bastards.[141] The metropolitan parishes of Middlesex were precocious in developing petty sessions, and it is reasonable to suppose they were more common in the urban areas, where population growth increased demand for access from the parish officers. They also served as rudimentary police offices: for example in 1730 Middlesex quarter sessions recommended that justices should hold weekly petty sessions for the discovery and prosecution of street robbers, the suppression of brothels and gaming houses, and the regulation of constables and the watch in pursuance of these tasks.[142] Similarly in 1783 Hertfordshire quarter sessions encouraged frequent petty sessions for charging constables 'to apprehend and carry before the Magistrates all suspicious and disorderly Persons, to be examined and dealt with as the Nature of their Causes may require and as the Law directs'.[143] At Hackney in Middlesex, there were even two levels of petty sessions in mid-century, one for the Tower division which met at Whitechapel and one for the parish of Hackney itself which met fortnightly at the Mermaid or the Blue Posts taverns.[144] In the countryside their development was more uneven. Some justices were content to maintain casual arrangements with other nearby JPs whereby they only met occasionally for dispatch of the 'double justice' work. For example the Rev. Dr. Henry Yate, a JP who officiated in the Malvern Hills border district between Hereford, Gloucestershire and Worcestershire around 1800, often took settlement and bastardy examinations himself and made orders with a colleague later, although he seems to have sat with another justice occasionally to expedite the process.[145] However he did collaborate with two other justices in a 'special sessions', held at Ledbury in December 1801, when they heard several cases brought by the excise officers and committed a man accused of stealing a gun for trial at the next meeting of quarter sessions.

Whether meeting regularly or not, in the performance of these functions the justices proceeded judicially, on motion or complaint; and as we have seen, their decisions in settlement and bastardy cases were subject to review by quarter sessions, and ultimately by King's Bench, if the parish officers decided to pursue the case. However, no juries were involved, few records were kept, and in practice the presiding magistrates had considerable discretion, provoking traditionalists to equate petty sessions with 'an unheard of system of tyranny'.[146] Certainly Landau commented that in the eighteenth century petty sessions were 'acquiring an extra-legal monopoly over many of the powers allocated by statute to two justices, and altering the relation between the justices and those they governed'.[147] The development of a divisional corporate existence provided the opportunity to assume command of local administration, and some JPs were keen to take up the reins of government. In Kent at least the JPs meeting in petty sessions during the early eighteenth century became quite imperious, in so far as they issued summonses and orders to alehouse keepers and parish officers designed to give their meetings a monopoly of the work which had to go before two justices, and made detailed regulations for their conduct. Over the next few decades Kentish petty divisions put on institutional flesh: all the divisions appointed permanent clerks, several had regular chairmen, and at least one promulgated rules and ceremonies for supplicants to attend their worships, which were to be enforced by the clerk and his doorkeeper.[148] It is not clear how far other counties followed suit in the assumption of similar powers and pretensions, because records of petty sessions have rarely survived, although there are passing references to such meetings in many magistrates' diaries, and they clearly tended to chime with the 'clubbable' culture of Georgian gentlemen.[149] For example during the later 1760s and 1770s a group of Surrey magistrates met every month at the Sun Inn in Kingston, where they bespoke dinner afterwards.[150] References in the Cheshire quarter sessions minutes show that there too the JPs were holding 'monthly meetings' in their divisions throughout the eighteenth century, although the term 'petty sessions' does not seem to have been used until the early nineteenth century.[151] But central government initiatives undertaken in the 1820s and 1830s which were associated with the further extension of summary jurisdiction and the reform of the poor law effectively curtailed the ad hoc arrangements for divisional meetings, where they survived, and established petty sessions everywhere as 'a generally recognized administrative unit'.[152]

Even a century before this, every county commission developed at least the embryo of a divisional command infrastructure, for by statute the JPs in every division had to hold 'special' sessions for 'the Execution of some particular Branch[es] of their Authority', where they exercised more purely administrative authority.[153] The highways act of 1691 prescribed such a meeting every four months for the magistrates to charge the surveyors of the highways and examine them about the condition of local roads and bridges, including one in January for appointing the new year's officers.[154] And statutes of 1729 and 1753 established special 'Brewster' sessions in September of each year for the JPs to summon alehouse-keepers and issue licences on the basis of their judgement as to the applicants' behaviour and standing.[155] Evidence suggests the provisions of these statutes were carried through. Two of the Cheshire JPs held a special session for appointing surveyors at Sandbach in January 1728.[156] More detail is provided by the notebook of William Hunt, a JP who lived near Devizes in Wiltshire. In the 1740s Hunt regularly attended sessions like these for the nearby hundred of Swanborough, when he sat with a colleague at the Horse and Jockey in West Lavington or the Green Dragon in Market Lavington. They also held annual sessions for appointing the overseers of the poor (from lists submitted by the parish or township) and for approving parochial rates and accounts.[157] Here too, there is evidence of administrative aggrandizement: like the justices of Kent and Gloucestershire, Hunt and his colleagues absorbed the administration of the land and window taxes into their petty sessional meetings, thereby co-opting the tax commissioners who were not JPs into a consolidated institution of local government.[158] On these occasions the JPs were hardly acting as judicial officers reacting to plaints from below: the various statutes gave the divisional justices considerable powers of initiative and compulsion, and they were hardly accountable for their decisions.[159] In these circumstances moralists felt obliged to issue stern warnings against sliding into habits of oppression and corruption, and even conscientious decisions were liable to be misunderstood.[160] Reviewing the licensing sessions held before two JPs at Hackney in Middlesex during the mid-eighteenth century, proceedings which required difficult choices between competing applicants, one scholar has said 'many of the justices' decisions must have seemed both arbitrary and capricious'.[161] And like the petty sessions in Kent, these meetings provided opportunities for proactive administration not sanctioned by law. Even in Gloucestershire, for example, a county where petty sessions were relatively undeveloped before 1800, the licensing sessions were used to promulgate general regulations restricting the operation of alehouses, although this clearly went beyond the magistrates' legal authority.[162]

As with the growth of summary jurisdiction generally, the devolution of poor law administration and related issues to divisional sessions and individual JPs implies diminishing public engagement with the justices in the 'court' of quarter sessions. As we have seen, the meetings of quarter sessions were formally supposed to be gatherings of the county, and according to the justices' precept the sheriff made public proclamation of the day and place they would be held. As Burn's *Justice* declared 'all persons may attend the sessions for the advancement of public justice, and for the service of the king'.[163] Certainly like a court, the formal judicial proceedings were open, to the extent that the opening ceremonies, jury trials, and appeals hearings were held in public.[164] But it is virtually impossible to assess the overall attendance at proceedings of this kind. Obviously prisoners in the custody of the county gaoler were conveyed to the sessions, and individuals bound over to appear on recognizances had virtually no choice but to attend ultimately, because of the threat of estreat, by which defaulters were threatened with Exchequer process to recover the sums specified in their bonds.[165] The principal officers were also expected to be present, especially the clerk of the peace, who organized the proceedings, and the high sheriff, who was formally the chief of ceremonies. The presence of all these, together with the various jurors, parish officials, lawyers, clerks, and attendant javelin men, must have guaranteed some popular interest, aside from those whose relatives or friends were involved.[166] But in the eighteenth century the coroners, high and petty constables, surveyors of highways and other local officials frequently failed to turn up unless they had particular business, and many studies have revealed only a thin attendance by the justices themselves, at least before the end of the century.[167]

Besides the development of justice work 'out of sessions', another cause of the diminishing relevance of quarter sessions as a point of contact between government and the common people was a growing disinclination among leading county families to act in the commission.[168] In Gloucestershire, for example, the diary of the Rev. Francis Welles, a conscientious JP who attended the county quarter sessions regularly from 1715 to 1756, shows that sometimes only two justices were present on the first morning, and there was difficulty in finding a chairman. Attendance by the aristocracy was exceptional.[169] Cheshire's experience was a variation on this theme. The Cheshire quarter sessions had averaged around eight justices per session in the early seventeenth century, and in 1678 the average attendance was about nine, out of 43 in the commission overall.[170] At this time the meetings invariably attracted some of the leading county families, such as the Mainwarings, the Shackerleys, the Leicesters and the Cholmondeleys. Half a century later, in 1729–31, the numbers on the bench had not changed much, for an average of ten JPs attended each session.[171] This made Cheshire slightly unusual, because George II's reign was something of a nadir in quarter sessions attendance elsewhere, as the fire of local party conflict went out with the proscription of Tories.[172] Admittedly, in Cheshire as elsewhere, the commission had grown considerably by then, numbering 79 in 1727, so there were many more inactive JPs, although some scions of the prominent families were still riding to sessions more than occasionally, including two generations of Mainwarings, and a baronet, Sir Charles Duckinfield. However 40 years on, the Cheshire bench was at a much lower ebb: average attendance at quarter sessions was only five, none of the heads of the leading families came, and a respectable showing was only achieved by the regular presence of a couple of clerical justices.[173] Indeed on at least two occasions meetings had to be adjourned because only two JPs appeared.[174] And this was at a time when the Cheshire commission numbered more than 140 JPs in total. In these circumstances quarter sessions could hardly be regarded as a representative meeting of the county.

Under these conditions the magistrates' administrative proceedings inevitably became rather cosy, and were liable to ridicule:

> THREE or four Parsons, three or four 'Squires
> Three or four Lawyers, three or four Lyars;
> Three or four Parishes, bringing Appeals,
> Three or four Hands, and three or four Seals;
> Three or four Bastards, three or four Whores,
> Tag, Rag, and Bob-Tail, three or four Scores;
> Three or four Bulls, and three or four Cows,
> Three or four Orders, three or four Bows;
> Three or four Statutes, not understood,
> Three or four Paupers, praying for Food:
> Three or four Roads, that never were mended,
> Three or four Scolds – and the Sessions is ended.[175]

It was a common practice in many counties for the JPs to adjourn to the parlour of a nearby inn to conduct 'the county business'; that is paying accounts, appointing or confirming officers, and making orders relating to the general governance of the county.[176] This habit of meeting in private 'over their wine and walnuts' might not have excited much comment among contemporaries, had it not been for the fact that the JPs in quarter sessions were actually disposing of far more administrative power than their predecessors of the sixteenth and seventeenth centuries. Up and down the country, much of the administrative business done at sessions was ceasing to involve the judicial machinery of juries, indictments, plaints and petitions, but was taking the form of direct orders by the justices. Some counties even assumed a quasi-legislative authority, in so far as they issued general orders for such matters as the suppression of popular customs and entertainments, the prohibition of hawkers and peddlars, the licensing of alehouses, the relief of the poor, the direction of justices in their divisions, and even the re-organization of local government areas according to the convenience of the resident magistrates.[177]

The decision of the Berkshire justices at Speenhamland in May 1795, whereby they ordered that labourers' wages should be supplemented from the poor rate according to a tariff linked to the price of bread, was only the most famous of these 'extra-legal' magisterial orders.[178] Indeed, examples can be found throughout the eighteenth century. For instance, the Middlesex justices' persistent attempts to suppress fairs and plays and systemize the licensing of alehouses were inspired by the campaign for the reformation of manners which dated from the proclamation issued by William III.[179]

Such imperious behaviour did not pass unnoticed. In 1759 a correspondent of the *Gentleman's Magazine* complained of the practice by which 'the legislature of the court of quarter sessions' collected money for and erected new 'gratuity' bridges without the sanction of common law or statute, merely 'for private convenience and communication of neighbouring houses'.[180] And in 1822 Cobbett drew attention to substantial amendments in the administration of poor relief made by 'two squires' and 'five parsons', meeting in a private sessions of the Hampshire quarter sessions.[181] But they were certainly encouraged in several areas by an accession of legitimate power via parliamentary statutes. For example, on 25 April 1693 the Cheshire bench imposed a sixpenny rate on the townships of Malpas, Boughton, Olton Lowe and Fordham for repair of the highways, as they were authorized to by a statute of 1691; legislation which also required them to fix the rates of carriage between London and the main centres in the county.[182] From 1700, counties could raise rates to cover the costs of removing and transporting vagrants, and later legislation enabled them to reward constables and others who undertook the duty, powers which inspired the Hertfordshire quarter sessions to farm the business out to the county treasurer. This must have assisted the process of professionalizing constables, for they earned large sums by enforcing the laws against all kinds of itinerants and strangers.[183] Table 2.2 shows that the Cheshire bench may have been less active in prosecuting vagrancy before the nineteenth century, but they continued to raise money for the improvement of the county's transport infrastructure. Besides the regular orders for setting the carriage tariffs, several sixpenny rates were levied in 1729–31 and 1769–71; although unpopular, they helped to supplement the requirement for statute labour until the nineteenth century, when quarter sessions seems to have preferred the procedure of presentment by a JP and the levying of a fine.[184] Indeed, the 1691 highways act and subsequent legislation along the same lines passed during the same decade gave the JPs much greater initiative in relation to the roads, for in addition to levying a rate, they were given powers of compulsory purchase for enlarging or widening the highways in accordance with a national minimum.[185] Admittedly, the Cheshire justices were careful to treat property owners with respect. Thus in 1731 when the surveyors of the highways reported that a road was too narrow for traffic under the statute of 8&9 William III, the quarter sessions summoned the owners of the adjoining land to appear at the next sessions and 'shew cause' why the highway should not be enlarged out of their land. But their power was clear: a similar order made in October 1772 for treating with the owners of land adjoining a bridge was simply annotated 'Order for purchasing a Road adjoining to Brickdale Bridge'.[186]

The clearest accession of direct power to the justices in quarter sessions was authorized by the County Rates Act of 1739.[187] Under a succession of Tudor and Stuart statutes, besides the regular parish rates which were earmarked specifically for the relief of the poor and poor prisoners, the county justices were only able to raise money in a piecemeal fashion by levying 'collections' or 'assessments' in particular sums for set purposes, such as repairing roads and highways, maintaining prisons, and establishing houses of correction.[188] As Table 2.2 shows, in Cheshire before 1740 collections were raised mainly for the maintenance of bridges and public buildings such as gaols and houses of correction, after due presentation by the grand jury. Thus in 1727 quarter sessions ordered several sums of money to be raised for the repair of five bridges and cawseys, the shire hall and the county gaol, levying each hundred with its customary share of the total, amounting to no more than a few pounds in each case.[189] In addition each hundred had to pay its allotted proportion of the 'quarterly pay' for the county, a sum which totalled only £200 a year in the early eighteenth century. Clearly, leaving aside the burden on the local officers who were required to collect so many different amounts, these arrangements for raising money imposed considerable financial restrictions on the justices' freedom of action. The statute of 1739 therefore empowered quarter sessions to levy one consolidated rate 'for such Sum or Sums of money as they in their Discretions shall think sufficient' in lieu of all the previous rates.[190] Such moneys were supposed to be spent only on the purposes earmarked for the previous rates, and parishes or townships could appeal against over-assessment, with provision for removal of the action into the court of King's Bench by *certiorari*. But litigation was made liable to triple costs in the event of its failure, and the statute gave the justices considerable discretion by permitting them to levy another rate 'from Time to Time', after three-quarters of the previous rate had been spent, rather than just once a year.[191] Such provisions virtually amounted to parliament writing a blank cheque for the county justices to spend in public works. Certainly it has been observed that this act gave the JPs 'extensive powers of taxation', and Table 2.2 shows that henceforth in Cheshire payments to contractors multiplied as quarter sessions was able to invest freely in the improvement of the county's infrastructure.[192] Indeed, the clause which appeared to be designed to check improvident expenditure by providing that money could not be spent on the repair of bridges until the defect was presented by the grand jury was easily evaded by the expedient of justices making presentments 'on their own view', an administrative short-cut sanctioned by statute in 1773.[193] It also seems significant of the changing conditions in local government that the County Rates Act gave the justices in quarter sessions draconian powers over the officers charged with levying the rate, in so far as high constables and petty constables could be committed to the county gaol without bail for defaults in collecting or accounting for the money.[194]

Under these more positive financial conditions the county business offered real scope for creative government. In most counties the attendance of JPs improved from the final decades of the eighteenth century as the greater gentry families re-asserted their role as leaders of the localities.[195] But it is likely that in Cheshire as elsewhere in the early nineteenth century, there was an increased emphasis on administrative efficiency and membership of a consolidated propertied elite with shared ideals about public policy, which diminished the importance of inherited social status.[196] Certainly, as the statistics for payments of bills suggest, the justices who were on the Cheshire bench in the early nineteenth century were much more ambitious and innovative than their predecessors. In 1816–18, taking advantage of a further draught of parliamentary power for improving houses of correction, they raised several large loans by mortgaging the rates.[197] Indeed, although much of their effort continued to be devoted to roads and bridges, like many late-Georgian benches, they responded to parliamentary encouragement by devoting considerable administrative energy to the establishment or improvement of the county's facilities for administering justice and punishment.[198] In October 1814 they ordered the construction of a new sessions house and grand jury room at Knutsford, and in 1816 they considered taking steps towards adding a house of correction and lock-up house to the project 'for the confinement of Prisoners during the Midsummer and Michaelmas Quarter Sessions'.[199] In the same year two JPs who had been appointed by quarter sessions to inspect the house of correction at Middlewich presented it as not being 'sufficiently large and convenient for the reception classification and employment of the different descriptions of Male and Female Offenders usually committed thereto' and recommended the construction of another facility in a more central location which would be 'sufficiently capacious'.[200] Moreover, in September 1818 the Cheshire bench made a proposition to the quarter sessions in adjoining counties for building a lunatic asylum under the provisions of the 'late' act of parliament.[201] So even before they took the lead in establishing a county police force, these initiatives are sufficient to demonstrate a new found will among the Cheshire JPs 'to initiate, direct, and plan, rather than respond to parochial neglect or local complaint'.[202]

The change in the nature of the magistrates' proceedings that had occurred by the early nineteenth century is clear. With the encouragement of parliament, the 'court of quarter sessions' had begun to assume the proportions of a county executive, rather than a judicial body. Moreover, like every ambitious executive, they were developing a professional bureaucracy. Certainly a tendency to depart from the principle of relying on unpaid service and to appoint salaried officials has been noticed in several areas.[203] Most common was the appointment of a treasurer to manage the larger revenue streams and organize a regular system of expenditure and accounting, a development encouraged by the 1739 Rates Act.[204] Already in 1730 Cheshire had a treasurer on £10 per annum; his salary was increased to £20 in April 1731, and by 1817 it had reached £200 a year.[205] Moreover, by this time the office had been thoroughly professionalized: the incumbent treasurer was Mr. Henry Potts, a partner in the firm of Leek and Potts, solicitors, who were also retained to carry out the county's legal business.[206] Indeed, the late-Georgian magistrates of Cheshire appeared to have a much greater establishment to support them than their predecessors of a century earlier. Obviously with additional houses of correction there were more gaolers, and the employment of increasing numbers of special constables has already been mentioned. Under contemporary ideas about penal policy the prisoners required religious instruction as well as punishment, so the bench also retained a chaplain for Chester castle gaol, who was paid £40 per annum from 1817.[207] Equally, the ever-increasing burden of bridge maintenance ultimately required expert superintendence. Burn had recommended the employment of professional surveyors, and in 1816 the Cheshire sessions appointed salaried surveyors of the county and hundred bridges for the various hundreds.[208] They took over the role of the grand jury in respect of reporting disrepair and arranged for the necessary repairs. Only in the area of price regulation is it possible to detect a minor contraction in the county establishment: inspectors for the price of cereals sold in the county markets had been appointed following the act of parliament passed in 1770, but returns of prices were discontinued by the early nineteenth century after legislation made alternative arrangements.[209]

These widespread trends towards magisterial initiative, diminishing popular participation, and executive professionalization in the eighteenth-century experience of quarter sessions – so clearly confirmed by the proceedings of the Cheshire bench – are obviously significant for the themes of this book. It has been argued by seventeenth-century historians that the broad participation typical of local government in English society before 1700 allowed scope for the application of shared, normative, values.[210] Of course medieval and early modern communities were hardly idylls of peace and harmony, and there was a considerable 'increase in governance' during the seventeenth century. But although patterned by the particular circumstances of central government policy, local social structure and the community's relative cohesiveness or disunity, a system of local government which depended largely on unpaid service and personal initiative by its members could never be entirely patrician. Even if they were wealthy farmers or substantial shopkeepers, the wide measure of initiative, discretion and semi-independence allowed to the officers of the hundreds, townships and parishes must have encouraged an understanding that the institutions of government were susceptible to influence from the grass-roots.[211] Certainly, by resorting to the JPs and the sessions and using their legal processes the English people 'invited the state in'; their participation therefore represented 'an increase in its collective power rather than the distributive power of the executive'.[212] Or, to put it a simpler way, relatively lowly people shared in the process of governance. Moreover, by proceeding through judicial forms in open court the king's justices helped 'to teach men the very nature and forms of government'.[213] And the lesson was obvious – government proceeded via the hallowed forms of the common law, law administered with the community's consent, signified by its presence and participation. And in theory under this culture of governance everyone – even the JPs – was equally answerable to the law, even if they were not so equal in practice.

By contrast, at the end of the eighteenth century, the proceedings of the justices of the peace appear to have been remote and oligarchic, and at the lower levels effectively autonomous. At the apex, magistrates in sessions enjoyed virtually unlimited power to levy rates; met behind closed doors to direct administrative initiatives in accordance with the latest legislation; and employed salaried professionals whose livelihoods depended on their favour. At the grass-roots individual JPs mediated disputes or dispensed summary justice according to their own ideas, prejudices, or interests, with very little accountability to the higher law courts; and petty or special sessions appointed officers, made general regulations, and co-opted the administration of state taxation into their calendars. Under these conditions local government must surely have appeared to be the exclusive province of their worships, the consolidated elite of property owners, and their servants. The new lesson of county governance was surely not about law, as much as power, and positive administration from above. And whether it took the form of constitutional powers given to justices or commissioners under statute, magisterial quasi-legislation from the sessions bench, or the decisions of a squire or parson sitting in his front parlour, the origin and symbol of that power and authority was clearly the Westminster parliament.[214]

So by 1800, their commands might well be taken for law, just as parliament's were. The popular identification between magisterial power and parliamentary legitimization can be seen most clearly in the assumption that the orders which introduced precise scales of poor relief at the end of the eighteenth century partook of statutory authority.[215] Indeed, it would have been hard for the people to miss the growing symbiosis between the parliament at Westminster and the magistracy from the later eighteenth century. As we shall see later, in the 1770s, 1780s and 1790s county magistrates took the lead in promoting and utilizing new legislation for improvement of local prisons.[216] The evidence for Cheshire and other counties suggests that the most active justices responded eagerly to fresh parliamentary initiatives, and many more simply thirsted for copies of the new statutes to display in their justice rooms.[217] Besides promulgating the statutes, they also answered private ministerial requests for data on a range of subjects, thereby acting as 'so many superior sources of information for legislation as well as agents for its implementation'.[218] Admittedly, although a trend for quarter sessions to appoint permanent chairmen assisted its flow, the channels of central-local communication were not wholly new, and it is clear that there was greater central direction of local government in Tudor and Stuart times than in the eighteenth century.[219] Nevertheless, in the counties JPs were appointed and dismissed on the advice of the lord lieutenant, who was often close to the government, and in some places the deputy lieutenants (always JPs) continued to serve as 'conduits for central government authority'.[220] Indeed, despite the traditional emphasis on JPs' independence, and the decline in the coercive power of the central government with the weakening of the privy council after 1660, there were enduring official and unofficial links between the magistracy and the centre, and no doubt communication became more interactive in a period when politics and government were staple fare for the growth of the press.[221] Certainly the JPs' connections with Westminster became more noticeable at the grass-roots under late-Georgian conditions of hyperactive legislation, and radical reformers were able plausibly to caricature the justice of the peace who executed so many different acts as 'that retailer of oppression to every administration'.[222] They were no longer so much judicial officers acting under law as statutory instruments with very general powers. Here, in the dynamic reciprocal connections between magistrates, parliament, and activists among backbench MPs and ministers, were the lineaments of a state which was parliamentary and localist, rather than centralized and bureaucratic. But it had travelled a very long way from the medieval culture of self-government under the common law and built decisively upon some of the Tudor-Stuart trends towards legislative activism and administrative intervention. I shall return to these themes later, but it is appropriate now to consider another major shift in the nature of governance during the eighteenth century: the decline of civil litigation.

# 3
# Going to Law: The Rise and Fall of Civil Litigation

> The courts were cultural as well as legal institutions.
> C. Harrison, 'Manor Courts and the Governance of Tudor England'
> in C.W. Brooks and M. Lobban (eds.), *Communities and Courts in Britain 1150–1900* (1997), 45.

> The monstrous Increase of the Expense of Law Suits, arising from the extravagant Fees of counsel, Officers, Stamp Duties, &c &c ... have very nearly destroyed the Law, and deprived the Subject, of his most valuable Birthright; for it is the same Thing to the Subject, whether Right be denied him, or so high a Price be set upon it, that he is unable to purchase it.
> *Reflections or Hints Founded upon Experience and Facts, touching the Law* (1759), 71.

Almost Everyman – and more women than expected – went to law in England before the eighteenth century. Civil litigation was a common, almost universal experience in some areas, and many people appeared as prosecutors of suits as well as defendants, at least above the level of the desperately poor.[1] One reason for this was the availability of courts for hearing private pleas. As suggested in the last chapter, courts were the characteristic institutions of governance in medieval times, and the prerogative to administer justice between party and party was fundamental to lordship and kingship.[2] Just as the king's courts heard pleas of the crown, so they also entertained suits between party and party, as did the hundred and county courts, manorial courts, church courts, and the courts which sat in virtually every incorporated borough. Together they provided a complex web of overlapping jurisdictions which allowed individual access to law and authority from almost every doorstep.

But the experience of taking a dispute to court became much more exceptional in the course of the eighteenth century, and has never returned to the 'hyperlexis' levels of the Tudor-Stuart period.[3] This chapter attempts to consider the significance of the rise and fall of mass participation in civil litigation. The English propensity for litigiousness was already marked in the Middle Ages, and recourse to the law increased still more in the later sixteenth century, remaining at a very high level until the end of the seventeenth. So around 1700 the English would have taken access to justice for granted: like serving as a constable, overseer, or churchwarden, widespread use of the civil courts must surely have imprinted appreciations of 'law' as a culture of governance which was generally amenable to individual initiative and negotiation. Moreover, although the desired outcome was hardly guaranteed, it is arguable that the ability to maintain a personal prosecution in court would have been an empowering experience, especially for people below the social elite: and it seems that even 'illiterate and educated peasants and townsmen' were able to 'use and manipulate … courts for their own purposes'.[4] If that was so, then the recession in English litigation may well have had profound implications for relations between government and the governed. Before considering those implications, however, it is necessary to outline the range and scope of the courts, as well as the ebb and flow of their business.

## Patterns of litigation

Understanding the rise and fall of civil litigation in English society requires an appreciation of the web of courts which were available for hearing the complaints of individual litigants. First, there were the central courts of Westminster Hall, which were accessible from most parts of England for suits worth more than 40 shillings through the arrangement of *nisi prius*, whereby actions were started in London but tried by the assize judges when they came round on their circuits. Secondly, several provinces had preserved their own alternative versions of the Westminster courts which heard civil suits as well as pleas of the crown: in Wales the 'great sessions' of the county palatine of Chester and the other circuits served this purpose, and there were also more limited palatine or duchy jurisdictions for Durham and Lancaster, as well as the Council of Wales and the Welsh Marches and the Council of the North at York.[5] In the third place there was a whole separate network of ecclesiastical courts for spiritual causes, ranging from those of the archdeacons and bishops in each diocese to the provincial courts of York and Canterbury. They heard interpersonal suits relating to wills, tithes, promises and breakdowns in matters of marriage, and sexual defamation. Fourthly, where they survived the communal courts of the hundreds were also able to entertain private pleas, and every manor had a court baron (and/or possibly a court leet) which could hear the suits of the lord's tenants. If these courts were not sufficient, a fifth layer was made up of the various borough courts, often called the mayor's court, the guildhall court, or simply the court of record or of pleas, as well as a range of more curious names. They could only deal with pleas which arose within their liberties, but many country people had business in their nearest town or city, and together their jurisdictions covered most of the country: '[v]ery few people in the countryside lived more than a half-day's horse ride from a court of record in a major market town, and most lived much closer, perhaps even within walking distance'.[6]

As far as we can tell from research, with the partial exception of some of the hundred courts and manorial courts, which were threatened by price inflation and tended to survive and prosper only where they coincided with urban development, virtually all these tribunals were heavily used in the two centuries before 1700.[7] The practice of litigating over debts and broken promises had been institutionalized and firmly established among English people during the later Middle Ages; and although there was a decline in the number of lawsuits during the economic and political crises which set in from the mid-1400s, with the return of economic prosperity and rising commercial activity around the time of Elizabeth I's accession the courts became busier than ever before.[8] In the principal common law tribunals of Westminster Hall – the King's Bench and Common Pleas – sampling has shown that cases reached a historic peak around 1600 which was more or less maintained until the final quarter of the seventeenth century, despite a temporary recession during the Civil Wars. However, a steep decline set in around 1680, reaching a nadir after 1750 when the two courts together were hearing only about a sixth as many cases as they had 70 years previously, and they remained relatively depressed until the end of the eighteenth century. Although there was a significant revival after 1790, by contrast with the sixteenth century, this hardly kept pace with increasing population and economic activity, for around 1830 the rate of central court litigation per head of population was less than half what it had been in 1606.[9] A broadly similar pattern has been tracked in Chancery, where the rate of new litigation seems to have been running at around 5–6,000 bills of complaint a year between 1610 and 1700, but then declined by over two-thirds over the course of the eighteenth century, before increasing again in the early nineteenth. Here too the recovery hardly matched the post-1800 demographic and economic take-off, however, since aggregate levels of new bills coming into the court in 1820 were only at about 40 per cent of the levels achieved in 1700.[10]

The great contrast between the litigiousness of the Tudors and Stuarts on the one hand and the relative 'hypolexis' of the Georgians is rendered still more significant by the extensive social reach of the courts before 1700. In their hey-day the principal customers of the central courts, like the constables, jurors and churchwardens who animated the law locally, were drawn from the 'middling sort' of English society; the 'ordinary people' who constituted 70 or

80 per cent of the population and were broadly 'middling' in the sense that they were by no means wealthy but not destitute either.[11] As Christopher Brooks has pointed out, 'provincial farmers, merchants, tailors, miners, and occasionally even labourers, could find legal representation and use the courts'.[12] But far fewer people were going to law after the early eighteenth century; and there are clear signs that the barristers, attorneys and officers who depended on the central courts elaborated working practices and increased fees to suit high-value metropolitan cases and their wealthy clients. Certainly there was a two or threefold rise in the average costs of a lawsuit between the later seventeenth and mid-eighteenth centuries, and the limited data which is available for quantifying the social and geographical origins of litigants suggests that even the provincial gentry – those without a London address, and presumably without the extraordinary wealth signified by metropolitan business or official interests or a second house in London – were partially deterred from going to law.[13] Indeed, in the first half of the eighteenth century, when the aggregate of litigation was declining most sharply, there was a spate of complaints about the difficulty of affording justice, especially among provincial people of modest means. As one critic maintained:

> the great Charge, and Delay of Justice, is not only injurious to all sorts of Suitors, but perfectly deprives the poorer sort of Justice, who (tho' they were sure of having it all again) cannot be so much in Disburse as a Suit requires, or cannot stay so long for their money as the tedious Rules of the Courts oblige them to, before they can recover it.[14]

It is significant of popular engagement with the courts that another claimed their growing expense and delays 'have very nearly destroyed the Law, and deprived the Subject, of his most valuable Birthright'.[15] Complaints like these demonstrate the persistence of a culture of litigation which depended on using the courts as of course in matters of recovering small debts and prosecuting trespasses and breaches of promise, and was profoundly disappointed in its expectations.

Studies of local courts have revealed a similar pattern of high participation and subsequent recession. There were over 200 active courts of record in the English boroughs during the early modern period, and together their jurisdiction extended over large parts of the countryside.[16] Certainly they were very heavily used, contrary to previous assumptions about the mass transferral of litigation from local courts to Westminster Hall.[17] Muldrew has shown that in Tudor and early Stuart times local borough courts were more important centres of litigation than the central courts, in so far as the rate of litigation per head of population covered by them was much higher, reflecting their proximity and comparative cheapness.[18] In the Norfolk sea-port borough of

King's Lynn, over a four-year period during the mid-1680s it is likely that virtually every household was a litigant in the Guildhall court, including a majority who appeared as plaintiffs at least once, and many people who sued again and again. Moreover, such litigation was hardly confined to the town elite: over 60 per cent of the litigants were relatively poor, in so far as they were not subject to property taxation, and nearly half of them appeared as plaintiffs in their own right. One man who was resident in an almshouse, a mere patten maker by trade, sued five times, while the borough records also identify two plaintiffs as labourers, who each appeared four or five times.[19] And the poorest plaintiffs took action against people from all levels of the community, including the very wealthiest. The explanation for this high incidence and broad social penetration of litigation was the universal reliance on oral promises in this thriving commercial centre, whereby credit was extended in virtually every transaction, and even relatively humble people depended on initiating an action in the court for routine settlement of debts, either for goods sold or for simple services like borrowing a horse to ride to Ely. It is true that the overwhelming majority of these suits did not proceed beyond the initial stages of filing a suit, and only a tiny proportion went to final judgement. But the court at King's Lynn was nevertheless intimately connected with the local community, and poor litigants were frequently present in person.[20] Moreover in towns the size of Lynn, even if suits did not proceed to final judgement, the fame of an arrest, or the non-appearance of a plaintiff when the defendant had appeared to answer the plea, would likely result in severe popular discredit. In this sense, because proceedings ultimately became public, even incomplete suits involved some measure of substantial popular participation and judgement.[21]

In addition to King's Lynn, studies for other courts in Great Yarmouth, Exeter, Shrewsbury, Bristol, Taunton, Chester and Norwich suggest that levels of litigation in borough courts were very high generally in the later sixteenth and early seventeenth centuries.[22] The rising economic activity of this period meant that more transactions were made on credit and more debts therefore had to be recovered via the law. In some of the substantial towns it appears there was an average of up to two suits for each household every year around the end of the sixteenth century, and there were more still in the very largest urban centres, such as Bristol, Norwich and London. Fragmentary evidence also suggests that levels of litigation were high in some manor courts, especially those of unincorporated market towns, such as Witney in Oxfordshire, Tiverton in Devon, and Thirsk and Northallerton in North Yorkshire. The pattern of usage may have been matched in courts which served smaller urban centres, such as Battle in Sussex, where most of the 100–150 male residents sued in the High Court of Battle Abbey.[23] If all the estimates for rates of litigation in local and central courts are extrapolated to the whole of England, then it appears that there would have been at least one lawsuit per household every year around 1600, a rate which has never been achieved since.[24]

But again, all this changed after 1700. In fact, many of the borough courts which have been studied show that the social incidence of litigation had been falling somewhat from its peak during the seventeenth century, in so far as absolute numbers of actions did not match the population growth which continued down to 1650. But most of them were still attracting high numbers of suits in the later 1600s, and it was not until the eighteenth century, when absolute numbers of suits fell to unprecedented low levels, that the decline in litigation would have become 'socially obvious'.[25] In King's Lynn, for example, the number of new actions commenced in the Guildhall Court dropped from around 1,000 in 1700 to 160 in 1750, a figure which was less than a tenth of the caseload recorded for 1685. Taunton borough court was diminished from around 400 actions in 1670 to less than 50 after 1710.[26] And in Shrewsbury's *curia parva*, around 1730 the level of new business was only 5 per cent of what it had been in the early seventeenth century, following a steady decline from the time of the Restoration.[27] Less dramatic recessions had set in by 1750 in the municipal courts of Newcastle, Exeter, Great Yarmouth, and Bristol.[28] It is unlikely that borough jurisdictions like these ever recovered much of their business during the later eighteenth century, and parliamentary enquiries show that most were moribund in the 1820s.[29]

Although new local small-debt courts attracted many litigants in the nineteenth century, the decline of the old urban jurisdictions is doubly significant for the arguments of this book. For by contrast with the courts of requests, or of 'conscience', which were founded in some developing urban centres during the eighteenth century, and the new system of county courts which replaced them in 1847, it has been argued that the older courts were 'much more firmly rooted within the local community'. They depended on local juries, were accountable to borough and city corporations, and lay mayors and aldermen sat alongside lawyer recorders as judges.[30] Given their high level of community participation, it is probably no coincidence that some borough courts appear to have been relatively lenient with poor debtors, in so far as they were less likely to be sued to judgement than defendants of middling wealth. Certainly the juries in seventeenth-century King's Lynn tended to award only moderate damages, despite high claims from plaintiffs, and there is evidence that other local courts encouraged compromise settlements too.[31] The courts of requests and county courts, on the other hand, were utilized enthusiastically to collect small debts from the poor, even to the extent of sending substantial numbers of destitute people to prison, where over time a culture of disciplinary correction tended to displace the notion that indebtedness was merely a matter of misfortune, rather than a moral failing which approximated to crime.[32] Admittedly, the overall picture of these new courts in action is a complex one: there were individual cases in early nineteenth-century courts of requests where plebeian plaintiffs recovered debts against the odds, and both courts of requests and county courts could be very flexible in allowing minors, servants and especially wives direct representation. Nevertheless close analysis shows that at the same time they overwhelmingly favoured men and women of property against working-class defendants.[33] Moreover, the administration of courts of requests was much less participatory than that of the traditional local courts: Blackstone condemned them as tending to the creation of 'a petty tyranny in a set of standing commissioners', and there were complaints to parliament that commissioners oppressed the poor.[34] Their principal defender, the bookseller William Hutton, who was a commissioner of the Birmingham court of requests in the 1770s and 1780s, was hostile to local juries because they were drawn from 'the shop, the street, and the alehouse', and he clearly believed that one of the court's major functions was to correct what he regarded as the endemic fecklessness and deceit among 'the lower ranks'.[35] Some Victorian county court judges were less narrowly prejudiced, but several were overbearing and erratic in their courtroom conduct, and these courts were so frequently hostile to jury trials that they soon became a 'rarity'.[36] So it is probably no exaggeration to say that the decay of the ancient borough courts in the eighteenth century meant that one of the principal ways in which relatively humble lay people participated actively and successfully in the administration of civil justice – and thereby helped to govern interpersonal relations – was lost irretrievably.

Interestingly, the church courts were also losing clients at a rapid rate in the early eighteenth century, and with their decline the interaction of the law with plebeian women diminished. Most studies of the 'instance' litigation (as distinguished from the official or 'correctional' jurisdiction, which was almost moribund by 1700) have tracked the rise of defamation suits for words alleging sexual misconduct, a species of litigation which came to predominate in all the church courts during the Elizabethan and early Stuart periods, and ultimately became colonized by women.[37] In a legal regime which normally reflected patriarchal values, these courts were almost unique as sites available for negotiating disputes among women of relatively modest means, especially wives. No doubt this is why defamation suits survived in diminished but still substantial numbers at the ecclesiastical courts into the 1700s, despite seventeenth-century popular and political challenges to the established church. For example there were about 120 actions of this kind a year in the church courts at York around 1720, and nearly 70 were initiated at the Consistory Court of London in 1715. However all the principal courts examined extensively – those for York, Wells, and London – experienced a major decline in defamation business by mid-century.[38] Although a few women were still suing for words in some provincial church courts every year during the early 1800s, and the jurisdiction generally underwent a rather slower death than historians have assumed, the overall levels of litigation were insignificant in the context of rising population.[39] Moreover, in the only church court which seems to have made a partial recovery, as in the central courts of Westminster Hall, the revival of litigation was socially disproportionate: the London Consistory Court attracted new clients in the second half of the eighteenth century, but it only survived as a centre of interpersonal litigation by becoming the most fashionable divorce court in the country, which catered primarily for unhappy couples of wealth and high status.[40]

So there were multiple points of contact with courts and legal processes which were used very heavily in the two centuries before 1700, but they were virtually disconnected from the majority of English people in the first half of the eighteenth century and never fully re-established. What does the rise and fall of civil litigation say about 'law' and relations with government? General and active involvement with court proceedings may have had great significance for the positive experience of authority. For example in King's Lynn 'On many court days the poor would have been present in the hall with their betters, and would also have spent much time talking to lawyers, or entering complaints with the court clerk'. Imagining the court in this way therefore 'gives a very real illustration of equality before the law'.[41] Indeed it is possible that going to law meant much more than simply using the court as an instrument for achieving an individual remedy. Certainly in a society which placed so much emphasis on the enforcement of rights and duties in the courts, as early modern England did, it could have quasi-political resonance. In such a legalistic context the courts may be interpreted as primary sites for 'the discourse about good and bad states of society'; whether the issue was the payment of a debt, the performance of a promise, restoring personal reputation, or respecting local rights of common, maintaining an action meant that the prosecutor was participating actively in the continuous exchange of ideas about the 'right' ways of ordering society.[42] In this sense virtually every adult male in Tudor-Stuart England – apart from those who were excluded by mental incapacity – could take part in such a discourse of government through the courts. Moreover, although married women were disqualified from suing at common law by the doctrine of coverture, some were able to litigate in a more than nominal sense through the courts of equity, as well as in the church courts.[43] The studies of litigation summarized previously show that the result was a complex social exchange, which included a wide range of colourful perspectives. By contrast, after 1700, one supposes the recession of litigation meant that the discourse of the courts must have been much more monochrome in character. However, perhaps it is important to pause before assimilating the individual experience of litigation to the wide-angle lens of modern sociologists. Most litigants were acting in their own personal interest after all: they were not necessarily sincere in their protestations of fair dealing, or seeking to achieve harmonious relations with their opponents in court; and it is hardly conceivable that they were seeking consciously to advance the interests of their class or sex. At this point, it is necessary to consider more carefully the variety of motivations for taking a dispute to court, and observe the experience of litigation at close range.

## Motives and meanings: The experience of litigation

Why did people sue in the courts? Some historians have suggested that the litigiousness typical of early modern English society was expressive of widespread interpersonal intolerance, malice, and the furtherance of discord, and was most definitely not motivated by any desire to use the authority of the law to promote justice, order or harmony. Such a view tends to read the sixteenth and seventeenth-century proliferation of lawsuits as a breakdown in the social cohesion of local communities under pressure from population growth, economic individualism and post-Reformation religious uncertainty.[44] Certainly, Bernard Mandeville, writing in the early eighteenth century, believed there were plenty of 'selfish and litigious' people, and there is no doubt that suits were used sometimes to vex an opponent, or even to carry on a preexisting argument or feud.[45] Around this time Christine Churches has uncovered ample evidence of 'spiteful enemies' among the litigious inhabitants of the prosperous port of Whitehaven in Cumberland. James Lowther, the lord of the manor and local entrepreneur, was involved in several long-lived suits with residents of the town against whom he harboured grievances. For example, a claim for a small debt which he prosecuted against a Whitehaven apothecary was just one episode in a long-running vendetta, and actions against a local farmer for trespass and non-payment of tithes were actually motivated by revenge for the defendant's previous objections to the Lowthers' modifications of customary procedure in the manorial court.[46]

Moreover, vexatious suits were hardly confined to the secular courts, or to aggressive merchant capitalists. Indeed, many contemporaries and some modern historians believe that the availability of actions for defamation in the ecclesiastical courts gave far too much scope for the encouragement of a neighbourhood culture of plebeian disorder which depended on suspicion, malicious gossip, and ritual humiliation.[47] Again, it is not hard to find confirmation for such opinions. A good example is the case of *Grant v. Russell*, which was decided before the Consistory Court of London in 1700. It was a fairly typical suit between two married women of Wapping: Mary Grant sued Lucy Russell for defamatory words, she having allegedly called Mrs. Grant a whore in public. But the real issue seems to have been an argument over a debt of £30 which Mr. Grant owed to Mr. Russell, for which the former had been arrested at common law, and the defamation case was most likely brought as retaliation.[48] Here surely the suitor was just 'trying it on', and like serial killers with a divine mission, the claims of principle by serial litigants need not be taken too seriously.[49]

However, whatever the merits of the particular issues in these technically 'vexatious' cases, it is difficult to dismiss even litigation like this as frivolous sport, or casual oppression, which signifies nothing beyond the propagation of malice or individual self-interest. Most people in early modern times seem to have been touched in some degree by the prevailing 'culture of reconciliation', whereby going to law against a neighbour or acquaintance had to be justified according to ethical principles, and a degree of restraint was ultimately necessary.[50] Expressions of these ethical constraints are relatively rare after 1750, given the decline in the experience of litigation, but they were still current among those privileged groups able to use the courts. For the Sussex shopkeeper Thomas Turner in 1764, contemplating his parish vestry's re-appointment of two 'litigious' men as surveyors of the highways, the temptation for 'executing law to the utmost' ought to be tempered by 'justice, equity, or charity'.[51] Around the same time the Reverend William Cole, rector of Blecheley in Buckinghamshire, was embroiled in petty disputes over trespassing livestock with a vexatious neighbour. But although he was not above *threatening* to sue, ultimately he resolved to 'sit down under my injury, rather than suffer the greater one of going to law', declaring that he had never yet had occasion to fee a lawyer against one of his parishioners.[52]

It is probably significant of normal ethical expectations in relation to litigation that litigants themselves often attempted to brand their opponents as vexatious. Thus the brewer James Pew, responding in 1734 to a prosecution in the archdeaconry court of Surrey for encroaching on the churchyard of St. Mary Rotherhithe with his malt kiln, alleged the suit was carried on 'out of sheer vexation' in an attempt to make him surrender a piece of disputed ground.[53] Pew sued successfully for a prohibition by the court of King's Bench. So it was probably an unusual litigant who had no conscious self-justification for going to law. For example Mary Grant was Lucy Russell's serving maid, and her husband was Mr. Russell's apprentice.[54] No doubt the accusation of 'whore' had been flung at Mrs. Grant in the context of a quarrel over the arrest of her husband, perhaps signifying dishonesty in money matters, rather than sexuality. But faced with the intransigence of the Russells over the debt, Mary may well have felt justified in taking her mistress to the Consistory in the hope that the threat of prosecution and public penance would make her relent. As a poor married woman the ecclesiastical court was the only tribunal available to her, and the predominance of women litigants in cases like hers may have given her confidence. Even the hard-nosed James Lowther regularly legitimated his dubious legal chicanery as a fair response to previous harassment in the courts by his enemies in Whitehaven: 'it is a piece of justice that is due to litigious people to serve them in their own kind'.[55] And such protestations of self-righteousness should not be dismissed as mere superficial piety: for Lowther, the larger issue at stake in his campaigns at law seems to have been maintaining respect for what he firmly believed was his legitimate power and status as the lawful lord of the manor. In other words, he regarded many of the cases in which he was engaged as battles in a semi-political campaign, where the main issue was ensuring the continuance of his patrician hegemony against social inferiors and business rivals, who might be encouraged by his forbearance, even in a suit over a few pounds. As the historian of this imbroglio has put it, from his point of view: 'if merchants and masters had only deferred to his guidance and direction then town, harbour and trade would have been quietly and agreeably governed for the benefit and prosperity of all'.[56] For their part the townspeople of Whitehaven went to law because they wanted to have their say in the government of their community, and resisted the local magnate's pretensions to oligarchy. So even seemingly vexatious litigants might be promoting a vision about order and justice.

Lowther and his opponents utilized the courts fairly self-consciously to negotiate their competing ideas about the legitimate ordering of their community in matters of business, politics, and religion. Perhaps this approach to litigation was exceptional, however. The great bulk of common law suits during the 'boom' years of the sixteenth and seventeenth centuries were about 'specific rights and dues', especially actions for unpaid debts and broken agreements, and it seems reasonable to assume that many were genuinely commenced for the limited purposes alleged: redressing a simple case of material injustice.[57] An eighteenth-century example is the case of *Cook v. Keep*, tried before Sir Dudley Ryder in June 1754. Mrs. Cook was a widow who had continued the family farm after her husband's death in 1751. Three years later she was the plaintiff in an action at the Middlesex *nisi prius* sessions for nearly £40 allegedly due for quantities of corn, oats and beans sold on account over several years to a corn factor named Keep. Presented with a demand for the money, the defendant had said 'Damn the account'. Faced with this unreasonable behaviour, she needed the authority of the court of King's Bench to assert her rights and recover the debt, and was duly satisfied by a verdict in her favour.[58] Admittedly, this case was relatively unusual in so far as the issue of right was so clear, and the case went to trial, rather than out of court settlement. One wonders whether Keep did not compromise because he anticipated misogyny from an all-male jury. Certainly relatively few cases commenced were fought through to a verdict and award: normally a complaint was sufficient to bring the defendant to account and the case proceeded no further. In this failure to follow through, one can perhaps discern aggregated traces of the cultural imperative for reconciliation which has been mentioned previously. According to this view litigation was a necessary evil at best, and the prosecutor should be prepared to sacrifice some portion of his or her right in the interest of restoring good relations.[59] Nevertheless, the assertion of a property right remained the basis of actions like *Cook*, and whether ameliorated by consciousness of the need for reconciliation or not, by itself it constituted a statement about fair dealing in social relations and government in a commercial society. By prosecuting for the value of her cereals Mrs. Cook was silently affirming a fundamental cultural value: people should keep their promises and pay their debts, and in the last resort the courts should force them to do so. As will be seen, the presence of these basic ideas behind the simple act of going to court was revealed by reaction to the rising expense of litigation.

According to the prevailing ideology about the rule of law, every Englishman should have been able to tell his story and enforce his right, if he could prove it to the satisfaction of his peers. So in a society where wealth, status and gender normally produced very unequal personal relations, poorer male suitors and virtually all female litigants must have felt genuinely empowered by the ability to maintain a case against the grain of property and patriarchy. To put the point more generally, while the courts remained broadly accessible the law could serve as 'powerful solvent on the deferential posture of ordinary people'.[60] This was not just a matter of theory, even in the years when popular engagement with the law was declining. Another case heard by Dudley Ryder was an action of trespass prosecuted at the Hertford Assizes in August 1754 by Joseph Durham against a man called Fisher. At the trial counsel for the prosecution proved that Fisher had entered Durham's close with dogs and trampled his corn, but on the surface it is hard to see this as a great victory, since the jury only awarded 5s. damages and no costs, which must have left the plaintiff severely out of pocket. Indeed, it is clear the case could not have been brought for strictly material reasons, because late seventeenth-century statutes had made it very difficult to recover full costs and damages in minor trespasses.[61] However the real issue was opposition to the gentry's exclusive legal right to take game wherever they liked. The defendant was a gentleman's servant employed to course game for his table, and Durham had obviously had enough of his repeated depredations. His principal aim was to obtain a certificate from Ryder to the effect that the trespass was 'willful and malicious' according to the statute, thereby winning a legal instrument which could be deployed in any subsequent proceedings. Ryder was typically cautious at first, but he was persuaded to issue the certificate on the bar's assertion that it was customary where the trespass was deliberate, and the other judge on the circuit confirmed this was normal practice.[62] Thus the farmer proved his point against the local gentry.

The authentic political significance of litigation can be read in the largely negative reactions of oligarchs and patriarchs to what they perceived as the potential rebelliousness of the English people. Suits of the David *v.* Goliath variety must have been more frequent before the turn of the eighteenth century, given the relatively low costs of going to law, and their importance is attested by the complaints of grandees on the receiving end.[63] After having to compromise with a tradesman who sued him for full payment in return for work done on a saddle, James Lowther rightly anticipated the setback would encourage other inferiors to take him to court, and therefore determined to be 'a little stricter upon people'.[64] Moreover, in the immediate aftermath of the English Civil War explicit connections were made between litigation and revolution. Certainly, whatever the prosecutor's conscious motive for going to law, the image of a poor tenant or servant arguing his rights in court was often believed to be powerfully subversive of the natural social order; and the threat seems to have been even more keenly felt in the case of women suitors. It has been shown, for example, that husbands who were sued for maintenance by their estranged wives in the Elizabethan court of requests positively squealed at what they saw as the court's connivance in allowing wives 'unbrydled libertie', and generally deplored the prospect of women 'being boldened though sufference' of their claims.[65] Indeed even Anthony Benn, recorder of London under James I and an advocate for every *man*'s right to the rule of law, thought women should be excluded from the courts because of their opportunism and vanity: in his experience they 'would be thought wise in speaking and fayer to be seen'.[66]

As Benn's ingenuous comment about the 'shifts and Importunytes' of women in court reveals, whether he liked it or not, many inhabitants of early modern England were not shy about taking their chances to 'negotiate' with the law by deploying their own wiles and strategies. Common law trials were highly amenable to personal suasion or popular opinion because they depended on the litigants, the parties' witnesses and local sentiment as sources of information; juries were susceptible to such influence, and even professional judges were not immune. In these circumstances there was considerable scope for representations of behaviour which appealed to 'unofficial norms' beyond the letter of the law.[67] Of course the most famous exemplification of such a transaction in eighteenth-century trials is the 'pious perjury' of criminal juries, whereby stolen goods were deliberately undervalued in order to allow thieves to escape the penalty of death which applied formally to some species of larceny.[68] Here the value-judgement that death for petty theft was disproportionate punishment could ameliorate the law, according to the discretion of the jury and its opinion about the circumstances and characters represented in court.

There is no reason to doubt that similar transactions occurred in civil cases where lay juries made decisions about verdict, costs and damages, as they did in most local courts and the *nisi prius* sessions of the central courts.[69] Certainly the power of juries to decide damages gave them great scope to make decisions on the basis of their judgement about the culpability and 'character' of the parties, rather than the facts at issue. Thus in *Knowlys v. Castleton*, an action for slander at the Middlesex sessions maintained by a Hampstead publican against a neighbouring competitor, the jury accepted the clear proof that the defendant had spoken the words in question – alleging that the prosecutor kept a bawdy house. But they only awarded 1d damages, thereby effectively giving their verdict according to the public reputations of the protagonists, a comparison which told heavily against the plaintiff, who was represented as having associated with highwaymen, as well as prostitutes.[70] More famously, the jury in the trial of the duke of Norfolk's action against John Germain for 'criminal conversation' with his duchess only awarded the duke 100 marks in damages, rather than the £100,000 claimed, 'Upon Which they had a severe Reprimand from the Court, for giving so small and Scandalous a Fine'.[71] In this case the jury was doubtless taking notice of the duke's own notorious adultery and other lapses, and conveying its sense that the parties were almost equally morally reprehensible.[72]

The important point to be made here is that the availability of discretionary judgements, and the parties' natural tendency to express themselves, invested litigation with significance beyond the purposes of the principals involved. Inevitably, cultures and sub-cultures, values and beliefs, rubbed up against each other in the courts as the participants embellished their stories, directly and indirectly, with or without the court's approval. And they were bound to rub off: sometimes 'unofficial norms' blended with the 'official' culture of the courts to influence decision-making, and occasionally they might even become established practice. For example Clive Holmes has shown how witchcraft proceedings in the sixteenth and seventeenth centuries expressed complex interactions between popular beliefs, the preoccupations of interested clergymen and magistrates, and the administration of the law; and these exchanges influenced both elite and popular attitudes.[73] Something like this went on in every court, as it still does today, although the balance of power between lay participants and lawyers has shifted in favour of professional legal culture. Judges and counsel are hardly intellectually autonomous, however, and in early modern England there was more scope for creative jurisprudence which read their opinions and prejudices into the administration of law.

This was especially true of jurisdictions which proceeded by equity, or 'conscience', where 'shared principles of justice' were supposed to be applied and substantive law was relatively inchoate.[74] As Tim Stretton has observed of suitors litigating in the Elizabethan court of requests, which attracted a broad cross-section of contemporary society, the parties implicitly acknowledged the absence of a jury by constructing their bills and answers according to what they thought the Masters of the court wanted to hear, assuming the 'high moral standards' of the clergy's sermons and prescriptive literature. But the Masters were hardly fools, and their experience would frequently have enabled them to glimpse quite different standards and cultural practices which lay behind the parties' stories. Thus Margaret Dier complained that a lodger had got her daughter with child 'upon a devilishe minde to satisfy his luste'; but her own evidence suggested she had condoned their sexual relations in the hope of marrying her off to the man in question.[75] Moreover, although they usually disagreed about the facts in question, and embroidered or economized with the truth, the protagonists' carefully composed accusatory and exculpatory narratives revealed and affirmed contemporary ideals of behaviour in marriage, household and family. So in these cases, as in others, litigation proceedings 'cut through the boundaries that separated different groups within society, in a cultural as well as a legal sense, transporting ideas back and forward between the highest courts in the land and the humblest subjects in town and province'.[76]

This function of litigation as a conduit for continuous cultural exchange and negotiation, as well as the direct affirmation of individual rights, can be seen most clearly in defamation proceedings at the ecclesiastical courts. Because such actions came to be dominated in most places by plebeian women – the wives and daughters of tradesmen, shopkeepers and artisans in urban centres, or of husbandmen and yeomen in the surrounding countryside – in the seventeenth century the church courts were partially colonized by their habitual modes of expression and personal interaction.[77] These women's reputations and prospects were vulnerable to street or alehouse gossip about unchastity, normally expressed as accusations that they were 'whores', 'queans', or 'bawds'; and they went to the courts to restore their sexual reputations and bring their accusers to a private settlement or a public penance imposed by the judge. As the case of *Grant v. Russell* suggests, however, many sexual defamation cases were expressions and escalations of quarrels which had little connection with actual sexual conduct.[78] Laura Gowing has argued persuasively that both women and men used sexual insult as a highly-charged weapon to bring the power of conventional moral expectations to bear on women with whom they were in conflict over other matters. By so doing they were hardly subscribing to contemporary magisterial and clerical campaigns for moral reformation, but rather adapting the authority of elite messages about respectability for their own particular purposes.[79] While slander of this kind obliquely acknowledged the reality of normal patriarchal values, whereby feminine honour was centred in control of sexuality, the defamation proceedings in the ecclesiastical courts reproduced the language and relations of a sub-culture of people who used sexual insult routinely in all sorts of economic, household and neighbourly disputes.

This plebeian culture can still be glimpsed in defamation suits before the London Consistory Court during the eighteenth century. In trinity term 1700 Frances Gale sued her neighbour Ann Pearce, alleging she had been called a whore. Ann admitted the charge, but said she was provoked. According to her story, one day in May of the same year she had been crossing the street to a chandler's shop with the aim of purchasing a pint of small beer when she encountered Frances and her sister, who were standing outside the door of their house. The two women allegedly accused her of borrowing and failing to return a muslin apron, and talked darkly of laying an indictment for a 'robbery', whereupon she said 'she hoped they did not counte her for a theife'. After this, it appears the argument escalated, with the two women saying 'if she was not a Theife she was a Whore', and taunting her further by jeering 'she was as Common as the high way, and ... they never kissed any, or tooke any new milled money of any under the Cherry tree or in the house of office'. Ann thereupon responded in kind, to the effect that any woman who accused her of such behaviour must be a whore herself.[80] A slightly different example is the 1752 case of Hannah Burkinsher against Joseph Ward, which appears to have arisen from another neighbourly dispute, this time in Marylebone, but one with an economic twist. Again, Mrs. Burkinsher alleged Ward had called her a whore. For his part, the defendant alleged that he came across Hannah late at night by a back-door adjoining the courtyard near her house; asked whether she was waiting for someone, she flew into a passion and said loudly 'What you call me a Whore do you', to which Ward said he replied 'no, I don't call you a Whore but I think it would be much more decent for you to be in your own House at this time of Night'. He also claimed that the real cause of the dispute was the 'Spite Enmity and Malice' the Burkinshers bore towards him because he had refused to allow Hannah's husband John a lease of his stable yard, and that they had offered to drop the suit if he relented.[81] Of course there were also cases where the details imply that the central issue *was* an authentic suspicion of sexual incontinence; and Hannah Burkinshaw's sharp reaction to Joseph Ward's question may well have been a genuine expression of women's sensitivity towards attacks on their chastity. But it is evident that because sexual insult was actionable in the ecclesiastical courts, and the processes were advantageous for them, women took the opportunity to mobilize official authority in a wide range of their quotidian disputes.[82] As a result the courts reproduced their distinctive culture as much as they influenced it. Indeed, some litigants were involved in tit-for-tat suits, and witnesses called to support the parties' stories were regularly tendered questions which deliberately impugned their own sexual reputations. In these circumstances it is easy to agree with Tim Meldrum that the church courts themselves were not only being used by vulnerable women to restore their damaged prospects; in effect they were also an extension of 'street, shop or stall' as another arena for plebeian arguments in the language of sex.[83]

It therefore appears that participation in lawsuits had informal representative functions, beyond the surface issues at stake. The various studies of litigation in the ecclesiastical courts, local courts, and central courts at Westminster have shown that when participation was widespread even those groups normally excluded from taking active roles in the institutions of government, such as married women, copyhold tenants, and people with insufficient wealth to pay tax, found active voices as prosecutors, not to mention their appearance as witnesses. So in the later sixteenth and seventeenth centuries the courts and their processes were primary sites for whole cultures of living and ordering, as well as individuals, to negotiate their consent to justice and law. But of course representation and consent through the courts was hardly possible when litigation receded from the general population. It is necessary now to consider the implications of the eighteenth-century decline in access to the courts.

## The law world we have lost: Complaints, explanations and consequences

Given the constitutional and cultural resonance of the rule of law in England, it should be easier to understand the impact of the rising costs and increasingly labyrinthine processes which placed the courts beyond the reach of most potential litigants during the early eighteenth century. It was not just that relatively poor people could not collect their debts, or redress other injuries: rather they felt cheated, in so far as they were excluded from what they understood as their birthright of equity before the law. Of course grumbles about the difficulty and expense of access to justice had a long history in England, but the literature of complaint in the eighteenth century conveys a fresh sense of bitterness and impotence. For example a correspondent of the *London Magazine*, writing in 1740, bemoaned the inability of people with modest means to prosecute their rights in the courts:

> A little *German* Prince may as well go to War with the Grand Monarch, as a poor Man contend with one who is very rich. What avails the clearness of a Man's Right, and the Justice of his Cause, if he is not able to go thro' the Expense of the Suit? A man that has not Strength to hold out to the End of his Journey had better sit still, and save his Money and his Constitution.[84]

Where poor men do sustain a lawsuit, they are portrayed as honest innocents bamboozled out of their rights by a conspiracy of prohibitively high costs and mysterious processes. In this nightmare vision of the rule of law authority figures are irredeemably corrupt, unscrupulous lawyers connive at delays and procedural derailments, and only litigants with long purses and dubious motives can gain any advantage. Thus a satirical poem of 1738 told the story of a north-country fisherman, whose nets and tackle were damaged by a neighbouring farmer's cow when it became entangled. The fisherman indicted the farmer for a nuisance at the county quarter sessions, but the farmer bribed the jury, and he lost. Then, on advice of counsel, he tried the case at *nisi prius* in York, where the jury gave a verdict in his favour. But the farmer then took the case to Westminster Hall on the advice of his lawyer, and two perjured witnesses testified against the fisherman. As a result the fisherman lost his case again, with the consequence that he had to sell his boat and nets to pay the costs. Finally, he made his complaint in equity to Chancery, and after many terms waiting, won a decree in his favour, with damages and costs. But the upshot of the whole web of suit and counter-suit was that both were ruined; the farmer had already sold his cows and sheep to maintain the litigation and ultimately had to go to jail, while the fisherman was left with nothing. The moral is clear: the law is a labyrinth where most ordinary people fear to tread, since it is administered to serve wealth, rather than justice:

> Thro' various Paths oblique they Draw,
> To the fell Market of the Law.
> At length they reach the noted Hall,
> Where Mercenary Tongues do bawl,
> Like Priest in black each Lawyer plies,
> And Client serves for Sacrifice.[85]

Certainly, many contemporaries blamed the lawyers and officers who controlled the courts for the increasing costs and procedural delays which rendered litigation unaffordable. And the litany of complaint about the prohibitive expense and unpredictable results of litigation in the eighteenth century is matched by evidence that conditions in the courts more and more favoured litigants whose wealth and experience enabled them to exploit its shortcomings. Sir James Lowther had frequently come off worse in the law campaigns which he fought early in the century, having to suffer the indignity of reverses at the hands of tradesmen and lesser freeholders, as well as substantial merchants. But 30 years later the 'dilatoriness' of the law was being used as a handy weapon in the complex business dealings of Whitehaven merchants, who maintained suits in Chancery simply to weaken their opponents and avoid settling debts. They were serious and learned litigants, for whom lawsuits were 'business by other means'. To his considerable satisfaction, Lowther even found that his hard-won knowledge of law procedures allowed him to manipulate the protagonists from behind the scenes.[86] In these cases lesser folk appear only as witnesses and deponents in affidavits, roles which certainly provided some experience of the litigation process, and occasionally endowed them with a limited authority, but hardly matched the positive agency of going to law in their own right.

Indeed in Chancery by the early nineteenth century businessmen or professionals (especially the former) accounted for a majority of the prosecutors and defendants, whereas they had formed only about a quarter of the court's client base in 1627. They were not always litigating over their professional affairs, but their prominence is indicative of the court's social regression. There was also a significant increase in the proportion of litigants who came from London and its environs – up from around 15 per cent to nearly 40 per cent.[87] It appears that in Chancery, as in King's Bench, Common Pleas, and the Exchequer, the decline in litigation partly took the form of significantly fewer suitors from the provinces, and especially rural society.[88] As mentioned previously, if the profile of litigants is compared with that for a century earlier the smaller freeholders and minor gentry are conspicuous by their absence. When all the statistics for the social and regional origins of lawsuits are taken into account, one has the impression that in the eighteenth century the central courts concentrated their resources on the high-value work derived from the wealth concentrated in London and (to a lesser extent) other growth areas of English society, such as the developing industrial areas in the north like Whitehaven.[89] Significant numbers of relatively small-value suits were still being initiated in the 1790s, but it is doubtful whether many were taken much beyond the point of taking out a writ.[90] Since the regional courts appear to have virtually priced themselves out of the market for small claims too, this amounted to a considerable ebb in the tide of justice.[91]

Admittedly, there is some partial evidence of declining demand, but demographic, social and economic changes are not sufficient to account for the general recession in litigation.[92] Rather, decisions made by the legal establishment seem to have moved the law up-market. The relatively depressed state of the agricultural sector before the middle of the eighteenth century and the drift to consolidated country estates may be one of the reasons for falling litigation from the provinces, given the central courts' previous dependence on broad prosperity and tenurial fragmentation in landed society.[93] But rapidly rising population and the general expansion of the economy after mid-century should have resulted in many more lawsuits than there were, suggesting that potential litigants were deterred from going to law by problems on the 'supply' side. 'Legalization' inseparable from the work of professional lawyers seems to have been important. Evidence from some of the local courts suggests the crucial factor in their recession, which began earlier than the decline at Westminster, was the incursion of lawyers from the end of the sixteenth century, which resulted in multiplication of fees with novel forms of action and the full introduction of elaborate legal procedures, such as special pleading, demurrers, repleadings and motions in arrest of judgement. By the mid-seventeenth century the borough court of Shrewsbury was thoroughly professionalized in this way: whereas it had been common for litigants to represent themselves, or employ local craftsmen who doubled as inexpensive attorneys, most case were conducted by barristers and professional attorneys, who charged the standard fees. The numbers of suitors declined in parallel with the growth of this lawyerly regime, although it appears that the introduction of a stamp duty on the various stages of legal proceedings by statute in 1694 was the 'final straw' for many Shrewsbury litigants.[94] In the central courts too the introduction of stamp duty must have had a negative impact on the amount of fresh litigation, although there are clear indications that the lawyers and sinecurists who depended on the supply compounded the problems by hiking their fees, and data for the work of barristers suggests they maximized their returns by multiplying motions and appearances.[95] Indeed, in Chancery, the court most notorious for glacial progress of cases, there was a marked rise in the ratio of court work to active cases during the early eighteenth century, just as the number of new suits was falling steeply.[96] Significantly, it was in the 1720s and 1730s that complaints about declining access to the courts reached a crescendo in the press and in parliament, resulting in an official enquiry into central court fees and statutes which forced legal documents to be written in English (rather than Latin and Law French), and established the registration of attorneys.[97]

There are indications that rising costs and further elaboration of proceedings also contributed to the disappearance of defamation suits in the church courts.[98] Certainly complaints along these lines formed part of the early eighteenth-century press and parliamentary campaign against the ecclesiastical jurisdiction, and even Convocation had lamented the courts' 'dilatory and expensive methods of procedure'.[99] As mentioned earlier, the eighteenth-century decline of litigation was socially disproportionate in these courts too. The litigants who remained were drawn from a much narrower segment of English society. Besides suits for divorce *a mensa et thoro*, an increasing amount of 'ecclesiastical' business occupied the London Consistory Court, but most of it was simply administrative, in the sense of non-contentious work which was generated by the administration of church fabric and land, the clergy, and of the church generally. The most pronounced area of growth occurred in the form of applications from parishioners who sought permission to build burial vaults and monuments for the exclusive use of their families, or for the allocation of family pews: 30 of the 50 'ecclesiastical' cases for 1749–53 concerned affairs of this kind, compared with only 14 similar items (out of 36) for 1699–1702.[100] Obviously, the promoters were people of considerable means, for besides feeing the proctors for their services and paying the court fees, they would often be required to pay carpenters and stonemasons to carry out the work. Women were not as dominant in these affairs as they had been in suits for words, but widows and other female executors were frequently named as promoters, and in mid-century most originated from the upper social echelons of parishes in country Middlesex, Essex, or Hertfordshire. For example in May 1753 Dame Emma Susannah Hudson petitioned for a faculty to appropriate a pew in the parish church of Sunbury in Middlesex to the exclusive use of herself and her family. The clerk's entry described her as 'a Principal Parishioner and Inhabitant of the parish', and this was not merely a matter of form, because it also explained that she had given £100 towards rebuilding the church. Since the pew was given 'in consideration of her being a great Benfactress', like most of the other petitions for appropriating the fabric of the church to private use, this application was effectively a property transaction, as well as a public declaration of outward conformity to the church.[101] Moreover, like a suit for defamation, it certainly represented an assertion of honour in the face of the community, although the increase of this kind of business suggests that for Dame Emma and her ilk honour consisted principally in a public display of social differentiation, rather than adherence to the norms of the community.[102]

As was noticed in the case of JPs adjudicating interpersonal quarrels, increasing consciousness of social differentiation may have compounded the problems of gaining access to justice. It is possible that this impacted most in London, the crucible of elite opinion and fashion, and the centre of the early eighteenth-century campaign for the reformation of manners. Certainly the parallels between the decline of binding over for opprobrious words at the Middlesex sessions and the fall in defamation suits at the London Consistory court suggest a growing reluctance on the part of the capital's magistrates and ecclesiastical lawyers to encourage legal action over such issues, rather than any sudden growth of politeness from below. It has been pointed out that there are many examples in the law reports of judges dismissing interpersonal insults as too petty for their attention, and there are indications that feminine quarrelling was especially liable to elite trivialization, judging by critical comments made by Whitlocke Bulstrode, the chairman of the Middlesex quarter sessions in 1718. Bulstrode was adamant that the law should be used to reform popular morals, but he believed the common law descended too low in prosecuting a scold, who was but a 'silly Woman [who] only makes a noise amongst her Neighbours'.[103] In this context it is interesting that by the mid-eighteenth century Middlesex recognizances tended to be based on accusations of violence, rather than slanderous words: one suspects that London JPs were anticipating their country cousins by rejecting what they regarded as petty disputes between people of little consequence.[104]

So the rapid decline of defamation cases at the London Consistory was probably not just a matter of exclusively high costs. Widespread and unashamed prejudices against 'indecorous' suits and coarse suitors were revealed by the early nineteenth-century enquiries into the ecclesiastical jurisdiction, and it is likely that they took root first in the London church courts establishment. The bishop of London between 1723 and 1748, just when defamation cases declined most steeply, was Edmund Gibson, who also actively supported the campaign for the reformation of manners. In his *Admonition against Prophane and Common Swearing* he complained about the 'wild, unthinking, profligate Part of Mankind', and encouraged personal restraint and 'Christian Conversation'.[105] For Gibson the courts' legitimate role was the suppression of 'lewdness' among the laity generally: his *Codex Juris Ecclesiastici Anglicani* (1713) advocated their re-invigoration, and in 1733 he defended their disciplinary powers against a powerful parliamentary attack.[106] In this context, and since he was a vigorous administrator and advocate for administrative reform in the church, it would hardly be surprising if his influence tended to discourage litigation which contradicted his public statements about the need for improvements in personal manners.[107] This was certainly what was happening in virtually every diocese a century later, when the church courts were under attack again. Politicians complained about corruption and oppression, bishops were embarrassed, and judges either refused to entertain 'common' defamation cases or deterred them by denying costs to the prosecutor.[108]

Whatever the causes of the decline in recourse to the courts were, its implications seem clear. With the loss of a broad national clientele for the law courts, the range of civic voices must have been reduced too: if litigation can be construed as a discourse of government, then after the middle of the eighteenth century it was increasingly a conversation dominated by members of the business, professional and propertied elites, rather than one which involved the population generally.[109] There is evidence that marginal groups in English society lost power and agency. In the case of the church courts Laura Gowing has argued that early modern women were uniquely empowered by the availability of actions for defamation.[110] Certainly the jurisdiction had features which were particularly advantageous for women, in so far as the parties were not required to give evidence, and the truth of an allegation was no defence. A prosecutor was not therefore subjected to damaging cross-examination as to her previous sexual conduct, and success was virtually certain if there were two reliable witnesses to the insult. By contrast, until 1891 the common law left women virtually unprotected against sexual slander unless damage could be proved, and although the loophole was closed by statute in that year, women's reputations remained disproportionately vulnerable to courtroom attack.[111] Moreover, seventeenth-century women's threats to have their opponents 'carted' or do penance suggest they had good collective consciousness of the law and individual confidence in their ability to appropriate it in support of their rights.[112] But while traces of popular consciousness about the potential for suing people who called women whores remained in the early nineteenth century, the scope of such awareness diminished with the decline in the frequency of suits.[113] The surviving church court litigation tended to represent the values and interests of the propertied, especially men. In the London Consistory Court the decline of defamation resulted in a partial de-feminization of the court as divorce cases came to predominate, and the results show they represented a normal culture of marital relations which advantaged husbands, rather than wives.[114] Wives' complaints about adultery were less likely to succeed than men's, and they were disproportionately vulnerable to accusations of disobedience and infidelity. Indeed, as the action for criminal conversation became popular in the court of King's Bench, separation suits in the Consistory seem to have been subordinated to it: they therefore became part of a species of litigation which supported male commerce in women's persons as *property*, and rendered their roles as mere submissive ornaments in the ideal patriarchal household.[115]

Similar tendencies can be observed in the secular courts. In King's Bench itself, the only one of the central courts which increased its caseloads in the eighteenth century, deliberate modifications were made to accommodate elite interests. Lord Mansfield famously relied on special juries of merchants to advise and adjudicate commercial disputes.[116] It is less well known that he also used special juries of 'gentlemen of fortune' in some other cases, especially prosecutions for *crim. con.*, where jurors were expected to understand and enforce gentlemanly notions of honour. In fact elite juries like these were available on motion from one of the parties after 1730, and there is evidence that they advantaged the more powerful parties to a suit, such as landlords in litigation with their tenants.[117] Moreover, in a context where by 1750 the courts' principal customers were drawn from a narrower cross-section of the community than previously, it may be no coincidence that the common law judges seem to have been increasingly insensitive to typically plebeian issues, such as claims of commoners' and customary rights, and the enforcement of apprenticeship regulations against capitalist manufacturers. Exceptionally, Lord Chief Justice Kenyon and his King's Bench puisnes were roused to revive the offences of forestalling, engrossing and regrating against merchants in the context of widespread dearth at the end of the century.[118] But it is clear that Kenyon's Cokean paternalism was out of step with both his predecessor and successor, not to mention the *ton* of the Westminster bar, whose social associations and self-image were becoming increasingly elitist, to the point where they tended to disparage barristers who mixed with the *hoi polloi* at the Old Bailey.[119] By 1800 barristers expected their colleagues to regard themselves as members of a consolidated ruling class made up of the propertied and politely educated, thereby 'raised above the common herd of men', and with appropriately conservative values. Indeed, it may be significant of the cultural gulf which had opened between people of small property and the lawyers' world centred on Westminster Hall that early nineteenth-century radical reformers doubted their independence, and preferred to represent themselves.[120]

Certainly in Chancery, it is probably no accident that in the eighteenth century the court generally connived at complex (and expensive) conveyancing strategies which were intended to preserve large estates in the hands of approved male descendants, to the detriment of widows' rights of dower, the interests of younger children, and a free market in land.[121] Here was a form of private ordering with which the courts were very comfortable. The perspective of the Chancery lawyers may have been narrowed by their experience, for high-class conveyancing work was a good source of income for London chamber counsel, and trust or estate cases were the longest-running (and therefore most profitable) suits. As a junior barrister Mansfield had once earned a fee of three hundred guineas for advising on the family settlement of his patron the duke of Newcastle; and Lord Chancellor Eldon, who consistently gave the established practice of learned conveyancers as justification for rules which departed from equity, had started his professional life as the pupil of a Lincoln's Inn lawyer specializing in 'great conveyancing'.[122] But exceptionally the courts were prepared to overrule the legal logic of contracts which tended to make married women femes sole with respect to pin money and maintenance allowances, substituting new rules of construction which limited their control over such property.[123] Indeed, the twists and turns of judicial rulings relating to settlements suggest an abiding adherence to the 'deeper structures' of patriarchy and aristocracy which hardly conformed to the evolving plural interests of a 'polite and commercial' people. In this crucial area at least, eighteenth-century legal history is a story whereby elite cultures were almost subliminally represented as public policy.[124]

Important as they are, rather than changes in legal remedies and doctrines, in this book I am primarily interested in the political and social implications of falling participation in the courts, and especially what appears to be a marked reduction in the exchange of cultures and values via the primary institutions of government. As we have seen, in the eighteenth century ordinary people were increasingly likely to encounter government in the personage of a justice of the peace, rather than a court: and this was unlikely to be an empowering experience. Moreover, poor people seeking to negotiate their rights and interests against their betters were disadvantaged as massive draughts of private legislation created new statutory commissions with important powers beyond the reach of the courts. But I will consider localist legislation and 'parliamentary government' in general later. For the moment it is appropriate to turn to participation in the administration of criminal justice, and particularly the generation of public concern about robbery and violence. From this perspective it is possible to discern clearly the importance of politeness and professionalization as developments which discriminated against popular involvement in the business of government, and the use of legislation as an instrument for resolving 'social problems' with sovereign 'law'.

# 4
# Crime and the Administration of Criminal Law: Problems, Solutions and Participation

> ... it is a very piercing Lamentation, that the inoffensive wise, and useful part of Mankind, how much soever they are entitled to Protection from all illegal Violence and Molestation, ... yet know not whether travelling Abroad, or walking in the Streets, or dealing in their Shops, or resting in their Beds, they may be out of Danger from *these Monsters*.
> G. Ollyffe, *An Essay Humbly offer'd, for an Act of Parliament to prevent Capital Crimes, and the Loss of so many Lives; and to Promote a desirable Improvement and Blessing in the Nation* (2$^{nd}$ edn., 1731), 4–5.

> ... nothing hath wrought such an Alteration in this Order of People [i.e. 'the Commonalty'] as the Introduction of Trade. This hath indeed given a new Face to the whole Nation, hath in a great measure subverted the former State of Affairs, and hath almost totally changed the Manners, Customs, and Habits of the People, more especially of the lower Sort. The Narrowness of their Fortune is changed into Wealth; the Simplicity of their Manners into Craft; their Frugality into Luxury; their Humility into Pride; and their Subjection into Equality.
> H. Fielding, *An Enquiry into the Late Increase of Robbers*, ed. M.R. Zirker (Oxford, 1988), 69–70.

> without *energy* in government to enforce, no well-digested *police* can be established ...
> J. Hanway, *The Defects of Police the Cause of Immorality, and the Continual Robberies Committed, particularly in and around the Metropolis* (1775), v.

There is abundant evidence of unprecedented public sensitivity to crime in eighteenth-century England. Certainly the mushroom growth of London, the repeated social and economic disturbances caused by the return of soldiers and sailors from wars, and the supposedly corrupting effects of unprecedented personal wealth, appeared to be serious grounds for concern about rising crime rates. But the totals of indictments were relatively low by modern standards: it is clear that anxieties about crime were magnified and focused by the growth of the press; and perhaps in turn by higher expectations of personal conduct created by increased public exchange and developing middling consciousness.[1] Before 1700 the vast majority of people's knowledge of crime was confined to their limited personal experience, or to comments and advice in sermons and assize or quarter sessions charges. But with the proliferation of newspapers and magazines knowledge about localized criminality could be shared all over the country. And it was hardly objective knowledge: commercial imperatives ensured that columns had to be filled and readers' interests, tastes and prejudices had to be catered for; while editorial policies varied according to particular markets and opportunities, as well as the changing availability of alternative stories and the strengths and weaknesses of competitors.[2]

The commodification of crime reporting is an example of the rich and creative commercialization of English society typical of the eighteenth century.[3] However, the burgeoning 'public sphere' of eighteenth-century print discourse and associations was not wholly inclusive or creative. In much of the alarmist literature about crime there were conjunctions between reports of robberies and expressions of distaste and disapprobation for the supposedly degenerate habits of the common people – 'the idle, vagrant and loose Tribe' – who were ultimately labelled as 'the criminal class'.[4] Of course worries about the morals of the poor had a long history, but urbanization rendered them more frightening, and again, they were broadcast and focused with the development of a periodical press which catered for a polite readership. So even before Enlightenment rationalism became a dominant mode of discourse, crime was beginning to be identified as a social problem which was susceptible to 'policy', and there was public discussion about legislative solutions.[5]

It is the argument of this chapter that these currents of public and polite opinion about crime and the common people had decisive effects on the administration of criminal law. As suggested previously, community discretion and private prosecution of offences were primary features of medieval justice and government, and it has recently been argued that the eighteenth century was the 'golden age' of discretion in the administration of criminal law.[6] But while large elements of discretion certainly remained in decisions about prosecutions and punishment after 1700, and in some ways their scope was even extended, here I want to draw attention to the coincidence of enduring departures in quite another direction, towards more control by authorities and professionals.[7] As early as the second decade of the century, faced with some signs of moral panic about crime in the metropolis, the central government instructed officials and lawyers to achieve more certainty in exemplary prosecutions; an intervention which helped in the progressive lawyerization of the criminal trial and the development of evidentiary rules. And as has been pointed out already, there was also a trend towards more professionalization in policing, first in London, but later in other centres of rapid urban population growth.[8] From the second half of the century there was also a significant public retreat from supporting bodily punishments involving participation by the community in favour of more orderly and 'rational' penal contexts, governed by rules and officials. All these points are relatively well established, although their combined significance has not been appreciated. It is important to understand that while they were all associated with genuine concerns about crime and managing the urban masses, together they also represent the beginnings of 'de-communalization' in the administration of justice, consistent with new visions of law as a vital instrument of the 'civil power' conceived in opposition to the common people.[9] Indeed, it seems the people were not to be trusted with the law.

## Crime as a 'social problem': Public opinion and the degeneracy of the common people

The easy link between crime and poverty was hardly invented by eighteenth-century newspapers. As Roger North pointed out, the statutory provisions made for the poor in the sixteenth and seventeenth centuries were partly directed to 'the Prevention of common beggars, Thieves, and Offenders, supposed to spring from Poverty'.[10] Fears about wandering vagrants were commonplace in Tudor-Stuart England, and warnings about their potential depredations were conveyed down the great chains of authority constituted by parliaments and privy councils, judges and magistrates, clergymen, churchwardens and constables.[11] But the Georgians had their own distinctive and worrisome slant on the issue. They believed that criminality was proliferating wildly as morally weak individuals were dazzled by the fabulous commodities and life styles generated through commercial prosperity, and they feared the relative freedom from the usual social constraints enjoyed by labourers and craftsmen in the anonymity of the city. Crucially, although they were expressed in several settings, these anxieties were given their widest currency by another characteristic of the first age of consumption: the unprecedented market for reading matter of all kinds, including commentary on the nation's faults, as well as its triumphs.

Perhaps most famously, Bernard Mandeville's notorious satire *The Fable of the Bees* (1714–24) shows that with rapidly increasing wealth and urbanization from *c.* 1680 there was sharpened awareness of the potentially corrupting influence of luxury and emulation on the masterless poor, principally in the metropolis, which was the centre of the new public discourse facilitated by newspapers and monthly magazines. Conventionally, in another pamphlet Mandeville recommended more effective prosecution and punishment of crime, but his attitude towards criminality was highly exceptional in so far as he accepted the inevitability of new forms and dimensions of crime and vice as evils which were largely inseparable from a flourishing centre of commerce and conspicuous consumption.[12] For him, it was sheer hypocrisy to condemn materialism and narrow self-interest in the poor, when the very same instincts inspired the prosperity of the rich and the growing economic strength of the kingdom. So crime had to be dealt with, but there is no element of panic in his writings. As John Langbein has suggested in a slightly different context, for Mandeville crime was nasty but inevitable, and countering it was akin to collecting garbage.[13] However more often contemporary social commentators worried and railed against what they saw as a swelling tide of moral corruption which offended conventional pieties and sensibilities, endangered their prosperity and comforts, and ultimately seemed even to threaten the social order.

Certainly, there was plenty of material for alarm.[14] Although not all were equally interested, by the 1720s more or less detailed reports of 'remarkable' crimes, criminal trials and executions were carried by the London newspapers, and following the staples of foreign affairs and domestic politics they were reproduced in several of the papers founded in major cities and country towns.[15] Accounts of crime and punishment were especially welcome in the intermissions between wars, when editors needed to find material which might compensate partially for the absence of the 'patriotic sensationalism' engendered by British naval and military exploits.[16] Indeed, although there is good evidence that rates of prosecutions for property crimes increased markedly during the intermissions between wars, probably reflecting real increases in breaches of the law with endemic underemployment, at such times changing editorial priorities must have helped to magnify further the fear of crime.[17] Moreover, the newspapers' reporting of robberies and rogues inevitably conveyed subtle and not so subtle hints about the social contexts and implications of rising crime against property.

For example in the early 1720s, a time of semi-continuous hysteria among the reading public already rocked by the rampant corruption uncovered in the wake of the South Sea Bubble and shocked again with the unfolding news of a high-level Jacobite conspiracy, the weekly *London Journal*'s reports of more humble crimes and criminals developed several complex themes which ultimately rose to a discordant and terrifying crescendo. In September 1722 there were stories of hardened and desperate thieves resisting the law. Two 'Fellows of the Town of Deptford' were apprehended stealing iron from an anchor-smith's yard and committed to Maidstone Gaol, 'a place they are well acquainted with, as having been there twice before'. And 'a noted Dear-stealer' was taken in Whitechapel after a ferocious struggle, during which he defended himself with an axe and received a mortal cut in the scull.[18] The following month the paper printed correspondence from Waltham Chase in Hampshire about the activities of the 'Waltham Blacks': not just brazen stealers of deer, but social bandits with a pseudo-gentleman leader – 'King John of the Blacks' – and a primitive programme of intimidatory social justice which included compelling the payment of tradesmen's and poor farmers' debts, punishing informers, and enforcing rights of common and timber waste against local landowners. The *Journal*'s correspondent hoped their 'lawless authority' would be rewarded with 'a deserved Punishment'.[19] The next issue included only a rather vague account of a 'Scotch Gentleman' who was robbed of money and rings by three footpads on his way into London from the north, and there was no more substantial reporting of crime before 8 December, when the paper reported on the searching of a house at Whitechapel which was suspected of being 'a Harbour for Pick-pockets, &c.'. It seems this suspicion of organized crime was well-founded, since 'all manner of Dresses for both Sexes were found, so that they could equip their Emissaries with proper Habits to cover their Designs, either in St. James's, the City, or Wapping'. Indeed, the editor added to the impression with some tantalizing heresay: ''Tis said, there are several Schools of this Nature in the Out-Parts of the Town, where many a Youth qualify'd himself for Tyburn'.[20]

Over the next six months the *London Journal* included more frequent and developed reports along these lines. Their collective message was clear. Highwaymen and footpads appeared to have colonized the roads and heaths leading to the capital, making them unsafe, especially for coaches carrying the gentry and the mails; taking a boat on the Thames meant risking sudden attack by the waterman or even a fellow passenger, if they should spy a full purse; and the poor residential and industrial areas spreading from the east end of London, such as Whitechapel, Bow, and Deptford, were nurseries for gangs of thieves and housebreakers who were bred to their trade from an early age.[21] The rebellious exploits of the Waltham Blacks also continued to fascinate, and seemed to multiply. Although 'King John' was reported in March as having declared he would avoid 'public affairs' until May, when he threatened a demonstration in defiance of legal moves to suppress his activities, there was news from Portsmouth of a copy-cat robbery, whereby smugglers with blackened faces gave a 'drubbing' to customs officers who had seized contraband wine.[22] Moreover, the reports of ordinary crime were more violent, and the editor's comments began to take on a note of alarm. In June there was an account that 'several disguised Persons' had destroyed deer and wounded the gamekeeper in a gentleman's park near Farnham in Hampshire; and the issue of 3 August included a report of a man committed to Newgate after grievously wounding his master and mistress, who had previously loaned him money. The paper related how he had confessed that after being refused another loan he obtained a dagger and had intended to murder them both before robbing their house and running away to Holland.[23] October brought further accounts of desperate violence: three footpads were taken and committed to the Marchalsea prison after robbing and shooting a servant for a mere 20d., and there was a report of another gang of footpads who had committed 'Several Robberies' in Lincoln's Inn Fields. They had 'dragg'd the Persons they attack'd over the Rails, and there strip'd and plunder'd them of what they found valuable about them'.[24] There was even a hint that all this was a spreading French disease. The *Journal* had recently carried a report of a gruesome robbery and murder near Calais, on the road to Paris, where several English gentlemen and their servants were killed in cold blood by a gang of French robbers, to prevent them being detected. Now the editor commented, 'Robbery and Murder seem to be as common among our Rogues here as in France, and we now hardly hear of the first without the Latter.[25] The next few issues seemed to bear him out, for they were full of further accounts of robbery, murder, and mayhem, including a burglary in Cheapside which was the work of 'a master of his business', a 'barbarous' assault on the customs officers at Portsmouth by '12 Persons being disguised and armed with Swords and Staves', and the discovery of the body of a gentleman in a ditch between Highgate and Hampstead, 'with his Throat cut from Ear to Ear, and his Handkerchief cramm'd into his Mouth'.[26]

As John Beattie has said, confronted with a rising stream of reports like this, it must have seemed to contemporaries that society was in danger of being overwhelmed with crime.[27] Moreover, the context and style of reporting can only have multiplied the psychological effects. The 'crime waves' represented in the *London Journal* and other newspapers at several points during the eighteenth century were not invented, in the sense of being quite unconnected with the incidence of prosecutions. Certainly we know the machinery of justice was operating at full stretch just at these moments, and private commentators and officials were equally alarmed. But it seems to me that the distinctive contribution of the press was to turn perceptions of rising crime into moral panic. Whether wittingly or unwittingly, repetition and context, editorial style and gloss, helped to shape the bare events into a commentary on the state of English society, and particularly the moral condition of working people. Certainly this is clear for the early 1720s. First, because of the details repeated, readers of the *London Journal* would have become more sensitive to the social context of crime: while there were exceptions, it was most frequently perpetrated by the poor against their betters, and in London particularly the poor seemed to be breeding gangs of professional criminals. Second, if these accounts suggested a threat to property and the social order, such fears can only have been confirmed by their juxtaposition with the exploits of the 'Blacks': apparently avowed social rebels who were also prepared to challenge the king's officers. And third, it cannot have escaped any reader's notice that there was rebellion at the top of English society too: in February 1723 the paper had printed special supplements devoted to the trial of the Jacobite conspirator Christopher Layer, and every week it carried an editorial by 'Britannicus' thundering against the Pretender, the bishop of Rochester, and the Papists, who were suspected of complicity in an armed conspiracy against the king.[28] In such a highly-charged political context, comments about English rogues conforming to French standards of casual violence and brutality may well have suggested that the times were out of joint, and the common people were out of control.

Nevertheless, the reports of crime in the *London Journal* ultimately conveyed confidence in the ability of the law to hold the ring, for the machinery of justice was represented as awful and inevitable, if somewhat irregular.[29] Many of the robberies were reported in the form of the arrest and committal to prison of the suspected offenders. For example in December readers were advised that two men had been taken by the thief-catcher Jonathan Wild at an alehouse in Fleet Lane and subsequently committed to Newgate, 'it being strongly suspected that they have been guilty of several Robberies both in Surry and Middlesex.', including the theft of money and a gold watch worth 70 guineas from a member of parliament on Hampstead Heath.[30] And although the Waltham Blacks seemed to disappear, there were accounts of the trials and condemnation of the Windsor Blacks by a special commission of judges at Reading, and of a group of Hampshire Blacks at the King's Bench in London. These reports made it clear that the prosecutions had been arranged and paid for by the government. The paper also took grim satisfaction in the death sentences handed down: one of the condemned Hampshire Blacks was said to be the keeper of an inn where they used to meet, and 'as he shared in their Plunder, is now likely to bear a Part in their Fate'.[31] Indeed, the *Journal* was subsidized by the ministry to provide space for 'Britannicus', who was the pamphleteer-bishop Benjamin Hoadly.[32] Its expressions of alarm about violent crime were balanced by a sense that the Lords Justices (regents in the absence of the king at Hanover) were firmly in command, and would crack down hard on violence against private individuals, just as they had in the case of the forest banditti. Certainly at the height of the 'crime wave' in November 1723 the paper reported their promises of a large reward for information leading to the conviction of those persons concerned in an 'outragious Attack upon the House of Mr. William Brown, in Wimbleton Warren', promising £100 and a pardon in the case of accomplices, 'except him, or those who shot into the House with Bullets'.[33] And in December successive issues highlighted their lordships' rational choice of those Old Bailey convicts who should be left to hang, rather than reprieved by the royal mercy. John Stanley, the worst offender, convicted of murdering his mistress,

> had an Education which promised a better Fate; but getting the Reins of Liberty too early into his own Hands, he plunged into Vice, and gratify'd very Appetite, as far as it was possible for one in his circumstances to do.[34]

This account of declension into sin re-inscribed the familiar moral and religious context of crime, by which any man might have fallen into similar errors, given the opportunity; and the report showed that the administration of justice appeared to be synchronized to deal with it. The law had selected those offenders who were morally irredeemable, those who virtually condemned themselves by their descent into hardened viciousness. The *London Journal* therefore represented the normal social construction of news about crime and the law: its reporting highlighted the conventional explanations and solutions of the propertied. Indeed the authorities seem to have responded in kind, because there was an increase in the proportion of capital convicts executed around this time.[35] Nevertheless, the press was generating a prototypical 'law and order' problem: crime was increasing, criminals were social deviants, and at this particular historical moment, an excess of 'liberty' among the common people appeared to be multiplying offenders.

As Nicholas Rogers has shown, at several points during the eighteenth century, especially in the aftermath of wars, 'crime waves' were accompanied by anguished public comment about the degeneracy of the common people and broad campaigns for improved forms of social regulation.[36] Most famously, in 1750 the novelist-magistrate Henry Fielding attributed the 'great Increase of robberies' he had noticed over the previous years to the tendency of tradesmen, artisans, and even labourers to be deflected from their assigned social role – honest labour and its modest fruits – by luxuries and entertainments which tempted them beyond their means and ultimately led to a life of crime. He also complained about the failure of the poor law institutions to inculcate habits of industry among able-bodied paupers, and characterized all these problems – social emulation, idleness, and a propensity to robbery and riot – as a crisis of insubordination among the common people.[37] As a London magistrate at the sharp end of the administration of criminal law, Fielding claimed his diagnosis was authentic: he had extensive first-hand experience of offenders, and insisted that 'few Persons, ... have made their exit at Tyburn, who have not owed their fate to some of the Causes before mentioned'.[38] But for the vast majority who did not have his exposure to criminality, the new discourse of law and order news must have helped to shape the prevailing ideas of rising crime as a serious social problem, and of the urban poor as 'deviants' from the developing ideals and expectations of the middling sort.[39]

Indeed, by the early 1780s, another period of acute concern about violent crime in the context of demobilization and high unemployment, the proliferation of provincial newspapers meant that concerns about metropolitan crime were reproduced for readers around the country via their 'London' pages; and the anxieties and explanatory frameworks in vogue at the time were further reinforced by reporting of local offences.[40]

Certainly it appears that in East Anglia and Essex during the 1780s the provincial newspapers' metropolitan pages reproduced a wave of rising public anxiety about violent property crime. In April–June 1782 the *Ipswich Journal* included several accounts of 'cruel murders and robberies' in the suburbs of London which were attributed to the discharge of convicts who had served their time of transportation in the hulks on the Thames.[41] These reports seem to have had a disproportionate impact, because in November the paper reported that the contractor for the convicts sent to the hulks had appeared before the court of King's Bench and attempted to demonstrate that few of the men discharged had re-offended, a circumstance that Lord Mansfield pointedly emphasized 'contradicted the general belief of the public'.[42] However the papers continued to make the easy connection between reported robberies by 'desperadoes' in gangs and what they called 'the floating academy at Woolwich'.[43] And their local columns included more and more accounts of equally desperate robberies which were uncomfortably close to home. There were even signs of panic. In February, the *Ipswich Journal* printed a notice that the Bury St. Edmunds corn market would in future be held at the earlier time of 12–2pm, following the application of buyers and sellers who were alarmed by 'the frequent robberies lately committed in the neighbourhood'.[44] The metropolitan authorities subsequently took emergency action to reassure the public. In June 1782 the Commons considered a bill for punishing buyers and receivers of stolen goods, as recommended by the grand jury at the Old Bailey sessions; in September, despite Mansfield's hint, the recorder of London declared that no more convicts would be sent to the hulks; and in the same month the king, 'taking into account the many daring and desperate robberies lately committed' proclaimed that no pardon or respite would be granted for such offences.[45] At the opening of the new session of parliament in December the king's speech referred to the necessity of 'a strict and severe execution of the laws' because of 'The great excess, to which the crimes of theft and robbery have arisen, in many instances accompanied with personal violence'.[46] As this anxiety continued to simmer over the next few years, the judges and the government sent an unusually high proportion of capital convicts to the gallows, and there was a parallel rise in prosecutions, suggesting that victims, magistrates and grand juries were acutely aware of the need to stifle rampant criminality.[47] Clearly there were special grounds for concern about soldiers and sailors returning from war at a time when transportation to

America was no longer available to remove convicts from the gaols: would the machinery of justice be able to cope? But the newspapers' emphasis on robbery with violence and the potential problem of old offenders being released into the community may have had played a part in precipitating a crisis. As Peter King has suggested, the moral panic represented in the reporting of 1782 anticipated full demobilization by six months, and there is a strong possibility that it was partially self-fulfilling.[48]

Anyone reading the *Ipswich Journal* in 1782–3 would have been alarmed about rising crime and might have believed that it was appropriate for property-owners and government authorities to adopt a policy of zero tolerance towards all degrees of criminal offences in the face of what appeared to be a major challenge to private property and the social order. The *Journal* was a well-established newspaper with wide circulation in its region, but during the 1760s it had been locked in a circulation war with the newly-founded *Colchester Chronicle*, and law and order reporting seems ultimately to have become one of the staple fields for competition between the two publications.[49] By 1783, with the gradual cessation of hostilities in America and Europe, the *Journal* was carrying a considerable variety of material relating to crime: besides reports of violent robberies, arrests, committals, and executions in London, East Anglia and elsewhere, it printed some of the most sensational trials and published many advertisements offering rewards for conviction or recovery of stolen property, as well as carrying notices for the formation and proceedings of private associations dedicated to prosecuting theft. In January the slight amount of space dedicated to local news was almost entirely taken up by crime: there were accounts from Ipswich of highway robberies, burglaries and attacks by footpads; in the neighbourhood of Hemlington in Norfolk readers were told that almost all of the farmers' houses had been robbed by 'a gang of villains'; in Norwich 'the wine-vaults of Messrs Bacon and Marshall were again broken open and several dozen of wine stolen'; at Hunstanton on the Wash customs officers and a regiment of dragoons were involved in a pitched battle with armed smugglers and their local supporters after a seizure of contraband goods; and from Chelmsford there was a report of a man murdered at West Ham for two gold rings, his knee and shoe-buckles. This last account included gruesome details from the surgeon's examination of the body for the coroner's inquest: 'several swan-shot were extracted from various parts of his body, the lungs were much torn, and near three pints of extravasated blood had lodged in the thorax'. Although there was no comment besides the jury's verdict of 'wilful murder, against some person or persons unknown', the bare report conveyed a dramatic sense of brutal violence whose origin was as yet unknown and unchecked.[50]

Such detail was not incidental: the attention given to crimes of violence in eighteenth-century newspapers serves to demonstrate the gradual construction of non-violence as a central norm of middle-class public opinion and identity.[51] Indeed, the pages of the *Ipswich Journal* rendered footpads in particular as faceless devils who suddenly appeared out of the darkness and cut down respectable and innocent people just going about their business:

> Last Friday night, between 8 and 9 o'clock, as Mr. Meadows, baker, at Boreham, was returning from this town [Chelmsford], he was met by two men, near Stump-lane, in the parish of Springfield, who, without speaking a word, knocked him off his horse, and otherwise cut and wounded him in so brutal a manner about the head and face, that 'tis feared he will lose the use of one of his eyes'.[52]

In this account, like so many others, the *Journal* was appealing to an unspoken moral consensus: men who behaved in such a brutal way were beyond the pale of civilized society. Without making an overt comment, by representing random crimes of violence from the perspective of bourgeois, law-abiding victims it was speaking for the honest farmers and decent country tradesmen who were its target constituency.[53]

Admittedly, some of the thefts reported appear trivial by contrast: two East Suffolk militia men suspected of robbing the mayor of Sudbury's shop were found in possession of 'several fowls, geese and turkeys', and 'an old and notorious offender' was committed to Norwich Castle for stealing two cheeses and four slices of bacon.[54] But there was a pronounced tendency at this time for the public notices of prosecution associations to lump misdemeanours together with much more serious and violent offences. For example the *Ipswich Journal* of 4 January 1783 included a notice from a meeting of the gentlemen, clergy and others of the hundred of Hartismere, Suffolk, held at the White Horse Inn on December 31, where the assembled property owners covenanted 'to enter into an agreement for the more effectually preventing horse-stealing, murders, thefts, burglaries, and petty offences'.[55] And in April the newly-formed association of the principal occupiers of rabbit warrens in Norfolk and Suffolk observed 'that those who are guilty of this species of robbery [i.e. robbing rabbit warrens], are the people who otherwise commit other felonious acts, – as sheep-stealing, horse-stealing, and house-breaking'.[56]

The prosecution associations' interest in minor crimes was a new development of the 1780s, and while their commitment to the rigorous prosecution of all offenders turned out to be somewhat rhetorical, notices like these must have suggested to readers that petty economic theft represented the same immoral tendencies as more serious criminal offences.[57] So the perpetrators were legitimate subjects for the law's attention, rather than sympathy and discretion. Moreover, as with the 'crime wave' of the early 1720s, the published life-stories of convicts executed around this time generally suggested their moral sense was overcome by opportunity and ambition, rather than poverty. For example two men were hanged for robbery with murder at Chelmsford in March 1783. The *Journal* reported that one was an Irish catholic who had worked 'honestly' as a baker but 'determined to rob the first person he could' on receiving a letter from his sweetheart telling to him to get money and meet her in London. He was penitent on the scaffold, and declared he was deluded into crime by his religion 'which taught him that it was an act of the Devil's not his own'. The other man admitted he had planned to murder his victim, a meat carter, some weeks before the crime, and 'his only motive, he declared, was making money of the meat, horses and cart, after which he intended to have gone abroad'. Before he died he thanked God for being detected 'as he had determined to have gone on in the same way, and might have had more murders to answer for'.[58] Readers can hardly have missed the collective meaning of such accounts: they suggested that the moral and social bonds which restrained the poor had loosened with visions of wealth and increased mobility; any poor man or woman might be tempted into crime on a sudden opportunity; and only the law stood between innocent respectable people and a deluge of violence. Assizes like that for Gloucester, which concluded with large numbers of capital convictions, therefore 'afforded a melancholy proof of the profligacy of the times'.[59]

So while the moral narratives of individual men and women's 'last dying speeches' played on broadly similar themes throughout the eighteenth century, by the 1780s the problem of immorality and disorder among the urban poor appeared to be of much larger proportions than it had assumed earlier. There was much less sympathy among the polite classes for the moral failings of plebeian convicts, and there was less confidence that the institutions and underlying principles which informed the criminal law were adequate for maintaining order.[60] Certainly in the aftermath of the American War, although they were alarming, the apparently growing incidence of robberies and murders all over the country might have seemed to be but one symptom of a strictly temporary social turmoil. But there were also reports of tumultuous mutinies among the sailors at Portsmouth and Plymouth; the garrisons of Jersey and Guernsey and Rotheram and Wakefield in Yorkshire refused to obey their officers' orders, and in various parts of the country mobs seized grain and sold it at cheap rates.[61] Reports of these events sometimes mentioned their proximate causes: food riots were occasioned by 'the high prices of the necessaries of life', discharged sailors naturally wanted their arrears of pay and prize money, and soldiers who had been enlisted for strictly limited terms were understandably provoked by rumours that their officers had sold them into service with the East India Company. But in 1782–3 there was a new anxiety that these events had deeper causes – and therefore more permanent implications – than the usual post-war coincidence of demobilization and high food prices, even if they were exacerbated by divisions among the parliamentary elite. It was only a couple of years since the Gordon riots had terrorized London for a week, and memories of the mob's attacks on the symbols and institutions of authority must have been fresh. Indeed another provincial newspaper, the *Newcastle Journal*, saw congenital insubordination among the common people as the root cause of contemporary disorder, although it was careful to fix the blame on the irresponsible opportunism of its political opponents:

> Riots and mutinies rather encrease than subside! – The reflux of the war seems to be more dangerous than the war itself. – The soldiers and sailors, seeing or hearing of their superiors quarrelling, follow their example, and the State malady becomes contagious! – Those Members of the State, who, in order to thrust themselves into power, strongly inculcated on the people the doctrine of self-government, now feel the effects, and see the evil of stirring up the multitude to affect a greater degree of power than they are capable of exercising with discretion. – Where all these things will end, no body yet knows; but all men of understanding can suggest to themselves the necessary effects of such causes. – May the great hand of Divine Providence interpose to save us from our numerous enemies, and our own vices and folly! Or we are undone.[62]

In other words, 'something should be done about it'. This diagnosis of a spreading 'contagion' of immorality and insubordination among the labouring population seems to represent the authentic scenario of an escalating moral panic which generates a 'social problem' and ultimately draws a 'law and order' response.[63] After mid-century, and certainly by the 1780s, growing anxiety about what was perceived as proliferating crime and violence, most likely grounded on the regular reporting of events in newspapers like the *Ipswich Journal*, tended to be generalized into concerns that the poor, when removed from the social constraints of small communities and tempted by the wealth of large towns and cities, were intoxicated by prospects of wealth and pleasure. Indeed a range of publications conveyed the impression that the metropolitan environment was creating a whole class of people who were habituated to crime from an early age.[64] The newspapers furnished most of the raw material and many of the other essential ingredients for such a view: through occasional bursts of hysterical comment like the one just noticed they also demanded official action. As they eclipsed other more traditional forms of crime and justice literature the nature of their reportage would only have increased public anxiety about crime and the inadequacies of official remedies.[65] However the sense of crisis was most fully fleshed out by essayists like Fielding, who supplied the essential ingredients of assumed moral consensus and a call for remedial intervention. Of course the preferred answer to the demands of any moral majority is law: and ultimately in this case it took the forms of the 'law and order' instruments developed by parliamentarians and middling opinion, and justice administered by the state, rather than the common law punishments which involved the discretionary consent of local communities at the grass roots. This conjunction between public opinion, social differentiation, and interventionist legislation is important for the subject of this book. Although taken for granted in modern western societies, it appears to have been virtually unprecedented before it occurred in eighteenth-century England. Certainly the 'reforming' legislation which ultimately transformed the administration of criminal justice in England was emblematic of a fundamental shift in the public expectations of law in society.

## Punishment solutions: Middle-class consciousness, the bloody code and the penitentiary

Despite the much increased sensitivity to crime, resulting in the kinds of panics described previously, nevertheless in the eighteenth century the permanence and general assertiveness of parliament and the established legitimacy of legislative intervention in the administration of criminal justice bred unprecedented expectations in the potential for remedial governance from the centre. It was believed that parliament could and should fix the crime problem by imposing appropriate punishments. As the Reverend George Ollyffe insisted (in 1731), the Leviathan of king in parliament could do anything because it represented the formal consent of the people:

> since with us no Punishment is first settled without the whole Legislative Power, and the People in general as represented in Parliament, as well as the Royal Power, are all concern'd in appointing divers kinds of Punishment, whether they are more or less severe, none can say there is any Thing done without the Nation's own Consent and Act.[66]

Ollyffe therefore expected parliament to pass new penal laws which would deal with 'the idle, vagrant and loose Tribe', who 'scruple no Mischief either with regard to Men's Persons or Properties, wheresoever they imagine they may extort any Prize, and yet escape the Lash of present Justice'.[67] Similarly, faced with what he saw as a crisis of authority in the 'wild notions of liberty' associated with the mobility, idleness and insubordination of the labouring population, Henry Fielding declared that the primary purpose of his tract was 'to rouse the CIVIL Power from its present lethargic State', and recommended several legislative measures to deal with crime and what he understood as its social causes.[68] For these authors, preventing crime, disposing of criminals, and governing the people who were liable to be tempted into crime were among the fundamental responsibilities of government, and penal legislation – the *leitmotiv* of the moral majority – was its primary weapon.

The post-Revolution state was set on a path of sustained legislative intervention in the administration of criminal law early in the eighteenth century, at a time when there was little concentrated public discussion about remedial changes.[69] Most importantly, in 1717, after almost a century of piecemeal experimentation, the Whig government legislated decisively to establish transportation to the American colonies as the main form of punishment for felony short of death. By this act the state signalled that it was prepared to take responsibility for those offenders it considered too incorrigible for branding and discharge into the community, and also transferred a significant measure of sentence decision-making from juries to professional judges.[70] A later act empowered local authorities to contract with carriers and merchants for transporting felons and required them to pay the costs of conveying their transportees to the ports.[71] These measures seem to have been the products of interests and authorities in London who were alarmed about the threat posed by crime in the metropolis, and who made their arguments behind the scenes. Subsequently, however, by their focused moral indignation and leverage with governments the essayists and the press more broadly seem to have played a crucial role in transforming English criminal justice from a popular to a professional regime.

So what did they recommend? Although there had been significant innovations in 'secondary' punishments like transportation and imprisonment with hard labour, and more extensive legislative schemes which aimed to tackle the supposed causes of crime by re-organizing the administration of poor relief and regulating the manners and leisure options of the working population, before the later eighteenth century the penal policies recommended by most public commentators were relatively conventional in their ultimate dependence on exemplary terror for dealing with the most serious offences and seemingly irredeemable offenders.[72] Until widespread doubts developed in the 1770s and 1780s it was broadly accepted that the deterrent potential of death on the gallows was the keystone of the criminal law, and after 1689 the penalty of capital punishment was attached to a variety of specific property thefts and their particular circumstances, even if by no means all offenders were hanged, or were intended to be.[73] Certainly, while they frequently connected criminality with irreligion, idleness, and vice, many pundits on crime wrote as if they believed that potential offenders could be terrorized into outward conformity with the law and the social order; and suggestions for dealing with the proliferation of serious crime frequently included aggravated forms of death and other physically painful punishments. Thus the author of *Hanging, Not Punishment Enough* (1701), argued that murderers, highwaymen and house-breakers should be broken on the wheel, hanged in chains and starved, or whipped to death.[74] Thirty years later, George Ollyffe went further: he too recommended breaking on the wheel, and a more painful form of hanging with slowly-tightening cords around the arms and legs; and he suggested such penalties should be applied to a greater range of capital offences.[75] Moreover, these pamphlets, like the better-known works of Mandeville, Fielding, and Michael Madan, argued for more rigorous application of the death sentence, on the grounds that the frequent exercise of mercy was 'false compassion' which only encouraged those likely to resort to crime with the prospect of escaping justice; for 'many will be found (as ill men easily flatter themselves) who will not fear a Law, that has sharp Teeth indeed, but does but sometimes bite'.[76] Indeed, the teeth were sharpened by parliament in 1752, when another wave of concern about violent street robberies around London resulted in legislation which ordered the bodies of murderers to be delivered to physicians or surgeons for dissection, or at the trial judge's discretion, to be gibbeted in chains as a standing object of terror to observers.[77]

The administration of such 'sanguinary Laws' was not just a matter of simply deterring crime by physical terror and taking retribution on the condemned, however. For most of its advocates the deterrence value of capital punishment depended on the presence of the common people. In this it too formed a continuity with other traditional participatory forms of government, traces of which we have identified already. But in the eighteenth century the people were expected to behave properly: ideally they should be empathetic witnesses in a solemn moral lesson which supposedly restored the health of the body politic by the convict's public repentance and confession, while affirming individual subordination to the social order and lawful authority through the communal infliction of death.[78] And here lay a problem, for while they accepted the necessity for exemplary punishment, several commentators complained that the apparently growing moral depravity and insubordination of the people meant that they disrupted its theatre and drowned out its authorized messages, or at best sympathized with the plight of the condemned, instead of contemplating his crimes. This was most clearly evidenced by the behaviour of the crowds at Tyburn, the usual place of execution for London and Middlesex. Rather than affirming the justice and utility of the proceedings by attending with awe and solemnity, it was said that hangings at 'Tyburn Tree' frequently took place in an atmosphere of popular licence, riot and carnival. Mandeville famously described how the procession from Newgate to Tyburn was 'one continued Fair' of noise, confusion, and 'Nastiness', occasioned by the presence of a vast crowd of idle apprentices, prostitutes, thieves and pickpockets, as well as the former companions of the prisoners, all roaring drunk and keen to excel each other in ribaldry and disorder.[79] And the presence of such an audience provided an opportunity to the prisoner: Fielding complained that rather than a day of shame, a thief's execution was his 'Day of Glory':

> His procession to *Tyburn*, and his last Moments there, are all triumphant; attended with the Compassion of the meek and tender-hearted, and with the Applause, Admiration, and Envy of all the bold and heartened.[80]

Outraged newspaper reports suggested this behaviour was not confined to the London crowds. Indeed, some accounts of the more famous hangings represent a back-handed appreciation of the celebrity criminal's ability to attract an unruly crowd and easily arouse their worst instincts, thereby subverting the whole performance. Thus in April 1739 'the famous [Dick] TURPIN' was executed at York in front of 'the greatest Number of Spectators ever known in the Memory of Man, several having come 38 Miles on no other Account'. Naturally, he took the opportunity to stir up anti-authoritarian feelings by laughing in the face of death and generally playing the hero, rather than the penitent villain. And it seems he understood precisely how to invert the moral of the whole performance. He was clad all in white, the cart was followed by four men with white gloves, and he carried himself 'as if he was going to a Wedding [rather] than to his Execution'.[81]

While some prisoners did die penitent, such a display of misrule was not unique, and simple disorder was very common.[82] Of course the experience of public execution therefore begs an important question: how – and why – was this allowed to happen in what was one of the most powerful states of western Europe? Thomas Laqueur has argued that in England the authorities actually took little trouble to orchestrate executions as theatrics of power. Usually there were few soldiers, and a poor display on the part of the sheriff and the officials, who appeared with 'mean Equipages' and were mounted on 'scrubby Horses'.[83] Tyburn itself was just a shabby open space at the western margins of London. This was no mere administrative lapse. Rather the panoply of government was understated because public hangings above all, represented the consent of the people to the law: their overwhelming numbers, their forbearance of rescue, and their intimidatory guarantee of equal treatment for rich and poor offenders symbolized popular subscription to the ultimate expression of sovereign government.[84] Here was a time-hallowed 'economy of power' by which the people felt themselves to be the law. But the criticisms of the press imply that in the eighteenth century there were rising expectations of behaviour which cast traditional execution carnivals as evidence of the common people's bestiality, rather than fulfillment of their traditional role in lawful punishment.[85] Middle-class sensibility rejected outright the experience of public executions as legitimate expressions of the unified body politic – where polite ladies and gentlemen administered justice together with butchers and prostitutes – and their fastidiousness symbolized the beginning of the end for the unbounded community at law.[86]

The difficulty was that the values implicit in newspaper reports of crime, and explicitly associated with 'the sober, careful, and wiser Part of the Nation' who were most frequently represented as its victims, did not seem to be shared by the crowds who attended executions.[87] Indeed, for conservative advocates of exemplary deterrence the people were the problem, not the law. The 'bloody code' of judicial death and other violent exemplary bodily punishments was compromised, not vitiated, by social change, in so far as the common people could no longer be trusted to participate in the administration of justice. So the state should step in to vindicate the majesty of the law. Fielding took such an analysis furthest by grounding his arguments about crime and the poor in a legal and historical dissertation on the declension of the English polity, whereby the balanced constitution of hierarchical society had been destroyed by the corrupting power of wealth and mobility on the 'commonalty', with the result that a golden age of minimal crime and social harmony had been lost.[88] According to this view the frankpledge system of the Anglo-Saxons, which he believed had effectively prevented theft, had been rendered redundant by the 'wanderings' of the poor from the supervision of their communities. Since the common people were now so abandoned in their libertine viciousness, they should be only the subjects of law, rather than its agents. Hence he argued that their disruptive presence should be excluded from executions, which ought to be staged privately, or at least in a highly controlled environment, like those in Holland, with all the majesty which elaborate state ritual could conjure up, to work on 'the Minds of the Multitude'.[89] Others recommended isolating the prisoner from supporters and other convicts, denying the succour of drink and exhorting Christian penitence, and generally increasing the representation of officials at the place of execution. Some such changes were introduced around mid-century, at least in London and Oxford. But at Tyburn the attendance of the crowd continued to be attended with so 'many inconveniences' that in 1783, by order of the sheriffs of London, the procession through western London was abolished altogether, and henceforth convicts were executed outside Newgate prison, where it was supposed the crowd would be more controllable and awed by the officially contrived circumstances.[90]

The abolition of the procession to Tyburn, which provided an example for several other provincial authorities, was a major step in the exclusion of the common people from participating in legal punishment with officials.[91] The infliction of corporal punishment in public also declined. In London and its environs there were increases in the overall number of whippings with rising population and a retreat from transportation after 1750. But the tradition of whipping offenders through the streets declined in favour of private floggings and public whippings were described as 'extraordinary' in 1790. Moreover a pelting in the pillory – completely unmediated popular justice which might lead to maiming or even death in extreme cases – was subjected to more control by local authorities and severely restricted by legislation in 1816.[92] Critics particularly deplored the frequent brutality and disorderliness of the crowds who attended the pillory as uncivilized behaviour which they regarded as quite inappropriate for the proper administration of justice.[93] Belief in the power and legitimacy of exemplary violence survived into the nineteenth century and afterwards, but ordinary people were progressively excluded and the rituals of punishment were focused on the imagination, symbolizing the criminal law's concentrated engagement with the individual, rather than the need to acknowledge the consent of body politic.[94]

The central story of this fundamental shift, by which a regime organized around 'the hanging tree' was ultimately replaced by one grounded on the penitentiary, is well known. But it is not sufficiently appreciated that the arguments among conservative and progressive penal 'reformers' represent considerable intellectual common ground, in so far as late eighteenth-century critics of the bloody code were even less comfortable with popular mores and the experience of popular participation in punishment than those who wanted to purify and maintain the theatre of death. Like most commentators, they argued that where capital punishment had to be inflicted, it should be 'the most solemn and affecting scene, that can be exhibited'.[95] But the principal project of the later Georgian penal reformers was the transformation of the mores and manners of men and women by suitable socialization and discipline, and frequent public executions were emphatically unhelpful. It was not just that death was a wholly disproportionate punishment for most crimes of property, and that the culture of public hangings became disreputable in polite circles, even provoking revulsion in the 1780s and at other times when the authorities determined to crack down on crime waves by mass executions of convicts.[96] Rather the law was wholly failing in its didactic enterprise. In such cases hangings set an example of cruelty which only confirmed the common people in their interpersonal brutality because the laws themselves 'teach them to think, that the life of a fellow-citizen is of little value'.[97] They also reflected poorly on government, implying a degree of incivility and unreason in the rulers which was not commensurate with an enlightened society. For Samuel Romilly and William Eden, both common lawyers like Fielding but with more progressive aspirations for law, justice should be seen to value the individual by emphasizing moderation in punishment, while its measured application to offences encouraged industry, politeness and sensibility in human relations.[98] Eden looked forward to an age when 'the selfish passions are softened into an habitual acquiescence in the general dispensation of Law', while Romilly recommended penal institutions which would address the disadvantages of criminals who were simply ill-educated, indigent, or led astray by others.[99]

Indeed, the advocates of imprisonment at hard labour certainly had far higher ambitions for the law than traditionalists: they wanted to use criminal sanctions to re-fashion society according to the values of the urban middle classes, and this meant reforming popular culture at a microscopic level. In their hands, law was more than just rules and processes for maintaining a modicum of order: it was a purposive instrument of governance. Achieving their human engineering ends would require more intensive and professional forms of punishment as 'treatment', where the people were individual patients to be cured, rather than citizens to be consulted.[100] The cure consisted in nothing less than substituting good bourgeois values for the lifestyle of 'violence, riot and dissipation' typical of hardened criminals.[101] And the primary site for achieving such a transformation was the 'penitentiary', where the offender would be quarantined from further moral infection and made to see the error of his ways. In the optimistic words of Sir William Blackstone, their principal legal architect, 'Penitentiary Houses' were intended to be '[experimental] Houses of Confinement & Labour', and their name signified 'the [hope] of Reformation which may be indulged from their Establish[ment]'.[102] Blackstone's followers dreamed of a complex system of correction and discretionary rehabilitation: while 'the fiercest and most ungovernable spirits' would be subdued by solitary confinement and regular labour; offenders who appeared to be redeemable would be isolated from their 'infectious companions' and subjected to improving religious and industrial disciplines with the aim of creating 'valuable members of society'.[103] Of course the prototype of such a totalizing regime was mapped out by the Penitentiary Act of 1779, a complex statute drafted by Blackstone, and sponsored by Eden as a junior government minister.[104]

The Penitentiary Act authorized the construction of two experimental national prisons along the lines envisaged by the ascetic and philanthropist John Howard, author of the influential *State of the Prisons*, first published in 1777. In this book Howard distilled his non-conformist piety and middle-class discipline into a recipe for saving the wretched inmates of the prisons he had visited up and down the country. His main aim was to reform existing conditions, rather than extend the application of incarceration. But while he drew attention to the disease, corruption, and human waste which were features of English houses of correction (or 'bridewells') and county and city gaols, his observation of European prisons which were places of cleanliness, work and religious reflection were attractive to those critics of the existing penal regime who were beginning to argue for the extension of imprisonment at hard labour. His emphasis on the improving discipline of labour appealed to the instincts of those influenced by contemporary materialist thinkers who denied original sin and believed the mind of the criminal could be transformed by a regimen of work. Again, for them crime was regarded as a moral disease which was endemic among the poor: just as their lack of hygiene led to typhus, so their lifestyles drew them to robbery and violence. So like the reforming doctors who recommended cleanliness and quarantine for hospitals, the advocates of imprisonment with hard labour believed that solitary confinement would prevent the contagion of 'criminal values', and accustoming the body to industry might habituate the mind to order and godliness.[105] Certainly for Howard, 'Solitude and silence are favourable to reflection; and may possibly lead them to repentance', and he repeated with approval the maxim of the 'rasphouses' in Holland 'Make them diligent, and they will be honest'. Most of all, however, he recommended their efforts to inculcate ideas of religious duty, and he wished aloud

> that *our* prisons also, instead of echoing with profaneness and blasphemy, might hereafter resound with the offices of religious worship; and prove, like these, the happy means of awakening many to a sense of their *duty* to God and *man*.[106]

While penitentiaries were not built before the nineteenth century, the principles and prejudices on which they were founded had been gaining ground in the eighteenth century with the developing notion that the associative experience of the common people was a source of moral corruption. Conventionally enough, the author of *Hanging not Punishment Enough* believed 'in common Persons so much Roguery is learn'd among Numbers', and he therefore prescribed isolation cells for prisoners awaiting trial, 'to make their Confinement more uneasie'. Mandeville also wanted them to be locked up by themselves, that they might be denied the support of their fellows, and at Newgate solitary cells were constructed for the condemned.[107] Moreover, the reforming philanthropist Joseph Hanway had long recommended institutional confinement as a solution to 'the dissolutions which prevail among the lower classes of the people', and in the 1770s he argued for the solitary confinement of convicts in purpose built prisons.[108]

Long term imprisonment was not generally favoured, however, until transportation to America ran into difficulties and the idea of imposing a regime of improving labour was incorporated into thinking about prisons for criminals, as well as workhouses for the poor. In his pioneering *Principles of Penal Law* (1771) Eden himself had opposed simply locking up offenders as tending to make them an economic burden on society, and like most thoughtful contemporaries he was very critical of the 'secret tyranny' perpetrated in existing prisons.[109] Nevertheless he did recommend temporary imprisonment with forced labour as a suitable punishment for non-violent theft: 'a mode of punishment, which, by inducing a habit of industry, and by the effects of that habit, would be equally beneficial to the criminal and the public'.[110] Certainly short spells of enforced labour in houses of correction had been prescribed for wilful idleness since the sixteenth century, and occasionally this productive remedy was extended to people convicted of lesser felonies, presumably because they were thought to need more rigorous treatment than the usual punishments of whipping or burning in the hand.[111] Indeed, 'The employment of the poor was the favourite panacea of early eighteenth-century reformers'; and in the reign of Queen Anne there were several attempts by interested parties in the city of London to substitute corrective labour for felonies which attracted benefit of clergy.[112] In 1706 a statute passed which provided for a period of hard labour (six months to two years) in houses of correction or workhouses for clergyable felonies, at the discretion of the judges.[113] In proposing such a regime to the corporation of London, the secretary of state opined that it would serve as 'A proper means to breake them [i.e. offenders] of their idle and wicked Course of Life. As also by the Example thereof to deter others from the like Courses and ill practices'.[114] In fact the judges tended to favour transportation for felony rather than imprisonment after the implementation of the Transportation Act in 1718, but the idea of forcing felons to labour remained current, and 40 years later Henry Fielding also advocated applying a modified poor law solution to punishing crime.[115] He proposed a strict regime of separation, prayer and 'the hardest and vilest Labour' in a county-wide Middlesex house of correction for the idle, vagrants and petty criminals which would sit alongside a county workhouse for the honest poor. The scheme anticipated the penitentiary in so far as it was intended for 'Correction of the Mind' as well as the body.[116]

The substantive reasons for the failure to build state penitentiaries in the eighteenth century were fear of the expense and local opposition to the centralizing tendencies expressed in the wave of legislative proposals introduced during the later 1770s which culminated in the Penitentiary Act.[117] But there can be little doubt of widespread persuasion about the association between crime and 'the problem' of popular culture, and the attraction of legal instruments for reconstituting the individual offender's psyche which underwrote these schemes seems to have extended beyond the reformers already noted. In the course of the American war imprisonment at hard labour for terms of several years had been authorized by an act of 1776 which established labour gangs on the Thames, as well as by the Penitentiary Act itself, and these measures were straws in the wind. While parliament's acceptance of them probably owed much to the enforced interruption of banishment to America, they were both initiated by Eden and drafted by Blackstone: even the earlier statute specifically declared that the aim of putting offenders to work was so that they might be 'reclaimed from their evil Courses', while the Penitentiary Act itself expressed the hope that solitary imprisonment, labour and religious instruction 'might be the Means under Providence, not only of deterring others from the Commission of the like Crimes, but also of reforming the Individuals, and inuring them to Habits of Industry'.[118] Moreover, the new punishment options provided were certainly used, albeit in a makeshift way at first. There seems to have been a considerable rise in sentencing non-capital criminals to terms of imprisonment during the war years, at least on the evidence of Surrey, where the judges sentenced almost 90 per cent of convicts in this category to terms of labour in the prison hulks or in existing houses of correction.[119] Indeed, with rising gaol populations after the end of the American War these government-led shifts towards what their advocates claimed were 'the Means best calculated for reforming as well as punishing Individuals' were taken up enthusiastically by several local authorities; and the state itself invested in major penitentiaries during the early nineteenth century.[120] So ideas about the 'problem' of crime and the common people became policies, and the policies were transformed into purposive laws. The reasons for the translation of the new penology into institutional forms are indicative of the changes in local government outlined earlier in this book.

Admittedly, in part the new 'carceral regime' became established in some English gaols and houses of correction because transportation to Botany Bay (facilitated by a provision of the Penitentiary Act which authorized transportation to suitable places other than America, and confirmed by another statute in 1784[121]) was never able to meet as much of the demand for non-capital punishment as transportation to America had during the middle years of the century. Since rising population around the end of the eighteenth century led to increased numbers of offenders, and conveying more than a minority to the south Pacific was economically impracticable, imprisonment perforce became the staple punishment for criminals who were not regarded as incorrigible or dangerous.[122] But perhaps the key reason for the ultimate success of a form of imprisonment which aimed to impose middle-class conceptions of morality on the common people was that by the later eighteenth century there appears to have been a clear conjunction between advanced bourgeois opinion in the localities and some leading parliamentarians who had a new commitment to public service and the ability to translate their convictions into legal instruments. William Eden is the obvious exemplar of the new lawmakers in the case of prison reform, but Thomas Gilbert, the poor law reformer, also played an important role. In 1782 he was responsible for legislation which tightened up the administration of houses of correction by requiring their inspection by local JPs, the separation of prisoners according to gender, prohibition of the sale of alcohol, and enforcement of up to 12 hours of productive labour a day.[123] This act had an immediate impact among some sympathetic members of the Lancashire magistracy, especially the Manchester

Unitarian Thomas Butterworth Bayley, son of a textile manufacturer, who led a successful campaign to reform the county's prisons, culminating in the construction of new gaols at Lancaster, Preston and Manchester which introduced the disciplines outlined by the Penitentiary Act.[124] And in Gloucestershire Sir George Onesiphorus Paul, a scion of the wool manufacturing industry, pushed forward the construction of the county's own penitentiary and introduced the new regime of prison 'police' into all the local prisons, adding his own emphasis on humiliating rituals of enforced sanitation to the prescription of solitary confinement, religion, and labour. Indeed, here as in some other counties there was a clear symbiosis between the plans of local JPs and parliamentary initiatives, for while the Lancashire magistrates deployed the act of 1782 and further permissive legislation passed in 1784[125] to set up prison inspection committees and raise money for repairs and new construction work by borrowing on the security of the rates, in Gloucester and elsewhere the county obtained its own act of parliament to authorize its reforms. Subsequently the Gloucester Act and Paul's *General Regulations for Inspection and Controul of all the Prisons, together with Rules and Orders for the Government of the Houses of Correction, within the County of Gloucester* (1790) became a blueprint for other local authorities to follow, even leading to a general Prisons Act in 1791 after a magistrates' convention in London.[126]

While they remained a minority experience among English prisons in the eighteenth century, the development of intensive penal institutions is important because they represent several elements of a larger change by which the criminal law – and I would argue the administration of public law generally – was infused with a new instrumental and substantively more rigorous character. Three points deserve emphasis here. First, as suggested a moment ago, the movement for prison reform illustrates how, under the influence of advanced opinion, the leaders of some local authorities were keen to take advantage of parliamentary facilities to forge new statutory instruments of governance, either by utilizing general legislation or by obtaining a private act. The new prisons were built by local magistrates, rather than the central government, but they acted through the agency of the sovereign state.[127] Indeed, the history of what may be described accurately as 'penal policy' for the first time in the eighteenth century is a prime case of the opinion-led legislative positivism which is taken for granted in modern western societies.[128]

Secondly, in principle if not always in practice, the new penal institutions were anti-discretionary instruments of the state, in so far as they were supposed to be governed by detailed rules which would be enforced by supervising magistrates, who were in turn answerable to the king's judges for their conduct.[129] Certainly this vogue for management was partly a reaction against the corruption which traditionally prevailed in English prisons, where unsalaried gaolers were left to milk the prisoners for fees if they could pay and usually neglected those who could not, while running profitable schemes for supplying provisions and liquor and allowing inmate subcultures to impose their own vicious forms of regulation. John Howard had complained bitterly about the 'wickedness, disease, and misery' which flourished under these conditions, and he recommended much closer magisterial attention to 'economy and government'.[130] But the plethora of rules and accountability arrangements which were included in the Penitentiary Act and its practical analogues were also a product of Enlightenment ideas about rational authority which thoroughly permeated the new reforming penology. While they found their most extreme expression in Jeremy Bentham's abortive 'Panopticon', Henry Fielding had been thinking along the same lines half a century earlier, for he stipulated that his proposed Middlesex workhouse and house of correction should have salaried officials, who were charged with implementing a detailed system of rules, and they were to be accountable to the magistrates and the lord chancellor for defaults.[131] Moreover, the emphasis on control from above which permeated thinking about prisons also influenced the administration of transportation when it was renewed in 1787, for in New South Wales the convicts and their keepers were subjected to imperial control and penal discipline in the name of the crown.[132] Here was 'a distinctive relationship between prisoner and state' which substituted continuous executive supervision for discretionary power. I shall have more to say about discretion in the next section, but at this stage it appears that in England after 1750 the availability of discretionary participation in the administration of punishment was becoming confined to judges and county magistrates, who were usually trusted to make the right decisions. Certainly there was less scope for discretionary interventions from the community: for with the gradual declension of public forms of bodily punishment and their replacement by transportation and imprisonment the people lost the chance to signal their consent or dissent in the justice of the proceedings.

Thirdly, as I have attempted to show in this section, the establishment of the new prisons symbolizes the ultimate establishment of the widespread conviction that the roots of the 'crime problem' lay in the immorality and insubordination of the common people. As Michael Ignatieff has pointed out, the inmates of Paul's prisons were principally men and women convicted of relatively minor offences by summary proceedings – breaches of contract by farm labourers, embezzlement of tools and goods in agriculture and industry, lesser forms of poaching and theft, bastardy and paternal desertion of families. And it is probable that the offenders confined in late eighteenth-century reformed prisons like his were also largely the younger convicts, who were convicted for the first time. Indeed, although not new offences, these petty crimes and misdemeanours were punished with a new rigour and concern for the maintenance of order and authority because men like Paul believed that early intervention was essential to prevent the inevitable moral slide into a career of more serious criminal offences.[133] For Paul attention to such seemingly trivial digressions was simply good economy in government: 'if it be by Correction of the smaller Crimes that the greater are prevented, when we dispense with the smaller, we become responsible for the greater that ensue'.[134] In fact by the 1780s, with increasing doubts about the deterrence value of common law traditions of public punishment and continuing anxiety about apparently ever-increasing levels of crime, there was a tendency among public commentators to identify a section of the labouring population in England as a 'criminal population' or the 'dangerous classes', whose very habits of life required sustained corrective attention.[135]

Finally, this tendency to social labelling helps to explain why, in addition to the offences mentioned already, the new penal instrument at the disposal of the magistrates was brought to bear on other aspects of plebeian behaviour which were thought to be associated with criminality. Chief among these was the prosecution of interpersonal assault. Although assaults could be treated as private trespasses rather than crimes, research has shown that some JPs were tasking a harsher attitude towards those who were brought before them for assault as a breach of the peace.[136] While the vast majority of cases were still 'settled' by individual justices, the statute of 1778 which allowed them to impose costs on parties summarily convicted also provided for commitment to imprisonment at hard labour on failure to pay.[137] And where such cases were sent for indictment, at Quarter Sessions in Essex and in Surrey from around the later 1770s the presiding magistrates and juries took an increasingly severe line, finding proportionately more offenders guilty and either imposing substantial fines or sentencing them also to terms of imprisonment under the new penal regimes. In cases of manslaughter too, near the end of the century judges began to impose custodial sentences on convicts (unless the offender was a gentleman), rather than simply branding and discharging them, as has been the previous practice. So it appears that by the end of the eighteenth century casual interpersonal violence among the labouring population was being regarded as a legitimate subject for exemplary justice and correction by the criminal law, whereas previously it had tended to be viewed as a largely private matter, suitable for discretionary settlement. This shift has been aptly described as 'an assertion of the role of the law and the courts in creating and preserving social order'.[138] The next section discusses further 'assertions' of this kind in the earlier stages of criminal law administration.

## Policing and prosecution solutions: Professional law enforcement

In this chapter I have been attempting to show how under the influence of 'public opinion', from the mid-eighteenth century the criminal law became a positivist instrument in the service of a new ideology about the degeneracy of the common people which amounted to a social pathology of crime. As V.A.C. Gatrell has argued, the corollary of that ideology was an overriding concern for social order, and in the nineteenth century the primary expression of the demand for order was professional policing under the direction of the state.[139] Of course it would not be at all accurate to describe Georgian England as a 'policeman state'; certainly there was no uniformed, statutory, paid police force anywhere in England before the establishment of the Metropolitan Police in 1829. But the burden of recent research on policing in the eighteenth century has emphasized important continuities with the early Victorian age, especially in London, rather than an abrupt shift with the foundation of 'the new police'.[140] It is now evident that tendencies towards the professionalization of constables were much more advanced than had previously been thought, and there is also evidence for the eighteenth-century roots of the new policing 'project' for disciplining the common people.

It will be recalled that in the early seventeenth century village constables generally continued to fulfil a traditional 'interhierarchical' role, in the sense that they were unpaid locally-appointed notables who were imbricated with their communities' distinctive cultures of order and had considerable discretion in carrying out their duties, although they were formally responsible for carrying out the instructions of the king's justices. Moreover, the constable was more a general civil officer than a local policeman in the modern sense, for he had acquired a range of administrative duties besides his principal responsibility for maintaining the peace.[141] By contrast, as seen previously, in Cheshire at least by 1817 the quarter sessions records reveal the regular employment of special constables who were paid by the magistrates specifically 'to execute warrants in felony', and a county police force was established after 1829.[142] Indeed the professional police force was envisaged as a powerful instrument of active authority. Historians of policing have pointed out that the most committed architects of the 'new police' emphasized the need for surveillance and regulation of the working population with a view to moral reformation, a project which is aptly described as 'preventive policing'.[143] But although the changes in the theory and practice of policing during the period covered by this book were very considerable, they were also complex and uneven across the country. In fact it appears that while many counties continued to resist legislative initiatives for the establishment of professional police forces well into early Victorian times, in the metropolis new ideas and central government action were anticipated by grass-roots innovations which were already transforming the experience of 'law enforcement' a century earlier.

In the cities of London and Westminster, as in the other large towns and cities in England, what we would call everyday policing – patrolling the streets, apprehending people for breaches of the peace, and bringing them before judicial officials – depended principally on two sets of officers, the constables and the watchmen. Like their country cousins, these officers were supposed to be locally-nominated householders, men who were obliged to serve without pay in their parish or ward precinct for a year under the provisions of the Statutes of Winchester, which had made local communities responsible for apprehending felons.[144] However, it is clear that by the later seventeenth century many London householders were becoming reluctant to take their turns as constables, probably because of the multiplication of their duties, the rising expectations of 'respectable' citizens, and unwillingness to neglect their normal occupations. As a consequence, in the City of London from the later seventeenth century there was increasing resort to paid substitutes, and it has been shown that by 1730 at least half of these deputy constables served for several years, effectively becoming career policemen.[145] A similar drift towards professionalization can be observed in the case of the watchmen. The London watch already consisted largely of paid men by the early seventeenth century, because householders were even more reluctant to serve as lowly night watchmen than as constables. But it was increasingly difficult to force defaulters to pay the fines which were the basis for hiring substitutes, and for this reason after 1700 the process towards the creation of dedicated bodies of watchmen was accelerated from above. Under the impact of complaints about the inadequacies of the watch in the face of what was thought to be the rising incidence of robbery and burglary, especially during the 1720s and 1730s, both the genteel vestry of Westminster and the Corporation of London took steps to provide for regular quotas of paid watchmen in each parish or ward. Ultimately over the next half century the night watch was re-structured across London and urban Middlesex by a series of acts of parliament which empowered the raising of a dedicated local rate, with the result that the shift towards paid, professional watchmen was institutionalized at the parish or ward level, or (more rarely) was placed in the hands of a turnpike trust or a paving commission.[146] Like some of the other changes in the exercise of local government described previously, these were decisive developments in the growth of administrative power; and they were generally led by the more wealthy inhabitants, who tended to prefer 'more formal arrangements for law enforcement' which advanced their interests and preoccupations.[147] More particularly, although the nomenclature of the officers remained the same, they represented the beginnings of a distinctively 'modern' approach to policing crime and disorder. As in the case of providing for effective street lighting, which was also the subject of legislative action around this time, the civic authorities were assuming new statutory powers 'as a way of bringing the streets under surveillance and control'.[148]

Seen from this perspective, it appears that 'community self-policing' had largely been eliminated from London by 1750.[149] Certainly, this was no mere administrative shift: the professionalization of constables and watchmen provided the London authorities with a new instrument of legal authority that could be used in the service of more positive government. Admittedly, there is evidence from the early eighteenth century that watchmen regarded themselves as servants of their neighbourhoods: some took care to light householders they knew to their dwellings, or intervened to save them from prostitutes whom they knew to be pickpockets.[150] But constables may have had a different allegiance: unlike watchmen, they were sworn officers of the crown, who were directly responsible to magistrates, and in the City of London they were paid additional allowances for accepting extra duties, such as apprehending vagrants and beggars, or attending the Old Bailey sessions. Some even carried out active policing missions which were probably ordered from above: for example in 1693 one man led a group of watchmen in the suppression of after-hours drinking and the arrest of a peer's servants.[151] Indeed, like the societies for the reformation of manners, who used paid full-time informers as the instruments of their campaigns against vice, the City of London authorities ultimately discovered that paid men could be used to carry out more extensive 'policing' duties.[152] This was not just a matter of expanding surveillance over the streets by establishing regular patrols and constructing watch-houses at strategic points, important as those developments were. The increasing resort to paid deputy constables for policing purposes allowed the City to concentrate large forces at hangings and other public punishments, thereby facilitating effective crowd control through the intimidation of numbers. In the later eighteenth century, when as we have seen concerns about riotous crowds competed with rising crime as sources of panic, 'extra' policemen were frequently hired for special events, and large numbers of constables could be concentrated when trouble was anticipated at public punishments or on other occasions which attracted potentially unruly crowds. For example in April 1783, at the height of the post-war panic about crime and public disorder, the Corporation of London ordered the City marshals (who were salaried officers from the 1770s) and constables to patrol the streets in force in case the large bodies of discharged seamen who had assembled to demand their prize money became unruly.[153] It is perhaps indicative of contemporary consciousness about the enlarged scope of legal authority that newspapers commented on the presence of 'the whole civil Power' on occasions like these.[154] Although there was as yet no institutionalized central control over London's daily policing, there was a growing consciousness that the arrangements for hiring constables and watchmen had transformed the potential for effective management of the people.

This consciousness is reflected in the language used by social commentators, as well as in newspaper reports. Writing in 1796, the London magistrate Patrick Colquhoun distinguished between 'those particular branches of Police which may be denominated *municipal regulations*' and 'that branch which is connected with the *prevention* and *suppression* of crimes'.[155] Here he touched on a crucial shift in contemporary thinking about 'police'. Originally the word had been imported from the French, but Englishmen were careful to avoid using it as a subject noun because of its association with the hated example of the French police, who supposedly personified the threat to liberty normally identified with centralized state officials. Rather the term was normally used as a synonym for the general business of domestic government: in Johnson's definition it meant 'The regulation and government of a city or country, so far as regards the inhabitants'.[156] However from around the middle of the eighteenth century there was a clear tendency for writers on law and government to use the term 'police' more positively, and especially when they discussed the roots of crime and the 'problem' of popular morals. For example in 1775 Joseph Hanway published *The Defects of Police the Cause of Immorality and the Continual Robberies committed, especially about the Metropolis*, a book which called for more active regulation and religious instruction of the common people, especially in reformative prisons and workhouses. He also advocated 'a regular body of police' in the form of a salaried metropolitan establishment of magistrates and constables, to be paid for by a tax on popular entertainments.[157] Such usage had already led naturally to further semantic development, whereby 'policing' was identified more narrowly with securing the urban streets and suppressing those activities and associations thought to encourage crime. Thus in a tract which described his own improvements in policing the metropolis since 1753, Sir John Fielding had described a plan of 'police' for Westminster and metropolitan Middlesex which involved not only breaking up gangs of street robbers and burglars, but also suppressing popular gaming, apprentices' and servants' balls, and begging and prostitution. In addition he emphasized the importance of employing 'some principal acting Magistrate' like himself; a justice of the peace who would be 'handsomely subsisted' to collect public information about crimes and 'disorders' of these kinds and co-ordinate and encourage the 'civil Power' of constables.[158] Indeed, although most writers on policing continued to avoid the French bogey by discussing constables and watchmen rather than 'the police', their proposals for more active policing depended fundamentally on the two principles at the heart of the French system: professionalization and central control.

In 1796, as its full title suggests, Colquhoun's *Police of the Metropolis* was concerned self-consciously with policing in the narrower, more modern sense of deterring crime and prosecuting criminals.[159] Moreover its principal recommendations were inspired largely by the comparatively recent establishment in metropolitan Middlesex of several central police offices, presided over by stipendiary magistrates (including Colquhoun himself) who kept regular hours of business and had small squads of paid constables at their disposal.

The institution of an active justice who was partly remunerated out of government funds and accountable to ministers was a very significant policing initiative, which seems to have originated in the 1730s with the adoption of Thomas de Veil, who sat at Bow Street, Covent Garden, as the 'court JP'.[160] But the Bow Street office only became a centre of active policing under Sir John Fielding and his older half-brother Henry, successively magistrates there from 1748 to 1780, and who were supported by undisclosed government salaries. By virtue of his connection with the government the senior magistrate at Bow Street became the de facto chief magistrate of the metropolis, the officer held responsible by the ministry for maintaining order on the streets and dealing with any emergencies. Besides introducing a centralized country-wide system for reporting crimes and advertising stolen goods in the *Public Advertiser*, their distinctive contribution to the policing of London was to inaugurate an embryo criminal investigation force by maintaining several part-time constables who gathered evidence, and were ready to pursue offenders at any time, even beyond London.[161] Admittedly, the size of this force was tiny in the early years – there were only four in 1757 – but similar 'rotation' offices were established in adjacent parts of the capital, and some of those also had constables on call for pursuit.[162] Forty years later Colquhoun counted a total 117 such 'stipendiary officers of police' in eight offices.[163] He argued for an extension of 'premiums and gratuities' for constables, watchmen and patrolmen, to ensure their dedication to duty, and the unification of the various 'organs of Police which at present exist, in such a manner, by a general superintendence, to give equal encouragement, and to instil one principle of universal energy into all its parts'.[164]

Central government had been thinking along these lines too. Although the Fieldings' policing experiments had not received as much financial support as they had requested, it appears that by 1785 the government was persuaded of their virtues and wanted to go much further. As we have seen the Gordon riots of 1780 had contributed to a sense of crisis about maintaining order, and concerns about policing were compounded by the aftermath of the American War. The foundation of the Home Office in 1782 also contributed to more concentrated thinking on law and order issues, in so far as it gradually assumed responsibility for addressing the 'social welfare and discipline' aspects of government.[165] It was on behalf of the Home Office that in June 1785 the solicitor general, Sir Archibald Macdonald, introduced a parliamentary bill promoting a new scheme for securing the peace in the City of London, Westminster and Southwark, principally by establishing district police offices under a three-man metropolitan commission 'in whose hands should be concentrated the whole power of the police', including the divisional magistrates, constables, watchmen and other 'peace-officers'.[166] Macdonald's stated aim was to reduce the incidence of robbery and burglary by making discovery and punishment certain, but the bill's provisions would have introduced unprecedented measures of 'preventive' policing. Officers would be given wide powers of search and seizure, as well as powers of surveillance over publicans and pawnbrokers, and a range of tradesmen dealing in precious metals and other commodities frequently supplied by theft. In addition, the laws against vagrancy were to be extended, allowing for arrest and summary conviction of people 'notoriously suspected of being Thieves', as well as prostitutes, people gaming in public, and anyone else judged to be 'loitering about', even in daytime.[167] Perhaps unwisely, the solicitor general explicitly acknowledged the ambitious nature of these proposals – he said the bill amounted to 'a total reformation ... in the regulation of the police'; but he also emphasized its correspondence with the central principle which had animated the piecemeal police reforms made since the beginning of the century: 'that public business of any sort, would never be adequately and effectually performed, unless those to whom the performance was committed, were paid for their trouble'.[168]

In the event, the government's management of this wide-ranging initiative was inept, and the bill was left to wither in the face of sustained opposition from the Corporation of London, which identified it as a threat to the City's powers and privileges. Indeed it was the explicitly centralizing tendency of the measure, rather than the idea of a paid magistracy, which made it so obnoxious to the City and most of its other critics. The superintending commissioners and their peace officers were recognized as a major extension of the powers of the state at the expense of local civil authority, and inevitably comparisons were made with the police of Paris.[169] Ultimately the plan was imposed on Dublin, where the centralization of policing had proceeded further.[170] The traditional English aversion to encroachments on the power of local elites helps to explain why a watered down version of the 1785 bill was passed into law in 1792 as the Middlesex Justice Act. That act was brought in by a government lawyer and seconded by the Home Secretary, and it applied the model of the Bow Street establishment of stipendiary magistrates and paid detachments of constables to found seven more police offices in Westminster, metropolitan Middlesex and Southwark. But it did not touch the City of London, and created no unitary policing authority; and of course it was debated at a time when the French Revolution was strengthening conservative opinion. So although like the 1785 bill it created new legal powers for the active detention and summary imprisonment of 'ill-disposed and suspected Persons and reputed Thieves', it passed with a large majority.[171] Its opponents emphasized the constitutional significance of this legislation, however. The Whig leader Charles James Fox, who was also MP for Westminster, pointed out that the formal appointment of magistrates with crown salaries and who were therefore 'to a certain degree, under influence', was 'to introduce a new principle [of police]' which overturned the tradition of magisterial detachment and threatened 'perverting the law to oppression'. But he saved his most passionate language for the substantive clause that enabled summary conviction of 'any suspicious Person', not only because it reversed the usual burden of proof, but also because it was plainly directed against the poor:

> the clause was against every principle of criminal justice and altogether repugnant to the law of England. ... No man should, in a country governed by laws, be permitted to say, I know what I cannot prove; more especially, I will imprison a man for what I know I cannot prove, merely because he is in a situation that will not enable him to procure bail. ... [I]t was an attack on the best principle in our constitution, namely, that the law is no respecter of persons.[172]

Here Fox perceived the new legal tradition which was the substantive burden of that growing body of statutes applying summary proceedings: poor 'suspects' had to account for themselves before police magistrates and were easily convicted of crimes involving possession of goods presumed to be stolen.[173] Indeed Bruce Smith has drawn attention to a series of eighteenth-century statutes which expanded the summary jurisdiction of magistrates in circumstances relating to the theft of specific goods common to London life. In these cases constables were empowered to arrest suspects and bring them before a magistrate, where they in turn were required to prove their ownership. If the accused could not they were to be adjudged guilty and fined or committed to prison. Thus it is possible to identify a clear trajectory by which an alternative structure of policing and prosecution was developing strongly alongside the established system. Crucially, under these summary arrangements, the decisions about prosecution and conviction were made by officials.[174]

Certainly the policing of the metropolis seems to have been transformed in its structure and scope over the course of the eighteenth century, and the impact of this for the grass-roots experience of the law deserves to be emphasized. It was not just that with parochial establishments of paid constables and watchmen and the development of the police magistrates' forces 'London already had a sizeable police force before Peel's 1829 act'.[175] Although its centralizing potential did not emerge all at once, with the Middlesex Justice Act parliament created an increasingly professional establishment of magistrates who were accountable to the Home Secretary and had unprecedented administrative powers to enforce the law. Another similar office was created at Wapping in 1798, and the police establishments of all these officers were increased in subsequent years. Moreover, horse and foot patrols were expanded in the decades after 1790, following precedents set by Sir John Fielding and his successors at Bow Street. Ultimately the Metropolitan Police Act widened this breach in the eighteenth-century constitution by fully centralizing control of the 'new engine of power and authority' and introducing street surveillance of an unprecedented intensity. But the engine was built from materials developed steadily over the previous century, and with power derived from Georgian parliaments.[176]

As David Philips has suggested, in the long run the worst fears of traditionalists about the oppressive potential of the new police were not realized.[177] Professional policing spread beyond London after 1800, however. Stipendiary magistrates were introduced in Salford hundred (1805), Manchester (1813) and other industrial towns; and while there was resistance to central government initiatives for reformed policing in many of the rural areas, there were also several grass-roots movements for professional police under local control like the one in Cheshire.[178] Moreover, as this chapter has attempted to show, the development of professional policing was just one of a barrage of changes which together made significant inroads into the traditional administration and substance of criminal law, and helped to transform the experience of government.[179] Indeed, in the contested 'reform' of policing it is possible to identify with peculiar clarity the departures from consensual and participatory modes of governance that are the primary subject of this book.[180] For one early nineteenth-century critic, observing the policing of the metropolis by stipendiary officers and magistrates under central authority, it seemed as if a form of government limited by England's 'ancient institutions and laws' was being abandoned in favour of foreign ideas which tended to a despotism of executive and legislature.[181]

Leaving aside the 'preventive', surveillance function of the new police, the drive for professional policing at the end of the eighteenth century was one element of a range of ideas about crime and punishment inspired partly by thinking which became associated with Cesare Beccaria's *An Essay on Crimes and Punishments*, first published in English in 1767. Beccaria did not write much on the details of policing, but he promised to deal with crimes by making their punishment 'scientific'. Instead of depending on occasional exemplary terror to compensate for the discretionary decision-making steps in process that allowed many offenders to escape prosecution and punishment, he advocated a system which would facilitate a code of moderate punishments more proportionate to the offence by making their application virtually inevitable. Under such a plan, ideally in the eyes of the potential criminal the process of law should appear 'inexorable' rather than 'arbitrary': in other words apprehension, prosecution and punishment had to follow the commission of an offence in regular succession. And of course for that to happen, besides controlling the arrangements for policing, the state had to assert its 'right of punishing' over the individual's subjective participation in the process of prosecution, whether he was a mere victim of crime, the officiating magistrate, or even the sovereign with the power to pardon.[182]

From the perspective of government, the ordinary victim of crime was potentially the weakest link in this chain. In England the common law principle of private prosecution was held dear, however, especially at a time when memories of the Stuarts' repressive use of the criminal courts were fresh. Although carried on in the name of the crown, the prosecution of interpersonal offences remained largely a matter of individual choice and action throughout the eighteenth century. And as Mandeville and Fielding complained, despite the criminal sanctions applying to misprision (i.e. concealment) of felony and 'theftbote' (agreeing not to prosecute a thief on return of the property) many victims failed to prosecute offenders, either out of compassion, indolence, poverty, fear, or self-interest.[183] Moreover, even if the victim proceeded, without professional advice and presentation of the case the prosecution was susceptible to failure because of procedural error or some other 'quibble'. In these circumstances, which were exaggerated into alarmist claims about large numbers of the guilty being 'vomited back upon society', disciples of Beccaria like Bentham and Colquhoun would have liked to establish a state prosecution office which would take control of prosecutions on behalf of the crown.[184] But such an active empowerment of executive influence over the prosecution process was never seriously contemplated in parliament before the mid-nineteenth century, and then resisted successfully. In theory at least Everyman and Everywoman had the right to set the law in motion, and the accused should have the advantage of every doubt.[185]

In fact, however, although the principle of private prosecution had to be preserved, if only to symbolize the consent of the common people to the criminal law, some significant compromises were made. Early Georgian governments were somewhat insecure in the face of actual and anticipated threats to the Hanoverian regime, and authorities partly anticipated Beccaria by responding to the moral panics described earlier with a range of practical inducements to make victims take their complaints to court, and to strengthen the hand of the prosecution in serious or sensitive cases. Firstly, beginning with a statute passed in 1752, parliament passed a series of acts which provided for the reimbursement of legal costs to prosecutors, initially only in successful cases of felony and for those who petitioned and alleged their poverty; but eventually to all prosecutors and witnesses in serious misdemeanour cases as well as felonies, whatever the outcome.[186] Such payments probably only made a marginal difference to the number of prosecutions undertaken, since before 1818 there was no compensation for the time and trouble undertaken by the victim in arranging the prosecution, and for many these inconveniences were likely to be very burdensome, if not prohibitive. They therefore had little impact on the discretionary implications of retaining private prosecution of the criminal law.

More important was a second, earlier initiative, by which parliament established large rewards for the successful apprehension and conviction of selected capital offenders. Following a precedent established by the Rump Parliament, between 1692 and 1750 legislation established substantial rewards (£10–£40) for apprehending and successfully prosecuting persons guilty of highway robbery, counterfeiting and clipping the coinage, shop-theft, housebreaking and burglary, horse-stealing, sheep-stealing, assisting in the return of stolen goods without prosecuting, and returning from transportation.[187] In addition, at times of high public anxiety even larger rewards were offered by executive action, operating through royal proclamations. The most remarkable of these extraordinary executive incentives to prosecute was that offered in 1720 and continued until 1745, by which another £100 on top of the statutory £40 reward was offered for the conviction of robbers and murderers within a five-mile radius of Charing Cross, thereby covering all of Westminster and the City, plus the suburban approaches into London.[188] A similar reward was proclaimed in February 1749, at the height of another post-war 'crime wave', and it may have been effective, because within a couple of weeks newspapers reported that nearly 20 house-breakers and street-robbers were taken up.[189] Despite such claims, in the short term rewards were clearly a sign of administrative weakness in government, and they were abolished in 1818.[190] But for London they were of lasting significance because the enduring existence of large incentives to catch thieves helped to accelerate the tendency towards professional policing as substitute constables and 'thief-takers' made a lucrative trade out of prosecuting criminals, sometimes earning the princely sum of £140 per head. It is true that 'policing' of this private enterprise kind tended to corruption, for criminal entrepreneurs like Jonathan Wild combined prosecuting for profit with organizing theft and returning stolen goods for gratuities.[191] Also there were several major reward scandals, whereby prosecutions which had led to execution were found to have been fabricated by thief-takers.[192] But the thief-takers broke new 'law enforcement' ground. Although few were free of nefarious practices, in the course of their prosecuting activities during the 1690s they took on a detective role relatively unknown to the early modern constables and watchmen, especially in the detection and apprehension of people who were involved in coining and clipping activities. Moreover, at this time they frequently worked under the instructions of the treasury, the mint and the sheriffs of London in breaking up coining operations, especially by conducting raids and searches with constables. While the balance between their genuine crime-busting activities and more corrupt enterprises may have shifted towards the latter during the 1720s and early 1750s, both the public and the authorities continued to utilize their services for the apprehension and conviction of offenders. Indeed, despite their dubious reputation for corrupt dealings on the side, in their detective functions and in their links with state and city authorities the thief-takers were the authentic predecessors of the Fieldings' Bow Street 'proto-police'.[193]

Henry Fielding numbered thief-takers among 'the most honourable Officers in Government', and from the perspective of this study the most important government initiative in the prosecution of crime was the third: the gradually increasing participation of local and central government officials.[194] The development of professional policing in the metropolis has been described already. Here it is only necessary to emphasize the point that the increasing involvement of paid watchmen, constables, thief-takers and police magistrates like the Fieldings in the apprehension, public examination and committal of suspected offenders and reporting of offences created and sustained prosecutions which would not have occurred otherwise.[195] In this sense, in Georgian London at least, as Hay has said for a later period, 'the private prosecutor had begun, slowly, to turn blue'.[196] Indeed it has been argued that the model of public prosecution pioneered by London police magistrates and sanctioned by some of the statutes authorizing summary process meant that by the early nineteenth century the cherished principle of citizen initiative in ordinary criminal proceedings was actually an 'illusion'.[197] However for most of the eighteenth century perhaps the most visible aspect of that long drawn-out change was not so much the initiation of prosecution proceedings by the 'police' – which does not seem to have been occurring much outside Bow Street before the 1790s – rather it was the development of pre-trial public hearings at which the magistrates sifted the evidence and examined the accused and other parties to the alleged offence to see if there was a case which would stand up in court. This was happening in the City of London from 1737 at the latest, when the aldermen decided to sit in rotation at the Guildhall to conduct judicial business brought to them by the public, as well as at Bow Street under De Veil and the Fieldings.[198]

Certainly the development of a 'judicialized' pre-trial committal process – in practice the origin of the modern magistrates' court – meant that the charges against some accused individuals were dismissed, most frequently because the evidence proved to be insufficient and the prisoner brought witnesses to his good character. Moreover the public nature of the pre-trial hearings encouraged more formalism and the intervention of defence lawyers in a few cases, ultimately providing extra legal protection for the accused.[199] But on the other hand the purpose of examining in public was to allow for corroborating identification of the accused and the stolen goods, and to open the possibility of clearing up other offences he or she may have committed by pre-advertising for victims of similar offences to attend.[200] Moreover, if the 'facts' appeared to support a prima facie case of guilt then because of the publicity and participation of the magisterial office the victim must have been under unprecedented pressure to prosecute the charge. Indeed, the provisions of the Marian committal act which required the magistrate to take penal recognizances of material witnesses to a felony with the condition that they appear at the trial appear to have been strictly enforced in mid-eighteenth century London.[201] John Langbein has shown how a poor City shopkeeper who was bound over to prosecute a theft from his shop in 1754 was terrified that he would be fined by the lord mayor for failing to turn up at the trial, he being ill at the time. And it appears that under the influence of interventionist justices like Sir John Fielding prosecutors had only limited discretion in the framing of indictments, being advised, for example, to avoid capital offences in order to maximize the chances of a conviction. The London magistracy even granted immunity to some offenders on condition they would become 'crown witnesses' and impeach their associates in crime, therefore effectively selecting who should be prosecuted and who should not.[202] Here indeed were the beginnings of a major change in the culture of criminal prosecution, a shift towards more official control.[203]

The central government was directly involved in this process too. As Langbein and Betttie have shown in considerable detail, the unprecedented growth in the resources and activities of the executive during the early eighteenth century helped to professionalize the administration of justice by stimulating the growing involvement of lawyers in the prosecution of felony. Partly this was a result of the tendency – first evident after 1714 – for ministerial anxieties about threats to the state to merge with public panics about violence and street crime. From the early years of the Hanoverian regime the under secretaries of state were instructed to invest time and Treasury funds in the prosecution of people who were perceived as enemies of the regime – typically active jacobites, suspect printers, publishers and editors, and those involved in serious riots, including the 'Blacks' prosecuted in the early 1720s.[204] Furthermore, apparently encouraged by the predilections of a king accustomed to the state-led criminal prosecution system of Hanover, around this time the government also intervened decisively in ordinary felonies by taking control of the prosecution in a few high-profile crimes of violence, and promoting the conviction of some London gangs of street robbers and criminal racketeers, most notably the infamous Jonathan Wild, whose trial (in 1725) was choreographed by the assistant solicitor to the treasury. By the mid-1720s ministers were already initiating the beginnings of the ongoing correspondence and co-operation with Westminster magistrates in matters of crime and public order which later developed into the semi-institutionalized 'court justice' arrangements of De Veil and the Fieldings.[205]

What was crucial about these executive interventions in the ordinary administration of criminal proceedings was that the government's financial assistance normally resulted in the management of the pre-trial aspects of the prosecution by a 'solicitor': a professional litigation manager who would organize the evidence and the witnesses and – in some instances – engage a barrister to present the case in court. Indeed, as their business, and their exposure to crime increased from the end of the seventeenth century, several of the departments of state – the Treasury, the Mint, and the Bank of England – appointed an officer who took responsibility for the investigation and prosecution of criminal offences, and increasingly they tended to fee counsel too. Similarly, the solicitor for the City of London was prosecuting felony in the 1730s, and it seems these institutional prosecutions progressively influenced private prosecutors, because after mid-century there is evidence from various parts of the country of solicitors and attorneys prosecuting cases for private individuals. Criminal litigation work like this was especially common among those practitioners who became magistrates' clerks, or who managed the associations for the prosecutions of felons which proliferated in provincial centres and rural areas after 1770.[206] It now appears that it was the combined impact of assiduous magistrates, prosecution solicitors and reward-hungry thief-takers in some trials during the 1730s that led to changes which ultimately transformed the English criminal trial from a contest between 'citizen equals' to a fully lawyerized exchange in which ordinary people took a much less active part.[207]

Professional prosecution begot professional defence. Following evidence of a trickle of criminal cases prosecuted by counsel from the beginning of the century, several historians have drawn attention to the relatively sudden appearance of counsel partially representing defendants in felony trials at the Old Bailey and in the Surrey assize proceedings from the mid-1730s, despite the longstanding judicial prohibition against their appearance, other than to speak on issues of law.[208] Langbein's astute detective work has now revealed that this important shift in courtroom practice followed hard on the heels of a series of scandals by which innocent defendants were prosecuted on the initiative of unscrupulous thief-takers and 'Newgate solicitors' who invented evidence and coached witnesses with the aim of profiting from convictions. Also the practice by which London magistrates keen to break up gangs admitted accomplices' evidence against their fellows in return for immunity from prosecution was probably adding to the anxiety about the dangers of unsafe convictions on perjured evidence. In these circumstances he conjectures that the common law judges who presided at the Old Bailey and in the crown courts on the Home circuit must have come to realize that the intervention of interested quasi-professionals in the preparation of cases had tipped the balance of the criminal trial in favour of the prosecution, to the extent that there was a growing danger of juries being persuaded to convict by an accumulation of unsafe or insufficient evidence. Their response was to facilitate further professionalization. Confronted with such major flaws in the operation of the trial process, it appears that individual trial judges decided to permit barristers to stand in for defendants by examining and cross-examining witnesses, therefore 'evening up' the balance of justice and enabling more rigorous testing of the prosecution evidence.[209]

However it was taken, such a decision was a momentous one for the future development of the criminal trial, and for the representation of lay voices. Certainly it was the presence of counsel for the defence in a growing number of cases – especially after the 1780s when their numbers expanded considerably – which seems to have been ultimately responsible for the increasing application and full development of exclusionary rules of evidence which became standard by the nineteenth century.[210] Although defence barristers were not permitted to speak directly on behalf of their clients before 1836, and even in 1800 two-thirds of the trials at the Old Bailey had no lawyers, the growing practice of challenging the prosecution by cross-examination facilitated the gradual development of the trial process into a formally-structured and sequenced dialogue between 'cases' for the prosecution and the defence, helping to consolidate modern ideas about the prosecution's burdens of production and proof with the underlying presumption of innocence.[211] Ultimately the trial's purpose was transformed into providing the defence with the opportunity to test the prosecution's case.[212]

Already by the 1750s at the Old Bailey the early consequences of this shift were becoming clear. In the case of Elizabeth Woodcock, tried in October 1754 for stealing a few shillings from a drunken man in an alehouse, Lord Chief Justice Ryder stopped the case after the witnesses for the prosecution had been heard, the victim's evidence having been undermined by the counsel for the prisoner.[213] Directed verdicts like this suggested that the burden of adducing sufficient evidence lay with the prosecution, and allowed the accused to remain silent. The application of the privilege against self-incrimination to criminal defendants followed naturally, and was firmly entrenched in the nineteenth century. Even in 1790 the leading defence counsel William Garrow was confident enough of this principle – and of his powers – to rely upon his own judgement as to when his clients had a case to answer. Defending the coachman William Hayward, who was accused of stealing a chariot harness from his former employer William Champion Crespigny esquire, his questioning of the prosecution's witnesses inferred that the harness was a legitimate perquisite in lieu of unpaid wages, while Crespigny was mean-spirited and vindictive. He thereupon declared 'I shall call no witnesses in such a case; and I advise the coachman to say nothing', after which the judge directed the jury to return a verdict of not guilty.[214]

Leaving aside arguments about the improved prospects for defendants, under these conditions it appears that lay voices were progressively controlled and partially muted by the presence of the lawyers, both at the committal hearing and the trial. By the 1820s, when the impact of the lawyers' work was becoming apparent to contemporaries, the defendant was often substantially excluded from the proceedings; witnesses were clearly being selected and carefully prepared for what they would prove according to the solicitor's brief; and members of the jury were reduced to interested but passive spectators of the trial: they voted, but had no active voice. In other words, the criminal trial was well on the way to assuming its modern forms.[215] Parliament put their seal on this process in 1836 with the Prisoner's Counsel Act, which established the rights of persons accused of criminal offences to be fully represented by counsel, who in cases of felony could 'make full Answer and Defence'.[216]

It is possible to gain a sense of the transformation in the proceedings which accompanied professionalization by comparing the increasingly formal conduct of early nineteenth-century trials with those of a century earlier. Before 1700 the absence of lawyers was regarded as fundamental because felony trials were organized around the principle that judges and jurors had to make their discretionary decisions about verdict and (especially) sentence on the basis of an unmediated exchange between the defendant and the prosecutors. As Langbein has shown very clearly, pre-trial and trial were structured to force the accused to speak and exculpate himself.[217] Above all, judge and jury needed to decide whether the gravity of the offence and the circumstances and character of the accused deserved death or some lesser sanction, such as transportation or imprisonment. That was usually the main purpose of the trial. Essentially, at a time when the lack of investigative policing meant that most alleged offenders were caught red-handed, little incriminating evidence was excluded, and there was no presumption of innocence, the trial was an opportunity for the accused to respond to the victim's accusation, and for judge and jury to assess his or her explanation for each fact alleged, before making their determinations. So prisoners were required to conduct their own defences – as cross-examiner, witness and advocate – with the result that the proceedings normally amounted to a 'rambling altercation' between the prosecution witnesses, the defendant, and the judge.[218] For example William Davison, a servant, was tried at the Old Bailey on 11 October 1732 for stealing books from his master, Duncan Macqueen, a Westminster attorney. The trial started with Macqueen telling the court how having missed some of his law books he found several of them at the local bookshop, and the bookseller had identified Davison as the man who had sold them. But Davison thereupon interjected, claiming that he had sold them for Macqueen's use and that the money was spent on 'necessaries' for the house. He also maintained that Macqueen was in debt, had already pawned a silver seal, and had secretly moved the rest of his household goods to avoid their being distrained. Macqueen then admitted he was in 'difficult circumstances', upon which the defendant shot back 'And when I was before Justice De Veil [i.e. at the committal hearing], you trod upon my Toes, and whisper'd [to] me, that if I would say no more, you would be easy', thereby suggesting that the prosecutor had been anxious to compromise the affair to avoid paying the costs. After this Charles Marsh, the bookseller, gave his evidence. He testified that following the discovery of the books at his shop Macqueen had allowed Davison to return to his employment, but had threatened to prosecute Marsh for receiving stolen goods unless he used his influence to recover the rest of his books, which had been sold to another bookseller. At this Marsh said he had told Macqueen 'I thought it was very strange, that he should still harbour a Man whom he pretended had robb'd him', thereby insinuating that the whole affair was an elaborate blackmail designed to recover goods which had been honestly but reluctantly sold under financial pressure. It is likely that the judge stopped the trial at this stage, because the report concludes abruptly with a verdict of not guilty without the usual defendant's account, or witnesses to his character. Davison had effectively exculpated himself in his cross-examination, even though he had run the risk of self-incrimination.[219]

Admittedly, such a spirited defence was relatively unusual: when confronted with the usual prosecution evidence, which found them caught in the act of a theft, identified by accomplices, or found with stolen goods, defendants most frequently had little to say for themselves. But that was probably because they were guilty, at least before the scales were tipped against defendants by professional prosecutors. Indeed, in the context of so many trials where the defendant was caught virtually red-handed, the unmediated victim versus prisoner contests seemed fair to many contemporaries.[220] Widespread public doubts only clearly began to appear when accumulated experience of the arts and partisanship of prosecution lawyers began to be suspected of creating circumstantial cases that would have failed without their efforts.[221] Indeed it is important to understand that decision-making on the basis of observing direct altercations between the protagonists genuinely represented the historic participatory tradition of the common law criminal trial. Justifying the common law rule against defence counsel in his *Treatise of the Pleas of the Crown*, published in 1721, William Hawkins insisted:

> It requires no manner of Skill to make a plain and Honest Defence, which in cases of this Kind [i.e. in serious criminal cases] is always the best; the Simplicity and Innocence, artless and ingenuous Behaviour of one whose Conscience acquits him, having something in it more moving and convincing than the highest Eloquence of Persons speaking in a Cause not their own. ... Whereas on the other Side, the very Speech, Gesture and Countenance, and Manner of Defence of those who are Guilty, when they speak for themselves, may often help to disclose the Truth, which probably would not so well be discovered from the artificial Defence of others speaking for them.[222]

Hawkins's apparent faith in the unvarnished transparency of guilt or innocence has mostly been ridiculed by nineteenth and twentieth-century commentators, but without denying the substantive achievements of justice wrought by counsel in criminal practice, such views are clearly anachronistic.[223] His position clearly had its roots in the origins of the trial by jury as a mechanism for the community to discover its own knowledge about the crime and the protagonists.[224] Although by the eighteenth century the jury was hardly expected to have eye-witness evidence of the crime itself, the encouragement of an unstructured altercation and relatively unfettered jury access to all kinds of incriminating evidence represented contemporary faith in the jurors' ability to make decisions about the protagonists' characters and community standing on the basis of their immediate impressions and previous (usually extensive) experience of sitting in judgement on similar cases. By contrast with their modern counterparts, who sit on juries for one case and consider prosecution and defence 'cases' passively and inscrutably before rendering their verdicts, these jurors were effectively expert witnesses, as well as lay judges, for they even conveyed their impressions to the court before the case was closed, through extensive informal discussion with the judges.[225]

Given its inquisitorial and subjective character, this kind of interactive vernacular fact-finding by the jurors was still akin to the 'unofficial knowledge' central to the operation of the medieval jury, who were expected to investigate the circumstances of the crime for themselves.[226] Certainly there were still traces of the more active and participatory roles of medieval juries in the early eighteenth century. For example, jurors would often interject, especially when witnesses were telling their stories.[227] Examination of just one Old Bailey session can produce several instances. In *R. v. Richard Marshall et al*, for burglary and receiving stolen goods, tried in October 1732, the principal witness was John Griffin, alias 'King John', who had turned king's evidence in return for immunity from prosecution. He related how on the night of 27 September he and Marshall had twice burgled the house of Henry Carey in Cold Bath Fields, but after being disturbed on the second occasion by a woman calling out 'Who's there', Marshall went back again by himself to get more booty. One of the jurors was obviously unconvinced, because he asked how the defendant had the nerve to go back a third time, and Griffin thereupon explained that they had left some of the household goods outside the premises, so there was little danger of discovery.[228] And at the same sessions, in the trial of Thomas Headly and Henry Chapman for a highway robbery on George Young, an apothecary, a juror intervened in the trial with a pointed question and challenge to the evidence of a witness who had given the prosecutor a character for honesty and good standing, confidently relating a personal exchange with Young which suggested that he – and the witness – were not trustworthy at all. The judge clearly thought this was a legitimate contribution to the proceedings, for he did not intervene or put the juror on his oath (as his successors did later in the century); and no doubt such an injection of doubt from within their own number assisted in the jury's eventual decision to acquit the prisoners.[229] It is true that judges were normally able to control jury prejudices and apparently wayward decisions by their positive instructions, but there are even examples of late seventeenth-century juries arguing with the bench over issues of fact and law, and not only in cases which were influenced by political partisanship.[230]

So, like the defendants themselves, the jurors were remarkably active participants in criminal trials before the proceedings were colonized by the lawyers. Indeed contemporary sessions charges tended to celebrate the constitutional role of juries, even describing them as 'the Representatives of the People of England'.[231] But although its formal decision-making power was not diminished, and its autonomy increased somewhat, the jury was largely silenced as an active voice by the professionalization of the criminal trial, beginning in the mid-eighteenth century.[232] It was probably no coincidence that in 1738, just as barristers were being allowed to intervene in criminal trials and began to control the jury's access to the evidence and the defendant, a ruling in a civil suit effectively removed the civil jury's theoretical right to decide a case according to their personal knowledge, thereby subjecting them to formal judicial control and an order for a new trial in case of private knowledge being disclosed as an influence on the verdict.[233] Indeed, eighteenth-century judges began the process that Simpson has described as 'the progressive dethronement of the jury' by formulating new rules of law which restricted the scope of jury decision-making.[234] Moreover, there were legislative attempts to ensure that criminal trial juries were socially exclusive, and some civil juries were carefully selected for their elite status.[235] As seen previously, Lord Mansfield used special juries of merchants to advise and adjudicate commercial disputes, and he also deployed special juries of gentlemen in some other cases.[236] In fact these developments appear to have been symptomatic of a more general process, by which virtually all vernacular forms and expressions of knowledge were progressively devalued. As Malcolm Gaskill has suggested, in the eighteenth century progressive social differentiation meant that 'opinion generated by custom, memory, rumour and local knowledge, and the popular modes of demonstrating that opinion, no longer carried as much weight', and he has shown that this was clearly reflected in several criminal law proceedings. Rational rules about the admissibility of evidence were accompanied by social prejudices about its origins and modes of expression. An analysis of criminal trials at the Old Bailey which featured medical testimony suggests from mid-century 'the growing authority of expert testimony and a concomitant restriction of nonprofessional opinions'.[237] In cases of murder even 'quasi-professional' medical testimony was preferred to the vernacular observations and beliefs of lay people, and as we have seen hearsay – the currency of community values – was in the process of being excluded.[238]

Here was a clash between a culture of common sense typical of everyday life among ordinary people, as opposed to more scientific Enlightenment ideas about degrees of probability which attach to various forms of testimony, ideas associated with the discourse of the educated middle classes.[239] Their effects on the jury have been closely observed. As Barbara Shapiro has shown, empirical standards of proof associated with John Locke and other philosophical writers were current among legal thinkers at the end of the seventeenth century, and after 1750 phrases like 'beyond reasonable doubt' and 'to a moral certainty' began to be used by judges in their instructions to jurors about the standards of proof required for conviction. Certainly by the 1820s, when Thomas Starkie's *Practical Treatise on the Law of Evidence* was published and widely assimilated, jurors were expected to apply rational tests of probability, and to avoid deciding on 'light, trivial and fanciful suppositions, and remote conjectures'.[240] Moreover, the criminal trial court was well on the way to its modern 'bifurcation' into separate spheres for lawyers and jury, with the flow of information strictly regulated by the professionals.[241]

By the later eighteenth century, then, profound shifts in the administration of criminal justice were underway. I would argue that taken with parallel changes in law enforcement and punishment – centering on policing and the penitentiary – they betoken new attitudes and fresh ambitions for positive governance. It was not just that correcting plebeian culture was regarded as the primary mission of the criminal justice 'system', as it was being elaborated in new penal and policing 'solutions' to the growing crime 'problem'. In addition lay people were being marginalized from the administration of justice in favour of professionals and officials, despite its origins and continued ideological associations with the participatory traditions of the common law. This was hardly a coincidence. Certainly some of these shifts were the practical consequences of genuine concerns about what was perceived as a rising tide of criminality, especially in the major urban centres, and in London above all. Indeed in the early years of the century many anti-crime measures were adopted in a piecemeal, ad hoc, fashion that can hardly be characterized as any coherent 'policy'. But from their beginnings these changes were also connected with the tendency for polite opinion to coalesce around criticism of some principal features of popular culture, such as casual physicality and the legitimacy of violence in interpersonal relations, and social ordering by folklore, intuitive knowledge and gossip. Moreover, while some of the early shifts in the administration of justice described here were implemented by the direct action of individual authorities, rather than through parliamentary legislation, the establishment of permanent parliamentary sessions after 1689 provoked a considerable increase in the corporate self-consciousness of the governing elites in English society, and enormously augmented their capacity for governance. These subjects will be considered in the following chapter.

# 5
# Parliament, Legislation and the People: The Idea and Experience of Leviathan

> It is too often found that new Proposals, varnished Over with popular Pretences, are but selfish Projects.
> Roger North, *A Discourse of the Poor* (1753 [written *c.* 1688]), 85.

> ... every member of the other House takes upon him to be a legislator
> Lord Chancellor Hardwicke in the House of Lords, 24 May, 1756.
> (*Parliamentary History*, xv. 736).

> ... there is a large amount of individuality in the statutes of the eighteenth century. Each statute was, to a large extent, a law by itself.
> Sir William Holdsworth, *History of English Law*, xi. 372.

> Once the Crown had been painfully brought under the law, it was parliament which began its own democratic form of despotism.
> J.H. Baker, *Introduction to English Legal History* (4th edn., 2002), 151.

Although not all the initiatives which were transforming the administration of justice between 1690 and 1820 were implemented in the form of legislation, it should be clear from much of what I have written about local government and 'law enforcement' that acts of parliament had an unprecedented place in the experience of government during the eighteenth century. Indeed, there was a 'dramatic rise' in the output of legislation during the eighteenth century: whereas around 2,700 acts were passed in the two centuries between 1485 and 1688, nearly 14,000 reached the statute book in the 100 years or so from the Glorious Revolution of 1689 to the Act of Union with Ireland in 1801.[1] In the context of what has been said in this book about more positivist government in the localities, declining participation in civil litigation and the administration of criminal law, and the gradual professionalization of policing and criminal prosecutions, on the face of it the massive increase in law-making from Westminster might seem to constitute part of a general transformation from common law traditions of self-government towards rule from above. Certainly in modern Britain parliament is a primary institution of government at the heart of the nation state, and the executive government usually imposes its will on the people via compliant parliamentary majorities who rubber-stamp their legislative instruments. But for the eighteenth century interpreting the massive increase in parliamentary law-making as the growth of the reach of the state is a hasty assumption. Traditionally eighteenth-century parliaments have been discussed as heterogeneous assemblages of country gentlemen with a sprinkling of government placemen and aristocratic clients, pulled in different ways by their separate interests and connections, rather than as cohesive legislative bodies composed of individuals defined by their allegiance to the centre. At the time legislative innovations in communications and local government were represented as grass-roots 'improvements'; and more positive policing and punishment of the poor have been regarded as the authentic reflexes of a properly 'reactive state'.[2] While several species of acts of parliament extended political authority over private interests and common rights, in general it is clear that many of the legislative initiatives that were transforming the scope and experience of government around the country were not initiated by ministries, or even by authorities and individuals with close institutional links to the centre. How then, should we integrate eighteenth-century legislative activism with the other trends towards positivist governance identified in this book?

This chapter attempts to nuance simplistic interpretations by taking a broad perspective on the politics, substance and experience of legislation in the eighteenth century. While Georgian 'members' of parliament were uniquely self-conscious about their status and power as part of the governing elite, and powerful sectional interests were able to deploy parliamentary legislation to overcome local resistance to their projects, it has been suggested that in some respects parliament became aware of the necessity to allow representative public access and symbolic participation in the decision-making processes of what was becoming self-consciously a national legislature.[3] In public at least parliamentarians acknowledged their trust to the nation: they frequently insisted that everything they did was dedicated to the national interest or, in contemporary phraseology, the public good. In this sense eighteenth-century parliaments claimed to represent all the people.[4] Nevertheless, it is important to consider how that trust was fulfilled in deeds as well as words, and also to assess how inclusive legislative machinery and processes were. There is considerable evidence that eighteenth-century parliaments conceived of the public and the community in relatively narrow terms – in practice identifying the interest of the public and the right to participate actively in government with the ownership of substantial property, rather than accepting older ideas of community defined by freedom under the law.[5] This raises the important question of how the legislative products of parliament's labours were received at the grass-roots of society, among people of slight property. It also remains to be seen whether the machinery and conventions for connecting parliament with 'public opinion' which developed during the later part of the century satisfied popular expectations for legitimacy in the creation and administration of law. First, however, it is necessary to consider how eighteenth-century legislative absolutism and activism were assimilated to contemporary political thinking.

## The politics of legislation: Parliament, sovereignty and the law

In the eighteenth century parliament became Leviathan. Parliaments made laws which facilitated compulsory purchase of property, gave unprecedented numbers of state servants powers of forced entry and search, automatically annulled binding ceremonies of marriage between consenting adults because they were informal, and even changed the calendar, removing 11 days from one year.[6] As we have seen, they also substituted summary processes of conviction for trial by jury in prosecuting a number of offences.[7] Above all, in 1689 and 1701 legislation altered the succession to the throne, and it became treasonous to profess allegiance to the previous incumbent and his heirs. Indeed as early as 1702 it was pointed out that the legislature disposed of 'Supream Power ... over all Causes, and over all Persons whatsoever; all Humane Rights are subject to it; when that has determin'd a Cause there is no remainder left'.[8] And yet the English were usually told they enjoyed enduring liberties under the law, and in terms which suggested the administration of justice by common law and the people's rights under the constitution were immutable. The language of politics inherited from the seventeenth century was built from a legal vocabulary centred on rights, after all. Even Lord Chancellor Hardwicke, a considerable legislator himself, reminded grand jurors 'the Laws of *England* are adapted, the best of any in the World, to the Security of the Property, the Liberty, the Lives of Men', and lauded 'the Guard of this Constitution, the Price of the Blood of your Ancestors', for preserving the protestant religion and the liberties of England 'safe and entire, amidst the various attacks that have been made upon them'.[9] It is not the argument of this book that the ideology of fundamentalist law and liberty that was such a dominant discourse around 1700 was merely rhetoric, so in the context of parliament's radical law-making capacity it would not be surprising if there were doubts about the growing extent of parliament's legislative capacity, even among the governing elites. And doubts there were, as well as fears of what parliament might do next.

Certainly much has been written on Country Whig and Tory suspicions about parliament's encroachments on the constitution under the early Hanoverians.

During the administration of Robert Walpole particularly (1722–42) there were growing complaints that the House of Commons was being corrupted into unconstitutional policies and legislative projects, especially the maintenance of a standing army in peacetime and the expansion of numbers and powers in the revenue collection service.[10] But it has been argued that in its principal ideological register, the opposition to Walpole was mainly concerned to ensure that parliament was composed of landed gentlemen, rather than officeholders and monied men, and frequently refreshed by elections, to maintain its independence from the executive.[11] The point here was to restore the 'virtue' of the legislature, rather than argue for rights against its power. Indeed J.G.A. Pocock has suggested that law and rights were less central to political discourse after 1688, as notions of resistance tended to fade.[12] However, many contemporaries educated in 'revolution principles' thought some of the products of the supreme power of parliament were potentially a threat to Englishmen's liberties under law. While admonitions about the right to resistance were mostly not serious, there was strong attachment to the idea and practice of government by consent, and around 1700 the experience of consent was associated principally with the institutions and traditions of the law.[13] As late as 1750 a critic of the Mutiny Bill complained about the maintenance of a large military establishment and warned against what he claimed was the growing habit for 'Ministers and their Implements' to resort to soldiers, rather than constables and justices, for keeping the peace: 'What must become of us, if the Sword of *Justice* cannot be wielded except by an Army? And what will become of us, if the Sword of the Army should be made Use of as the Sword of the *State?* For that of *Justice* would then be out of *Use*'.[14] Ultimately of course the Americans pressed issues and incidents like these arising out of positive government by statute to the point of Revolution. They proceeded to establish a novel form of constitution designed to prevent legislative absolutism by maintaining a separation between the powers of government, enshrining popular rights in a written constitution, and providing for a court to review acts of the legislature.[15] Here was a major common law challenge to parliamentary absolutism, which established popular rights and an enduring process of judicial review according to fundamental law. But what did it say about law and governance in Britain?

The clear implication is that there were ideological divisions over the nature and scope of parliamentary law-making in the eighteenth century, which went beyond the issues of corruption and representation to challenge the reach and capacity of legislation. This may seem surprising, because parliamentary sovereignty was hardly a novel idea in 1689; after all it had been asserted most clearly by the legislation of the Reformation Parliament, and statute had been a significant source of law and social regulation long before that.[16] But the notion of legislative omnipotence was not as firmly established in practice as the hindsight of whiggish history might suggest Certainly seventeenth-century Whig constitutional theorists like Algernon Sidney, Henry Nevill and John Locke had maintained the supremacy of parliament, but theirs was a minority view before 1689, and as they developed their arguments in opposition to claims about the divine rights of kings they tended to represent the power of parliament in a negative sense, as a check on the power of the crown.[17] At this stage there seems to have been no conception of parliament as an instrument of government in a modernizing, positivist, mode. Rather the instinct, even among radical thinkers, was for government by institutionalized consent, as a defence against anarchy and arbitrary power. Writing in his *Second Treatise*, Locke maintained that establishing a sovereign authority to make and enforce laws for all people was the essence of society, but added significant qualifications about the need for such an authority 'to govern by established standing laws, promulgated and known to the people, and not by extemporary decrees', and made pointed injunctions against any tendency towards 'absolute arbitrary power'. Moreover, he warned that if the legislative power was to rule by arbitrary will, or act against its trust to protect life, liberty and property, the bonds of government would be dissolved, and the people would be free to form new arrangements.[18]

Admittedly, Locke's thoroughgoing contractarian ideas were relatively untypical, even among Whigs, and the Revolution of 1688-9 appeared to consolidate seventeenth-century arguments for parliamentary sovereignty. In 1689 Sir Robert Atkyns maintained 'The Parliament is of an absolute and unlimited power in things Temporal within this Nation'.[19] Atkyns was a common lawyer, and like most other Whig lawyers, he justified his arguments by precedents and appeals to the notion of the ancient constitution, by which it was claimed that from time immemorial the legislature of king, lords and commons had enjoyed transcendent power as the constituent body of the three estates of the realm.[20] After 1689 even moderate Tories accepted parliamentary supremacy on the basis of custom, precedent and prescription, by analogy with legal tradition. These doctrines were essentially backward-looking and defensive, implying a conservative role for the legislature.[21] Indeed, although the Revolution legislation of 1689, the act of Succession (1701), the Regency Act (1706), and the Act of Union (1707) all appeared to be clear demonstrations of parliamentary supremacy, there was a world of difference between accepting parliament's right to secure the protestant succession and the rights of subjects, and realizing the full positive implications of legislative sovereignty. The Glorious Revolution and its legislative appendices had been regarded as a victory for law and limited government, after all. While many eighteenth-century people accepted that parliament was the highest institutional authority in the land, they were hardly prepared for the practical implications of its growing authority.[22]

This can be seen most clearly by analysis of some important constitutional controversies which animated parliamentarians and pamphleteers during the early years of the century. For example in 1701 the majority in the House of Commons extended the pretensions of parliamentary privilege by claiming the power of arrest over some Kentishmen who had petitioned for a vote of supply to wage war with France. The legislative power was not at issue here, but hostile reactions demonstrated the depth of conservative thinking about law and parliament, and a pamphlet accused the Commons of offending against 'that fundamental Liberty of our Persons which by *Magna Charta*, and several other Statutes, as well as the most ancient Customs and Laws of the Land, we are entitul'd to'.[23] The idea was that some law was of fundamental status and should even control the subsequent acts of parliament. It was frequently expressed with reference to historic statutes and resolutions which were supposed to have secured subjects' rights, especially the 39th chapter of Magna Carta, as glossed by Sir Edward Coke.[24] Some near-contemporary constitutional legislation was also believed to have a similar standing, as evidenced by similarly pious references to the Act of Union with Scotland and the Triennial Act of 1694. Indeed, in 1716 the abrogation of the Triennial Act's provisions for electing a new parliament every three years touched off a storm of protest which centred on claims that by extending its life the existing parliament was exceeding its authority. Several opponents of the new Septennial Bill insisted that 'frequent and new parliaments are required by the fundamental constitution of the kingdom', and 24 peers protested against it on these grounds. Admittedly most speakers seemed to mean that the proposed law was contrary to the spirit of the constitution, as evidenced by ancient usage, rather than a legal nullity. But in the Commons Sir Robert Raymond, formerly solicitor general under Queen Anne, went so far as to argue that any law passed after the parliament had been sitting beyond three years would need confirming in a new parliament, and his comments were echoed by at least two other speakers.[25]

The Septennial bill passed into law, however, and the extended parliament continued to pass statutes which posterity accepted as legally valid, despite continued complaints about the act's constitutional irregularity. As J.W. Gough has argued, this did not mean that a majority of the House of Commons and the House of Lords thought, like A.V. Dicey two hundred years later, that parliament could enact anything at all, but it does seem to constitute a straw in the wind, tending towards more positive governance, and utilizing parliament's legislative capacity as its primary instrument.[26] In 1716 the ministry and its supporters claimed they were taking exceptional measures, in desperate circumstances. As we have seen, the times were troubled. The Hanoverian succession to the throne was patently insecure, at least as demonstrated to contemporaries by serious rioting in London and some provincial cities at the time of the king's coronation, by the armed rebellion of 1715–16, and by the continuance of Jacobite-Tory demonstrations through the 1720s and into the late 1730s.[27] The Septennial Act, passed in the immediate aftermath of the rebellion, was only one of a series of legislative measures taken by the Whig government which identified threats against the regime in popular disorder and extra-parliamentary politics. Two years earlier they had passed the Riot Act, another statute which provoked considerable controversy, in this case because it extended the power of magistrates to render any assembly of more than 12 people a felony, merely by proclamation, even if the meeting did not tend to sedition or serious disorder.[28] In so far as it reversed the common law's emphasis on protecting the subject within the king's peace it has been represented as 'a law to abolish law', and opponents of the government claimed it was contrary to the spirit of the constitution because it was so oppressive.[29] In 1723 the infamous Black Act became law. This remarkable statute automatically criminalized anyone appearing armed and disguised in any deer park or on the road, and also created a host of other loosely-defined capital felonies, to the extent that a modern authority described it as 'in itself a complete and extremely severe criminal code'.[30] Until recently it was believed the Black Act was of a piece with the rest of the eighteenth-century Bloody Code, albeit it addressed the special propertied interests of the Walpole administration.[31] But without denying these continuities, it was enacted with other legislation passed after the Atterbury Plot, and there is now strong evidence that it was brought into parliament following intelligence that the Waltham Blacks had been recruited to the Jacobite cause.[32] Indeed, like the legislation which (in 1718 and 1720) established Transportation as an answer to the crisis of crime in London, it was the product of a government which had 'the political will and capacity' to act positively in response to emergencies which threatened the public interest, whether they consisted in robbery, riot or rebellion.[33]

What I am suggesting is that although it by no means had a legislative programme, in appropriate circumstances the Whig government of this period was prepared to govern, in a positive sense, with the aid of its unprecedented law-making capacity. Following the precedent of the annual Mutiny Act (first passed in 1689), which legislated for a standing army while openly admitting its legal unorthodoxy, ministers showed they would compromise constitutional shibboliths in the cause of what they identified as pressing necessity. And in so far as successive eighteenth-century parliamentarians and their clients followed suit, the practice of government after 1689 seems to constitute a departure from seventeenth-century ideas about the limiting powers of precedent law, custom and the ancient constitution, although those ideas died a slow and lingering death. Such a shift can be observed in progress by studying the career of Henry Fielding, whom we have encountered previously in this book in his capacity as a Westminster police magistrate and lobbyist on criminal justice and social policy. It will be recalled that in his tract on the causes of rising crime, Fielding urged the 'civil power' to use its strength by enacting new laws to deal with crime and what he saw as its social causes.[34] However, Fielding's most recent editor has pointed out that his discussion of the need to restore the balance of the ancient constitution was reminiscent of the opposition to Walpole in the 1730s, wherein (*inter alia*) Lord Bolingbroke and his supporters accused the Whigs of increasing the power of the executive at the expense of parliament's independence.[35] Bolingbroke was no lawyer, and although he talked of the ancient constitution and fundamental law, they were conceived broadly, in terms of a balanced polity, the English 'spirit of liberty, transmitted down from our Saxon ancestors', and the original contract between prince and people, which limited the acts of government to furthering the public good.[36] This in itself was a significant departure from traditional common law thinking about the constitution, which looked for legal precedents to determine legitimate decision-making.[37] Indeed, like Bolingbroke's carefully-targeted arguments, Fielding's comments about the pristine nature and subsequent corruption of Anglo-Saxon society were ultimately derived from the Whig canon of early eighteenth-century opposition theory, which highlighted the constitutional importance of a free parliament against a regime illegitimately empowered by public credit and influenced by commercial individualism.[38] But in the 1740s he became a writer for the government, and gained a position as a magistrate under the Pelham administration, and in these circumstances he could hardly disparage the power of modern executive government. On the contrary, the practical emphasis of his writings around 1750 was approval for positive legislation that contributed to the welfare of the public, as he saw it. Thus, in addition to calling for legislative reform of the poor law and the administration of justice, he defended the Riot Act against accusations that it was oppressive and derogatory of common law. Rather for Fielding, magistrate and would-be legislator, it was 'the most necessary of all our Laws, for the Preservation and Protection of the People'.[39]

So despite powerful doubts grounded in Whig theory and expressed in opposition practice, the actions of eighteenth-century administrations and their supporters suggest that if they acknowledged any limits to parliamentary powers of law-making, they were bound by less tangible ties than the iconic statutes and common-law principles said to represent the historic provisions of the ancient constitution. It is true that at least until mid-century there was occasional opposition to selected legislation on the grounds that it was contrary to 'the laws of the land'. For example in 1749–50 bills relating to the discipline of the army and navy excited trenchant criticism that their provisions for applying martial law to officers on half-pay were unconstitutional because they contradicted Magna Carta and generally failed to respect the common law. One opponent even insisted that the discretionary powers proposed to be given to courts martial could not be 'law' but were rather 'absolute Power;

and therefore was such a thing to be enacted, no Man is oblig'd to obey it'.[40] Also legislation which appeared to run counter to the law of God as declared by scripture or the canons of the Church was sometimes opposed on the grounds that it was sacred and therefore beyond the power of human law. The Marriage Act of 1753 was subjected to objections of this kind because it could nullify a free contract sanctified by an ordained clergyman. But in parliamentary debate they were simply swept aside by the government's law officers, who asserted confidently that 'the supreme legislature' could regulate any contract at all if such interference was conducive to the public good.[41] Indeed, the 'regime Whigs' who governed for most of the eighteenth century appeared to believe in strong parliamentary government grounded in an ideology of social and commercial progress; or at least they accepted the legitimacy of pragmatic legislative intervention in the broad spirit of the law's historical adaptation, as 'social problems' and commercial or imperial opportunities presented themselves.[42]

Of course even the most positivist advocates of parliamentary power were aware that every act of government depended ultimately on the implicit consent of the governed. The fiction that all the people were represented in parliament was of considerable provenance, and parliamentarians routinely acknowledged their obligation to act in the interests of the people.[43] This meant there were practical limits to the exercise of sovereignty. In Edmund Burke's formulation, 'no ... given part of legislative rights can be exercised, without regard to the general opinion of those who are to be governed', and as Lord Hardwicke admitted (in the context of the unpopular Militia Act of 1757, which provoked riots up and down the country), in extreme cases of resistance statutes would have to be repealed, or not implemented.[44] But representing the people also conferred the authority to govern, and there was no obligation to follow any particular opinion, even that of a great city or province of Empire. Burke himself famously declared he was not bound by his electors' advice, and in the case of the British government's treatment of America he acknowledged 'the unwieldy haughtiness of a great trading nation, habituated to command'. Here was no substantial limit to the pretensions of those who claimed they divined the interests of the public. Certainly, by 1777, through the habitual exercise of its legislative power, parliament had grown into a 'mighty sovereign'.[45]

Most of the leading lawyer-legislators understood this was a fact of life, even if it was sometimes destructive of the common law, and bent their efforts to making sure that parliamentary law-making was conservative and rational. But they were unsuccessful, even according to their own judgements. Condemning clumsy attempts to remodel the militia, Hardwicke, the prime mover of the Marriage Act, complained bitterly about the legislative activism of the House of Commons, pointing out that 'our statute books are increased to such an enormous size, that they confound every man who is obliged to look into them'. He recommended a return to modes of law-making which had prevailed in 'old times', whereby the judges in the House of Lords had considered the necessity and appropriateness of proposed statutes in the context of existing law, with the result that few passed.[46] Blackstone too complained 'every man of fortune thinks himself *born* a legislator', and as we have seen he was famously critical of the 'specious embellishments and fantastic novelties' which statute had made in common law, especially in the area of criminal justice.[47] But he also understood, with Locke, that the power of giving law to society constituted the assumption of sovereignty, and admitted parliament 'can ... do every thing that is not naturally impossible', including changing the provisions of the constitution itself.[48] The author of the *Commentaries* was acutely aware of the tendency to read the Revolution of 1688 as a foundational re-statement of the constitution which simply abrogated any need to respect the historical development of the law, and gave a licence to wholesale legislative innovation.[49] So, like Hardwicke, he was concerned to constrain parliament against 'wantonly' interfering with standing rules of law, in his case by educating lawyers and parliamentarians to appreciate the historical rationality of previous legal development and therefore avoid disrupting it. For Blackstone, to be legitimate, English law had to conduce to its historical role of furthering life, liberty and property, and lawmakers as well as lawyers needed to appreciate their historic social trust. After all, as he insisted on several occasions, only the legislature could lose or destroy the spirit of liberty, which had infused the constitution since the time of Alfred.[50]

The crisis in relations with America was arguably the greatest test of the new emphasis on extensive parliamentary sovereignty because it raised in a very practical way the issue of what was the legitimate scope of law-making in the English tradition. Crucially, there was a marked disjunction in constitutional and legal thought between Westminster and the American colonies, a disjunction that helps to reveal the profound shifts in the context and meaning of law in eighteenth-century England. Like many of their contemporaries across the Atlantic, the colonists were slow to realize that in the aftermath of the Revolution of 1689 the king in parliament was transforming itself into an absolutist sovereign along Bodinian lines. But the crucial difference in their situation was a more extensive tendency to continue looking at law and politics through a seventeenth-century lens, even in the 1760s and 1770s.[51] In the northern colonies especially, many of the Americans lived by the 'old constitutionalism' of Coke and John Pym, according to which law set restraints to arbitrary power, while for their part the ministers of the crown appeared to behave as if law was simply what parliament commanded.[52] Hence, viewed from the perspective of a Pennsylvania lawyer, the British government's insistence on parliament's power to give law to America was to assert 'high prerogative doctrine' in contradiction to the rights and legal principles which had been guaranteed at the time of the Glorious Revolution.[53] Indeed, as J.P. Greene has suggested, the Americans' patriotic pride as Englishmen was based upon their consciousness of inheriting freedom under English law, and by contrast with the situation in England itself, this was consolidated by a semi-democratic political culture which depended on widespread popular participation in local common law courts and representative assemblies. In such a context American lawyers, who were frequently among the leaders of the resistance to Westminster, tended to read the common law tradition in a fundamentalist sense, as setting limits to sovereign authority and guaranteeing popular consent to government.[54] Moreover, such opinions had real social depth. At the grass-roots, the local communities' involvement in legal processes and institutions fostered a common belief that their active consent formed the essence of law; and in Massachusetts they reacted to the legislative acts of the imperial parliament by taking direct action to enforce what they saw as the rule of law.[55] Clearly, here, in pre-revolutionary America, the law world which was disappearing in eighteenth-century England continued to flourish and inform the practice of government.

Thus for the Americans, articulating a basic principle of common law thinking, the Stamp Act of 1765 was illegal because parliament's claim to tax the colonies had not been established by custom or precedent and therefore not secured their consent.[56] And the redcoats sent to patrol the streets of Boston could be no more legal, since the Mutiny Act which authorized them was simply unconstitutional. Indeed for Massachusetts patriots, if the magistrates needed any help enforcing the laws, then the legal way to proceed was to enlist the aid of the people, in the form of the *posse comitatus*, rather than the military: for if it was to be legitimate, according to this view, law must be based on popular consent, rather than command.[57] By contrast, at Westminster the colonists' resistance to metropolitan authority tended to harden understandings about the extent of parliament's legislative capacity: if it was truly sovereign over the British polity, its laws could reach anywhere, and touch any sphere of government; if not, then sovereignty meant nothing.[58] According to Lord Mansfield, parliament had to insist on its power in this point, or effectively abdicate.[59] So although the Stamp Act was repealed by the Rockingham ministry, it was accompanied by another act along the lines of the Irish Dependency Act of 1720 which declared unequivocally the right of parliament to legislate for the American colonies. There was only a moderate resistance to this doctrine in the parliamentary debates at Westminster, although it included some prominent figures. Lord Camden, then lord chief justice of Common Pleas, argued that there were customary and consensual limits to the power of the legislature, but he was flatly contradicted by the lord chancellor, who insisted 'Every government can *arbitrarily* impose laws on all its subjects', and pointed to the Revolution settlement as positive evidence of parliamentary sovereignty.[60] In the Commons, Blackstone was representative of mainstream opinion on the issue, albeit tending to impractical measures. He spoke against the repeal of the Stamp Act on the grounds that dependents must obey sovereign laws, and subsequently moved an amendment that repeal should only apply to those colonies which rescinded their resolutions denying parliament's right.[61] But most discussion centred on the pragmatic question of whether it was expedient to force an unpopular tax on the Americans. The rising generation of leading lawyers and politicians had few doubts about unlimited parliamentary power, and objections of principle were left largely to the radical press.[62]

Radical thinkers recognized the trend revealed by the American crisis towards using statute as an instrument of authority and argued that there were limits to what parliamentary legislation should do, even if most ultimately admitted the practical extent of its power. In the 1770s Granville Sharp condemned the current vogue for parliamentary omnipotence as 'a kind of Popery in Politics', and argued against Blackstone that natural law considerations must restrain 'the modern rage of act-making', particularly where civil liberties were abridged or due process under law set aside.[63] In moving for repeal of the Declaratory Act John Wilkes also claimed that the scope of parliamentary legislation was limited, but he concentrated less on residual individual rights and more on the need to recognize the popular origins of parliament's power, referring pointedly to the Middlesex election controversy of 1769, when the House of Commons had declared him ineligible to sit in parliament, even though he had won a majority of the votes.[64] Indeed, although they continued to insist that some substantive and procedural law was inviolable, by the third quarter of the century radical thought was tending towards reform of the franchise as a solution to corruption in the House of Commons, rather than opposing legislation with fundamental law. In this sense the preferred process for negotiating consent to government was certainly beginning to approach modern electoral forms, rather than the traditional juridical ones, at least on the British side of the Atlantic. But traditional attitudes towards what was legitimately 'law' could hardly be swept away overnight: even the advocates of parliamentary democracy reminded their readers that legislation should be exceptional:

> The business of ancient ANNUAL PARLIAMENTS was to make a *few wise* laws, expressed with a simple dignity and a clear conciseness: not a multitude of discordant unconstitutional laws, loaded with redundancy of words and perplexity of matter.[65]

Certainly the supporters of Wilkes put their faith in the courts, rather than in parliament, when it came to articulating what they regarded as fundamental constitutional rights. And in his opposition to general warrants their spokesman, 'the Father of Candor', insisted that parliament's proper role was to declare the common law, rather than pass positive statutes, which he said were 'not so venerable in the eyes of the world', and more liable to further amendment.[66] In the context of what they saw as the imposition of oppressive laws on America the radicals warned that the imperial muscles of parliament would be flexed at home too, and lead inevitably to 'the same measure of slavery'.[67]

Despite the failure of legislative attempts to coerce the Americans and the resurgence of radical criticism, opinion on the issues underlying the American war showed that by 1780 the doctrine of unlimited parliamentary sovereignty was broadly acknowledged across the English political elite. This was true among old Tory landowners as well as the heirs of the Whig governing families. For Tories the supreme authority of the king in parliament was a logical progression from the divine right of the monarchy and non-resistance to its power.[68] Indeed it has been argued that the power of the state became more generally respectable from the 1780s as the 'corrupt' methods of parliamentary management associated with Walpole and North gave way to administrative rectitude under the younger William Pitt, assisted by the 'apotheosis' of the king as national figurehead.[69] That power was expressed above all by a growing self-consciousness about the legitimacy of executive government in the 'national' interest, tending ultimately to authoritarian measures which offended the heirs of the Whig constitutional tradition.[70] Certainly Pitt was a determined and innovative law-maker; although interested in reform of the franchise early in his parliamentary career, he recognized few limits to the reach of legislation. Most famously, in the 1790s his government passed repressive anti-libertarian laws which suspended Habeas Corpus, prohibited public meetings for petitioning constitutional change, made speaking or writing against the government seditious libel, and brought challenges to the authority of the king in parliament Leviathan within the scope of the treason laws.[71] When debating these bills he was accused of ultra-positivist views along the lines of the conservative legal writer and anti-Jacobin placeman John Reeves, who maintained there were no constitutional limits to the power of government, and that subjects had no rights of resistance.[72] Defending the Treason and Sedition bills of 1795 against the opposition's threat of popular resistance, Pitt himself declared 'We trust whatever attempts may be made to resist their operation, the power of the laws themselves will be found sufficient to defeat them and to vindicate their Rights'.[73]

Indeed, in their hostility towards popular radicalism the ministers and their supporters betrayed a tendency to identify the interests of the state and the reason of 'law' in opposition to the people: as the bishop of Rochester said in debate over the Treasonable Practices Bill 'he did not know what the mass of the people in any country had to do with the laws but to obey them'.[74]

Admittedly these extreme positions were articulated in the heat of argument, and the Two Bills themselves were enacted as temporary measures conceived in fear of a social revolution, rather than any permanent abridgement of civil liberties.[75] But they do represent a remarkable incidence of the ministry's confidence in the authority of parliamentary statute as an instrument of government, even in the face of contrary judgements in the courts.[76] Although his style of government is best known for incremental administrative reform, and his admiration for Adam Smith may have tempered any desire to interfere strongly in economic affairs, like North Pitt evinced a thoroughly positivist attitude to law-making, even before 1789, especially in fiscal policy.[77] In this area at least the growing reach of the state under the pressure of war finance was very evident, and in the mid-1780s newspapers and caricaturists represented the 'Free-Born Briton' as enraged and groaning under a mass of taxes and duties, bound in every direction 'By Act upon Act'.[78]

The practice of government was buttressed by conservative theory. Alarms caused by resurgent radicalism, the American revolutionary challenge and the still more dangerous doctrines and examples of the French Revolution required a restatement of constitutional orthodoxy in the form of 'a high doctrine of sovereign authority' which stressed the irresistible power of legislation and downgraded fundamentalist or consensual ideas about law.[79] In philosophical discourse William Paley interpreted the law of the land in terms of duty, obligation, obedience and submission rather than rights.[80] Indeed for Paley, legislation was to the laws of England as revelation was to morality: they were precepts handed down from a supreme will. Like Burke, he recognized the pragmatic necessity to respect opinion and govern in the interest of the whole society, but he insisted this meant the law-making capacity should be unlimited: for all laws and customs must be equally mutable in the interests of public utility. So while the obligation of obedience depended ultimately on benevolent rule, it was suggested that a parliament of landowners moderated by wealth and talent was eminently well qualified to make laws in the interests of all the people; and there was emphatically no appeal from the acts of the supreme legislature.[81] Burke, turned reactionary political theorist after 1789, agreed. Following the influence of Sir Matthew Hale and Blackstone he was more inclined than Paley and most other contemporaries to dwell on the historical evolution of law, and using their ideas he adapted Coke's doctrine of the 'artificial reason' of law into a theory of inherited constitutional wisdom. But while he was strongly influenced by the common law thinking of these authors, and he acknowledged English liberties under law 'as an *entailed inheritance* derived to us from our forefathers', crucially, Burke argued that the 'collected reason of ages' which informed the constitution could not be apprehended by any individual, or even any single generation. Rather he entailed the inherited power of the ancient constitution on the unified sovereign of king in parliament as its legitimate heir and sole trustee. So while he was hardly in favour of innovation in government, in his writings and in parliament the author of the *Reflections* argued powerfully for practical legislative sovereignty, severely limited the role of the common people in government, elevated aristocracy, and more generally dignified the authority of states as being of divine origin.[82] Ironically, therefore, in Burke's great conservative polemics parliament had the potential (if not the licence of its author) to assume the trappings of Hobbes's Leviathan. Such authoritarianism had already influenced legal scholarship, as it was expressed in the lectures of Blackstone's successor as Vinerian Professor of English law at Oxford, Robert Chambers. By contrast with the *Commentaries*, Chambers's lectures hardly mentioned the rights and liberties of Englishmen and their historical achievement, but rather stressed the primacy of the monarch in parliament and the duties of subjects, tracing their submission to the social necessity for law and order. It is likely that he was partly inspired by the Tory politics of Samuel Johnson, who assisted in their composition. Certainly under this optic, in civil society the natural rights of men had been fully subordinated to the supremacy of government, and the subject's primary role was to obey: even when acting in error the legislature 'has a *civil* right to obedience from its subjects, whose execution of its laws is only ministerial and who are considered not as agents but as instruments'.[83]

By the latter part of the eighteenth century, then, there was increasingly broad recognition that the power of the state could overrule all other interests and 'laws' – public or private – and its legitimate expression was identified as parliamentary statute. But the question remained: what were the appropriate circumstances for the exercise of such power?[84] Although few contemporaries would have agreed with the more radical claims that parliamentary legislation which contravened natural law by enacting things 'mala in se' (or evil in themselves) was null and void, there was a growing understanding that parliament had most discretion in 'things indifferent', which were not prescribed by the law of nature or the law of God.[85] As we have seen, power also carried responsibility. In the latter case the judgement to be made was how far the law conduced to promoting 'the welfare of the society, and more effectually carrying on the purposes of civil life'.[86] This kind of test tended to be applied to criticize the criminal law. Certainly it was perfectly legitimate to pass laws which attached penal sanctions to murder and theft because they were crimes by natural law, but as William Eden pointed out, over the centuries the English statute book had accumulated a range of criminal laws against 'indifferent' actions, ranging from taking excessive interest for lending money to being in the company of 'Egyptians'. Many more, of course, had been added in the eighteenth century: Eden singled out laws directed against smuggling, negligence by watermen, the destruction of industrial machinery or manufactured cloth, going into French or Spanish territory after transportation, and the obstruction of customs and excise officers. He accepted that statutes like these had their own rationale in 'the *temporary* advantage of that particular community for which they are enacted', just as the Elizabethan penal laws against harbouring Catholic priests were produced by the fear of Catholic plots. But by comparison with statutes arising from 'the general obligations of humanity', he argued that such 'positive laws' should necessarily be of limited duration, and cautioned legislators generally against inappropriate use of power.[87] More particularly, according to Samuel Romilly, criminal laws should be derived only from 'humane and rational principles': the promotion of public rather than private interests, and proportioning penalties to fit the gravity of the offence. Romilly also complained about criminal statutes 'which have been, for the most part, the fruits of no particular design, but of sudden and angry fits of capricious legislators'. He doubted that 'justice and morality are matters of positive institution' and insisted 'If laws operate in violation of the feelings and understandings of men, they are unjust and unwise, by however legitimate an authority they are enacted'. Indeed, he complained 'every novice in politics is permitted, without opposition, to try his talents for legislation, by dealing out death among his fellow-creatures; and laws of this kind commonly pass as of course, without observation or debate'.[88] In this detail modern scholarship has proved him wrong, but it is clear that both Romilly and Eden felt that the individual construction and piecemeal aggregation of criminal statutes was hardly an ethical science.[89] Their concern was just one species of more general contemporary criticism about parliament's developing legislative capacity.[90]

In asking why systematic reform of the criminal law had not been undertaken by parliament, Romilly took note of parliament's 'fatal indifference for the public good', and preoccupation with 'interested pursuits'.[91] Of course it is well known that most of the Bloody Code was designed to protect the various forms of private property which became more exposed with commercial development in the eighteenth century; and petty crimes which affected country gentlemen were a principal target of that other species of legislation which facilitated summary jurisdiction by JPs. But it is not sufficiently understood that the general utility of parliament for advancing particular propertied interests was the primary reason for the increase in legislation after 1689. Improved access to the legislature meant that minority (usually elite) interests and temporary initiatives could be given the force of law, despite entrenched local opposition.[92] After all, a turnpike act was as binding and could be as permanent as the Act of Settlement, unless the legislature passed another law.[93] The propertied elite and upper middle classes of Georgian England gradually became aware that parliament could become a great law-making engine, therefore facilitating their multifarious 'improvements' and interventionist schemes of development. It is appropriate now to leave the realm of political discourse and consider more directly the characteristics of eighteenth-century legislation, especially acts which were specific to localities or individuals.

## 14,000 acts: The substance of legislation

Just as the imperial parliament presumed to make law for its Atlantic colonies, so it could also make law for a parish, a highway, or a private estate. In fact the history of Georgian government is 'imperial parliamentarianism' in progress.[94] Its spectacular reach developed unawares: regular parliaments had been necessary to work the financial machine which subsidized the continental wars fought after 1689; and it was gradually understood that parliaments which could guarantee millions in war finance could be 'imperial' at home as well as overseas. Indeed, besides parliament's capacity to enact general legislation in what was perceived as the public interest, ultimately many among the propertied realized the utility of parliamentary law-making for progressing their own particular schemes.

It has been argued that eighteenth-century parliaments were relatively reluctant to pass acts of national scope. Certainly 'general' acts constituted a minority of the overall legislation, and measures of local or particular application were more likely to pass, especially before 1715.[95] Even later parliaments remained shy of broad measures which interfered with property rights. The most usual subjects for general law-making were the raising of public revenue, the regulation of international trade, and the prosecution of war: pressing necessities in a century of semi-continuous warfare.[96] However Joanna Innes has shown that parliament was also responsible for a substantial body of general laws which might be categorized together as 'social policy' measures, applying as they did (for example) to the regulation of the poor, vagrancy, and the practice of imprisonment for debt, as well as the more familiar preoccupations with the prevention and punishment of crime.[97] These acts were not necessarily sponsored by ministers, but it was common for their authors to consult the law officers or judges, especially in criminal justice legislation, and officials were sometimes involved behind the scenes.[98] Indeed it has been suggested that the important 'social welfare' measures introduced into parliament in the early 1750s constituted part of 'a modest programme of administrative and social reform' that owed its original impetus to the concerns of the Pelham ministry in the wake of the peace of Aix-la-Chappelle. Although they hardly had ready-made 'policy' to apply, at mid-century ministers and sympathetic back-benchers 'increasingly saw the necessity of statute for the daily government of the nation', and parliamentary committees were put to work to hammer out the instruments of government.[99]

There are some clear continuities between the social legislation of the Pelham ministry (which taxed spirits, and aimed to suppress bawdy houses, gaming dens, and disorderly alehouses, in addition to attaching extra penalties to the punishment of murder, modernizing the calendar, naturalizing Jews and regulating marriage) and the earlier organized agitation for the 'reformation of manners', which was associated with societies founded for that purpose in the 1690s. The Societies for the Reformation of Manners themselves constituted another chapter in the long history of attempts to govern personal morals and manners by law, dating from late medieval times.[100] Yet it is possible to discern new departures in the relations between law and moral reform during the eighteenth century, and these are symptomatic of changes wrought by the growing centrality of parliament. First, with the breakdown of the correction jurisdiction of the ecclesiastical courts, although often still supported by prominent clergymen, attempts at moral reformation tended to become the province of voluntary groups who looked to the secular legal authorities for intervention, rather than to the church. Second, eighteenth-century moral reformers and their supporters were most concerned with what they saw as links between poverty, crime and popular indiscipline in the large cities, especially London, rather than undifferentiated sin. And third, they increasingly regarded parliament as the most appropriate forum for promotion of their causes and sought redress by legislative regulation of those activities they associated with disorder, rather than dealing with offences against religion. By the 1780s and 1790s, when William Wilberforce's Proclamation Society was stimulating a further burst of moral reform, the promotion of new legislation was central to its activities, and recruitment of a membership associated with government and parliament was clearly a deliberate strategy for achieving them.[101] In the 1690s, the Reformation of Manners societies were only able to achieve parliamentary support for new laws against profanation of the sabbath, swearing and blasphemy – all regarded as direct insults against God – and action against drunkenness and prostitution depended on the grassroots activities of informers and JPs. By contrast, although informers remained important, the later successful campaigns for the regulation of gin consumption and places of public entertainment marked the moral activists' growing strength among MPs and the apparent potential of fresh legislation as a primary instrument of broad social control.[102]

The increasing scope of legislation did not go unnoticed. Commenting on a 1752 bill which sought to restrain crime and disorder by reducing the number of popular establishment for dancing, the performance of music and plays, the *Gentleman's Magazine* remarked on the extent to which the legislature was proposing to interfere with the everyday lives of the common people, and doubted it was good policy. For such an act would 'deny all amusements to the lower ranks of people, and ... throw all those now engaged in exhibiting such amusements out of that way of getting their bread'.[103] But as in the case of the Stamp Act, when their laws engendered resistance, righteous parliamentarians insisted on their power. Confounded by riotous opposition to the 1736 Gin Act and other 'Discontents', the would-be poor law reformer William Hay wondered 'whether this Nation is for the future to be governed by a Mob, or by the Legislature' and argued that unpopular legislation should be enforced by arms.[104]

Historians have also drawn attention to the propensity of eighteenth-century parliaments to shape legislation that aimed primarily to advance economic development by the extension of criminal sanctions protecting commercial and industrial forms of private property. For example, as Blackstone noted, a 'multitude' of statutes protected new forms of commercial property and inflicted capital punishment on almost any species of forgery.[105] Among these, the Forgery Act of 1729 stands out because it was so 'sweeping and general', in an age when most statutes were narrow and specific. The measure was enacted in response to a high-profile case wherein a stock-jobber was convicted for a sophisticated attempt to obtain thousands of pounds by creating fictitious bills of exchange drawn on some prominent members of the London financial community. Certainly in substance the act was one of a long series which protected commercial instruments, but its principal significance for the history of eighteenth-century law lies in its official provenance. Like the Transportation Act and the Black Act, the Forgery Act was sponsored by government lawyers who were active in the criminal courts and identified problems that they were prepared to address with new law. Indeed, contrary to historiographical convention, this statute was the product of 'considerable deliberation', rather than the reflex of a legislature which applied the death penalty lightly. As with the Marriage Act of 1753, it represented the work of lawyer-legislators who had been assimilated to the culture of positive government and regarded statute as its primary instrument. Like the moral reformers, they were animated by righteous indignation, in this case at the threat which individual dishonesty among businessmen posed to the system of credit and exchange that sustained the nation's commerce. In such a context they believed it was appropriate for the legislature to take an inflexible stand.[106]

Forgery was a crime that threatened the business of the wealthy, and the prosperity of the nation, above all. So did the 'embezzlement' of industrial materials, and this too was the subject of a significant body of general legislation in the eighteenth century. As several historians have shown, in many trades workers had control of the materials used to manufacture goods, and claimed customary rights to wastage or damaged goods as perquisites, or perks. Thus dockyard workers claimed 'chips', or off-cuts of timber, coal miners insisted on a regular allowance of coal, and weavers retained 'thrums', or scraps of thread left on the loom after spinning. The so-called 'putting-out' system of manufacture – where products were made up by cottagers supplied with raw materials from merchant capitalists – was particularly liable to takings which the workers legitimized as customs of the trade, and which formed part of the complex wage negotiations between employer and employee.[107] Long before 1700, employers who felt this practice went beyond acceptable bounds could maintain a civil action against their employees. However in the eighteenth century a series of statutes treated such appropriation as criminal embezzlement and subjected offenders to the summary jurisdiction of magistrates.[108] An act of 1749 in particular has been treated as transforming breach of contract into a criminal offence.[109] In fact, as in the case of forgery, there is continuity as well as change in this statute, as compared with Tudor-Stuart law, because previous acts had given magistrates some similar powers.[110] What remains significant is the sheer volume of such legislation during the eighteenth century, the accelerating (if not always consistent) trend towards stipulating automatic and harsher punishment, rather than restitution, and the practice of placing the burden of proof on the defendant, while empowering the prosecutor.[111] Certainly, statutes passed in 1777, 1784–5 and 1791 constituted a major erosion of workers' rights because they gave inspectors powers to search their employees' premises on mere suspicion of embezzlement and facilitated the creation of an industrial police force in the north-west worsted region.[112] All this is ample testimony to the enormous increase in the scope and rigour of penal legislation as it ramified across the whole range of industrial relations.

While it is not clear that the various acts which dealt with embezzlement were part of a conscious parliamentary attack on the customs of trades, after 1760 these laws formed the basis of intermittent employers' campaigns against customary perquisites.[113] In this they can legitimately be considered alongside other major legislative changes which have been interpreted as destructive of established popular usages that claimed the status of rights under the law. First, as the foregoing discussion of perks suggests, there were significant shifts in the law of master and servant, a complex of custom, common law and medieval/Tudor-Stuart statutes which had been used by trades and previous governments to maintain order and relative stability against social and economic change. Indeed in the eighteenth century two of the central pillars of this historic edifice – apprenticeship regulation and magisterial wage-fixing – came under serious pressure from attitudes which underwrote the new political economy usually associated with Adam Smith's *Wealth of Nations* (1776). Down to mid-century justices still occasionally fixed wages, and new legislation regulating wages was enacted for particular textile industries, but an act of 1757 inspired by clothiers' arguments about freedom of contract entirely eliminated wage-fixing in the weaving industry. The Spitalfields Act of 1773, which regulated wages for the London silk-weavers, was exceptional, in so far as it was passed to redress widespread disorders in London. Indeed the foundational wage-regulating provisions of the Elizabethan Statute of Artificers were finally repealed in 1813.[114] The same act's restrictive apprenticeship clauses were generally disliked by eighteenth-century parliaments, as evidenced by progressive exemption for particular trades and a recommendation for complete abrogation by a Commons' committee in 1751. After partial repeal in 1809 they too were swept away entirely in 1814, even in the face of a popular petitioning campaign for their revival that garnered over 300,000 names, but which was probably doomed by anti-Jacobin prejudices.[115]

Although its direct application was very limited by 1800, the repeal of the Elizabethan legislation of 1562–3 constituted a decisive rejection of time-honoured claims that a skilled artisan's apprenticeship gave him a form of customary property right in the exclusive practice of his trade.[116] Significantly, these arguments were still articulated in the quasi-republican rhetoric of the ancient constitution:

> the apprenticed artisans have, collectively and individually, an unquestioned right to expect the most extended protection from the Legislature in the quiet and exclusive use and enjoyment of their several and respective arts and trades, which the law has already conferred upon them as a property, ... and it is clearly unjust to take away the established property and rights of any one class of the community; unless, at the same time, the rights and property of the whole commonwealth should be dissolved, and parcelled out anew for the public good.[117]

Even food rioters thought they had legal rights as consumers which could not be taken away by statute, but the marketing of food is the second major area where historians have identified eighteenth-century legislation in opposition to grass-roots customary interpretations of the law. As Edward Thompson famously demonstrated, the laws regulating markets – enshrined in medieval and Tudor-Stuart legislation that codified common law – helped to inform broad ideas about customary right.[118] Like the custom of trades, in this area popular apprehensions of 'the law' formed a bulwark for the poor against unrestrained market forces – especially middlemen ('forestallers', 'regrators' and 'engrossers') who speculated by buying large amounts of grain for resale, thereby forcing up prices in times of dearth, and who were routinely castigated by sympathetic magistrates as 'great Offenders'.[119] This body of law was frequently the inspiration for direct action enforcing the 'moral economy', in the form of self-legitimating popular demonstrations that encouraged magistrates to intervene, forced bargains with dealers or simply appropriated grain for sale at fair prices. Eighteenth-century governments were sensitive to these pressures, frequently responding to riots in ways which buttressed the popular claims. Certainly the privy council issued proclamations against the marketing offences down to 1766, and as late as 1795 Lord Chief Justice Kenyon thought the common law prohibiting them was 'co-eval with the constitution', thereupon inspiring a spate of prosecutions.[120] But here too members of parliament were increasingly swayed by the ideas of political economy, and the crucial statutes were repealed in 1772.[121] The moving spirit of their abrogation was Edmund Burke, who consistently advocated freedom of trade in provisions, castigated the old laws as 'barbarous', and ridiculed their supporters for simplicity and ignorance.[122] Adam Smith likewise compared popular concern about engrossing and forestalling to fears of witchcraft, and lamented their baleful influence over government, which he believed had prevented the establishment of a 'reasonable' system in this area, just as it had in religion.[123] Indeed upon a petition to revive the statutes in 1787 one MP inveighed against the temerity of the petitioners in returning to the issue after the legislature had spoken; their petition was nothing less than 'an affront to the House'.[124]

Despite the importance of general acts like these, the overwhelming majority of acts passed in the eighteenth century consisted of measures that applied to particular localities or interests. But here too the volume and aggregate scope of legislation demonstrates the unprecedented importance of parliamentary governance and its radical consequences for what was taken to be 'law'. Enclosure is a case in point. Among the 10,000 or so 'specific' acts passed between 1689 and 1800, over 2,000 related to enclosure of land, the third and most famous category of legislation which historians have considered as destructive of customary rights in law.[125] Most of the land in England was enclosed before 1750, but previously enclosure was achieved principally by 'agreement' among the landholders, where one or a small number owned most of the property. Eighteenth-century parliamentary enclosure is usually regarded as a process by which small owners opposed to change were compelled to submit to the interests of the larger landowners whose improving instincts had the approval of parliament.[126] Certainly, the parliamentary process for approving these acts was skewed towards men of big property: as the Hammonds put it 'suffrages were not counted but weighed', and a majority of small proprietors could be overborne by one or two magnates who held most of the acreage.[127] It is important to understand that the history of parliamentary enclosure is exceedingly complex, however. There were two distinct waves: the first in the 1760s and 70s, involving principally the enclosure of open-field arable land in the midland counties with clay soils; and the second during the years of war between 1793 and 1815, when parliamentary enclosure spread more broadly into East Anglia, Somerset, and the north of England, and involved relatively more cultivation of wastes and heathlands. Evidence for Buckinghamshire and some midland counties suggests the first wave was dominated by bills driven by a few landholders, who were able to have their way without much opposition. M.E. Turner says 'these early enclosures proceeded through Parliament with haste and quite unmolested'.[128] Indeed in 1781 the Lord Chancellor, Thurlow, commented on the ease with which private bills like these passed, 'to the great injury of many, if not the total ruin of some private families', and criticized MPs for their 'criminal inattention' to such business.[129] It is possible that other parliamentarians were concerned too, because there was a temporary hiatus of successful enclosure acts in the early 1780s, with success rates dropping from over 80 per cent to 50 per cent, and a tightening up of the standing orders about the maintenance of public roads.[130] But the output of acts revived again in the 1790s and reached new peaks in the early nineteenth century, after the passing of a general act designed to simplify procedure.[131]

Even where there was determined opposition from the smaller landowners, evidence suggests that parliament was frequently unwilling to heed their objections, unless they held a very substantial proportion of the land.[132] West Haddon in Northamptonshire was a village dominated by common-field agriculture with a broad spread of land ownership and land use, including many small owners and cottagers who depended on their rights of common to supplement their livelihood. It was the subject of two unsuccessful enclosure bills in the early 1760s, and a third which became law in 1764. J.M. Neeson has shown that the larger landowners were in favour of enclosure, but a clear majority of the owners were opposed. They were the smaller men, and although they petitioned against the bill on second reading, alleging enclosure would be 'very injurious ... and tend to the Ruin of many, especially the poorer Sort', they were easily outmanoeuvred by stacking the select committee with MPs from neighbouring counties. Ultimately the bill passed without a division. Many of the lesser landowners who opposed it sold their land within a year, and there were major riots in 1765, after the last common field harvest, when the materials ready for fencing the enclosed fields were torn down and burnt in a carefully organized demonstration of resistance.[133]

The second wave of parliamentary enclosure in the war years of 1793–1815 was different from the first in some respects. In these years generally the projectors' aim was to extend the scope and efficiency of arable farming, rather than convert land to pasture, which was the most common motive in the 1760s and 1970s.[134] And in this case there were many more owners of smallish estates involved, possibly including previous opponents of enclosure who had been frightened by the large financial risks of improvement, and were more encouraged at a time of high cereal prices.[135] But the broader spread of ownership in these cases seems to have engendered more opposition. In Buckinghamshire at least the parliamentary enclosures undertaken in this period were characterized by 'a hard core of peasant resistance in the open field parishes well into the nineteenth century'.[136] Given the high price of food, there was even more opposition from landless commoners, cottagers and other relatively poor people whose access to common rights was their primary defence against poverty. At Burton Latimer in Northamptonshire the parish was enclosed by legislation in 1803. On this occasion there was a petition against the bill, but unlike the West Haddon petitioners two-thirds of these opponents were landless commoners, principally weavers, artisans, labourers and servants. Together with a few small farmers, tradesmen and artisans who held small parcels of land, they protested that enclosure would 'take away from the poor a Wold or Common of nearly 800 acres which provides them with fuel and sustenance for their cattle'. The proponents of the bill had arranged for their solicitor to stack the select committee with 'friends', and the House of Commons as a whole was not disposed to take much notice of opponents to enclosure, especially landless or land-poor men and women (who were generally not able to come to Westminster to press their claims in person).[137] By way of compensation the enclosure commissioners merely allocated a small plot of land whose rents were to be applied to the relief of the poor. As in the case of West Haddon, the immediate consequence for them was rural proletarianization.[138]

The broader 'legal' significance of enclosure by eighteenth-century parliaments deserves emphasis. Although enclosure had proceeded a long way before 1700, much land remained in common fields, especially in the midlands, and the parishes in these areas tended to be heavily populated because they were economically attractive to people of modest wealth. In total almost a third of the agricultural land in England was enclosed by legislation between 1750 and 1820, plus large areas of wasteland; and enclosures were similarly disruptive and provocative of resistance in areas where the wastes provided essential grazing. As Hay and Rogers have commented, this process largely resulted in the obliteration, within a generation, of the 'lived law' which had been the essence of manorial custom for 500 years.[139] By virtually abolishing common rights it also simply imposed a narrow definition of lawful property: rights of ownership were recognized, but customary rights of usage were not, with economically fatal results for many.[140] Even the improving agriculturalist Arthur Young admitted that the poor could be forgiven for incomprehension in the face of such legislative omnipotence. He believed they might justly say 'Parliament may be tender of property: all I know is, I had a cow, and an act of Parliament has taken it from me'.[141] Young was also appalled by the powers of compulsion parliament gave to the enclosure commissioners who worked out the details of awards, 'a despotic power known in no other branch of business in this free country'.[142]

It has been said that acts passed under 'private bill' procedure like enclosure legislation were essentially grants of privilege: they did not lay down general rules, but applied only in particular cases, and often for limited periods.[143] Georgian parliaments were notoriously shy of what nineteenth-century people would called reform: that is, general changes according to predetermined plans. But as opponents of enclosure were well aware, even statutes of limited scope were binding on all those affected, and in the aggregate many types of specific legislation effected important changes of a general nature. As David Lieberman has pointed out, 'A sovereign legislature which annually enacts a steadily growing number of private enclosure bills is making public policy as much as if it enacted a general law establishing a separate administrative procedure for the purpose'.[144] Moreover, despite the frequency of preambles pointing to improvements and public benefits, contemporaries were well aware that lawmaking of this kind was often undertaken for narrowly private advantage.[145] Indeed, commenting on the numerical significance of legislation relating to personal estates and enclosure, which together account for over 5,000 separate acts over the eighteenth century (or more than a third of the total legislation), Julian Hoppit says it demonstrates 'the extent to which legislative activity was being used by the upper echelons of society to further their particular interests'.[146] Much the same could be said of another large class of specific acts which was less obviously about exclusive advantage: those relating to communication projects.

The multifarious acts concerning projects for improving communications by roads, bridges, harbours, rivers and canals formed nearly a fifth of all legislation passed during the eighteenth century: together they amounted to more than 2,000 acts in all. About three-quarters of these related to turnpikes; indeed the remarkably high success rate of turnpike bills after 1714 suggests that road improvement projects of this kind were especially favoured by MPs once they became familiar. It is true that these acts were normally of temporary duration only, and so much of the total consisted of renewals.[147] But it is nevertheless fair to say turnpike legislation was common by 1720, and there was a veritable 'Turnpike Mania' of new law-making in the 1750s and 1760s, when nearly 400 acts of this type were passed.[148]

What was happening in these cases was that groups of local projectors were obtaining parliamentary authority to levy a compulsory toll for maintenance of a stretch of road. They usually alleged it was in such poor repair that the existing legal arrangements for statute labour and magisterial intervention financed by fine were insufficient.[149] Thus in 1697 the gentlemen and inhabitants of Reigate and Horley in Surrey petitioned parliament, claiming their roads were 'not passable without danger, nor can they be repaired by any Law now in Force, for that the Charge will exceed any legal Assessments'.[150] More rarely the positive economic benefits of turnpiking were adduced, as in the case of the petitioners for improving the roads through the Vale of Berkshire in the Thames Valley, who after complaining about the 'Badness' of the roads around Wallingford, maintained

> ... in case a good Road be made through the Vale, and an easy Communication opened to the River of *Thames*, and Cities of *London* and *Westminster*,

it must necessarily be productive of good Effects, not only to the Vale of *Berkshire*, but many other Parts of the Kingdom.[151]

Legislation was necessary in these instances because by common law highways were places where all people had free passage, and only the crown could grant the right to levy a toll. The common law recognized the power of the crown to grant any person the right to take a toll in consideration of undertaking to maintain a passage, although the case law shows this was highly unusual before the eighteenth century, and the application of tollgates to long segments of highway was a radical innovation.[152] Turnpike acts gave a set of named commissioners, or trustees, a monopoly right to levy tolls on this basis, and therefore enabled them to raise loans or subscriptions on the security of the tolls.[153] Unlike canals, turnpikes were not intended to facilitate private profit, because the highways were not privately owned, and raising share capital was therefore prohibited.[154] However trustees were often investors, thereby acquiring an interest in the project's financial returns, rather than improvement of the road; and jobbery was frequently alleged, especially against trustees who were road contractors, or lawyers, and therefore eligible to acquire lucrative business.[155] Moreover like all eighteenth-century parliamentary legislation, and especially that enacted under private bill procedure, turnpike acts were disproportionately susceptible to the private interests of the powerful. It was notorious that the routes of new turnpike roads were unduly influenced by the preferences of local landowners, sometimes to the extent that major highways underwent considerable diversions from the direct route between principal cities.[156] On the other hand poor smallholders and independent artisans, who felt the impact of tolls most keenly, were the least likely to benefit from improvements to the highways, since they did not generally travel by carriage or convey goods by heavy wheeled transport, and it was increased traffic of this kind which was causing the roads to deteriorate.[157] Certainly from the perspective of poor opponents, who observed elite merchants and other prosperous investors and their interested supporters among the gentry somehow helping themselves at the expense of the helpless majority, a turnpike act was simply illegitimate and underhand: it was 'a thing Clandestinely purchased'.[158]

In the early stages of the turnpike movement there was significant popular opposition to the passage and implementation of the legislation. Admittedly, as in the case of enclosure, only a minority of bills provoked counter-petitions, but that is hardly surprising, because they were often passed with remarkable speed, leaving little time for effective communication with all the stakeholders and the organization of a parliamentary submission.[159] Where the inhabitants did manage to petition against turnpike legislation, in the Severn Valley and the West Riding of Yorkshire analysis of the local social environment suggests that the persistence of open field arable agriculture was a key factor in much of the opposition. In these places communal modes of production and manorial government were still the norm, and repairing the roads by parochial labour remained possible. Transferring the costs of road maintenance from the community to individual users and creating a new form of property investment in tolls by act of parliament must have been quite alien to the common people in these places.[160]

Where petitions did not succeed, or the anti-turnpike interests were insufficiently sophisticated or organized to make a parliamentary submission, opposition sometimes took the form of riotous destruction of tollgates by mobs. Most famously, there were major turnpike riots in the vicinity of Bristol during 1727–8, 1731–2, and 1749, following the passage of legislation and the erection of gates on the roads around the city.[161] The most prominent perpetrators of these disturbances were the miners who lived in Kingswood Forest on Bristol's eastern outskirts: independent cottagers who either mined coal themselves or transported it on horseback to the city. Their principal grievance against the turnpikes was of course the toll, which impacted on their livelihoods. But they also objected to the large powers given to the turnpike commissioners for appropriating materials from common land, alleged that the bad condition of the roads was caused by willful abuse on the part of the local landowners, and castigated the magistrates for not enforcing the existing legal arrangements for communal repair. It is true that these men were relatively unusual: as forest dwellers they were beyond the constraints of the country elite, and as independent miners they had a remarkable sense of self-identity. But their grievances were certainly shared elsewhere, and there is evidence of widespread support for the rioters in many of the affected areas.[162] For example the Bristol anti-turnpike riots of 1749 were instigated by the 'country people' from the south and west of the city; Somerset farmers and labourers who resented having to pay to attend the Bristol markets.[163] Here and elsewhere there were signs of gentry encouragement for the rioters, and traditional rites of disguise, special dress and behaviour which signified community solidarity.[164] There were also widespread riots in the West Riding of Yorkshire in 1752–3, inspired by small commodity producers and farmers. Indeed there had been a spate of anti-turnpike rioting in Herefordshire and Gloucestershire in 1734–5, and there small farmers and farm servants were clearly the main protagonists. They included Thomas Reynolds, the son of a Ledbury farmer, who was taken by the authorities and felt the full force of the law. To avoid the inconvenience that he had not destroyed any gates he was prosecuted under the Black Act; and he was tried at Westminster, rather than Hereford or Worcester, because it was feared a local jury would be too sympathetic. Since he would not give evidence against the other rioters he was not reprieved, and subsequently suffered at Tyburn.[165]

The riots in the Bristol area were successful in rendering the relevant acts of parliament nugatory, for they prevented the establishment of turnpikes for 20 years. It is therefore hardly surprising that in such disturbances the government apprehended a deliberate challenge to the law and the authority of parliament. Lord Hardwicke, then lord chief justice, and the presiding judge at Thomas Reynolds's trial, said of the Ledbury riots (in 1735):

> For my own part I have some time look'd upon this sort of rising as one of the worst symptoms in the Kingdom; and have thought it my duty in the few charges I have made to take particular notice of them, and to inculcate into men's minds the dangerous consequences that must follow from suffering people to get the better of the Laws, and, as it were, to overrule the Acts of the Legislature.[166]

For Hardwicke, who was of course one of the Whig government's inner circle, the success of the turnpike rioters, like that of the Waltham Blacks, represented a 'displacement of authority', an open and humiliating subversion of government which could not be suffered to stand.[167] The government was therefore very active: it provided rewards for information leading to the conviction of the leaders of the Bristol anti-turnpike risings and arranged for the special prosecution of those who were apprehended at the expense of the crown. Ultimately, however, their primary weapon in defence of the turnpike laws was more legislation: successive statutes were passed in 1728, 1732, and 1735 which imposed penal, and finally, capital sanctions against the destruction of turnpikes.[168] Two of these acts were obtained at the behest of the turnpike trustees in the Bristol area, thereby providing a further demonstration of the special parliamentary influence wielded by the turnpike projectors.[169] Indeed it seems that parliament was prepared to go to virtually any lengths to satisfy the interests of property and uphold the authority of its determinations. Since it was usually difficult to obtain convictions of alleged offenders under the normal process, whereby they were tried before a local jury, the 1735 act provided they could be tried in an adjacent county. So as in the case of the Black Act, faced with what appeared to be entrenched opposition to its laws, parliament simply overturned the usual procedures in criminal trials, thereby sacrificing the common law ideal of the local administration of justice.

The turnpike species of specific legislation is also remarkable because, like the enclosure acts, it created new statutory authorities with wide-ranging powers; in this case the boards of trustees responsible for managing the turnpike. Until mid-century they were nominally under the control of the local JPs in quarter sessions; but their powers were extended from the 1740s and by the 1770s they were 'extensive and virtually unchecked'. Under the terms of the legislation trustees were usually empowered to set up gates for collecting tolls, appoint collectors and surveyors, mortgage or lease the tolls in advance, co-opt new trustees, compulsorily purchase land, and divert the course of the road.[170] Although these powers were given for 21 years in the first instance, no trust was ever refused a renewal act, and parliamentary supervision was limited to protecting investors by giving creditors first call on the income from tolls.[171] Certainly the turnpike trusts' membership was hardly exclusive: many acts named hundreds of local property owners as trustees, probably with the intention of binding the majority of the local property owners to the project. The statutes also frequently specified relatively low property qualifications for acting as a trustee, and in 1773 a general consolidating act established minima of only £40 p.a. in freehold land or personal property of £800. These provisions formally enfranchised propertied people of quite modest wealth; there were even complaints about trusts falling wholly into the hands of mere farmers and carriers, with the result that in 1822 parliament made a freehold estate worth £100 a year obligatory outside the metropolitan area.[172] But it is dangerous to use the names and qualifications listed in the individual statutes to make generalizations about the broad social spread of devolved parliamentary authority. In fact effective management of the trusts was usually confined to a narrow clique of less than a dozen, and with the exception of the trusts in the vicinity of London, where lesser men were clearly important, most trusts seem to have been controlled by members of the local elites, typically the lesser gentry and clergy in the countryside, or the merchants, master manufacturers and other professional men in the cities and industrial areas.[173] While it is anachronistic to dwell on the obvious shortcomings of these authorities in action, it is appropriate to suggest that they represented one element of a general eighteenth-century trend towards investing virtually unrestrained administrative powers in the hands of polite and propertied people and their dependants.[174]

Besides the turnpike and enclosure statutes, there were several other large bodies of highly specific legislation which established authorities with significant powers. The statutory courts of requests or courts of conscience have already been mentioned.[175] Their stated rationale was to overcome the slow process and prohibitive costs of recovering small debts in the common law courts, especially from the 'undeserving poor' in manufacturing areas. This was the principal complaint of William Hutton, commissioner of the court at Birmingham, who maintained 'This is the only Court which can recover money where there is none, by commanding the future time, and the person of the debtor ... another instance of its usefullness to trade'.[176] Around 50 such courts were established in London and many provincial urban centres by separate acts between 1689 and 1800, following early precedents in Newcastle, Bristol and Norwich. A court of this kind had been established in the

City of London during the sixteenth century.[177] But their proliferation after 1750 was unprecedented, and despite protestations about serving the public interest by promoting credit, trade and industry, the courts of requests were not simply neutral tribunals for hearing small claims. They were empowered to commit defaulters to prison, and in many cases the promoters and acting commissioners were manufacturers, businessmen and professionals who had strong vested interests in enforcing payment of small debts to control their servants and ensnare poor customers with easy credit. Indeed, their advocates evinced a clear hostility to what they regarded as the idle and feckless habits of the labouring poor, which they believed required moral correction, as well as redress for the resulting indebtedness.[178] Confronted with unsavoury evidence of oppressive use of imprisonment by the Halifax court, in 1786 parliament intervened with general legislation regulating all the small debt courts.[179] However while this act restricted the power of imprisonment for debts of to a notional maximum period, it also gave the courts discretionary powers to impose longer spells of incarceration where the offender appeared to conceal assets, and its other main provision was to set a relatively low property qualification for the commissioners. Certainly, like Hutton and clerical magistrates, some of the small debt commissioners saw themselves as propertied paternalists, rather than petty tyrants; but whatever their inclinations, parliament ultimately trusted them to do the right thing, largely independent of control by the common law.[180]

A combination of moral, religious and economic attitudes informed the enactment of another body of legislation, that which established local corporations for the management of the poor.[181] These were yet more statutory authorities, in this case incorporated bodies of commissioners (usually called 'guardians' and 'directors') who took over the usual parochial arrangements for administering poor relief. Several acts establishing authorities of this kind passed in the 1690s and early 1700s, and there were 200 or so before the Poor Law Amendment Act of 1834 created a more uniform system of poor relief. As has been suggested previously, disciplining the labouring classes was a central project of eighteenth-century polite society, and in constituting the poor law corporations parliament shared fully in the contemporary concerns about inculcating habits of industry and correcting idleness, as well as ongoing humanitarian and economic interests. In this case the enduring instrument of legislative intervention was the workhouse, which the sponsors and supporters of these acts believed had the potential to ameliorate poverty and reduce the poor rates.[182] Some of the legislation empowered groups of parishes in cities and rural areas to join together for the purpose of administering poor relief, thereby saving the expense of inter-parochial settlement litigation. The prototype of these poor law unions was that established at Bristol in 1696, but there were other influential exemplars at Shrewsbury (1783), and in the unions of rural parishes in Norfolk and Suffolk (1756–85) and in Shropshire (in the early 1790s).[183] After 1750, with rapidly rising population, many single parishes in London and provincial cities also formed new poor law authorities by applying for the parliamentary incorporation of their churchwardens and overseers (sometimes with the addition of others elected by the inhabitants or vestry).[184] But whether they covered one parish or more, all these local authorities were given significant powers to fulfil their stated purpose of providing for 'the better Employment, and maintenance of the Poor'.[185]

Since the poor law corporations were empowered to receive the poor rates and raise loans on their security, like the turnpike trusts they developed into considerable financial interests, and their governors were not always compassionate.[186] By granting them extensive administrative powers, and effectively allowing the corporations independence from the control by the justices, parliament risked encouraging instincts for repressing the poor, rather than relieving them from poverty. Naturally most of these acts conferred powers to compel paupers to enter a workhouse, but the corporations were also given wide-ranging authority to make by-laws for the government of the poor, and specific disciplinary powers of summary punishment over the inmates of the workhouse, including solitary confinement and whipping.[187] Moreover the legislation usually provided guardians with extra administrative authority to apprehend vagrants and beggars found in their locality and send them to the workhouse, provisions which effectively enabled them to detain indefinitely people who were not formerly paupers but deemed to be idle.[188] These were powers of compulsion beyond appeal to the common law courts, and they significantly extended the reach of the state over the liberties of the subject.[189]

It is misleading to call such a wholesale transferral of discretionary authority 'careless apathy' on the part of parliament, for several parliamentarians were committed to detailed schemes of reforming poor relief, and compassion continued to inform attitudes to the poor generally until the 1790s, especially in the countryside.[190] Indeed like all of the statutory authorities created in the eighteenth century, for better or worse, the corporations of the poor represented administrative policy, rather than the culture of common law: a scheme of positive government designed to achieve specific outcomes, instead of a system of checks and balances. Certainly some of the workhouses were genuine 'pauper palaces', which provided thoughtfully for the maintenance of the poor.[191] However the disciplinary instincts of many workhouse projectors were evident to those who were on the receiving end, and the common people clung to the older legal arrangements for relief, wherein they perceived their freedom. In East Anglia the poor associated the workhouses and their supporters with imprisonment and loss of their legal status as free-born Englishmen. Rioters attacked the new Suffolk houses; Norfolk anti-workhouse petitioners asserted their right to 'our laws and libertys', as against arbitrary punishment by the corporation; and outdoor relief was repeatedly asserted as an important right under the law.[192]

The poor law corporations established in urban areas formed part of a whole series of new statutory urban authorities, which in the aggregate became a third major category of local legislation, in addition to the enclosure and turnpike acts. The bulk of these were urban improvement acts. From the mid-eighteenth century a trickle of specific acts establishing commissions for 'improving' towns and cities, most commonly by paving, lighting, watching, and cleansing the streets, swelled into a flood, reaching over 500 by the 1830s.[193] In some cases they combined one or more of these tasks with the administration of the poor law, and like the poor law corporations, they might be connected with the existing local authorities by including magistrates or office-holders *ex officio*.[194] The distinctive structural characteristic of the poor law corporations was the common provision for some limited electoral element. Existing municipal corporations were increasingly frequently criticized because they were regarded as unrepresentative of propertied opinion and potentially corrupt; parliament clearly felt that a tincture of representative democracy was necessary to legitimize at least the most expensive provision of local government. As Langford has pointed out, while only a minority were elective bodies, and elite opinion was decidedly unfavourable to authentically popular participation, all the improvement commissions involved some limited extension of authority beyond the landed classes to a broader propertied elite.[195] Thus at Tewkesbury in Gloucestershire the improvement commission established in 1786 included prosperous tradesmen, shopkeepers and manufacturers, and at Southampton and Taunton improvement authorities augmented the existing ruling elites by representing retired business and professional people. In these places the new institutions of government entrenched a consolidated elite of genteel property owners who were the natural leaders of their societies.[196]

Although their constitutions provide grounds for claiming that the urban improvement and poor law authorities facilitated some expansion of the ruling class to incorporate middling wealth, the proliferation of statutory authorities was accompanied by a considerable restriction of rights and opportunities for participation among people beyond the charmed circle delimited by parliament. As already seen in the case of the legislation creating enclosures and turnpikes, as well as the poorhouses, those so qualified were often given the power 'to direct and control the propertyless', largely independent of legal restraint.[197] In these circumstances it is hardly surprising that towns with a relatively broad franchise resisted attempts to establish statutory improvement commissions: certainly, from the perspective of the poorer inhabitants they frequently appeared to be self-interested conspiracies of the rich.[198] But in the eighteenth century people who opposed these new arrangements for governance were swimming against the tide of a spreading mentality by which public life was identified firmly with the progressive interests of property.[199] It is one of the major themes of this book that such thinking gradually overturned traditional ideas about law and liberty, and the collision of these cultures can occasionally be glimpsed in contemporary events.

For example the London parish of St. Pancras established a poor law authority and built a new workhouse by act of parliament in 1805, following an agitation led by a substantial businessman. The original constitution of this corporation set a relatively modest property qualification for acting as a director (£30 freehold in land or £1,000 personal estate), and it included provision for the vestry to elect three new directors in the case of vacancies. Ultimately the existing 60-odd directors named in the act were given office for life, however; they also had the power to co-opt new members, and to levy unlimited rates on the parishioners, without consulting them. After a few years of suffering this absolute rule the administration of the poor law directors offended the local inhabitants who had to pay for it, and at a public meeting held at the Adam and Eve, Tottenham Court, on Wednesday 30 July 1817, the vestry resolved to apply to parliament for amendment of the statute, insisting

> the Act of Parliament of the 45th of the present Reign, known by the name of the Directors Act, is inimical to the true and general Interests of the Parish in as much as, it contravenes the Common Law of the Land, by taking all parochial Government from the hands of Officers well known and recognized by the Law, and vesting all Authority in the hands of those who hold their Offices for life, are elected by their own body, and are responsible to none but themselves.[200]

These complaints read like an authentic lament for the culture of citizen office-holding associated with the early modern parish.[201] Certainly the traditional administration of vestry and parish officers had been unable to cope with the massive expansion of population in St. Pancras at the end of the eighteenth century, and the parishioners accepted the need for some reform. But a significant body of the inhabitants was clearly offended by the secrecy and lack of public accountability institutionalized by statutory authority. A committee of the vestry complained that the act rendered the administration of poor relief 'the most effectually independent that can be imagined, of the inquiry and controul of the parishioners, of the correction of the common law of the land, and of liability to punishment of the directors and their officers'.[202] Indeed distrust of parochial decision-making was fundamental to all the schemes for reforming poor relief. The poor law corporations, like the other statutory improvement and policing commissions, worked through paid officers accountable to the directors, rather than through the church-wardens and overseers who were answerable to the justices in quarter sessions.[203] In the St. Pancras case the vestry claimed there was evidence of widespread waste, jobbery and fraud on the part of the new bureaucracy, and it was alleged that the poor were ill treated by the directors' 'hirelings'.[204] But parliament was adamant against the complainants' petition: at a time when advanced opinion was shifting towards more professional local administration there was no going back to the bad old days when everyone had a voice and executive responsibility was in the hands of the 'annual' parish officers who were obliged to serve. For their pains in 1819 the open vestry was dissolved by another act, also prosecuted by the business elite, which established a select vestry empowered to perpetuate itself by co-option.[205]

Thus despite their contemporary legitimacy as associations of propertied people, the local statutory authorities which proliferated in the second half of the eighteenth century marked a clear trend away from the participatory culture of government typical of the civil parish and the judicial arrangements for supervising it. On the contrary, as in the case of late-Georgian JPs in quarter sessions, the commissioners, trustees, directors or guardians created by parliament tended to behave more as executive boards, and did their work through paid bureaucracies. In this parliament was clearly reshaping English political culture in a recognizably modern direction, albeit in a piecemeal fashion. Was it also privatizing the business of law-making? At this stage it is necessary to take a more detailed look at the people, procedures and processes involved in passing legislation, especially acts which were locally specific.

## Making legislation: Representation, procedure and participation

The standard justification for modern parliamentary despotism is that under a universal franchise administrative powers are introduced with the 'democratic consent' of the governed, who are all represented in the legislature.[206] This idea of parliamentary representation has a long history; it was current by the sixteenth century, and was enthusiastically repeated by seventeenth-century advocates of parliamentary sovereignty. Thus George Petyt asserted:

> Every English-man is intended to be there [i.e. in Parliament] present (either in Person, or Procuration, and Attorny) of what Pre-eminence, State, Dignity, or Quality soever he be; from the *Prince* (be it *King*, or *Queen*) to the lowest Person in *England*. And the Consent of the *Parliament* is taken to be every man's Consent.[207]

Early modern parliaments were hardly democratic, but in the eighteenth century their increasing proclivity to legislate for all and sundry was legitimated by the claim that MPs and peers were qualified to divine the interests of the propertied classes, which were taken to constitute the public good. The question then arises, how precisely was parliament – and parliamentary law-making in particular – connected with, or influenced by, the people, and did its processes strive to achieve a measure of justice?

In a theoretical sense the democratic element of parliamentary governance was discharged by the House of Commons, because it was an elected body, and of course elections constituted one obvious point of contact between parliament and people.[208] However the constitutional arrangements for election were complex, and they severely limited participation. Naturally, the franchise was based principally on the ownership of property, but even so, in towns and cities it applied very inconsistently according to the vagaries of custom and politics. Moreover, as contemporary critics loved to demonstrate, the distribution of parliamentary boroughs was a matter of historical contingency, for there was little attempt to keep pace with recent urban development. As a result formal representation was spread very unevenly and irrationally, as compared with population density, and of course all over the country the great majority of humble people were not able to vote. These characteristics remained broadly the same between 1689 and 1832, in so far as there was no large scale tampering with the distribution of constituencies, or the extent of the franchise.

Nevertheless, the electorate had expanded in the seventeenth century, and throughout the eighteenth between one in four and one in six adult males was enfranchised.[209] These voters, or potential voters, were not just the landed, professional and business elites. Around two-thirds were modestly middling people: yeomen and tenant farmers in the countryside, shopkeepers and craftsmen in the towns and cities; it has also been estimated that up to 15 per cent were drawn from the labouring classes.[210] But did their votes count? The eighteenth century was the great age of electoral management: after the Septennial Act reduced the incidence of elections, aristocratic control settled over the smaller constituencies, and went on increasing.[211] In practice it was often applied to negotiate the nomination of members who were congenial to voters as well as patrons, thereby satisfying popular interests at the same time as avoiding the expense of a contested election. Indeed, despite claims of widespread deference to the social grandees, there is considerable evidence that electors could be robustly independent, or at least persuaded to register a principled protest vote. Certainly in the large boroughs with a broad franchise, where contests were more frequent and national issues animated opinion, middling tradesmen and craftsmen frequently participated in elections with a high degree of political engagement.[212]

Yet while electors were socially diverse and hardly supine in dealing with their betters, the fact remains that the instincts of the eighteenth-century governing elite tended strongly towards restricting popular participation in parliamentary elections. The Septennial Act significantly reduced the power of electors over their MPs, and there were several other legislative measures that bespoke a similar attitude. The 'last determination acts' of 1695 and 1729 gave parliament, rather than the courts, the exclusive right of determining the extent of the franchise in cases of disputed elections, thereby enabling the governments of Walpole and his successors to restrict constituency electorates in favour of Whig candidates.[213] In the City of London the City Elections Act of 1725, which restricted the electoral participation of freemen and strengthened aldermanic control, 'expressed a fear of open politics untempered by the sinews of patronage and magnate power'. Admittedly, these measures were motivated by party political ends, but there was a clear social dimension to London politics in this period, for the Whigs represented the big bourgeoisie and tory support was based on the middling manufacturers and craftsmen.[214] In 1725 the aldermen and their government allies were manifestly against the continued enfranchisement of what they called the 'Tory rabble'.[215] Indeed it has been argued persuasively that statutory limitation of the frequency of general elections in 1716 was prompted by negative elite reactions to the experience of enthusiastic popular involvement in politics during the previous 25 years.[216] Such prejudices were by no means confined to the period of the Whig oligarchy, however. Throughout the eighteenth century there was concern that price inflation had widened the scope of the county franchise to include undesirable 'ragamuffin' elements of the population. Although the principle of forty-shilling freehold enfranchisement was inviolable because of its popular symbolism, general legislation of 1712, 1745 and 1780 restricted its application to freeholders liable to pay local rates and land tax, thereby checking further downward growth in the shire electorates.[217] And in the case of borough electorates, where it was not distracted by partisan considerations the House of Commons decided disputed election returns in ways which consistently favoured 'the elimination of the authentically poor voter', normally by narrowing the franchise to ratepayers.[218] So while it is fair to argue that a significant degree of 'openness' and popular participation remained a characteristic of parliamentary representation throughout the eighteenth century, the abiding context of parliamentary intervention in the constituencies seems to have been an attitude of contempt, or at least lofty condescension, towards poor voters, which inspired a deep desire to avoid the unpleasantness of associating them in the business of government.[219] This is hardly auspicious of fair dealing for plebeian interests in the passage of legislation.

Before going on to examine parliamentary procedure for considering legislation it is appropriate to observe the evidence that eighteenth-century parliamentarians were becoming increasingly detached from the ideas, culture and life experiences of their poorer constituents. The importance of London can hardly be overstressed here. It is well known that after 1660 the leading members of the titular aristocracy were drawn to spend more and more time in the capital, to the extent that by the early nineteenth century the dukes of Devonshire were normally absent from their estates for three quarters of the year. Despite careful demonstrations of paternalism, especially in the context of electoral interests, such absenteeism clearly weakened their ties with tenants and labourers in the countryside.[220] The magnetic attraction of London was also felt by the leading county gentry who traditionally dominated the House of Commons, especially after 1689, when permanent sessions of parliament exposed more of them to the metropolis, and the development of the London season made rural society seem provincial. Under these conditions the influence of metropolitan standards over local ruling elites must have been magnified. For example Philip Jenkins's work on the landed elite of Glamorgan has shown that by the middle of the eighteenth century the gentry there had undergone a cultural transformation. By contrast with previous generations of Glamorgan landowners they were characterized by cosmopolitan values and interests associated with the tastes of London and the consolidated propertied elite it was helping to create, rather than the manners and mores of ordinary folk in their locality.[221] Indeed, in London itself the growing exclusiveness of the eighteenth-century parliamentary class is apparent from their concentrated migration into the new and fashionable squares west of the City, as far away as possible from the squalor of the East End.[222] Certainly there were still relatively humble long-term residents in some of the newly gentrified parishes, and it could be argued that the presence of peers and MPs enhanced their parliamentary representation, in a 'virtual' sense, by facilitating informal access. But in St. Marylebone, which by the 1760s was home to an aristocratic enclave centred on Cavendish Square, the grandees used their power to reconstitute parochial government by legislating a select vestry that restricted the influence of local tradesmen and lesser parish officers.[223] So it seems the presence of so many legislators in London and Middlesex could make for parliamentary 'service' of a very partial kind.[224]

Despite unfavourable examples like this and the formally unrepresentative nature of eighteenth-century electoral arrangements, nevertheless it is conceivable that with increasing demand for positive legislation parliament sought to deploy its overriding sovereign power in ways that allowed for a broad measure of access, participation and justice among competing interests. There is evidence of increasingly broad popular access to parliament, if not always just outcomes, in proceedings relating to general legislation and what might be called 'public' issues. Petitioning is a case in point.[225] It is true that by an act passed in 1661 the kind of 'tumultuous petitioning' on affairs of state which had led to the mobbing of parliament 20 years earlier was prohibited.[226] Henceforward large-scale political petitions were subjected to the control of local authorities in formally constituted meetings: assizes or quarter sessions in the counties or the common council of the corporation in the City of London. After the revival of radicalism in the 1790s similar constraints were extended to mass meetings called to petition for redress of grievances, and even more severe restrictions were imposed on public proceedings of this kind in 1819, in statutes which applied to industrial issues as well as state affairs.[227] However there were always multiple petitions on some controversial general bills, and there was a resurgence of petitioning parliament on major political issues in the 1780s, when there were petitioning 'campaigns' about Catholic relief, the movement for economical reform, the mooted reform of representation, and the abolition of the slave trade.[228] Moreover John Phillips has shown that many of the petitions which became a feature of national politics after the Wilkes affair included a significant degree of participation from people who did not have the right to vote for representation in parliament.[229] It seems this significant acceleration in activity carried over into petitions about general legislation, for in the mid-1780s there were hundreds of petitions of this kind during each session of parliament. Indeed, the early decades of the nineteenth century were marked by further major increases in the numbers of petitions relating to general legislation, and truly massive petitioning campaigns were fought over popular issues such as the bill of pains and penalties against Queen Caroline, the abolition of slavery, and various measures of Catholic Relief. By the 1820s some petitioning campaigns had burst their constitutionally defined local authority boundaries to become institutionalized and national in scope.[230]

How far all this made for greater popular agency in legislative processes is uncertain. Although the mass petitions occasioned major debates, and were frequently influential, the repeal of the apprenticeship clauses of the statute of artificers in 1814 showed that parliament was perfectly capable of ignoring a clear expression of popular opinion if the political conditions were unfavourable.[231] In the case of government financial measures the House of Commons was quite open about its exclusive power, and supply bills were not even printed. Indeed in an age of large-scale warfare the incidence and scale of taxation were even more controversial than usual, and from the early eighteenth century ministers refused to accept petitions against money bills creating new taxes, on the grounds that such opposition would render the business of government impossible. This practice, which was applied to exclude petitions against Walpole's Excise Bill and the Stamp Bill of 1765, ultimately became a settled rule, justified by Speaker Onslow in 1730 with the argument that in prospective financial matters the House of Commons was the best judge of 'what was for the advantage of the nation'.[232] Moreover as petitions multiplied MPs were increasingly disinclined to hear or discuss them, and the direct link between petitioning and parliamentary debate was finally severed in the 1830s, when the House of Commons took steps to ensure that they would no longer be discussed. Although prompted by the disruption to business, this measure was justified by some parliamentarians because it limited 'extrinsic pressure' on MPs' deliberations.[233] It should also be noted that while many of the early nineteenth-century petitioning campaigns did have a significant impact on legislation, most of them were initiated in response to previous parliamentary proceedings, and very few represented spontaneous outbursts of public opinion. Indeed it appears that parliamentarians themselves became adept at mobilizing extra-parliamentary opinion for their own purposes.[234] But the sheer scale of petitioning in the early nineteenth century does indicate that in a broad sense British people were being mobilized and politicized by unprecedented engagement with parliament.[235]

There are also indications that the practice by which parliamentary committees heard oral evidence from witnesses was becoming more common in the eighteenth century, especially after 1760. Besides the well-established procedure by which committees on local and private bills routinely heard interested parties (which will be considered later), it is known that from Tudor times at least representatives of particular merchant groups were summoned by the Commons and Lords to inform committees on general bills relating to particular branches of trade and industry.[236] There were broader committees of inquiry in the eighteenth century, and they may well have taken witness evidence; for example the inquiries into the conditions of metropolitan gaols in 1729–30 did so, although it is unclear whether the various committees of inquiry into crime and poverty also examined witnesses.[237] Committees of inquiry like these multiplied in number after 1780, and gave rise to much legislation.[238] Certainly by the early nineteenth century 'a tradition of witness interrogation' had become established as a principal feature of parliamentary enquiry into domestic government and remedial legislation.[239] Of course the most important question from the perspective of participation in law-making is: who was selected to appear, and how? In cases of general legislation and inquiries into broad issues the committees necessarily controlled selection, and there was no guarantee that all interested parties would be able to appear. On the contrary, Joanna Innes has given examples from the 1820s of committees on workers' combinations and friendly societies that were reluctant to hear evidence from plebeian sources. In one of these cases artisans' representatives won a hearing by determined petitioning and the assistance of sympathetic MPs, however, and they subsequently had a major influence over legislation.[240]

Thus both petitioning and witnessing appear to speak positively to the broad issue of exchange between parliament and popular opinion. There are other signs that this kind of conversation was on the increase, although progress was uneven. J.R. Pole has referred to important concessions that promoted more 'communication': tolerating the presence of strangers, printing proceedings, and above all, allowing the reporting and publication of debates.[241] Admittedly, from the sixteenth century, when the House of Commons regarded itself as 'the Common Council of the Realm', proceedings were formally confidential, and strangers were barred from entering the House by standing orders. But in fact they seem to have had relatively easy access to the lobbies and committee rooms and were known to penetrate the House itself. In general only the gatherings of large crowds provoked official intervention in Tudor-Stuart times, and in the eighteenth century strangers were excluded exceptionally, usually on occasions when matters of major political significance were debated.[242] Indeed it is well known that the Commons confirmed its ad hoc policy of admitting strangers in 1777, when Temple Luttrell declared 'candour, policy, gratitude, and duty to the people, whose representatives they were, called upon them to open their doors'. The standing orders against admitting strangers remained, but they were regarded as only a 'reserve power' after 1780.[243]

However the admission of newspaper reporters was resisted after the Commons' failure to suppress reporting of debates in 1771, when the newspaper printers were protected by the authorities of the City of London, and a policy of selectively excluding strangers was applied to restrict coverage of sensitive matters. The debates on the Royal Marriage Bill in 1772 were muzzled in this way, for example, as were the 1774 debates on American affairs. Moreover no note-taking was allowed before 1783.[244] So while parliament permitted interested members of the public to witness its proceedings, the right to report parliamentary debates in the newspapers was only grudgingly conceded. Many MPs and peers continued to believe that the people should only be informed about the outcomes of parliament's decisions, and not how those outcomes had been reached.[245] As in the case of petitioning, in their attitude towards newspaper reporting parliamentarians assumed a high notion of their right to discuss affairs free from popular influence. Even the young Charles James Fox, who generally favoured openness in his later career, maintained that there was no legitimate opinion outside the House of Commons: 'he knew nothing of the people, but through the medium of their representatives there assembled'.[246] Nevertheless newspaper reporting had extended the reach of parliamentary debates considerably by the end of the eighteenth century, and it continued to expand the scope of contact between public and parliament far beyond the major political issues.[247]

Parliamentarians were a little more liberal in publishing and disseminating the formal details of their proceedings. After all general laws and resolutions were orders, or at least declarations of intent, and in the case of local and specific bills interested people expected to be informed about the progress of measures which affected them directly. The *Votes and proceedings* of the House of Commons – a daily record of business transacted that was first published by the Long Parliament – had been suppressed after the Restoration, but publication was resumed in the 1680s and became permanent from 1689. In the 1730s 2,000 copies were printed daily, and the cost of distributing over 600 to MPs was covered by commercial sale of the rest, providing a substantial annual profit to the printers and the Speaker. Around that time at least 1,000 copies a day were sold to the general public, and many more copies of the king's speeches or addresses were distributed on occasions of great political controversy. There is evidence that copies of reports were also being printed for sale.[248] From 1742 the Commons began to publish its *Journals*, containing a fuller record of proceedings with some relevant papers such as reports and accounts; and by the 1760s they were appearing only a couple of years in arrears. The House of Lords also published its *Journals* from 1767. Indeed after the accession of George III there was a general increase in the amount of published material relating to parliamentary proceedings: long reports were published in a separate series of volumes, and there was more contemporaneous publishing of individual bills, reports, accounts and other papers.[249] The publication of these 'sessional papers' was made systematic after 1801 when Speaker Abbott instituted the scheme which led to the compilation of the 'Blue Books' in separate series. As Joanna Innes has suggested, although the circulation of these detailed materials was relatively exclusive, they were utilized by lobbyists and publicists whose special issue campaigns communicated some of them to a wider public, and by 1800 still more were being transmitted by the quality magazines and newspapers.[250]

Of course there were long-standing formal procedures for promulgating the legislative acts of parliament. Until the late fifteenth century statutes were proclaimed by the county sheriffs, and from early Tudor times the public acts were printed by the king's printer on a sessional basis and republished in commercial collections of 'statutes at large'.[251] But with the proliferation of legislation and the growing confusion which attached to the classification of local and specific acts, some of which had clauses which made them 'public' for certain purposes, it was increasingly hard for lawyers, not to mention ordinary members of the public, to keep abreast of the law.[252] Moreover the arrangements for bringing public legislation to the people's attention were inadequate, since almost all the sets of printed statutes distributed annually at the expense of the government were sent to parliamentarians themselves. The spread of knowledge about new law beyond this charmed circle was left to the newspapers, magazines, and other commercial publications aimed at magistrates and lawyers. As Simon Devereaux has noted, this lack of any systematic method of promulgation was an especially serious problem at a time when penal law was multiplying at an unprecedented rate, and in 1757 a newspaper essay commented: 'Our Laws are so incredibly numerous, and are passed in such Secresy, that they may be *literally* said to be Snares'.[253] By the 1770s advocates of reform were arguing that it was simply unjust to apply criminal sanctions where public knowledge about them was so doubtful. A more methodical administrative effort was inaugurated in 1797, when detailed arrangements were put in place to convey sets of the 'public general' acts to sheriffs, clerks of the peace and a proportion of the acting magistrates all over the country. However the main imperative for the initiative was a desire on the part of the government that the JPs, the criminal law's 'enforcers', should be kept up to date with parliament's latest products.[254] Under this early vision of centralized authority the people were merely the objects of the law. Thomas Hobbes would surely have approved the priority.

Whatever the intentions of ministers and MPs, it is clear that by the early nineteenth century the general increase in information about parliament had made for greater public participation in the consideration of broad national issues.[255] In particular the publication of debates had augmented the influence of the urban middle classes, who were regarded as the 'intelligent' and 'virtuous' part of public opinion, and whose opinions were taken seriously.[256] As seen, this influence was clearly apparent in the increased volume and impact of petitioning about major issues of public policy. But it is a different question to ask how far the people were positively involved in the making of legislation, especially of the local and specific variety.

It was argued by Holdsworth that the complex rules of parliamentary procedure ensured that the legislature was truly representative of all shades of opinion, and their elaboration under Speaker Onslow (1727–61) made it more so.[257] He was referring principally to issues of national politics, however, and his discussion of legislative processes is less reassuring. All the specific measures previously discussed were governed by private bill process because they affected private or local interests and were initiated by petition asking for some special privilege not available under existing law.[258] This procedure, which was broadly similar in both houses, certainly included elaborate 'judicial' features, which were designed to prove the truth of the promoters' allegations and consider the rights and interests of other parties, so that the legislation achieved a maximum of consensus among the stakeholders. Initially, petitions for bills were sent to committees tasked to ascertain whether a prima facie case had been made out for the bill and that it conformed to standing orders. In the Commons until 1773 counter-petitions could be heard at this stage. Then, after the principal reasons for and against the bill had been argued at its second reading, another select committee took the evidence of witnesses and heard arguments from its promoters and opponents. Petitions against the general principal of the bill could be heard in the house at second reading, and opponents were heard before the sponsors of the bill.[259] These provisions were hardly watertight against short-cuts however, and even if they had been, they had two features which made for a significant degree of inequality and injustice: the system was prohibitively expensive, and it was highly susceptible to the kind of interested influence typical of eighteenth-century parliaments.

First, the short-cuts. As Thurlow maintained in 1781, many private bills were routinely 'hurried through' select committees before anyone without special knowledge had noticed, even where they potentially had very deleterious effects on the property and rights of other interested parties.[260] This was occurring despite the House of Commons standing order of 1774, which stipulated that proper public notice of enclosure, turnpike and improvement bills should be given via advertisement in parish churches and newspapers and proclamation at quarter sessions.[261] Indeed it is not clear how these arrangements for publicity were guaranteed, especially in the case of petitions for enclosure bills, since they were no longer sent to committees after 1741.[262] Certainly in Northamptonshire several enclosure bills were still allowed to proceed after their failure to conform with the standing orders in this matter had been pointed out.[263] Turnpike bills were also likely to pass before anyone was able to react, given the rapidity of process.[264] This culture of haste and inconsistency seems to make a nonsense of all the procedural safeguards enshrined in the parliamentary standing orders, designed to ensure a broad measure of informed consent among stakeholders. The general problem was that procedural rules were not necessarily enforced, and were especially likely to become empty formalities where there was no formal opposition, and dedicated promotion on the other side. In these cases the Commons second reading committees actually consisted of the chairman only, who simply signed the bill, and in the house proceedings might be transacted in a few mumbled conversations around the Speaker's chair, while the rest of the MPs were distracted. As Sheila Lambert has admitted, it is doubtful whether committees which were named to consider unopposed private bills were ever 'real bodies'.[265] So by the realities of this process they often went through on the nod, with minimal attention.

Even if opponents were sufficiently informed and organized to resist legislative schemes of this kind before they became law, the expenses involved were likely to deter the less wealthy. The costs of private bill legislation were exorbitant because substantial fees were payable to officers at every stage, and it is notorious that they increased substantially in the eighteenth century with rising demand and the officers' multiplication of occasions for payments.[266] This explains why projectors had to call for subscriptions from a large number of other interested parties as one of the first steps in promoting a bill. Of course the enormous aggregated costs simply excluded individuals from initiating legislation of this kind, unless they were substantial property owners with funds to spare.[267] That did not matter much in practice because people of modest property hardly wanted to legislate for estate settlements, enclosures, or turnpikes (although they might have appreciated access to statutory divorce). But the need to pay procedural fees also acted as a deterrent, if not an absolute impediment, to mounting a campaign of opposition. It was not just that opponents had to pay the never-ending exactions of the parliamentary clerks. Clients of the sovereign legislature also needed to fee professionals to advance their causes. It was usual to employ solicitors to organize the preparation and presentation of petitions and counsel would be required to argue them if there was to be tolerable prospect of success.[268] Since their fees were proportioned to the generally prosperous circumstances of their clients – and parliamentary barristers took fees of hundreds of pounds – these imposts added hugely to the total costs. So the story that Sir George Savile interposed to save a poor man from being ruined by a private bill because his case went unheard in committee is plausible, even if the details may have been apocryphal.[269]

The important point about the Savile anecdote is that it shows the legitimate way to influence parliamentary legislation of this kind was to obtain the personal patronage of parliamentarians.[270] Indeed private bill procedure tended to render plebeian outsiders as mere supplicants, with little real agency in the business of government. Certainly the parishioners of St. Marylebone were able to petition against their aristocratic neighbours' attempts to destroy their open vestry: their access to the parish rates enabled them to afford the costs. But they only succeeded in delaying the project because they had the support of the duke of Portland, and it passed into law in spite of their opposition when he abandoned their cause. Portland was no white knight; he only helped them as long as the issue affected his material interest in obstructing the building ambitions of Lord Foley, who wanted to develop part of the Portland estate.[271] More routinely MPs and peers lent their legislative influence to their local connections among powerful manufacturers and traders, communications entrepreneurs, and industrialists, as well as their own fellow landowners. Among middling people the big bourgeoisie were most successful in lobbying endeavours of this kind, but even they were sometimes offended by the patronizing manner of leading parliamentarians.[272] Nevertheless it is true that local politicians often helped to ameliorate the more controversial features of improvement projects, as well as prefer them, and the treatment of some contested bills hardly conformed to the caricatures of nineteenth-century reformers. On the contrary there are well documented examples of lengthy and detailed discussions, as objectionable provisions were whittled away.[273] For example in 1721, among other negotiated changes, the inhabitants of 14 towns and villages close to a ford across the River Mersey were able to secure an amendment to the Mersey-Irwell Navigation bill which protected their access to a crossing. In this case they were fortunate that they lived in close proximity to the seats of two leading gentlemen, including

Sir George Warburton, MP for Cheshire.[274] Since parliamentarians' personal loyalties, connections and political affiliations were so widely spread, it has been argued plausibly that the 'clashing of interests' inseparable from commercial progress ensured a rough and ready kind of balance among competing social and economic stakeholders, none of which was permanently disadvantaged by the outcome.[275] However the usual result was a legislative output which represented the minimum of compromise among the most powerful parties. Clearly this was law for the haves rather than the have-nots.[276] Moreover, access to the law-making process was a matter of dependency and goodwill, rather than a citizen's right.[277]

Even with the best of intentions, in a parliament of landowners the inadequacies of private bill procedure left plenty of scope for little people to be crushed by the giants who animated the law-making Leviathan. But intentions were not always so good. Examples of damage caused by the unbridled self-interest of 'a few opulent individuals' have already been seen; they were most clear in the case of enclosure legislation, but were by no means absent from other species of local acts.[278] The reason that self-interest was able to predominate is that the customary ways of selecting committees promoted the influence of interested parties, rather than making for impartial discussion, despite their quasi-judicial machinery. In the Commons the chairman of the committees to whom the original petition and bill were committed (normally the same man) was usually the principal undertaker of the project in parliament, being the friendly agent of the promoters. Naturally when it came to constituting the other members of the committees he sought to name those whom he thought would be friends to the measure, and the rest would usually be made up by a blanket order adding all the MPs from the neighbouring counties.[279] In the case of powerful opposition developing from other local interests there were tried and tested techniques for packing membership and attendance to get the right result.[280] Admittedly, it was legitimate by contemporary standards for local members to decide local issues, and none of this would have mattered if MPs regularly rose above their private interests. But the evidence suggests that many did not. For example an analysis of Warwickshire enclosure bills before the Commons between 1730 and 1739 shows that in over half the cases a personal connection existed between the principal promoter of the measure and the MP who was guiding it through the Commons. Indeed there are several examples where the member was clearly a client or relative of the principal beneficiary.[281] Again, it may be objected that interested law-making of this kind was the essence of eighteenth-century landed society, and therefore uncontroversial. However some degree of impartiality *was* expected.[282] When he was an MP Sir Edward Coke had insisted that committee men should be 'no parties but indifferent', and in the eighteenth century William Paley wrote 'Parliament knows not the individuals upon whom its acts will operate; it has no cases or parties before it; no private interests to serve'. Paley was probably thinking mainly about penal law, but he clearly had a strong sense of the need to avoid 'laws made for particular cases and particular persons, and partaking of the contradictions and iniquity of the motives, to which they owed their origin'.[283] Ultimately MPs were expected to abstain from voting in divisions which affected them personally.[284] Plainly, these standards were not always maintained in the acts passed under private bill procedure.

Eighteenth-century legislation then, was increasingly imperial in its scope and legal supremacy, and could well be oppressive in its application to individuals, even if it did not typically represent a direct flexing of the central state's administrative muscles. As in the case of the general statutes that gave extra powers to magistrates, specific acts frequently created authorities with wide powers and relative immunity from correction by the courts. Indeed although they formally extended participation in government to include a broader range of property owners, these authorities generally exercised power in ways that superceded the quasi-republican culture of governance associated with the common law. Certainly parliament was increasingly open to the influence of public opinion, but the overwhelming majority of its acts were initiated by local combinations of private propertied interests. Moreover despite the increase in public engagement with its consideration of national issues, in the processing of legislation parliament could easily be partial and unjust, in so far as its procedures tended to privilege the most wealthy and powerful elements of English society. Given these leading characteristics of parliamentary governance, it is arguable that after 1750 the main species of 'law' was by no means saturated by ideas about the palladium of liberty, or the Englishman's birthright. In the later eighteenth century law was pre-eminently a service purchased by powerful vested interests.[285]

# 6
# Conclusion: An Imperial State? Governance, People and Law in the Eighteenth Century

> It is easy to see that all this is merely statuary; that it is merely an act of legislative power; such as would equally make it felony to eat buttered peas, or to wear leather breeches. It is, *sic volo, sic jubeo* [i.e, so I wish, and so I command].
>
> (Allan Ramsay, *Observations upon the Riot Act* (1781), 8.)

> ... his love for the constitution will be deeply wounded, when he perceive, that the LEGISLATURE itself, too frequently diminishes the POOR MAN's few remaining resources, and aggravates his multiplied miseries. *Their rights*, who have neither ability to be their own advocates, nor money to procure them ought surely, to be particularly guarded by the legislature; instead of being left, as they now are, to accident for the discovery, or to private humanity for relief.
>
> (Samuel Cooper, *Erroneous opinions concerning providence refuted, – the true notion stated, – and illustrated by the events which have lately happened to this nation: in a sermon, preached in the parish church of Great Yarmouth, on Friday February the 8th, 1782* (1782), 15n.)

> ... the spirit of both the executive and the legislative, in late years, has been radically changed. It has become theoretic, anti-popular, stern, savage, and arbitrary.
>
> (D. Robinson, 'The Local Government of the Metropolis, and other Populous Places', *Blackwood's Edinburgh Magazine*, 29 (1831), 82.)

In this book I have attempted to provide a fresh perspective on law and government in the eighteenth century by discussing changes in their cultures, processes and structures as they involved or impacted upon the people of England, especially relatively ordinary people. It is appropriate now to summarize my principal conclusions.

## Summary: From consent to command

One constant theme has been declining popular participation in the business of government. This can be observed at several different points. At the level of the county quarter sessions, which were the most important institutions of government in the localities, the evidence of Cheshire and several other counties suggests there was a marked deterioration in popular engagement with authority, as public judicial or quasi-judicial processes which required the presence or active involvement of the community were gradually abandoned, and more direct forms of administration took their place. For example individual magistrates tended to settle interpersonal quarrels on their own initiative, rather than binding them over to appear for a judicial hearing at the sessions. This is an important development because historians of Tudor-Stuart government have shown that a broad range of individuals utilized the legal procedure of binding over by recognizance to resolve their disputes: even relatively humble people therefore had initiative and some personal agency in the administration of justice under the law. Moreover, although sixteenth and seventeenth-century men and women might well be presented by officials for various infractions of statutes regulating personal behaviour, these prosecutions normally originated with unpaid local constables, men of middling status who were amenable to community pressures. By contrast their late Georgian successors were more likely to be subject to justice at the discretion of a local magistrate, either acting 'extra-legally' as an arbitrator between the parties, or applying summary justice under powers invested in him by statute. Of course it is true that quarter sessions still dealt with some criminal proceedings, and they certainly required the presence of the 'country' in the form of trial by jury. But here too there is evidence nevertheless of a shift in initiative from the grass-roots to the bench, for patterns of indictments in Cheshire and elsewhere show a transition from adjudicating minor interpersonal conflicts on the initiative of the victims to a sustained magisterial campaign against property crime. Indeed with the virtual disappearance of active lay constables, the JPs increasingly employed paid special constables who were directly accountable to the bench for their performance, and interested in maximizing their fees from arresting offenders. So in this sphere of government, as in so many others, it is possible to observe the beginnings of professionalization going hand in hand with diminishing popular engagement in the administration of justice. The growth of paid specialists who were primarily accountable to officials rather than the community is a second major theme of this study.

Having largely divested themselves of troublesome 'vernacular justice' by devolving it to individual JPs or to pairs sitting in petty sessions, throughout England and Wales quarter sessions benches became preoccupied with maintaining and improving the physical infrastructure of their counties. JPs were able to present local communities on their own initiative for not repairing roads and bridges, and then levy fines and contract with tradesmen to undertake the work. This business was recorded in the sessions minutes in the shape of common law processes, but they were actually fictions which disguised administrative intervention on the part of the magistrates. Indeed, executive intervention and the semi-professionalization of their activities are the hallmarks of the quarter sessions in the general administration of the counties, as well as their public judicial proceedings. Again, there was reduced popular engagement with government in proceedings of this kind, and very little scope for grass-roots individual agency. It is true that the eighteenth-century Cheshire bench continued to hear poor law cases as a court, and made judicial determinations. But the overwhelming bulk of this work consisted of appeals in cases of settlement, and the protagonists were the parish officers, who argued over which particular parish was responsible for the pauper's welfare, increasingly employing barristers for the purpose. Under such conditions the paupers themselves seem to have had little scope for personal initiative or agency. This contrasts markedly with administrative proceedings relating to the poor in the seventeenth century, when poor people can be identified as appearing personally before the bench to argue against bastardy orders, and the magistrates made original orders in response to the petition of individuals for poor relief, or to build cottages on waste land. After 1700 most of this work was devolved to the divisional justices, and was often institutionalized in 'petty sessions', where two or more JPs sat together.

Eighteenth-century petty sessions tended to acquire officers and became developed administrative units in their own right as they were given special responsibilities and powers by statute: powers which were sometimes used as the basis for extra-legal administrative aggrandizement. In this they echoed the administrative style of the quarter sessions themselves, for it is clear that over much of the country, as judicial process was abandoned, government by simple administrative order took its place, in some cases even tending to the assumption of quasi-legislative authority, most famously in the poor rate innovations of the Speenhamland magistrates in 1795. Arbitrary executive acts like this were clearly encouraged by empowering legislation which made magistrates virtually unaccountable at common law, exemplified above all by the County Rates Act of 1739. By the early nineteenth century the quarter sessions benches were largely behaving as county executives rather than courts, having embarked on extensive programmes of infrastructural improvement and developed the nucleus of their own professional bureaucracies. By contrast with proceedings according to the machinery of the common law this business was carried out behind closed doors, rather than in open court, in the presence of the community.

So at the level of 'local government', the evidence suggests that a marked declension in popular participation was linked with the corrosion of common law or broadly juridical processes by 'administrative imperialism' from above, as facilitated by the accession of extra powers and executive capacity derived from statute. The growth of positive governance by statutory instruments is another important theme which runs throughout the book. Of course legal processes which enabled ordinary individuals to apply the authority of government continued to animate the courts in their capacity as tribunals for hearing interpersonal suits. Indeed it has been demonstrated fairly clearly that by tradition the English were exceptionally litigious, especially in the sixteenth and seventeenth centuries, to the extent that quite humble people had access to this kind of justice via the plethora of jurisdictions which covered the country. However in the eighteenth century the volume of litigation appears to have declined very significantly, both at the centre and in the localities. Certainly many of the borough jurisdictions which had been so busy a century and a half earlier were quite moribund by the 1820s. It is true that during the eighteenth century some urban centres acquired new courts for suing small debts, but these tribunals had little of the community participation which was a feature of their predecessors: they had no juries, and poor individuals were often subject to oppression at the hands of the local elites. Moreover the 'instance' or civil litigation of the principal church courts also declined steeply in the early eighteenth century, and this is important because they had been very active in the later sixteenth and seventeenth centuries as sites for plebeian women to negotiate interpersonal disputes via suits for defamation. In London, where the Consistory Court had been dominated by this kind of business in Tudor-Stuart times, instance litigation simply went up-market, as the court became preoccupied by divorce cases between wealthy men and women, rather than actions for words among their social inferiors. Here too, therefore, the eighteenth century saw a marked diminution in access to the legal resources of government as the social reach of the courts contracted. In this sense 'the rule of law' was much less egalitarian in 1800 than it had been a century or so earlier.

Why were fewer people resorting to the courts? Litigation generally was becoming much more expensive and socially exclusive as professional lawyers concentrated on high-value suits, multiplied their fees and itemized more motions and appearances. At the same time they intruded their ever more complex culture into courts and processes which had previously been relatively free of their influence, and this 'legalization' most likely deterred potential suitors, especially the less affluent. But there are signs of social intolerance among the legal establishment too. Just as quarter sessions benches tended to distance themselves from the interpersonal quarrels at the grass-roots, so by the early nineteenth century the proctors, advocates, and judges who controlled the church courts were expressing considerable impatience with the unsavoury nature of defamation proceedings among plebeian women. In the early eighteenth century such prejudices were certainly encouraged by the bishop of London and other clergy and lay people who campaigned for a 'reformation of manners' among the common people. Thus 'politeness' seems to have combined with professional self-interest to limit the ability of ordinary people to access the courts and animate the law in their favour.

The significance of the recession in litigation is clear: if litigation is regarded as a discourse of justice and access to government, a complex but semi-structured conversation among all sorts of people about enforcing the right ordering of society, then those at the margins of English society were progressively silenced and disempowered. Plebeian women and men tended to lose individual agency and cultural influence in courts as suits became the preserve of business, professional and propertied elites. Indeed, the culture of litigation came to reflect closely the unequal balance of power in gender relations, as well as in wealth and status. For even in those jurisdictions where women had been able to evade the neutralizing effect of the rule of coverture, such as in equity and the ecclesiastical courts, by 1800 there was a return to outcomes which were essentially patriarchal, in so far as they tended to severely limit the power and autonomy of wives in the control of property and maintenance of reputation. Ironically, the business of 'going to law' was therefore rendered less fully representative of English society in the Age of Enlightenment; here, as in some other spheres of government, the extent of popular consent for its acts diminished.

Writing in April 1726, in the aftermath of the Atterbury Plot, the author of a newspaper editorial supporting the government suggested the people could no longer be trusted with a major role in state trials, for

> whoever considers the Nature of Juries, the Persons of whom they usually consist, the unhappy Prejudices by which they are too often misled, and their notorious Conduct in some late Instances, will think it dangerous to trust to them the Determination of Things, on whose Issue the Safety of the Constitution manifestly depends.[1]

Certainly, in the administration of criminal justice, as well as civil litigation, there is considerable evidence in the eighteenth century of elite distaste for popular participation and agency in government. And crucially, it is possible to identify the development of polite anxiety about popular cultures with the growth of a diffused 'public opinion' grounded upon newspaper reports of crime waves and commentaries which generated moral panics about the potential criminality of the common people. Admittedly, in the first half of the century the frequent publication of individualized 'last dying stories' which showed how convicts acknowledged they had taken a wrong moral turn suggested the people were not regarded as collectively incorrigible.[2]

Moreover the popularity of exemplary terror solutions and parliament's readiness to attach the penalty of public hanging to statutes intended to deal with property theft reveals an abiding expectation that ordinary people should signal consent to principal acts of punishment by their physical presence. Yet there was increasing public unease that the crowds who attended hangings were not playing their part in upholding the majesty of the law. Indeed the late eighteenth-century English penal reformers who followed in the wake of Beccaria wanted to refashion popular culture according to the mores of the rising middle classes, principally through the instrument of the penitentiary. Of course the idea of correcting the feckless habits of the poor by an institutionalized disciplinary regimen was hardly new: as Beattie has shown, penal 'reform' was not invented after 1750.[3] Nevertheless, given the newspapers' interest in crime and widespread canvassing of reforming options, the progressive realization of such schemes at the hands of several local authorities from the 1780s represents an important development in governance. Perhaps for the first time we can clearly identify genuine 'public policy', in the form of official plans for public advantage that were informed, for better or worse, by the identification and discussion of problems via the print media.[4]

If the penitentiary was one emerging instrument of what might legitimately be called a late-Georgian law and order policy, another was a new form of policing. Admittedly, the idea and achievement of the new police developed very gradually and unevenly, and the process was largely organic in its early stages. In London from the seventeenth century there was a trend at the grassroots towards career policemen in the form of semi-professionals who served as substitutes for citizens who wished to avoid taking their turn as constables and watchmen. But after 1700 rising public anxiety about urban crime encouraged metropolitan authorities consciously to accelerate this process by providing bodies of paid watchmen, and these forces were frequently institutionalized by local acts of parliament which empowered parishes or named commissioners to raise rates for the purpose. Officers were sometimes concentrated for crowd control, and from early in the century there were moves towards centralization in the form of police offices with attendant patrols. The central government acted in advance of opinion when it tried to establish a metropolitan-wide police establishment in 1785, and in the early nineteenth century there was also resistance to government-inspired reformed policing in the countryside. But a network of police offices under stipendiary magistrates was established in London by the Middlesex Justice Act of 1792, and the government's legislative initiatives clearly established the new principles of policing: surveillance and regulation of the urban poor by paid officers who were directly accountable to stipendiary magistrates or commissioners. As contemporaries recognized, these ideas represented major adjustments to the idea and experience of government under the law. Ultimately they reflected the sense of respectable people that the metropolitan poor were morally irredeemable, and only constant police vigilance on the streets could contain crime to bearable proportions.[5]

Other significant shifts in the administration of justice were connected with the moral panics about crime. Common law tradition had provided that individual victims, rather than the state, made the crucial decision about prosecuting ordinary crimes. Like trial by jury, and public punishment, this was one of the ways by which members of the community participated in and consented to the execution of justice by law. However, faced with unprecedented public concern, after 1714 governments attempted to make prosecution of criminal offences more probable by legislating financial incentives to victims, and (in London especially) officials intervened decisively to achieve more certainty in the results, both by formalizing public pre-trial committal hearings and by employing prosecuting counsel in sensitive cases. In the event the intervention of lawyers for the prosecution seems to have led to the judges allowing counsel to appear for the defence, and the gradual incursion of professional advocates ultimately transformed the criminal trial by making it a much more formal and structured affair, rather than an altercation between victim and accused. Indeed the creeping semi-professionalization of proceedings had important consequences: there was certainly less scope for discretionary decision-making by victims; and lay voices in court were partially silenced and disempowered as the lawyers imposed their own culture. Here again, government was self-consciously distancing itself from vernacular justice.

Above all, pamphlet discussions of the eighteenth-century crime and disorder social 'problem' reveal an enduring public expectation that parliament should develop legislative solutions. It is true that demonstrations of parliament's absolute sovereignty provoked surprise and unease in the early part of the century, and later occasioned full-scale rebellion among the more traditionally-minded American colonists. But in England the debates over the American crisis showed that after nearly a century of legislative experience the doctrine of unlimited parliamentary sovereignty had taken root among members of the governing elite. Statutory intervention, indeed, was a growing culture of positive government which challenged and ultimately supplanted older expectations about citizenship and *active* consent for the rule of law derived from popular participation in juridical processes and the cultural legacy of the common law. Although specific or local statutes were predominant among parliament's output, there were many general acts of parliament which may be categorized broadly as 'social policy' measures because of their attention to issues involving the poor and their regulation. Also a growing body of general legislation was dedicated to the promotion of economic activity by protecting commercial and industrial property with severe penal sanctions against appropriation. And of course there were several general acts which overturned popular apprehensions of the law relating to master and servant and markets. However in enclosure, as well as in poor law administration, urban development and the improvement of communications, eighteenth-century legislative practice normally favoured specific acts; especially the creation of piecemeal statutory instruments which empowered local elites, not excluding interested parties. This was particularist law-making. Typically under these measures commissioners, guardians or trustees were given powers of compulsion that offended against customary ideas about law, liberty and property. In all these areas too, and despite the enduring attraction of public displays of terror for the deterrence of crime, enlightened 'experts' normally preferred administration by paid professionals rather than continuing participation by parish officers representing their communities. The proponents of these schemes took it for granted that this kind of authority was appropriately rational for an enlightened age.

Parliament's positive commands therefore frequently created semi-autonomous zones where individual interests had wide powers of social ordering: in these cases it may be argued that the law had effectively been privatized, as well as particularized.[6] Certainly, in the eighteenth century the modern idea that parliamentary representation conferred the mantle of popular consent on all legislation was current; and perhaps this convenient fiction of government by the people may be regarded as a vestige of the demotic culture associated with the common law.[7] In reality representation was very limited, however: the electoral franchise was confined to a small fraction of the population, and parliament intervened on several occasions to restrict unwanted popular participation. Moreover the London-based parliamentary elite seem to have become increasingly detached from the cultures and preoccupations of humbler people. It is true that there was widespread involvement in petitioning parliament from the 1780s, and the multiplying committees of inquiry into government and broad social and economic issues routinely summoned witnesses. Also, after a struggle in the 1770s the right of newspapers to report debates was conceded, albeit grudgingly, and from 1769 there was a general increase in the publication of parliamentary papers and records of proceedings. But while these shifts seem to have enhanced public participation in issues of national politics, the evidence of legislative proceedings in those specific measures which formed the great majority of acts suggests that ordinary people were effectively denied access and agency. Certainly they had little chance of resisting unpalatable or oppressive measures. In these cases the private interests of wealthy and powerful stakeholders drove the process of law-making.

At the end of the eighteenth century, then, the institutions and processes of government in England, which had previously been dominated by common law forms and broadly judicial cultures, appear to have been much less accessible and intelligible than they had been a hundred years previously.

Moreover, despite some famous cases in the 1770s and 1790s where ministries were humbled in their actions against individuals, the exercise of legal authority was hardly generally power-constraining or quasi-egalitarian, given the emphasis on statute as an instrument which empowered property-owners, above all. It is hardly a coincidence that around this time Adam Smith declared:

> Laws and government may be considered … in every case as a combination of the rich to oppress the poor, and preserve to themselves the inequality of the goods which would otherwise soon be destroyed by the attacks of the poor …[8]

Indeed, despite the limited attempts to ensure the promulgation of new acts, at a time when a combination of legislative hyperactivity and litigious exclusivity rendered the law especially protean, distant and potentially oppressive, the common people found themselves rendered principally as merely the objects of law. In regard to the substance of new acts they were effectively the dependents of the legislators, being at the mercy of their goodwill, and in relation to the power of magistrates they were equally subject to the discretion of their betters. In other words, the working arrangements for government hardly conformed to contemporary expectations or official rhetoric about the libertarian character of the rule of law. With the passing of government by 'juridical forms' the kind of consent which depended on direct participation passed into oblivion. Many examples have already been given, but one more general point may be adduced. As Anthony Musson has shown in relation to labour law, under arrangements for government which were dominated by judicial processes and institutions even wholly statutory innovations were controlled by the courts, with the result that 'the law continued to receive definition from below'.[9] This was much less so in the eighteenth century, as proliferating statutory authorities were effectively insulated from the courts, or simply left alone by judges whose government-centred perspectives privileged the national interest. Overall, then, there are good grounds for suggesting that the prevailing cultures of governance tended towards a system of command, rather than consent. If this was so, what were the implications for relations between society and state, and where did 'the law' sit as ideology and culture, as the eighteenth century gave way to the nineteenth?

## The new 'empire of laws'?[10] Law, state and society in an age of empire and opinion

I have suggested that increasing middling consciousness of respectability and sensitivity to the perceived moral failings of the common people was one of the mainsprings of a process which progressively marginalized them from institutions of government and deployed penal law to 'correct' their behaviour. To be clear, I am not arguing for the birth of class, in the Marxian sociological sense, in mid-eighteenth-century England. In the provincial cities, towns and villages and of Georgian England, farmers and husbandmen, masters, journeymen and labourers lived in close proximity, and shared many cultural pursuits.[11] Yet I think it is possible to identify the rise of a virtual community of bourgeois respectability, constituted above all by the newspapers, pamphlets and novels of the eighteenth-century press, in the form of a growing discourse by which these middling people defined their moral and cultural values against what they regarded as the polluting influence of the commonality, as they imagined it to be in London particularly. Given a fresh 'law and order' gloss, the rule of law became a central pillar of this socially defensive public opinion, at the same time as it continued to inspire rhetorical declamations about birthrights. Indeed, conservative opinion of this kind became a mainstay of government, and of course it was massively reinforced by the experience of the French Revolution.

So by contrast with early modern conditions, in these circumstances the state was regarded as merely representative of 'the public', and institutionally separate, while consent for the law was associated primarily with the parliamentary franchise – even among radicals, who wanted to extend it.[12] For conservatives, law became an instrument for enforcing order and development, rather than a shared culture of rights and positive liberty. The emphasis on order was most apparent in the 1790s and the aftermath of the Napoleonic Wars, when repressive Tory legislation severely restricted participation in popular politics, to the extent that majority of the people were legally excluded from positive rights of free speech and assembly. Tories insisted unashamedly that rights of active citizenship did not extend beyond the parliamentary electorate.[13] Even the early nineteenth-century Whigs who passed the Great Reform Act were inspired by a desire to contain popular participation in government.[14] Among the propertied elites, whiggish ideas about liberty were in full retreat: for Robert Peel 'true liberty' was freedom from criminal interference with life and property, an idea with strong appeals for the emerging middle class.[15] Indeed, Gatrell has suggested that with increasing fear of the urban working classes, parliamentarians and public opinion were united in no longer perceiving the state as a potential threat to liberty. Rather they cleaved to the state as the bastion of order against the undisciplined and undeserving plebeians and as a positive source of opportunity for propertied people like themselves.[16]

Certainly by the 1780s at least the tenor of magistrates' and judges' charges was shifting from an earlier emphasis on the consensual nature of government and law to a greater stress on order and obedience to the state, in the context of alarm about the London mob and supposedly endemic criminality.[17] As late as 1780 Sir John Hawkins, addressing a metropolitan grand jury, was still able to declare 'although in common Speech we are frequently led to say, that the Laws are the King's Laws, ... yet are the Laws no less the Laws of the People than of the King'. But he also complained about the increasing prevalence of theft, claiming hyperbolically that in the environs of London 'scarce any one ... be his Condition ever so low, can call any Thing his own', and offering this as a demonstration 'of the increasing Depravity of the Times, and of the little Regard paid by the common People to the Laws of God'.[18] A decade later, after the shock of the terror in France, Sir William Ashurst outlined a much more positivist vision of the rule of law. He insisted on the necessity for 'general rules laid down by the governing power of the State' and dwelled on the importance of a 'coercive power ... to enforce the laws and rules of action as the wisdom of the State has thought fit to prescribe'. He also deplored the existence of 'men of dark and gloomy hearts, who would wish to overturn the general fabric of our Constitution'. His charge was duly printed in a broadsheet by order of the Society for Preserving Liberty and Property against Republicans and Levellers, and recommended to readers because it 'breathes so much the SPIRIT of the ENGLISH LAW, and is so well suited to CURB the LICENTIOUS SPIRIT of the TIMES'.[19] Indeed the judges were now broadcasting law as the state's prescribed antidote to modern liberal heresies. In 1796 Sir Nash Grose echoed Prime Minister Pitt and the bishop of Rochester when he told the grand jury of Hertford that the laws were intended primarily 'to preserve entire the Government of the country, as it has been constituted by our ancestors'. From Grose's point of view, rather than recognizing community values, laws and government simply informed 'the minds and morals' of the people below; so virtue consisted in obedience, and freedom was merely its reward.[20]

Ashurst and Grose were judges of the court of King's Bench and formerly practising barristers. But where did the lawyers generally stand in relation to the growth of parliamentary law and positive governance? While common law judges like Hardwicke and Blackstone did not welcome legislative activism, and lawyers normally thought of legal development as a continuous organic process, Michael Lobban has shown that the leading jurists of the period had a positivist conception of law which emphasized the sovereign as the source of legal authority.[21] Moreover, Douglas Hay's work suggests that *pace* Blackstone, by the turn of the century the 'high law' of Westminster Hall had conceded the virtual autonomy of magistrates in summary proceedings authorized by statute. The judges who made the crucial decisions were clearly acting in the interests of government, rather than justice, and there are good evidential grounds for doubting the famed independence of the eighteenth-century judiciary, because many judges were effectively lawyer-politicians, and some of the most senior ones behaved like ministers.[22] Perhaps it was no coincidence that the private law which was the bread and butter of barristers in Westminster Hall was largely left alone by parliament in the eighteenth century. Certainly, as Lobban points out, 'the growth of the regulatory legislation of the fiscal – military state did not elicit much of a legal response', in terms of remedies against the acts of officials.[23] It is interesting that the English bar elite survived and prospered in the eighteenth century, despite the dearth of litigation, and plausible to posit a Faustian pact between the leaders of the profession and the Westminster political class, especially since so many leading barristers were MPs and government placemen. By contrast with their sixteenth and seventeenth-century predecessors, these lawyers hardly claimed that the common law represented popular consent for government. On the contrary, it is clear that around 1800 barristers evinced a mindset of social superiority which closely mirrored their relatively exclusive clientele. Conduct manuals enjoined them to administer the laws so as to encourage respect for the constitution, therefore weaning the common people away from chimerical ideas about freedom of government engendered by 'the present spirit of liberty'.[24] Indeed radical barristers were in short supply at a time when promotion was so strongly influenced by politics, and whiggish constitutionalists like Lord Camden, who outlawed general warrants and spoke up for limits on the power of legislation, were a rarity on the judicial bench.[25] In 1792 Camden warned parliament that judges were highly susceptible to the influence of government, when it came to adjudicating cases of seditious libel.[26] It is tempting to conclude that the elite of the legal profession – the senior judges and law officers – had been assimilated to a culture of governance that identified law with the will of parliament, and preserved only a limited role for popular rights and participation.

It is true that 'the rule of law' survived beyond the eighteenth century, and of course its continued existence operated as a limiting factor on government, in so far as it guaranteed at least a minimum of popular consent for public policy, and some adherence to process and formalities.[27] Indeed the culture of common law was amenable to the pressure of public opinion, and in this context the courts were capable of extending civil liberties. For example Lord Mansfield's famous ruling in the case of the slave Somerset (1771) has been interpreted as a significant step in 'the emergence of a new English concept of freedom', in so far as it guaranteed a minimum level of protection from force for anyone living in England.[28] But the rule of law endured into the nineteenth century principally as one feature of a vaguely libertarian constitutionalist ideology, rather than in the form of a traditional juristic culture of active citizenship which animated and empowered large numbers of ordinary people.[29] The courts continued to be moved in the *name* of the people and their rights to law, but this was normally a severely attenuated conversation, which hardly involved plebeian voices. Certainly some of the middle-class radicals who were prosecuted for seditious libel in the 1810s used the theatre of the courtroom to appeal to the jury and the reading public, but their regular discourse was a grand narrative woven around iconic English constitutional landmarks, such as Magna Charta and the Bill of Rights, and the travails of seventeenth-century heroes like Hampden, Lilburne, Sidney and Russell. This was a story which was articulated to justify freedom of the press and enhanced political participation, and it hardly touched the law of the courts. On the contrary, courts and lawyers were normally distrusted by radicals because of their supposed servility to judges and deference to lawyerly culture, and they paid little attention to detailed case law when arguing their cases.[30] The printer Thomas Wooler, tried in 1817, was typical in his excoriation of 'learned' legal culture, which he compared with his own method of open reasoning, that did not depend on 'low artifice or petty cavil'.[31] Most of his fellows referred to law in what they regarded as a higher, less garbled strain. Thus according to William Cobbett, the radical version of the English constitutional tradition meant simply that 'the Laws of England and the Rights and Liberties secured thereby are *the birthright of the people*', and constitutional history therefore justified extension of the franchise.[32] However the evidence of this book suggests the practical implications of this ideal – that relatively humble individuals could access, animate and inform the law in the pursuit of their quotidian affairs – had a sharply diminishing general application to Everyman and Everywoman. They would have been even less recognizable at the frontier of British colonialism, where the rule of law was used to justify the violent imposition of order and the exploitation of indigenous people.[33] Of course this was an extreme case, but there is no doubt that around 1800 the conditions of law and government in England were converging with the consolidated elite's broadly 'imperial' and 'respectable' imperatives for order and development. Correspondingly, despite enduring official rhetoric and popular expectation, one suspects that the individual experience of law had little connection with patriotic ideas about the Englishman's birthrights. But this is a question for further research.

It has been the argument of this book that the law and governance became more exclusive and positivist in the eighteenth century. But it is important to emphasize again the point that there was a relatively new form of participation in 'law' matters, one that involved the construction of opinion through the proliferating consumption of print media. In 1743 the *Old England Journal*, an opposition newspaper, commended the freedom of the press because

> The *executive* power of the Government here, being absolutely independant [sic] of the people in every sense, and the *legislative* power being but partially and mediately dependant [sic] on them, the people of *England* without the *Liberty of the Press* to inform them of the *Fitness* and *Unfitness* of measures, approv'd or condemn'd by those whom they have *trusted*, and

*whom they may trust again*, would be in a blind state of subjection, as if they lived under the most arbitrary and inquisitorial Government.[34]

Certainly with the proliferation of print media, news and comment about trials and punishments became a staple of public attention, just as reports of parliamentary proceedings did. The Somerset *cause celebré* is a prime case in point.[35] However, as the evidence of moral panics about street crime shows, it is by no means sufficient to characterize the growing consumption of all sorts of commentary about 'law' matters in wholly positive terms.[36] For example, in addition to sensational reports of robberies and murders, there was plenty of titillating reportage about sex, marriage and divorce. As Lawrence Stone has shown, by the second half of the eighteenth century trials for adultery – actions for 'criminal conversation' in the court of King's Bench and for separation in the church courts – furnished the material for a mass of prurient accounts, some of which were collected in multi-volume editions.[37] Indeed, the growth of a consumer society produced a different culture of popular involvement in law and governance, one that depended on imagination and vicarious association through the consumption of printed matter, rather than active participation. In the present state of research the implications of this peculiarly modern culture are not clear.[38] While the regular generation of moral panics suggests the growth of the public sphere generated irrational outcomes, a convergence towards public pessimism about society, and considerable scope for manipulation of the public in the cause of 'law and order'; by contrast it is usually argued that the press provided opportunities for constructive public engagement in the 'reform' of law and the institutions of government.[39] It will be necessary to write another book to explore the social and cultural implications of what appears to have been a transition from direct participation in legal proceedings to a more mediated experience of law.

# Notes

## Chapter 1   Introduction: Law, Consent and Command

1. *The Parliamentary History of England*, xiv. 20.
2. *Charges to the Grand Jury*, ed. G. Lamoine (Camden Soc., 4th ser., 43, 1992), 380: charge of 9 Sept., 1767.
3. Compare Skinner's explication of English neo-Roman ideas about liberty in a free state (Q. Skinner, *Liberty before Liberalism* (Cambridge, 1998), chs. 1–2).
4. D. Hay, 'Property, Authority and the Criminal Law', in D. Hay et al (eds.) *Albion's Fatal Tree: Crime and Society in Eighteenth-Century England* (Harmondsworth, 1975), 58–9.
5. See D. Lemmings, 'Introduction', in D. Lemmings (ed.) *The British and Their Laws in the Eighteenth Century* (Woodbridge, 2005), 3–12.
6. For the broad thinking behind this approach, see J. Rawls, *A Theory of Justice* (Cambridge, MA, 1971), esp. 238, 313.
7. E. Bohun, *The Justice of Peace, his Calling and Qualifications* (1693), 74.
8. M. Shelton, *A Charge Given to the Grand-Jury, at the General Quarter-Sessions of the Peace, holden at St. Edmund's-Bury for the Liberty thereof, in the County of Suffolk: on the 19th of January, An. Dom. 1729/30* (1730), 28.
9. W. Bulstrode, *The Charge of Whitlocke Bulstrode, Esq; to the Grand Jury, and other Juries, of the County of Middlesex. At the General Quarter Sessions of the Peace, held, April 21st, 1718* (1718), 2–3.
10. See, e.g. T.R.S. Allan, *Law, Liberty and Justice: The Legal Foundations of British Constitutionalism* (Oxford, 1993), ch. 2.
11. Anon., *The History of the Late Great Revolution in England and Scotland* (1690), 3.
12. See e.g. T.B. Macaulay, *The History of England from the Accession of James II* (1906), ii. 213; G.M. Trevelyan, *The English Revolution 1688–1689* (1938), 16–19, 187, 201–3.
13. E.S. Morgan, *Inventing the People: The Rise of Popular Sovereignty in England and America* (New York, 1988), 45–6, 51–2; J.G.A. Pocock, *The Ancient Constitution and the Feudal Law: A Study of English Historical Thought in the Seventeenth Century* (Cambridge, 2nd edn., 1987), 49–50.
14. H. Nenner, *By Colour of Law: Legal Culture and Constitutional Politics in England, 1660–1689* (Chicago, 1977), xix; below, chap. 5.
15. E. Coke, *The Fourth Part of the Institutes of the Laws of England* (1644), 36 ('Of the power and jurisdiction of the Parliament for making of laws in proceeding by Bill, it is so transcendent and absolute, as it cannot be confined …').
16. C. Holmes, 'The Legal Instruments of Power and the State in Early Modern England', in A. Padoa-Schioppa (ed.) *Legislation and Justice* (Oxford, 1997), 285. I am not casting doubt on Clive Holmes's demonstration that the late seventeenth-century middling sort in the fenland villages of eastern England accepted the legitimacy of parliamentary statute. The point is rather that statutes were exceptional, and 'the law' was normally identified with judicial processes. See C. Holmes, 'Drainers and Fenmen: The Problem of Popular Consciousness in the Seventeenth Century', in A. Fletcher and J. Stevenson (eds.) *Order and Disorder in Early Modern England* (Cambridge, 1985), 166–95.

17 Cf. J. Brewer and J. Styles, 'Introduction', in J. Brewer and J. Styles (eds.) *An Ungovernable People: The English and Their Law in the Seventeenth and Eighteenth Centuries* (1980), 13–14.
18 See chap. 2 below, esp. sect. i. The phrase is Keith Wrightson's ('The Politics of the Parish in Early Modern England', in P. Griffiths, A. Fox and S. Hindle (eds.) *The Experience of Authority in Early Modern England* (Basingstoke, 1996: 12). For the scope of office-holding see M. Goldie, 'The Unacknowledged Republic', in T. Harris (ed.) *The Politics of the Excluded, c.1500–1850* (Basingstoke, 2001), who estimates that around 1700 a twentieth of the adult male population held parish office, and if the offices rotated as they were intended to then over a decade up to half might hold such office. In addition thousands each year served as jurors at the assizes and quarter sessions (161–2).
19 J. Sharpe, 'The People and the Law', in B. Reay (ed.) *Popular Culture in Seventeenth-Century England* (1985), 256.
20 For an interesting demonstration of 'communal ethics' informing judicial decisions in the context of medieval coroners' courts see S.M. Butler, 'Degrees of Culpability: Suicide Verdicts, Mercy, and the Jury in Medieval England', *Journal of Medieval and Early Modern Studies*, 36 (2006), 263–90.
21 G. Walker, *Crime, Gender and Social Order in Early Modern England* (Cambridge, 2003), 221–49. See also the work of Andy Wood, who has shown that early modern free miners developed particular ideas about liberties and rights through participation in their own customary courts and interactions with common law (A. Wood, 'Custom, Identity and Resistance: English Free Miners and their Law, *c*.1550–1800', in Griffiths et al (eds.) *The Experience of Authority*, 249–85; id, *The Politics of Social Conflict: The Peak Country 1520–1770* (Cambridge, 1999), esp. chs. 6–7).
22 See Allan, *Law, Liberty and Justice*, esp. 24–33; F.A. Hayek, *Law, Legislation and Liberty* (1982), chs. 4–5, 8.
23 C.W. Brooks, *Law, Politics and Society in Early Modern England* (Cambridge, 2008), 249, 277.
24 Brewer and Styles, 'Introduction', in *An Ungovernable People*, 16–17; A.J. Fletcher and J. Stevenson, 'Introduction', in *Order and Disorder*, 15–16. Of course there is also considerable evidence of crowds enforcing what they saw as the legal establishment at times of stress (see e.g. T. Harris, 'The People, the Law, and the Constitution in Scotland and England: A Comparative Approach to the Glorious Revolution', *Journal of British Studies*, 38 (1999), 31–7).
25 R. Shoemaker, *The London Mob: Violence and Disorder in Eighteenth-Century England* (2004), 113–33.
26 *The Newcastle Gazette*, 4 Oct., 1749.
27 Shoemaker, *London Mob*, 132. See also *A Foreign View of the Reigns of George I and George II: The Letters of Monsieur César de Saussere to his Family*, ed. Madame Van Muyden (1902), 130. See also M. Ingram, '"Scolding Women Cucked or Washed": A Crisis in Gender Relations in Early Modern England', in J. Kermode and G. Walker (eds.) *Women, Crime and the Courts in Early Modern England* (1994), 58–9.
28 E.g. *Newcastle Gazette*, 29 June 1748, 4 Oct., 1749, 29 Nov., 1749, 13 Dec., 1749, 13 Mar., 1751. Shoemaker, *London Mob*, 131–2.
29 G. Holmes, 'The Sacheverell Riots: The Crowd and the Church in Early Eighteenth-Century London', *Past and Present*, 72 (1976), 73–8, 84; N. Rogers, 'Popular Protest in Early Hanoverian London', *Past and Present*, 79 (1978), 84–7; G. Rudé, *Paris and London in the Eighteenth Century* (1952), 21, 28–9, 261–2, 298–302.

30 Brewer and Styles, 'Introduction', in *Ungovernable People*, 17; Fletcher and Stevenson, 'Introduction', in *Order and Disorder*, 20; E.P. Thompson, *Customs in Common* (Harmondsworth, 1993), 188, 209, 223. See, also for example, Herts. CRO, Panshanger, MSS., D/EP F150, ff. 5–6, Sir Edward Ward and Thomas Bury [judges] to Lord Chancellor Cowper, Taunton, 21 Mar., 1706: 'The Corporation here seem to befriend and Assist the Weavers, and give them some Colour of Assembling and Acting by themselves under pretence of some Instrument under their Commin Seale' (i.e. complaining of the Corporation's failure to support prosecutions against riots by local weavers).

31 S. Hindle, *The State and Social Change in Early Modern England* (Basingstoke, 2000), 15–16, 23–34; M.J. Braddick, *State Formation in Early Modern England, c. 1550–1700* (Cambridge, 2000), 162.

32 Hindle, *State and Social Change*, 89.

33 J. Brewer, *The Sinews of Power: War, Money and the English State, 1688–1783* (1989), 64.

34 The Crown's power to impress men for naval service rested on immemorial usage, but the Mutiny Act of 1705 provided for capital convicts to be enlisted in the army on condition of pardon, and from 1704 magistrates were empowered to conscript able-bodied men for the army if they appeared to be unemployed (2 & 3 Anne, c. 19; 4 Anne, c. 10).

35 Brewer, *Sinews of Power*, 83, 85, 101–14, 214–15.

36 'Short and plain REASONS against a General Excise', *Newcastle Gazette*, 11 Dec., 1751 (possibly paraphrasing C. Danvers, *The Second Part of an Argument against Excises; in Answer to the Objections of Several Writers* (1733), 19).

37 In the country justices of the peace heard excise cases. For examples of the forms used by JPs *temp*. George III, see Cornwall RO, MS. FS2/76: magistrates' book of precedents and forms, Penzance.

38 W. Blackstone, *Commentaries on the Laws of England* (Oxford, 1765–9), iv. 278.

39 D. Hay, 'Legislation, Magistrates, and Judges: High Law and Low Law in England and the Empire', in Lemmings (ed.) *The British and their Laws*, 72. See also P. King, 'The Summary Courts and Social Relations in Eighteenth-Century England', *Past and Present*, 183 (2004), 125–69. Although there is much of value in King's article, I find his aggregation of so many different magisterial functions and general use of the term 'summary courts' problematic.

40 King, 'Summary Courts', 131–4.

41 *Commentaries*, iii. 81–3, iv. 277–80. Lord Chief Justice Holt held similar objections (F. Dabhoiwala, 'Summary Justice in Early Modern London', *English Historical Review*, 121 (2006), 797).

42 D. Lemmings, 'Blackstone and Law Reform by Education: Preparation for the Bar and Lawyerly Culture in Eighteenth-Century England', *Law and History Review*, 16 (1998), esp. 214–15, 221–2, 230–1, 249–50; id, *Professors of the Law: Barristers and English Legal Culture in the Eighteenth Century* (Oxford, 2000), 321–3.

43 *The Parliamentary History of England*, xv. 725–6.

44 *Commentaries*, i. 10–11. See also D. Lieberman, *The Province of Legislation Determined* (Cambridge, 1989), ch. 2.

45 J. Innes, 'Parliament and the Shaping of Eighteenth-Century English Social Policy', *Transactions of the Royal Historical Soc.*, 5th ser., 40 (1990), 63–92.

46 J. Hoppit, 'Patterns of Parliamentary Legislation 1660–1800', *Historical Journal*, 39 (1996), 116–18; P. Langford, *Public Life and the Propertied Englishman* (Oxford, 1991), 175. See also J. Innes, 'The Local Acts of a National Parliament: Parliament's Role in

Sanctioning Local Action in Eighteenth-Century Britain', in D. Dean and C. Jones (eds.) *Parliament and Locality 1660–1939* (Edinburgh, 1998), 26–7, 39.
47  J. Innes, 'Politics, Property and the Middle Class', *Parliamentary History*, 11 (1992), 90–1.
48  E. Burke, 'Speech to the Electors of Bristol' (1774) in B.W. Hill (ed.) *Edmund Burke on Government Politics and Society* (1975), 156–8.
49  D. Eastwood, 'Parliament and Locality: Representation and Responsibility in Late-Hanoverian England', in Dean and Jones (ed.) *Parliament and Locality*, 68–75; Langford, *Public Life*, 188–90.
50  E. Burke, *Thoughts on the Present Discontents* (1770), in *The Writings and Speeches of Edmund Burke*, ed. P. Langford (Oxford, 1981), 295.
51  H.T. Dickinson, 'The Eighteenth-Century Debate on the Sovereignty of Parliament', *Transactions of the Royal Historical Society*, 5$^{th}$ ser., 26 (1976), esp. 199–200.
52  J. Brewer, 'The Eighteenth-Century British State: Contexts and Issues', in L. Stone (ed.) *An Imperial State at War: Britain from 1689 to 1815* (1994), 63–5. See below, ch. 5, sect. ii.
53  Innes, 'Politics, Property and the Middle Class', 291.
54  D. Eastwood, *Government and Community in the English Provinces, 1700–1870* (Basingstoke, 1997), 9.
55  See Lemmings, *Professors of the Law*, 328.
56  J. Innes, 'The Domestic Face of the Military-Fiscal State: Government and Society in Eighteenth-Century Britain', in Stone (ed.) *An Imperial State at War*, 97–101; J. Carter, 'Law, Courts and Constitution', in J.R. Jones (ed.) *The Restored Monarchy* (1979), 86, 90–1. Cf. J.S. Cockburn, *A History of English Assizes 1558–1714* (Cambridge, 1972), ch. 8.
57  I am using the term professional in a broad sense here to denote officers and others who performed specific services for payment, and make no judgement about standards of competence and training.
58  Hindle, *The State and Social Change*, esp. 29, 203, 204–7, 215–23.
59  See P.D. Halliday's comments in his useful review of Hindle, *State and Social Change* (*Law and History Review*, 20 (2002), 648).
60  Cf. Langford, *Public Life*; L. Davison et al (eds.) *Stilling the Grumbling Hive: the Response to Social and Economic Problems in England, 1689–1750* (Stroud, 1992), xxxi–xxxii.
61  L.E. Klein, *Shaftesbury and the Culture of Politeness: Moral Discourse and Cultural Politics in Early Eighteenth-Century England* (Cambridge, 1994), 21–2.
62  See J. Habermas, *The Structural Transformation of the Public Sphere*, trans. T. Burger (Cambridge, 1989); P. Langford, *A Polite and Commercial People: England, 1727–1783* (Oxford, 1989); P. Borsay, *The English Urban Renaissance: Culture and Society in the English Town, 1660–1760* (Oxford, 1989); R. Porter, *Enlightenment: Britain and the Creation of the Modern World* (Harmondsworth, 2000); P. Clark, *British Clubs and Societies 1580–1800: The Origins of an Associational World* (Oxford, 2000).
63  Klein, *Shaftesbury*, esp. 95–8, 206–12. See also idem, 'Politeness and the Interpretation of the British Eighteenth Century', *Historical Journal*, 45 (2002), 869–98.
64  P. Langford, 'Manners and the Eighteenth-Century State', in J. Brewer and E. Helmuth (eds.) *Rethinking Leviathan* (Oxford, 1999), pp. 289–90.
65  See below, chs. 3–4.
66  P. Fitzpatrick, *The Mythology of Modern Law* (1992), 62–4.
67  Ibid, 72–87.
68  C. Hanly, 'The Decline of the Civil Jury Trial in Nineteenth-Century England', *Journal of Legal History*, 26 (2005), esp. 259–66; below, pp. 120–5.

69  See below, ch. 5, sect. i; M. Ignatieff, *A Just Measure of Pain* (Harmondsworth, 1989), 75–8.
70  Fitzpatrick, *Mythology of Modern Law*, 89–91.
71  P. Stein, *Legal Evolution: The Story of an Idea* (Cambridge, 1980), 16, 35. See A. Smith, *Lectures on Jurisprudence*, ed. R.L. Meek, D.D. Raphael and P.G. Stein (Oxford, 1978), 205.
72  Stein, *Legal Evolution*, 26–9, 38, 48.
73  Lieberman, *Province of Legislation*, 154–8.
74  Ibid, 286–7.
75  E.g. *The Oxford History of the Laws of England*, ed. J.H. Baker.
76  R.M. Dworkin (ed.) *The Philosophy of Law* (Oxford, 1977), 2–3.
77  Ibid.
78  *English Liberty in some Cases worse than French Slavery, Exemplified by Animadversions upon the Tyrannical and anti-Constitutional Power of the Justices of the Peace, Commissioners of Excise, Customs, and Land-Tax, &c.* (1748), 55–6.

## Chapter 2   The Local Experience of Law and Authority: Quarter Sessions, JPs, and the People

1  G.V. Bennett, *The Tory Crisis in Church and State, 1688–1730: the Career of Francis Atterbury, Bishop of Rochester* (Oxford, 1975), 9, 14–15; W. Holdsworth, *A History of English Law* (1922–72), iv. 134; J.H. Baker, *An Introduction to English Legal History* (4th edn., 2002), 22–4; J.S. Cockburn, *A History of English Assizes* (Cambridge, 1972), 186–7.
2  See C. Russell, *Parliaments and English Politics, 1621–1629* (Oxford, 1979), 337.
3  See their commissions, as cited in every indictment (R. Burn, *The Justice of the Peace and Parish Officer* (2nd edn., 1756), ii. 29). I do not consider here the operation of those statutory bodies which were becoming an alternative face of eighteenth-century government in specific contexts: turnpike trusts, poor law corporations, and urban improvement commissions (See P. Langford, *Public Life and the Propertied Englishman* (Oxford, 1991), ch. 4). Some of their general characteristics are discussed in Ch. 5 below.
4  For the connections I am making between participation and consent see above, pp. 2, 5–6.
5  *English Liberty in Some Cases Worse than French Slavery* (1748), 55–6. This phrase was, presumably, adapted from Lambarde (see below, n. 22).
6  18 Ed. 3, st. 2, c.2; 34 Ed. 3, c. 1; 36 Ed.3, st 1, c. 12; Burn, *Justice* (2nd edn., 1756), ii. 30, 87. See also 2 Hen. 5, st. 1, c.4. For an outline of the early development of the office see A. Harding, *A Social History of English Law* (Harmondsworth, 1966), 68–73. Also J.R. Lander, *English Justices of the Peace 1461–1509* (Gloucester, 1989), ch. 1.
7  See e.g. Burn, *Justice* (2nd edn., 1756), ii. 79–80.
8  Blackstone bemoaned the decline of these medieval jurisdictions (W. Blackstone, *Commentaries on the Laws of England* (Oxford, 1765–9), iii. 82, iv. 278–9). Some leet courts remained vigorous into the seventeenth century, at least (W.J. King, 'Untapped Resources for Social Historians: Court Leet Records', *Journal of Social History*, 15 (1982), 699–705).
9  Cf. J.H. Baker, 'The Changing Concept of a Court', in idem, *The Legal Profession and the Common Law* (1986), esp. 156–65. For the attendance of constables see C. Fiennes, *The Journeys of Celia Fiennes*, ed. C. Morris (1947), 309; and for the

overseers see S. and B. Webb, *The Parish and the County* (1906), 31. Thus in July 1763 Thomas Turner and Thomas Carman, overseers for East Hoathly in Sussex, attended the quarter sessions at Lewes where they were concerned in two settlement trials (*The Diary of Thomas Turner 1754–1765*, ed. D. Vaisey (Oxford, 1985), 276–7).
10. Holdsworth, *History of English Law*, iv. 135–6.
11. See e.g. W. Hawkins, *Treatise of the Pleas of the Crown* (1721), ii. 209–10.
12. S. and B. Webb, *The Parish and the County* (1906), 306–8.
13. For expressions in the form of neo-Republican political theory, see M. Goldie, 'The Unacknowledged Republic: Officeholding in Early Modern England', in T. Harris (ed.) *The Politics of the Excluded, c.1500–1850* (Basingstoke, 2001), 179–80. Goldie argues that post-Renaissance theory re-conceptualized medieval practice (ibid, n. 180).
14. G. Lamoine, *Charges to the Grand Jury 1689–1803* (Camden soc. 43, 1992), 280 (orig. emphasis).
15. See Hawkins, *Pleas of the Crown*, i. 40; and forms of presentment in Burn, *Justice* (2nd edn., 1756), i. 571–2.
16. Lamoine, *Charges*, 478: charge of Henry Jodrell, Norfolk QS, 1793.
17. 2&3 Philip and Mary, c.8.
18. Chester RO, QJB 3/13, unpag.
19. Hawkins, *Pleas of the Crown*, ii. 35–6.
20. J.S. Morrill, *The Cheshire Grand Jury, 1625–1659* (Leicester, 1976), 18–19; C.B. Herrup, *The Common Peace: Participation and the Criminal Law in Seventeenth-Century England* (Cambridge, 1987), 100–1.
21. *Parliamentary History of England*, xix. 204: 29 Apr., 1777.
22. W. Lambarde, *Eirenarcha* (1581), 38.
23. K. Wrightson, 'Two Concepts of Order: Justices, Constables and Jurymen in Seventeenth-Century England', in J. Brewer and J. Styles (ed.) *An Ungovernable People: The English and their Law in the Seventeenth and Eighteenth Centuries* (1980), 26–32.
24. M. Ingram, 'Communities and Courts: Law and Disorder in Early-Seventeenth-Century Wiltshire', in J.S. Cockburn (ed.) *Crime in England 1550–1800* (1977), 133–4.
25. See A. Fletcher, *Reform in the Provinces: The Government of Stuart England* (New Haven, CT, 1986), ch. 4. Also, for a treatment that emphasizes the relative diligence and obedience of JPs in co-operating with central government, see A. Wall, *Power and Protest in England 1525–1640* (2000), esp. ch. 7.
26. Wrightson, 'Two Concepts', 33–7.
27. Fletcher, *Reform in the Provinces*, esp. 126–7.
28. Wrightson, 'Two Concepts', 43–4.
29. J. Kent, 'The English Village Constable, 1580–1642: The Nature and Dilemmas of the Office', *Journal of British Studies*, 20 (1981), esp. 27–30, 46; eadem, *The English Village Constable 1580–1642: A Social and Administrative Study* (Oxford, 1986), 14, 18, 21, 22–3. See also T. Curtis, 'Quarter Sessions Appearances and their Background: A Seventeenth-Century Regional Study', in J.S. Cockburn (ed.) *Crime in England 1550–1800* (1977), 140, 143, 144–6.
30. H. Langelüddecke, 'Law and Order in Seventeenth-century England: The Organization of Local Administration during the Personal Rule of Charles I', *Law and History Review*, 15 (1997), 76. Also 'the key problem with the Book of Orders was that JPs had wholly to entrust subordinate high constables and parish officers

of their division with its enforcement and that these men were even less willing (or able) to forward information' (H. Langelüddecke, '"Patchy and Spasmodic": The Response of Justices of the Peace to Charles I's Book of Orders', *English Historical Review*, 113 (1998), 1247). See also Wall, *Power and Protest*, p. 7: 'Compliance depended on JPs, but also on constables, overseers of the poor, and other lesser officials having the time an enthusiasm to attend to the issues'.
31  Essex Record Office, Q/SR 271/29 (online calendar).
32  Ingram, 'Communities and Courts', 132–3; K. Wrightson and D. Levine, *Poverty and Piety in an English Village: Terling, 1525–1700* (Oxford, 1995), 120.
33  Ingram, 'Communities and Courts', 130. See also Wrightson and Levine, *Terling*, 120.
34  Hawkins, *Pleas of the Crown*, i. 126–33; Burn, *Justice* (2nd edn., 1756), 466–93; S. Hindle, 'The Keeping of the Public Peace', in P. Griffiths, A. Fox and S. Hindle, *The Experience of Authority in Early Modern England* (Basingstoke, 1996), 218–22; R. Shoemaker, *Prosecution and Punishment: Petty Crime and the Law in London and Rural Middlesex, c.1660–1725* (Cambridge, 1991), 103–4.
35  Hindle, 'Public Peace', 224–5; Fletcher, *Reform*, 81; Wrightson and Levine, *Terling*, 122. See also J. Sharp, 'The People and the Law', in B. Reay (ed.) *Popular Culture in Seventeenth-Century England* (1985), 254.
36  Hindle, 'Public Peace', 225; Sharp, 'People and the Law', 254; Ingram, 'Communities and Courts', 116, n. 42.
37  The judges had ruled against discharging recognizances out of quarter sessions in the 1630s (N. Landau, *The Justices of the Peace, 1679–1760* (Berkeley, CA, 1984), 185–6). But the practice was not uncommon in Cheshire around 1600 (Hindle, 'Public Peace', 236).
38  See Burn, *Justice* (1755), ii. 387. Shoemaker provides several examples of hearings on recognizances (Shoemaker, *Prosecution and Punishment*, 111–13). There are also occasional references to individuals swearing the peace 'in open court' (e.g. J. Bailey, *Unquiet Lives: Marriage and Marriage Breakdown in England, 1660–1800* (Cambridge, 2003), 46).
39  Michael Dalton, author of the standard seventeenth-century manual for JPs, emphasized popular agency in the practice of binding over (Hindle, *State and Social Change*, 99–100).
40  For a convenient overview see Fletcher, *Reform in the Provinces*.
41  In addition to these broad categories, JPs also had a limited civil jurisdiction in adjudicating master and servant disputes, which was exercised summarily by individual JPs. See Holdsworth, *History of English Law*, iv. 139.
42  Besides the administrative studies of the Webbs (see especially *The Parish and the County*), and Holdsworth (*History of English Law*, x) the only substantial historical studies of the JPs for this period are E. Moir, *Local Government in Gloucestershire 1775–1800* (Gloucester, 1969); Landau, *Justices*; and D. Eastwood, *Governing Rural England: Tradition and Transformation in Local Government 1780–1840* (Oxford, 1994). There is also valuable information and insight in Langford, *Public Life*. See also D. Eastwood, *Government and Community in the English Provinces 1700–1870* (Basingstoke, 1997). By contrast with the seventeenth century, there is a dearth of county studies.
43  J. Rule, *The Vital Century: England's Developing Economy 1714–1815* (1992), 53, 106; H.C. Derby (ed.) *A New Historical Geography of England* (Cambridge, 1973), 166; C.B. Phillips and J.H. Smith, *Lancashire and Cheshire from AD 1540* (1994), chs. 2, 3. For the county administration and courts in the seventeenth

century see G. Walker, *Crime, Gender and Social Order in Early Modern England* (Cambridge, 2003), 13–18.
44  For Gloucestershire see Moir, *Local Government*, 45, 90, 110ff.
45  Landau, *Justices*, 240–1; Webbs, *Parish and County*, 425–33.
46  B.J. Davey, *Rural Crime in the Eighteenth Century: North Lincolnshire 1740–80* (Hull, 1994), xiv.
47  Chester RO, QJB 3/3, analysing sessions for 1678–1680.
48  Morrill, *Grand Jury*, 14; idem, *Cheshire 1630–1660: County Government and Society during the English Revolution* (Oxford, 1974), 9, 334.
49  Chester RO, QJB 3/8: sessions for 1729–31. See also Phillips and Smith, *Lancashire and Cheshire from AD 1540*, 118.
50  QJB 3/13: sessions for 1769–71; QJB 3/22, 3/23: sessions for 1816–18.
51  Landau, *Justices*, 263–4; Webbs, *Parish and County*, 429–33 and 480ff.
52  L. Glassey, 'Local Government', in C. Jones (ed.) *Britain in the First Age of Party: Essays Presented to Geoffrey Holmes* (1987), 160.
53  See e.g. their order of 13 July 1731, wherein they ordered the treasurers to pay the person or persons 'who shall take care of the Laying the Cushions Covering the Table & Sweeping and cleansing the Several Courts where the Quarter Sessions shall be held for this County' 5s at each sessions (QJB 3/8, unpag.).
54  Cf. Wrightson, 'Two Concepts of Order', 34, 300–3.
55  For estimated population totals see Phillips and Smith, *Lancashire and Cheshire from AD1540*, 66–70, 132–42.
56  For exemplification of inter-personal disputes in late seventeenth-century Cheshire, see T.C. Curtis, 'Quarter-Sessions Appearances and Their Background', in *Crime in England 1550–1800*, ed. Cockburn, esp. 135–43.
57  QJB 3/3: 12 Apr. 1680. See also P.B. Munsche, *Gentlemen and Poachers: The English Game Laws, 1671–1831* (Cambridge, 1971), 85–6.
58  The increase in grand larceny cases was part of a general trend across the country (J.M. Beattie, *Crime and the Courts in England, 1660–1800* (Oxford, 1986), 5, 220, 283–8, 309–11). A broadly similar pattern of declining attention to regulatory offences after 1700 and an increasing incidence of prosecutions for larceny towards the end of the century and after 1800 is apparent from the records of the Hertfordshire quarter sessions (*Hertfordshire County Records: Calendar to the Sessions Books*, ed. W. Le Hardy and G.L. Reckitt (Hertford, 1930–1939), vol. 7, p. xix, vol. 8, pp. xxxi–xxxii, 365–6, vol. 9, pp. xxviii, xxxi).
59  Davey, *Rural Crime*, 13–14, 22–4, 106, 109, 148.
60  Ibid, 148. The later eighteenth-century Salford (i.e. Manchester) quarter sessions bench was similarly preoccupied with property theft (G. Fisher, 'The Birth of the Prison Retold', *Yale Law Journal*, 104 (1995), esp. 1250–3).
61  Hindle, *State and Social Change*, esp. 97–100. See, e.g. S. Amussen, *An Ordered Society: Gender and Class in Early Modern England* (Oxford, 1988), 177–8; Landau, *Justices*, 245.
62  See Hindle, 'Public Peace', 224; Fletcher, *Reform*, 89–90; Landau, *Justices*, 187–8.
63  Shoemaker, *Prosecution and Punishment*, 231.
64  39 Eliz., c. 4.
65  Shoemaker, *Prosecution and Punishment*, 216.
66  See Chester RO, QJB 3/3. For 18th-century examples of JPs adjudicating marital disputes, see Bailey, *Unquiet Lives*, 38–46.
67  Landau, *Justices*, 245.

68 Beattie, *Crime and the Courts in England*, 138; id, 'Violence and Society in Early Modern England', in *Perspectives in Criminal Law*, eds. A.N. Doob and E.L. Greenspan (Aurora, Ontario, 1985), 36–60. See, more generally, N. Elias, *The Civilizing Process: Sociogenetic and Psychogenetic Investigation*, trans. E. Jephcott, revd. edn., ed. E. Dunning, J. Gousblom and S. Mennell (Oxford, 2000).

69 *The Justicing Notebook (1750–64) of Edmund Tew, Rector of Boldon* (Surtees Soc., 205, 2000), 16, 19, 33, 76, 92. For a full discussion, see G. Morgan and P. Rushton, 'The Magistrate, the Community and Maintenance of an Orderly Society in Eighteenth-Century England', *Historical Research*, 86 (2003), 54–77. Note also the e.g. of the Rev. Charles Coxwell JP in Gloucestershire, who prided himself on giving a patient hearing to all who came before him, admitted he was reluctant to implement the law in matters of petty crime, and signed his orders 'Minister & Magistrate' (Moir, *Local Government in Gloucestershire*, 126–7). By contrast, Eric Evans has argued that clerical magistrates tended to become distant from the poor, and by the early nineteenth century they were frequently reviled for hard heartedness (E.J. Evans, 'Some Reasons for the Growth of English Rural Anti-Clericalism, c.1750–c.1830', *Past and Present*, 66 (1975), 101–6). For the earlier clerical appointments see also C. Haigh and A. Wall, 'Clergy JPs in England and Wales, 1590–1640', *Historical Journal*, 47 (2004), 233–59.

70 In 1730 the lord mayor of London also settled the majority of assault cases which he heard (J.M. Beattie, *Policing and Punishment in London 1660–1750* (Oxford, 2001), 104–5). See also *The Justicing Notebook of William Hunt 1744–1749*, ed. E. Crittall (Wiltshire Rec. Soc., 37, 1981), 12–16. On 7 Dec. 1801 The Rev. Dr. Henry Yate granted a warrant in a case of assault 'with leave to settle the matter by mutual consent': Hereford CRO, BB88/1, examination book of Dr. Henry Yate, 1801–03 (complaint of Elizabeth Vaughan).

71 Shoemaker, *Prosecution and Punishment*, 42–3, 46; *Justicing Notebook of William Hunt 1744–1749*, 30.

72 Landau, *Justices*, 191–4; W. Paley, *The Law and Practice of Summary Convictions on Penal Statutes by Justices of the Peace* (1814), 73; 18 Geo. 3, c. 19.

73 In Kent at least petty sessions were not obviously very active in adjudicating criminal prosecutions (Landau, *Justices*, 222).

74 Munsche, *Gentlemen and Poachers*, 84–5, 87; Blackstone, *Commentaries*, iv. 175; sources cited in Table 2.1.

75 T. Skyrme, *History of the Justices of the Peace* (Chichester, 1991), ii. 122–3.

76 Cf. Moir, *Local Government in Gloucestershire*, 123–4.

77 Centre for Buckinghamshire Studies, Aylesbury, MS. DC 18/39/5: Diary of Edmund Waller, f. 8. I am grateful to Mr. Roger Bettridge, Buckinghamshire county archivist, for allowing me to examine his transcript of this document.

78 See Landau, *Justices of the Peace*, 343–4; Blackstone, *Commentaries*, iv. 277–9, 343–4. Cf. contemporary comment on the summary proceedings that applied to offences under the excise laws: 'the Method of Trial, in these Cases, is too much like the summary Progress [sic] of an *Inquisition*, a *Star-Chamber*, or a *Court-Martial*, and seems to be copied from Them' (*Newcastle Gazette*, 11 Dec. 1751).

79 W. Eden, *Principles of Penal Law* (1771), 58–9, n. For the Game Act see 10 Geo, 3, c. 19.

80 B.P. Smith, 'The Presumption of Guilt and the English Law of Theft, 1750–1850', *Law and History Review*, 23 (2005), 133–71.

81 See however, Peter King's analysis of summary proceedings in Essex, which reveals a different pattern of magisterial activity (P. King, 'The Summary Courts and

Social Relations in Eighteenth-Century England', *Past and Present*, 183 (2004), 142–3).
82  Wiltshire and Swindon Archives, 383/955, unpag.: justicing notebook of Richard Colt Hoare, 1785–1815.
83  Wilts. and Swindon Archives, A1260: summary convictions, 1698–1820.
84  Landau, *Justices*, 198–9; Brewer, *Sinews of Power*, 114.
85  It should be noted that summary proceedings did not always represent a transfer of jurisdiction to individual JPs from quarter sessions. Blackstone and Brereton both pointed out that the increase in summary proceedings before JPs had led to the decline of trial by jury in court leets. (See *Commentaries*, iv. 278; Brereton, *Subordinate Magistracy*, 4–5.)
86  For a similar decline of local participation in the punishment of affrays and regulatory offences at Shrewsbury in the early eighteenth century see W. Champion, 'Recourse to the Law and the Meaning of the Great Litigation Decline, 1650–1750: Some Clues from the Shrewsbury Local Courts', in C.W. Brooks and M. Lobban (eds.) *Communities and Courts in Britain 1150–1900* (1997), 193–5.
87  C.D. Brereton, *The Subordinate Magistracy and the Parish System Considered* (Norwich, n.d. [1827?]), 5. By 'parole authority' Brereton meant that the proceedings were by word of mouth, and decision-making discretionary in the magistrate.
88  *Justice in Eighteenth-Century Hackney: The Justicing Notebook of Henry Norris and the Hackney Petty Sessions Book*, ed. R. Paley (London Record Soc., 28, 1991), xxxi–xxxii. See also Landau, *Justices*, 195–6.
89  Smith, 'Presumption of Guilt'.
90  See H. Fielding, *Amelia* ed. M.C. Battestin (Oxford, 1983), 21–5; T. Smollett, *The Life and Adventures of Sir Launcelot Greaves* (Harmondsworth, 1988), chs. 11–12.
91  See, e.g., W. Shakespeare, *Henry IV*, part 2 ('Justice Swallow'); *Parliamentary History of England*, i. 943–4, 946–7: Dec. 1601 ('basket-justices').
92  *Gentleman's Magazine*, 20 (1732), 892: 'If the Number of *penal Laws*, and the Power of *these Magistrates*, were thought such Grievances in the Reign of that excellent Princess [Elizabeth I], what shall we say now, when the *former* are multiplied, and the *latter* extended almost *ad infinitum*, occasion'd by our Debts and Taxes' (*Craftsman*, 5 Aug., 1732).
93  For trading justices in Middlesex, see N. Landau, 'The Trading Justice's Trade', in N. Landau (ed.) *Law, Crime and English Society 1660–1830* (Cambridge, 2002), 46–70.
94  T. Gisborne, *An Enquiry into the Duties of Men in the Higher and Middle Classes of Society in Great Britain* (1795), i. 410. See also Fisher, 'The Birth of the Prison Retold', 1254, 1255, 1257, who cites popular criticism of Thomas Butterworth Bayley JP.
95  Gisborne, *Enquiry into the Duties of Men*, i. 410–12; H. Fielding, *The History of Tom Jones*, ed. R.P.C. Mutter (Harmondsworth, 1985), 327.
96  From Staffordshire 1740–1800 there were only 13 applications for criminal informations against JPs, and 11 cases of *certiorari* on summary convictions. This should be set against an estimate of 10,000 summary convictions and committals in the county over this period. (See D. Hay, 'Legislation, Magistrates: High Law and Low Law in England and the Empire', in D. Lemmings (ed.) *The British and Their Laws in the Eighteenth Century* (Woodbridge, 2005), 65–8; id, 'Dread of the Crown Office: The English Magistracy and King's Bench, 1740–1800', in Landau (ed.) *Law, Crime and English Society*, 21–33.) From Kent over six years in the 1740s there were apparently no applications to KB for criminal informations against

magistrates or writs of *certiorari* against summary convictions, and only one *certiorari* against an order of settlement (Landau, *Justices*, 7–8, 354). For the virtual autonomy of the JP's discretionary judicial and administrative powers see Holdsworth, *History of English Law*, x. 248–9, 251–2. And for the complex history of *certiorari* see Landau, *Justices of the Peace*, 345–53. Of course writs of *certiorari* were most frequently deployed on behalf of parish officers to challenge settlement judgements.

97  C. Brooks, 'Law, Lawyers and the Social History of England', in id, *Lawyers, Litigation and English Society Since 1450* (1998), 193; id, *Law, Politics and Society in Early Modern England* (Cambridge, 2008), 418–19; Landau, 'The Trading Justice's Trade', in Landau (ed.) *Law, Crime and English Society*, 54–6; Skyrme, *History of the Justices of the Peace*, ii. 23.

98  e.g. 12 Geo. 2, c.29, s. 24 (County Rates Act); 17 Geo. 2, c.5, s. 34 (Vagrancy Act); 18 Geo. 3, c.19, s. 10 (Payment of Costs Act). See also Blackstone, *Commentaries*, i. 342.

99  19 Geo. 2, c.21, s. 8; Burn, *Justice* (2nd edn., 1756), i. 334, ii. 494. See also Landau, *Justices*, 351.

100  Landau, *Justices*, 353–4.

101  *Commentaries*, i. 8–9, 25–6.

102  Moir, *Local Government in Gloucestershire*, 40. By 26 Geo. 2, c. 27, no act of two or more justices could be rendered null and void for failing to state that one was of the quorum (Burn, *Justice of the Peace*, 1755, i. 119). For the quorum see Baker, *Introduction to English Legal History* (4th edn., 2002), 25; Skyrme, *History of the Justices of the Peace*, ii. 9.

103  See J.A. Sharpe, *Crime and the Law in English Satirical Prints 1600–1832* (Cambridge, 1986), plate 74: Brit. Museum Satires, 8575.

104  *The Modern Justice, in Imitation of the Man of Taste* (1755), 3–4, 17.

105  For a recent analysis which emphasizes the high proportion of labouring people among applicants to JPs acting summarily see King, 'Summary Courts'.

106  *Commentaries*, iv. 356–7.

107  W. Stubbs and G. Talmash, *The Crown Circuit Companion* (2nd edn., 1749), i. 54; R. Burn, *The Justice of the Peace, and Parish Officer* (1755), ii. 388–9. See also Lamoine, *Charges to the Grand Jury*, 426–7: charge of Sir John Hawkins to Middlesex quarter sessions Grand Jury, 8 Jan., 1770.

108  P. King, 'Punishing Assault: The Transformation of Attitudes in the English Courts', *Journal of Interdisciplinary History*, 27 (1996), esp. 49–53; id, *Crime and Law in England, 1750–1840* (Cambridge, 2006), ch. 8; Beattie, *Crime and the Courts*, 609–10. For the prosecution and punishment of assault see also N. Landau, 'Indictment for Fun and Profit: a Prosecutor's Reward at Eighteenth-Century Quarter Sessions', *Law and History Review*, 17 (1999), 507–36.

109  King, 'Punishing Assault', 51, 61–74; id, *Crime and Law*, 265–7; Landau, *Justices*, 195–6. See, generally, ch. 4 below.

110  Davey, *Rural Crime*, 147–8.

111  Landau, *Justices*, 201–5; Gisborne, *Duties of Men*, i. 417.

112  Phillips and Smith, *Lancashire and Cheshire from AD 1540* (1994), 67, 133.

113  Beattie, *Crime and the Courts*, 42–6.

114  Chester RO, QJB 3/8: 7 Oct., 1729. See also *County of Buckingham: Calendar to the Sessions Records. Volume II. 1694–1705*, ed. W. Le Hardy and G. Ll. Reckitt (Aylesbury, 1936), xxxi–xxxii, 44, 248: payments of £2 to John Edgson in 1695 and £1 to Ralph French in 1700.

115  Chester RO, QJB 3/22. 555–8. See also J.C. Cox, *Three Centuries of Derbyshire Annals, as illustrated by the Records of the Quarter Sessions of the County of Derby from*

*Queen Elizabeth to Queen Victoria* (1890), i. 123: treasurer's accounts East. 1782 to East. 1783, including several sums (ranging from £11 12s 6d to £84 11s 0d) paid to named individuals for 'Apprehending and Prosecuting Felons'. The Worcestershire magistrate Rev. Dr. Henry Yate also employed 'Special Constables' in searches for stolen property and for executing warrants (Hereford CRO, BB88/1, examination book of Dr. Henry Yate, 1801–03 (unpag.)).

116  B. Keith-Lucas, *The Unreformed Local Government System* (1980), 67, citing QS resolutions of 14 Jan., 1828.
117  Keith-Lucas, *Unreformed Local Government System*, 66–7.
118  Shoemaker, *Prosecution and Punishment*, 164.
119  At the London Consistory Court around the turn of the century ordinary or 'mere office' prosecutions brought in the name of the judge after presentation by churchwardens were few in number, and largely confined to cases of unlicensed midwives, surgeons, or schoolteachers, matters which can be regarded as simple revenue collection (London Metropolitan Archives, DL/C 329, Office Act Book, pp. 135–85 (Hil. 1695–Mich. 1706)). See also M. Ingram, *Church Courts, Sex and Marriage in England, 1570–1640* (Cambridge, 1987), 373–4.
120  e.g. Chester RO, QJB 3/3: 15 July, 1679. Morrill, *Grand Jury*, 24. For exemplification of such meetings in Lancashire during the 1680s see Fletcher, *Reform*, 126–7.
121  Chester RO, QJB 3/3: 2 Oct., 1677; Ibid: 5 Oct., 1680. Kirkham was also presented for making an affray on Thomas Parker of Cholmondeley.
122  Chester RO, QJB 3/3: 10 July 1677.
123  *Hertfordshire County Records: Calendar to the Sessions Books*, ed. W. Le Hardy and G.L. Reckitt (Hertford, 1930–1939), vol. 7, pp. 202, 203–4, 210, 366.
124  Wrightson, 'Two Concepts', 45; Davey, *Rural Crime*, 122; Webbs, *Parish and County*, 470–3. 7 & 8 Geo. 4, c.38. For example at the Wiltshire quarter sessions for Hilary 1736, the hundreds almost all reported 'all well', and among the few exceptions all except one were presentments of parishes for failing to maintain their highways (*Wiltshire Quarter Sessions and Assizes, 1736*, ed. J.P.M. Fowle (Wiltshire Archaeological and Natural History Soc., 11, Devizes, 1955), 11–13).
125  There are occasional presentments of lists of constables for 'neglect', although their defaults are not normally specified. See e.g. Chester RO, QJB 3/5: 13 July 1697. Certainly in 1731 the quarter sessions attempted to discipline the constables of the townships by presenting many for defaulting in their duties during their term of office, usually on the grounds that they had not returned lists of freeholders (see QJB 3/8: 5 Oct., 1731). The presentments of constables in 1816–18 were largely for not paying over their proportions of rates and assessments.
126  e.g. Chester RO, QJB 3/8: 7 Apr. and 6 Oct., 1730. For the imposition of conditional fines on presentment by justices in Middlesex see also E.G. Dowdell, *A Hundred Years of Quarter Sessions: the Government of Middlesex from 1660–1760* (Cambridge, 1932), 94–7.
127  See e.g. Chester RO, QJB 3/23, pp. 659–63: 14 July, 1818; ibid, pp. 676–7: 20 Oct. 1818.
128  Webbs, *The Parish and the County*, 474–9. See e.g. Chester RO, QJB 3/22, pp. 73–4: 4 Apr. 1815 (orders for writs against four townships).
129  *Commentaries*, iv. 277–9, 343–4.
130  D. Lemmings, 'Blackstone and Law Reform by Education: Preparation for the Bar and Lawyerly Culture in Eighteenth-Century England', *Law and History Review*, 16 (1998), 212–55.

131 Burn, *Justice* (2nd edn., 1756), i. 126, 133; Fletcher, *Reform in the Provinces*, 91, 93, 135.
132 See Chester RO, QJB 3/3. Sometimes they simply considered the examinations previously taken by the divisional JPs but still made the order at sessions (e.g. 13 July 1680, *Buckley and Allen*).
133 For some of the strategies behind these cases see N. Landau, 'The Regulation of Immigration, Economic Structures and Definition of the Poor in Eighteenth-Century England', *Historical Journal*, 33 (1990), 541–71.
134 W. Hay, *Remarks on the Laws Relating to the Poor* (1735), 12.
135 Hay, *Remarks*, 12. For the relatively high rate of successful appeals see Cheshire QS minutes generally; also Landau, *Justices*, Table 10, pp. 250–1. In Cheshire in the early nineteenth century the court occasionally referred a case to King's Bench for a ruling, thereby behaving strictly like a lesser tribunal in the hierarchy of judicial authority (e.g. 13 Jan. 1818, *Worthington and family*, Chester RO, QJB 3/23, pp. 68–9; also 31 Mar. 1818, *Rushton and family*, QJB 3/23, p. 115 *et seq.*).
136 See e.g. *The Diary of Thomas Turner 1754–1765*, ed. D. Vaisey (Oxford, 1985), 276–7.
137 Motions for discharging recognizances in bastardy were excepted from this rule. See Chester RO, QJB 3/17, p. 44. Cf. Landau, *Justices*, 254–5. In Derbyshire barristers had a monopoly of all quarter sessions litigation from 1771 (Cox, *Three Centuries of Derbyshire Annals*, i. 12–13).
138 H.J. Pye, *Summary of the duties of a Justice of the Peace out of Sessions* (4th edn., 1827), ix–x. There are occasional explicit references to 'pettie' sessions in the seventeenth century: e.g. Hampshire, 1651 and 1666 (J.S. Furley, *Quarter Sessions Government in Hampshire in the Seventeenth Century* (Winchester, n.d.)), and late seventeenth-century Surrey (*County of Surrey. Quarter Sessions Records with other Records of the Justices of the Peace for the County of Surrey. Vol. 5* (Surrey Rec. Soc., 32, 1931), 30).
139 Fletcher, *Reform in the Provinces*, 122–35.
140 Glassey, 'Local Government', in Jones (ed.) *Britain in the First Age of Party 1680–1750*, 161–2. Cf. the summary in Skyrme, *Justices*, ii. 65–8, which tends to exaggerate the degree of uniformity in petty sessions administration around the country.
141 Blackstone, *Commentaries*, iv. 269.
142 Webbs, *Parish and County*, 401–6.
143 *Hertfordshire County Records: Calendar to the Sessions Books Sessions Minute Books and other Sessions Records with Appendices 1752 to 1799*. Vol. VIII, ed. W. Le Hardy (Hertford, 1935), 311–12.
144 *The Justicing Notebook of Henry Norris and the Hackney Petty Sessions Book*, ed. Paley, xxii–xxiii.
145 Hereford CRO, BB88/1: Yate's examination book, 1801–03 (unpag.). See especially examinations of Anne Jones and John Chambers, 18 Nov. 1801, Elizabeth Beard, 17 Nov. 1801, and Thomas Watkins, alias Haylins 11 Jan. 1802.
146 Brereton, *Subordinate Magistracy*, 4–6.
147 Landau, *Justices*, 9.
148 Landau, *Justices*, 212–13, 218–19, 226–8, 231–2.
149 In Gloucestershire the development of petty sessions was uneven before the nineteenth century (Moir, *Local Government in Gloucestershire*), 116–21.
150 *Deposition Book of Richard Wyatt, JP, 1767–1776*, ed. E. Silverthorne (Guidford, Surrey Rec. Soc., 30, 1978), vii.

151 See e.g. Cheshire QS for 15 Jul. 1729, when the surveyors for the township of Woodford were ordered to present their accounts to the next monthly meeting for Macclesfield hundred (Chester RO, QJB3/8, unpag.). For the term 'petty sessions' see Chester RO, QJB 3/23, p. 56: QS, 14 Oct., 1817.
152 Eastwood, *Governing Rural England*, 92.
153 Hawkins, *Pleas of the Crown*, ii. 42.
154 3 Wm. & Mary, c.12; Burn, *Justice* (2nd edn., 1756), i. 539–40.
155 2 Geo. 2, c. 28; 26 Geo. 2, c. 31.
156 *Quarter Sessions Records with other Records of the Justices of the Peace for the County Palatine of Chester 1559–1760*, ed. J.H.E. Bennett and J.C. Dewhurst (Lancashire and Cheshire Rec. Soc., 94, 1940), 209.
157 *Justicing Notebook of William Hunt 1744–1749*, 6–27.
158 Ibid, 9; Landau, *Justices*, 219–20, 228; Moir, *Local Government in Gloucestershire*, 119, 125–6.
159 See Holdsworth, *History of English Law*, x. 171–2, 184–5.
160 See e.g. Gisborne, *Duties of Men*, i. 424–6. Landau, describing incidents of Kent petty sessions' partiality in licensing alehouses, comments 'In giving petty sessions the discretionary power allotted by law to two justices, the justices of Kent endowed the majority in petty sessions with the full terror of administrative authority' (*Justices*, 221–2).
161 *Justice in Eighteenth-Century Hackney*, ed. Paley, xxvi.
162 Moir, *Local Government in Gloucestershire*, 120.
163 (2nd edn., 1756), ii. 420.
164 Webbs, *Parish and County*, 437–8.
165 N. Landau, 'Appearances at the Quarter Sessions of Eighteenth-Century Middlesex', *The London Journal*, 23 (1998), 30–52.
166 See Davey, *Rural Crime*, 80–1. Also *County of Surrey. Quarter Sessions Records with other Records of the Justices of the Peace for the County of Surrey. Vol. 5* (Surrey Rec. Soc., 32, 1931), 27–8.
167 Burn, *Justice* (2nd edn., 1756), ii. 423–8; Webbs, *Parish and County*, 422; compare E. Moir, *The Justice of the Peace* (Harmondsworth, 1969), 36. Landau, *Justices*, 262; Langford, *Public Life*, 392–3, 395, 401, 405; P. Jenkins, *The Making of a Ruling Class: The Glamorgan Gentry 1640–1790* (Cambridge, 1983), 88–9.
168 Langford, *Public Life*, 397.
169 Moir, *Local Government in Gloucestershire*, 90. See also Eastwood, *Governing Rural England*, 79.
170 Morrill, *Cheshire 1630–1660*, 9; Chester RO, QJB 3/3. For numbers of JPs in the county commissions 1680–1793 see Landau, *Justices*, 368.
171 Chester RO, QJB 3/8.
172 Langford, *Public Life*, 392–3, 395.
173 Chester RO, QJB 3/13 (1769–71).
174 Ibid: meetings of 4 Apr., 1769 and 24 Apr., 1770.
175 'A Country Quarter Sessions', *The Newcastle Gazette*, 19 Jul., 1749. The reference to bulls and cows alluded to the magistrates' order designed to control the prevailing distemper among cattle.
176 Webbs, *Parish and County*, 438–9; Davey, *Rural Crime*, 97.
177 Webbs, *Parish and County*, 535–50; G. Welby, 'Rulers of the Countryside: The Justice of the Peace in Nottinghamshire, 1775–1800', *Transactions of the Thoroton Society*, 78 (1974), 76.
178 Webbs, *Parish and County*, 544–50.

179 Dowdell, *A Hundred Years of Quarter Sessions*, 27–37. For the substance of the campaign see also R.B. Shoemaker, 'Reforming the City', in L. Davison et al (eds.) *Stilling the Grumbling Hive: the Response to Social and Economic Problems in England, 1689–1750* (Stroud, 1992), 99–120. See also Skyrme, *Justices of the Peace*, ii. 60–2.
180 *Gentleman's Magazine*, 29 (1759), 518.
181 Webbs, *Parish and County*, 551; *Cobbett's Weekly Political Register*, 21 Sept. 1822, 705.
182 3 Wm. & Mary, c. 12.
183 P. Slack, *The English Poor Law 1531–1782* (1990), 39; *County of Buckingham: Calendar to the Sessions Records. Volume II. 1694–1705*, pp. xxii, 314; *Hertfordshire County Records: Calendar to the Sessions Books Sessions Minute Books and other Sessions Records with Appendices 1700 to 1752*. Vol. VII, ed. William Le Hardy (Hertford, 1931), pp. xxvi–xxix, 36, 170, 171, 174–5, 286, 290, 296, 328; *Hertfordshire County Records: Calendar to the Sessions Books Sessions Minute Books and other Sessions Records with Appendices 1752 to 1799*. Vol. VIII, ed. William Le Hardy (Hertford, 1935), pp. xxxiv–xxxvi, 330–1, 334–5; *The North Riding Record Society for the Publication of Original Documents relating to the North Riding of the County of York. Vol. VII: Quarter Sessions Records* (North Riding Record Soc., 1889), pp. xii–xiii. For the efforts of the Northumberland quarter sessions bench to encourage constables in apprehending vagrants see *Newcastle Journal*, 14–21 Jan., 1764, 18–25 Oct., 1766.
184 Chester RO, QJB 3/4 (unpag.). See above, p. 40. S. and B. Webb, *The Story of the King's Highway* (1913), 36–8.
185 Webbs, *King's Highway*, 19.
186 Chester RO, QJB 3/8: Cheshire QS, 13 July, 1731; ibid, QJB 3/13.
187 12 Geo. 2, c. 29.
188 See Holdsworth, *History of English Law*, x. 169; preamble to 12 Geo. 2, c. 29.
189 Chester RO, QJB 3/12: 10 Jan., 1727.
190 12 Geo. 2, c. 29, s.1.
191 Ibid, ss. 1, 10, 12, 21, 24.
192 Langford, *Polite and Commercial People*, 694.
193 Webbs, *King's Highway*, 97–8; 13 Geo.3, c. 78, s. 24: General Highway Act, 1773.
194 12 Geo. 2, c. 29, ss. 8, 17.
195 Landau, *Justices*, 263–4; Langford, *Public Life*, 405–7. Cheshire quarter sessions also revived, attracting between ten and 12 justices for each of the principal meetings, including two baronets and many of the leading gentry families (Chester RO, QJB 3/22, 3/23). It should be noted that attendance was much higher – 13 to 17 usually – at the Knutsford sessions, while the Chester sessions rarely attracted the gentry elite.
196 Eastwood, *Government and Community*, 107–9.
197 See e.g. Chester CRO, QJB 3/22, pp. 371, 568: Oct. 1816, June 1817; QJB 3/23, p. 53: Oct. 1817; ibid, pp. 100, 222: Jan. 1818, July 1818. The relevant legislation was 24 Geo. 3, c. 55 (1784).
198 Eastwood, *Governing Rural England*, 244–6, 247–51.
199 Chester RO, QJB 3/22, p. 317: 16 July 1816.
200 Ibid, QJB 3/22, p. 670: 15 Oct., 1816.
201 Ibid, QJB 3/23, p. 231. 48 Geo. 3, c.96: Act for the better Care and Maintenance of Lunatics, 1808.
202 P. Langford, *A Polite and Commercial People: England 1727–1783* (Oxford, 1989), 694.
203 Webbs, *Parish and County*, 512–24; Glassey, 'Local Government', 163–4.

204 12 Geo. 2, c. 29, ss. 6, 7, 11.
205 Chester RO, QJB 3/8: sessions of 6 Oct., 1730, 27 Apr., 1731; ibid, QJB 3/22, pp. 423–4: session of 14 Jan., 1817.
206 Chester RO, QJB 3/22, pp. 366, 568: 15 Oct., 1816, 15 July 1817.
207 Chester RO, QJB 3/22, p. 420: 14 Jan., 1817.
208 Burn, *Justice* (2$^{nd}$ edn., 1756), i. 569–70; Chester RO, QJB 3/22: 9 Jan., 1816: appointment of Joseph Henshall, bridge builder, and three others.
209 See Table 2.1. The relevant legislation is 10 Geo. 3, c. 39 and 31 Geo. 3, c. 30. See also Holdsworth, *History of English Law*, x. 167.
210 Herrup, *The Common Peace*, 200–1; M.J. Braddick, *State Formation in Early Modern England c.1550–1700* (Cambridge, 2000), 27–8, 155–7.
211 For a similar point, but made on the basis of a survey of sixteenth and seventeenth-century manorial courts, see C.W. Brooks, *Law, Politics and Society in Early Modern England* (Cambridge, 2008), 277.
212 Braddick, *State Formation*, 162; also idem, 'Discussion: State Formation and Social Change in Early Modern England: A Problem Stated and Approach Suggested', *Social History*, 16 (1991), 7. For the concepts of collective and distributive power see M. Mann, *The Sources of Social Power: Volume 1. A History of Power from the Beginning to A.D. 1760* (Cambridge, 1986), 6–7.
213 See R. Isaac, *Transformation of Virginia*, 92–3 (epigraph to this chapter).
214 For statutory commissions see Glassey, 'Local Government', in *Britain in the First Age of Party*, 164–5; below, pp. 153–9.
215 Webbs, *Parish and County*, 547–8.
216 See below, pp. 103–6.
217 S. Devereaux, 'The Promulgation of the Statutes in Late Hanoverian Britain', in Lemmings (ed.) *The British and Their Laws*, 99–100; Moir, *Local Government in Gloucestershire*, 142–4.
218 Ibid; Langford, *Polite and Commercial People*, 694. See also D. Eastwood, '"Amplifying the Province of the Legislature": The Flow of Information and the English State in the Early Nineteenth Century', *Historical Research*, 62 (1989), 280–1, 283–4.
219 Eastwood, 'Amplifying the Province of the Legislature', 281–2.
220 J.M. Rosenheim, 'County Governance and Elite Withdrawal in Norfolk, 1660–1720', in A.L. Beier et al (eds.) *The First Modern Society: Essays in English History in Honour of Lawrence Stone* (Cambridge, 1989), 123–4.
221 J. Innes, 'The Domestic Face of the Military-Fiscal State: Government and Society in Eighteenth-Century Britain', in L. Stone (ed.) *An Imperial State at War: Britain from 1689–1815*, (1994), 100–1; id, 'Parliament and the Shaping of Eighteenth-Century English Social Policy', 67–8. See also Skyrme, *Justices of the Peace*, ii. 60.
222 T. Day, *A Dialogue between a Justice of the Peace and a Farmer* (1785), 18.

## Chapter 3  Going to Law: The Rise and Fall of Civil Litigation

1 I am using the term civil litigation in a broad sense to denote all interpersonal suits which were not pleas of the crown, and therefore encompassing common pleas in the secular courts and 'instance' suits in the ecclesiastical courts.
2 J.H. Baker, *An Introduction to English Legal History* (3$^{rd}$ edn., 1990), 10–11.
3 C. Muldrew, *The Economy of Obligation: The Culture of Credit and Social Relations in Early Modern England* (1998), 236.

4   Harrison, 'Manor Courts', in Brooks and Lobban (eds.) *Communities and Courts*, 45.
5   These last two did not survive: the Long Parliament abolished the Council of the North and restricted the jurisdiction of the Council of Wales, although the latter continued to hear civil pleas until 1689 (W. Holdsworth, *A History of English Law* (1922–72), i. 126–7, vi. 112; J.S. Cockburn, *A History of English Assizes 1558–1714* (Cambridge, 1972), 36–8, 40–2).
6   Muldrew, *Economy of Obligation*, 211. For their names see S. and B. Webb, *The Manor and the Borough* (1908), i. 340–1.
7   For the patchy survival of active hundred courts see Holdsworth, *History of English Law*, i. 75, 134; Webbs, *Manor and Borough*, i. 51, 55–7, 60–3; W. Blackstone, *Commentaries on the Laws of England* (Oxford, 1765–9), iii. 34–5. Recent research has identified some courts which remained 'robust' into the seventeenth century, however (C. Muldrew, 'Rural Credit, Market Areas and Legal Institutions in the Countryside in England, 1550–1700', in Lobban and Brooks (eds.) *Communities and Courts*, 169–70). For the activity of manorial courts see C.W. Brooks, *Law, Politics and Society in Early Modern England* (Cambridge, 2008), esp. 261, 265–6.
8   J.A. Sharp, '"Such Disagreement between Neighbours": Litigation and Human Relations in Early Modern England', in J. Bossy (ed.) *Disputes and Settlements: Law and Human Relations in the West* (Cambridge, 1983), 168; Muldrew, *Economy of Obligation*, 236; C.W. Brooks, *Lawyers, Litigation and English Society since 1450* (1998), 66–8.
9   Brooks, *Lawyers, Litigation and English Society*, 29–33; idem, *Pettyfoggers and Vipers of the Commonwealth: The 'Lower Branch' of the Legal Profession in Early Modern England* (Cambridge, 1986), 78–9.
10  H. Horwitz and P. Polden, 'Continuity or Change in the Court of Chancery in the Seventeenth and Eighteenth Centuries?', *Journal of British Studies*, 35 (1996), 30; H. Horwitz, *Chancery Equity Records and Proceedings 1600–1800: A Guide to Documents in the Public Record Office* (PRO Handbook 27, 1995), 29–30. See also M. Lobban, 'Preparing for Fusion: Reforming the Nineteenth-Century Court of Chancery, Part 1', *Law and History Review*, 22 (2004), esp. 398–409. For doubts about the meaning and consistency of all the statistics relating to the 'great litigation decline', see W. Prest, 'The Experience of Litigation', in D. Lemmings (ed.) *The British and their Laws in the Eighteenth Century* (Woodbridge, 2005), ch. 6.
11  Brooks, *Lawyers, Litigation and English Society*, 2, 187; A.L. Erickson, *Women and Property in Early Modern England* (1993), 14.
12  Brooks, *Lawyers, Litigation and English Society*, 15.
13  D. Lemmings, *Professors of the Law: Barristers and English Legal Culture in the Eighteenth Century* (Oxford, 2000), esp. chs. 3, 5; Horwitz and Polden, 'Continuity or Change in the Court of Chancery?', 42–52; Brooks, *Lawyers, Litigation and English Society*, 45–8.
14  *Proposals Humbly Offer'd to the Parliament, for Remedying the Great charge and Delay of Suits at Law, and in Equity* (3rd edn., 1724), 1–2.
15  See epigraph to this chapter.
16  Muldrew, *Economy of Obligation*, 211–12.
17  W.A. Champion, 'Litigation in the Boroughs: The Shrewsbury *Curia Parva* 1480–1730', *Journal of Legal History*, 15 (1994), 202, 207, 209–15.
18  Muldrew, *Economy of Obligation*, 203–4, 245; idem, 'Credit and the Courts: Debt Litigation in a Seventeenth-century Urban Community', *Economic History Review*, 46 (1993), 30.
19  Muldrew, *Economy of Obligation*, 249.

20 Muldrew, 'Credit and the Courts', 27, 28–36. It should also be noted that in Shrewsbury during the 1580s around one in three of the population were represented in litigation which had advanced to the stage where a writ been served on the defendant (Champion, 'Litigation in the Boroughs', 204, 209).
21 Muldrew, *Economy of Obligation*, 264.
22 The courts of the University of Cambridge were also increasingly busy in the late sixteenth and early seventeenth centuries, to the extent that in 1632–4 almost a quarter of the town's population was involved in interpersonal litigation, and participation was spread broadly across middling people (A. Shepard, 'Litigation and Locality: the Cambridge University Courts, 1560–1640', *Urban History*, 31 (2004), 10, 14–15, 20–4).
23 Muldrew, *Economy of Obligation*, 216–33; J.H. Baker, *The Common Law Tradition: Lawyers, Books and the Law* (2000), ch. 16, esp. 270, 284–5. See also Harrison, 'Manor Courts', 43–59.
24 Muldrew, *Economy of Obligation*, 234–5. By comparison, it appears there was one suit for approximately every 8.3 households in 1995 (Muldrew, *Economy of Obligation*, 394, n. 123).
25 Even in the 1690s Muldrew estimates that the annual average rate of litigation was 0.9 suits per household (*Economy of Obligation*, 241).
26 Muldrew, *Economy of Obligation*, 224, 241.
27 Champion, 'Litigation in the Boroughs', 205–7.
28 Brooks, *Lawyers, Litigation and English Society*, 40–1; Muldrew, *Economy of Obligation*, 216–38.
29 Webbs, *Manor and the Borough*, i. 343; Brooks, *Lawyers, Litigation and English Society*, 43. Cf. Prest, 'The Experience of Litigation', 138.
30 Brooks, *Lawyers, Litigation and English Society*, 107; J.P. Dawson, *A History of Lay Judges* (Cambridge, MA, 1960), 272–3.
31 Muldrew, *Economy of Obligation*, 260–3, 265–7.
32 G.R. Rubin, 'Law, Poverty and Imprisonment for Debt, 1869–1914', in G.R. Rubin and D. Sugarman (eds.) *Law, Economy and Society, 1750–1914: Essays in the History of English Law* (1984), 241–90; M. Finn, *The Character of Credit: Personal Debt in English Culture, 1740–1914* (Cambridge, 2003), ch. 5.
33 Finn, *Character of Credit*, ch. 6.
34 *Commentaries*, iii. 82; Brooks, *Lawyers, Litigation and English Society*, 42–4.
35 W. Hutton, *A Dissertation on Juries; with a Description of the Hundred Court: as an Appendix to the Court of Requests* (Birmingham, 1789), 43; idem, *Courts of Requests: their Nature, Utility, and Powers described, with a variety of Cases, Determined in that of Birmingham* (Birmingham, 1787), esp. 23, 24, 68–9.
36 P. Polden, 'Judicial Selkirks: The County Court Judges and the Press, 1847–80', in Brooks and Lobban (eds.) *Communities and Courts*, 250. See also idem, *A History of the County Court, 1846–1971* (Cambridge, 1999), chs. 1–2.
37 M. Ingram, *Church Courts, Sex and Marriage in England, 1570–1640* (Cambridge, 1987), pp. 299–300; R.A. Marchant, *The Church under the Law: Justice, Administration and Discipline in the Diocese of York 1560–1640* (Cambridge, 1969), pp. 61–2, 68, 71; J.A. Sharpe, *Defamation and Sexual Slander in Early Modern England: The Church Courts at York* (York, Borthwick Papers, no. 58, 1980), pp. 4, 8–9; L. Gowing, *Domestic Dangers: Women, Words, and Sex in Early Modern London* (Oxford, 1996), 32–8; T. Meldrum, 'A Women's Court in London: Defamation at the Bishop of London's Consistory Court, 1700–1745', *London Journal*, 19 (1994), 6, n. 36.

38  Sharpe, *Defamation and Sexual Slander*, 8–9; R.B. Shoemaker, 'The Decline of the Public Insult in London 1660–1800', *Past and Present*, 169 (2000), 101; P. Morris, 'Defamation and Sexual Reputation in Somerset, 1733–1850' (University of Warwick, PhD, 1985), Table IVA.
39  Morris, 'Defamation and Sexual Reputation in Somerset', 140, 213, 242–5; S.M. Waddams, *Sexual Slander in Nineteenth-Century England* (Toronto, 2000), 195–6.
40  D. Lemmings, 'Women's Property, Popular Cultures, and the Consistory Court of London in the Eighteenth Century', in M. Ferguson, N. Wright and A. Buck (eds.) *Women and Property in Early Modern England* (Toronto, 2004), 66–94; L. Stone, *Road to Divorce: England 1530–1987* (Oxford, 1990), pp. 43–4; S.M. Waddams, *Law, Politics and the Church of England: The Career of Stephen Lushington 1782–1873* (Cambridge, 1992), pp. 165–6. For declining litigation in the church courts generally see R.B. Outhwaite, *The Rise and Fall of the English Ecclesiastical Courts, 1500–1860* (Cambridge, 2006), ch. 9.
41  Muldrew, 'Credit and the Courts', 33, 36.
42  This idea of law as discourse is derived partly from S. Humphreys, 'Law as Discourse', *History and Anthropology*, 1 (1985), 251.
43  See Erickson, *Women and Property*, 115; Horwitz and Polden, 'Continuity or Change', 44–6; T. Stretton, *Women Waging Law in Elizabethan England* (Cambridge, 1998), ch. 6.
44  See especially L. Stone, 'Interpersonal Violence in English Society 1300–1980', *Past and Present*, 51 (1983), 31–2; idem, *The Family, Sex and Marriage in England 1500–1800* (1977), 98.
45  B. Mandeville, *The Fable of the Bees* (Harmondsworth, 1970), 241.
46  C. Churches, 'False Friends, Spiteful Enemies: A Community at Law in Early Modern England', *Historical Research*, 71 (1998), 56–8.
47  Stone, *Family*, 98.
48  London Metropolitan Archives, DL/C 149 (Allegations, Libels and Sentence Book, 1699–1702), ff. 58–63.
49  See T.G. Barnes, 'Star Chamber Litigants and Their Counsel, 1596–1641', in J.H. Baker (ed.) *Legal Records and the Historian* (1978), 7.
50  C. Muldrew, 'The Culture of Reconciliation: Community and the Settlement of Economic Disputes in Early Modern England', *Historical Journal*, 39 (1996), 915–42.
51  *The Diary of Thomas Turner*, ed. D. Vaisey (Oxford, 1985), 283.
52  *The Blecheley Diary of the Rev. William Cole*, ed. F.G. Stokes (1931), 88–9.
53  National Archives, KB101/1/6: affidavits in *Pew v. Creswell* (1734).
54  London Metropolitan Archives, DL/C 149, ff. 60–1.
55  Churches, 'A Community at Law', 56, 58, 59, 60, 72.
56  Churches, 'A Community at Law', 73–4.
57  M. Ingram, 'Communities and Courts: Law and Disorder in Early-Seventeenth-Century Wiltshire', in J.S. Cockburn (ed.) *Crime in England 1550–1800* (1977), 119–20, 122.
58  Lincoln's Inn, London, Harrowby MSS (Diaries of Sir Dudley Ryder), doc. 12, p. 36: 1 June, 1754.
59  Muldrew, 'Culture of Reconciliation', 938–9.
60  Brooks, *Lawyers, Litigation and English Society*, 195; E.P. Thompson, *Whigs and Hunters* (Harmondsworth, 1975), 261.
61  P.B. Munsche, *Gentlemen and Poachers: The English Game Laws, 1671–1831* (Cambridge, 1971), 13.

62 Lincoln's Inn, London, Harrowby MSS, doc. 19f, p. 2: 6 Aug., 1754.
63 For some sixteenth and seventeenth-century examples of plebeian vs. landlord quasi-political litigation over free mining, see A. Wood, *The Politics of Social Conflict: the Peak Country 1520–1770* (Cambridge, 1999), 210–12, 215–16, 220–3, 231–3, 241–4, 247, 252, 264–5, 285, 307.
64 Churches, 'A Community at Law', 55.
65 Stretton, *Women Waging Law*, 143.
66 W.R. Prest, 'Law and Women's Rights in Early Modern England', *The Seventeenth Century*, 6 (1991), 187, n.59. For Benn's comments on the rule of law see C. Brooks, 'Professions, Ideology and the Middling Sort in the Late Sixteenth and Early Seventeenth Centuries', in J. Barry and C. Brooks (eds.) *The Middling Sort of People: Culture, Society and Politics in England, 1550–1800* (Basingstoke, 1994), 126.
67 For this concept see L. Friedman, 'Lawyers in Cross-cultural Perspective', in R.L. Abel and P.S.C Lewis (eds.) *Lawyers in Society, Vol. 3: Comparative Theories* (Berkeley, CA, 1989), 14.
68 Blackstone, *Commentaries*, iv. 239. For examples see J.M. Beattie, *Crime and the Courts in England 1660–1800* (Oxford, 1986), 424–8.
69 See Muldrew, *Economy of Obligation*, 206 for the predominance of trial by jury in borough courts of record.
70 Lincoln's Inn, Harrowby MSS, doc. 12, p. 14: May 1754.
71 *The Tryal between Henry Duke of Norfolk, plaintiff, and John Jermaine defendant: in an Action of Trespass on the Case at the Court of Kings-Bench at Westminster, on the 24th of November, 1692* (1692), p. 20.
72 See L. Stone, *Road to Divorce: England 1530–1987* (Oxford, 1990), 314–15.
73 C. Holmes, 'Popular Culture', in S.L. Kaplan (ed.) *Understanding Popular Culture: Europe from the Middle Ages to the Nineteenth Century* (Berlin, 1984), 85–111.
74 G.J. Postema, *Bentham and the Common Law Tradition* (Oxford, 1986), 353.
75 Stretton, *Women Waging Law*, 209–12.
76 Stretton, *Women Waging Law*, ch. 8, quoting 211–12. Some litigation communicated distinctively *feminine* values: see M.R. Hunt, 'Wives and Marital "Rights" in the Court of Exchequer in the Early Eighteenth Century', in P. Griffiths and M.S.R. Jenner, *Londinopolis: Essays in the Cultural and Social History of Early Modern London* (Manchester, 2000), 107–29. See also Brooks, *Law, Politics and Society*, 277.
77 Gowing, *Domestic Dangers*, 61; Sharpe, *Defamation and Sexual Slander*, 17; Ingram, *Church Courts*, 304.
78 See above, pp. 64–5.
79 Gowing, *Domestic Dangers*, 114–19.
80 London Metropolitan Archives, DL/C 149, ff. 57–57v (*Gale v. Pearce*, 1700).
81 Ibid, DL/C 172, ff. 49–53 (*Berkinsher v. Ward*, 1752).
82 For the procedural advantages see below, p. 77.
83 Meldrum, 'A Woman's Court', 12–13. For consideration of the discrepancies between formal and underlying issues in church court litigation relating to marriage see J. Bailey, 'Voices in Court: Lawyers' or Litigants?', *Historical Research*, 74 (2001), 392–408.
84 *London Magazine*, 9 (1740), 387–8.
85 *The Law-Suit: or the Farmer and Fisherman* (London, 1738), 41.
86 C. Churches, 'Business at Law: Retrieving Commercial Disputes from Eighteenth-century Chancery', *Historical Journal*, 43 (2000), 937–54.
87 Horwitz and Polden, 'Continuity or Change', 49, 50.

88  Brooks, *Lawyers, Litigation and English Society*, 37–8; H. Horwitz, 'Chancery's "Younger Sister": The Court of Exchequer and its Equity Jurisdiction, 1649–1841', *Historical* Research, 72 (1999), 171–2; Lemmings, *Professors of the Law*, 93–5.
89  See Lemmings, *Professors of the Law*, 80–2, 93–5, 96–100.
90  Brooks, *Lawyers, Litigation and English Society*, 35, n. 22.
91  See Champion, 'Litigation in the Boroughs', 217–18.
92  For a survey of the 'external' influences on the levels of litigation between the mid seventeenth century and the early nineteenth, see Lemmings, *Professors of the Law*, 78–84.
93  Brooks, *Pettyfoggers*, 60, 94–5.
94  Champion, 'Recourse to Law and the Meaning of the Great Litigation Decline, 1650–1750: Some Clues from the Shrewsbury Local Courts', in Brooks and Lobban (eds.) *Communities and Courts*, 183–91; 5 Wm. & Mary, c. 21.
95  Lemmings, *Professors of the Law*, 184–9.
96  Horwitz and Polden, 'Court of Chancery', 31.
97  *Parliamentary History*, viii. 1071–8; *Report of the Lords Commissioners appointed to make a survey of the different courts in England, Wales, and Berwick-upon Tweed, – as to the Court of Chancery: Dated 8 November 1740. Parliamentary Papers (House of Commons), 1814–15*, vol. XI, pp. 5–152; 2 Geo. 2, c. 23; 4 Geo. 2, c. 26.
98  Lemmings, 'Women's Property, Popular Cultures and the Consistory Court of London', 84–5. Outhwaite emphasizes the rising costs of stamped paper, which would have impacted disproportionately on jurisdictions where proceedings were conducted primarily in writing (Outhwaite, *Rise and Fall of the English Ecclesiastical Courts*, 100).
99  E. Sykes, *Edmund Gibson, Bishop of London, 1669–1748: A Study in Politics and Religion in the Eighteenth* Century (Oxford, 1926), 150.
100  London Metropolitan Archives, DL/C39, ff. 1–381; London Metropolitan Archives, DL/C52, ff. 1–428.
101  London Metropolitan Archives, DL/C52 (Instance Act Book, 1749–54), ff. 362v–363.
102  For readings of sixteenth and early seventeenth-century funerary monuments see N. Llewellyn, 'Honour in Life, Death and in the Memory: Funeral Monuments in Early Modern England', *Transactions of the Royal Historical Society*, 6th ser. 6 (1996), 179–200. And for the introduction of family pews see M. Aston, 'Segregation in Church', in W.J. Shiels and D. Wood (eds.) *Women in the Church* (Oxford, 1990), 281–9.
103  *The Second Charge of Whitlocke Bulstrode, Esq* (1718) in *Charges to the Grand Jury 1689–1803*, ed. G. Lamoine (Camden Soc., 4th ser., 43 (1992), 118.
104  Cf. Shoemaker, 'Decline of Public Insult', 105, 117, 118–19; N. Landau, *The Justices of the Peace, 1679–1760* (Berkeley, CA, 1984), 204–6; above, ch. 2, p. 37. However Outhwaite has speculated about a transfer of actions for opprobrious words from the church courts to the magistracy (Outhwaite, *Rise and Fall of the Ecclesiastical Courts*, 101–2).
105  Sykes, *Gibson*, 195–6, 208–9; E. Gibson, *An Admonition against Prophane and Common Swearing* (7th edn., 1745), 13, 19, 22–3.
106  T. Isaacs, 'The Anglican Hierarchy and the Reformation of Manners', *J. of Ecclesiastical History*, 33 (1982), 406; [E. Gibson,] *Remarks on a Bill Now Depending in Parliament for the Better Regulating the Proceedings of the Ecclesiastical Courts. By a Right Reverend Prelate* (1733).
107  E. Sykes, *From Sheldon to Secker: Aspects of English Church History, 1660–1768* (Cambridge, 1958), 192–204.

108 S.M. Waddams, *Sexual Slander in Nineteenth-Century England: Defamation in the Ecclesiastical Courts, 1815–1855* (Toronto, 2000), 7, 56–7, 65, 66–7; Morris, 'Defamation and Sexual Reputation in Somerset', 236–8; Outhwaite, *Rise and Fall of the English Ecclesiastical Courts*, 99. In 1786 and 1812 Parliamentary critics condemned suits for defamation as founded in 'Malice and Resentment' or 'malice and revenge' (Outhwaite, *English Ecclesiastical Courts*, 122, 127).

109 For some theoretical arguments about doctrinal development and economic limits to accessing the courts, see G.R. Rubin and D. Sugarman, 'Towards a New History of Law and Material Society in England 1750–1914', in Rubin and Sugarman (eds.) *Law, Economy and Society, 1750–1914: Essays in the History of English Law* (Abingdon, 1984), 86–8.

110 Gowing, *Domestic Dangers*, 266, 268.

111 Waddams, *Sexual Slander*, 188–9.

112 L. Gowing, 'Language, Power and the Law: Women's Slander Litigation in Early Modern London', in J. Kermode and G. Walker (eds.) *Women, Crime and the Courts in Early Modern England* (1994), 33.

113 Waddams, *Sexual Slander*, 66, 182.

114 See however, J. Bailey, *Unquiet Lives* (Cambridge, 2003), 48: who suggests that the disadvantage of wives in the matrimonial cases she analysed was principally a consequence of their economic vulnerability, which prevented them from sustaining suits to advanced stages.

115 Lemmings, 'Women's Property, Popular Cultures and the Consistory Court of London', 78–82.

116 Juries of experts or men of substance were known before the eighteenth century, but procedures were formalized after 1700, special juries became increasingly common after their legality was confirmed by legislation in 1730, and usage was at a peak during the later eighteenth and early nineteenth centuries (J. Oldham, 'The Origins of the Special Jury', *Univ. of Chicago Law Rev.*, 100 (1983), esp. 140, n. 13; 3 Geo. 2, c. 25, sects. 15–17).

117 J. Oldham, *The Mansfield Manuscripts and the Growth of English Law in the Eighteenth Century* (Chapel Hill, NC, 1992), i. 93–9; id, 'Special Juries in England: Nineteenth Century Usage and Reform', *Journal of Legal History*, 8 (1987), 163, n. 20.

118 E.P. Thompson, *Customs in Common* (1993), pp. 132–43; D. Hay and N. Rogers, *Eighteenth-Century English Society: Shuttles and Swords* (Oxford, 1997), 104–5, 107–8; Oldham, *Mansfield Manuscripts*, ii. 932–3, 1317; Holdsworth, *History of English Law*, xi. 419–20; W.R. Cornish and G. de N. Clark, *Law and Society in England* (1989), 293; D. Hay, 'The State and the Market in 1800: Lord Kenyon and Mr. Waddington', *Past and Present*, 162 (1999), 101–62. See also ch. 5 below, pp. 146–7.

119 For Kenyon, see the biography by Douglas Hay in *Oxford Dictionary of National Biography*.

120 Hay, 'The State and the Market', 128–9; T. Ruggles, *The Barrister* (2$^{nd}$ edn., 1818 [first published 1791]), esp. xiii, 34; Lemmings, *Professors of the Law*, 223, 309–12; J. Epstein, *Radical Expression: Political Language, Ritual, and Symbol in England 1790–1850* (New York, 1994), 32.

121 S. Staves, *Married Women's Separate Property in England, 1660–1833* (Cambridge, MA, 1990), 27–94, 209–13. See also E. Spring, *Law, Land, and Family: Aristocratic Inheritance in England, 1300 to 1800* (Chapel Hill, NC, 1993); J. Habbakuk, *Marriage, Debt, and the Estates System* (Oxford, 1994), esp. 536–43. It should be noted that Habbakuk disagrees that the strict settlement operated to the disadvantage of younger children, but I find Spring's arguments more persuasive.

122 Lemmings, *Professors of the Law*, 40; Horwitz and Polden, 'Court of Chancery', 36–7, 53–4; R.A. Kelch, *Newcastle: A Duke without Money* (1974), 96, 99–100; Staves, *Married Women's Separate Property*, 43, 47, 56–9, 262, n. 51; H. Twiss, *The Public and Private Life of Lord Chancellor Eldon* (1844), i. 97–8, 102.
123 Staves, *Married Women's Separate Property*, chs. 5–6.
124 See Staves, *Married Women's Separate Property*, 173, 185, 197–8, 227–8.

## Chapter 4   Crime and the Administration of Criminal Law: Problems, Solutions, and Participation

1 See A. Silver 'The Demand for Order in Civil Society: A Review of Some Themes in the History of Urban Crime, Police, and Riot', in D.J. Bordua (ed.) *The Police: Six Sociological Essays* (New York, 1967), 20–4.
2 For the commercial advantages of sensational crime reporting and commentary, see e.g. D.T. Andrew and R. McGowen, *The Perreaus and Mrs. Rudd: Forgery and Betrayal in Eighteenth-Century London* (Berkeley, CA, 2001), ch. 3.
3 See generally, N. McKenrick, J. Brewer and J.H. Plumb (eds.) *The Birth of a Consumer Society: The Commercialization of Eighteenth-Century England* (1982); J. Brewer and R. Porter (eds.) *Consumption and the World of Goods* (1993); J. Brewer, *The Pleasures of the Imagination: English Culture in the Eighteenth Century* (1997).
4 G. Ollyffe, *An Essay Humbly offer'd, for an Act of Parliament to prevent capital crimes, and the loss of many lives* (2nd edn., 1731), 3; J.M. Beattie, *Crime and the Courts in England, 1660–1800* (Oxford, 1986), 631–2.
5 For the historical constitution of social objects or social problems see A. Hunt, *Explorations in Law and Society: Towards a Constitutive Theory of Law* (1993), 316. There were sixteenth-century precedents for the constitution of social problems and their legislative regulation (See W.R.D. Jones, *The Tudor Commonwealth 1529–1559* (1970), esp. chs. 6–9 and 11). The principal development in the eighteenth century was the broader scope of discussion because of the expanded public sphere (see D. Lemmings and C. Walker (eds.) *Moral Panics, the Media and the Law in Early Modern England* (Basingstoke, 2009), 4–5, 261–4).
6 See above, ch. 2; P. King, *Crime, Justice and Discretion in England 1740–1820* (Oxford, 2000), 1.
7 For the persistence of discretionary decision-making into the nineteenth century, especially in the localities, see S. Devereaux, 'In Place of Death: Transportation, Penal Practices, and the English State, 1770–1830', in C. Strange (ed.) *Qualities of Mercy: Justice, Punishment and Discretion* (Vancouver, 1996), 69–70.
8 Again I want to make it clear that I am using the term professionalization broadly here to signify performance of specific services for payment, and in some cases the appointment of officers who were accountable to and dependant on their superiors. There is no argument about improvements in training or standards.
9 See M.J. Braddick, *State Formation in Early Modern England* (Cambridge, 2000), 169–70.
10 R. North, *A Discourse of the Poor* (1753 [written c.1688]), 14.
11 J. A. Sharpe, *Crime in Early Modern England 1550–1750* (2nd edn., 1999), 141–2, 264; Braddick, *State Formation*, 150–4.
12 For his treatment of punishment and prosecution, see his *An Enquiry into the Causes of the Frequent Executions at Tyburn* (1725).
13 J.R. Langbein, 'Albion's Fatal Flaws', *Past and Present*, 68 (1983), 119.

14  In the account which follows I concentrate on newspaper reports, but of course there was plenty of other published material which must have raised sensitivity to crime, especially the collected 'sessions' papers of the Old Bailey criminal sessions, which appeared from the 1670s, and the biographies of condemned criminals such as the 'Accounts' of the 'ordinary' of Newgate. (See J.M. Beattie, *Policing and Punishment in London 1660–1750* (Oxford, 2001), 1–4. As these sources declined in popularity in the later eighteenth century, newspapers became the most important sources of law and order news (P. King, 'Newspaper Reporting and Attitudes to Crime and Justice in Late Eighteenth and Early Nineteenth Century London', *Continuity and Change*, 22 (2007), 74–5).
15  See M. Harris, *London Newspapers in the Age of Walpole* (Cranbury, NJ, 1987), 173–4; G.A. Cranfield, *The Development of the Provincial Newspaper* (Oxford, 1962), ch. 1 and 71–3; R.M. Wiles, *Freshest Advices* (Ohio, 1965), 249–50.
16  Harris, *London Newspapers*, 166; Cranfield, *Provincial Newspaper*, 70, 75.
17  See Beattie, *Crime and the Courts*, ch. 5, for the vexed issue of the relations between levels of indictments and 'real' crime rates.
18  *London Journal* (hereafter *LJ*), 15 Sept., 1722.
19  *LJ*, 10 Nov., 1722. See also Thompson, *Whigs and Hunters*, ch. 5.
20  *LJ*, 8 Dec., 1722.
21  *LJ*, 29 Dec., 1722, 16 and 23 Feb., 1723; 2, 9, 16 Mar., 1723; 13 July, 1723.
22  *LJ*, 26 Jan., 16 and 30 Mar., 1723.
23  *LJ*, 29 June, 1723, 3 Aug., 1723.
24  *LJ*, 5 Oct., 1723.
25  *LJ*, 21 Sept., 1723, 12 Oct., 1723.
26  *LJ*, 23 and 30 Nov., 1723, 21 Dec., 1723.
27  Beattie, *Crime and the Courts*, 213. For the correspondence between the incidence of newspaper reports about crime and popular anxiety in modern Britain, see P. Williams and J. Dickinson, 'Fear of Crime: Read All about It? The Relationship between Newspaper Crime Reporting and Fear of Crime', *British Journal of Criminology*, 33 (1993), 33–56.
28  For the events of the Atterbury and Layer conspiracies see G.V. Bennett, 'Jacobitism and the Rise of Walpole', in N. McKendrick (ed.) *Historical Perspectives* (1974), 82–90.
29  Cf. King, 'Newspaper Reporting and Attitudes to Crime and Justice', 95–6.
30  *LJ*, 29 Dec., 1722.
31  *LJ*, 8 June, 1723, 23 Nov., 1723; Thompson, *Whigs and Hunters*, 69–77, 148–55.
32  J. Black, *The English Press in the Eighteenth Century* (Philadelphia, 1987), 148.
33  *LJ*, 23 Nov., 1723.
34  *LJ*, 21 and 28 Dec., 1723.
35  Beattie, *Crime and the Courts*, 514, 516–17.
36  N. Rogers, 'Confronting the Crime Wave: the Debate over Social Reform and Regulation, 1749–1753', in L. Davison et al (eds.) *Stilling the Grumbling Hive: The Response to Social and Economic Problems in England, 1689–1750* (Stroud, 1992), 92.
37  Fielding, *Increase of Robbers*, ed. Zirker, 65–124.
38  Ibid, 68.
39  See Rogers, 'Confronting the Crime Wave', 78–81 for the role of the newspaper press in the mid-century panic; and R. Connors, '"The Grand Inquest of the Nation": Parliamentary Committees and Social Policy in Mid-Eighteenth-Century England', *Parliamentary History*, 14 (1995), 302–12 for the legislative response. In my view Connors gives insufficient weight to public opinion, as compared with the interests and initiatives of parliamentarians.

40 See P. King, 'Newspaper Reporting, Prosecution Practice and Perceptions of Urban Crime: The Colchester Crime Wave of 1765', *Continuity and Change*, 2 (1987), esp. 434–5.
41 *Ipswich Journal*, 1 June, 1782. Also ibid, 6 Apr., 11 May, 1782.
42 *Ipswich Journal*, 16 Nov., 1782.
43 *Ipswich Journal*, 14 Sept., 1782, 4 and 25 Jan., 1783; King, *Crime, Justice and Discretion*, 162–3.
44 *Ipswich Journal*, 1 Feb., 1783.
45 *Ipswich Journal*, 8 June, 14 Sept., 1782.
46 *Parliamentary History*, xxiii. 209.
47 Beattie, *Crime and the Courts*, 223–4, 582–5.
48 King, *Crime, Justice and Discretion*, 164–6.
49 King, 'Colchester Crime Wave', 439–42.
50 *Ipswich Journal*, 4 Jan., 11 Jan., 1783.
51 See S. Hall et al, *Policing the Crisis: Mugging, the State, and Law and Order* (New York, 1978), 67–8; J.M. Beattie, 'Violence and Society in Early-Modern England', in A.N. Doob, and E.L. Greenspan (eds.) *Perspectives in Criminal Law* (Aurora, Ontario, 1985), 36–60. Also, for statistical confirmation of the newspapers' concentration on crimes of violence, see King, 'Newspaper Reporting and Attitudes to Crime and Justice', 88–93; S. Devereaux, 'From Sessions to Newspaper? Criminal Trial Reporting, the Nature of Crime, and the London Press, 1770–1800', *London Journal*, 32 (2007), 10–11, 19–21; E. Snell, 'Discourses of Criminality in the Eighteenth-Century Press: The Presentation of Crime in *The Kentish Post*, 1717–1768', *Continuity and Change*, 22 (2007), 22–3, 25–6, 27.
52 *Ipswich Journal*, 12 Apr. 1783.
53 Cf. Snell, 'Discourses of Criminality', 29–30.
54 *Ipswich Journal*, 11 Jan., 1783.
55 A similar association for Framlingham in Suffolk bracketed horse-stealers and 'all persons guilty of committing murder, burglaries, robberies, thefts, felonies, petty larcenies, larcenies, and misdeeds whatsoever' (see *Ipswich Journal*, 18 Jan., 1783).
56 *Ipswich Journal*, 12 Apr., 1783.
57 P. King, 'Prosecution Associations in Essex', in 'Prosecution Associations and Their Impact in Eighteenth-Century Essex', in D. Hay and F. Snyder (eds.) *Policing and Prosecution in Britain 1750–1850* (Oxford, 1989), esp. 174, 202–4.
58 *Ipswich Journal*, 15 Mar., 1783.
59 *Ipswich Journal*, 5 Apr., 1763 [sic 1783].
60 Beattie, *Crime and the Courts*, 627–30; V.A.C. Gatrell, *The Hanging Tree: Execution and the English People 1770–1868* (Oxford, 1994), ch. 10; A. McKenzie, 'From True Confessions to True Reporting? The Decline and Fall of the Ordinary's Account', *London Journal* 30 (2005), 55–65; ead, *Tyburn's Martyrs: Execution in England 1675–1775* (2007).
61 *Ipswich Journal*, 11 Jan., 1 Mar., 22 Mar., 29 Mar., 5 Apr., 12 Apr., 19 Apr., 28 June, 1783.
62 *Newcastle Journal*, 19 Apr., 1783.
63 S. Cohen and J. Young, *The Manufacture of News: Social Problems, Deviance and the Mass Media* (1973), 344–5; Hall et al, *Policing the Crisis*, 273–82.
64 S. Devereaux, 'From Sessions to Newspaper? Criminal Trial Reporting, the Nature of Crime, and the London Press, 1770–1800', *London Journal*, 32 (2007), 12–19.
65 Snell, 'Discourses of Criminality', 28–35.

66  Ollyffe, *An Essay Humbly offer'd, for an Act of Parliament to prevent Capital Crimes*, 6–7.
67  Ollyffe, *Essay*, 3.
68  *Increase*, ed. Zirker, 73.
69  See J.M. Beattie, 'London Crime and the Making of the "Bloody Code", 1689–1718', in Davison et al (eds.) *Stilling the Grumbling Hive* (Stroud, 1992), 49–76.
70  Beattie, *Crime and the Courts*, 500–7; 4 Geo. 1, c. 11 (implemented 1718). See also J. Innes, 'The Role of Transportation in Seventeenth and Eighteenth-Century Penal Practice', in C. Bridge (ed.) *New Perspectives in Australian History* (1990), 1–24.
71  6 Geo. 1, c. 23, ss. 2, 3.
72  For some of the other innovations in penal and social policy see Beattie, *Crime and the Courts*, 492–500; 5 Anne, c. 6; Rogers, 'Confronting the Crime Wave'; J. Innes, 'Parliament and the Shaping of Eighteenth-century, Social Policy', *Transactions of the Royal Historical Society*, 5th ser., 40 (1990), 63–92.
73  See L. Radzinowicz, *A History of Criminal Law and its Administration from 1750* (1948–56), i. 3–8, 611–59; which should be read together with the comments of Langbein, 'Albion's Fatal Flaws', 115–19; and J. Innes and J. Styles, 'The Crime Wave: Recent Writing on Crime and Criminal Justice in Eighteenth-Century England', *Journal of British Studies*, 25 (1986), 420–30. For the persistence of capital punishment into the later eighteenth century and beyond see Gatrell, *Hanging Tree*, 6–7, 616–17.
74  *Hanging* (reprint, 1812), 9.
75  Ollyffe, *Essay Humbly offer'd, for an Act of Parliament to prevent Capital Crimes*, 8, 11.
76  Fielding, *Increase*, 164; *Hanging*, 9. Also Mandeville, *Enquiry*, 25; Madan, *Thoughts on Executive Justice* (1785).
77  Beattie, *Crime and the Courts*, 528–30; 25 Geo. 2, c. 37. For the origins of this statute see also H. Amory, 'Henry Fielding and the Criminal Legislation of 1751–2', *Philological Quarterly*, l (1971), 175–92.
78  R. McGowen, 'The Body and Punishment in Eighteenth-Century England', *Journal of Modern History*, 59 (1987), 651–79.
79  Mandeville, *Enquiry*, 20–4.
80  *Increase*, 167.
81  *Newcastle Journal*, 14 Apr. 1739.
82  P. Linebaugh, 'The Tyburn Riot against the Surgeons', in Hay et al (eds.) *Albion's Fatal Tree*, esp. 67, 112–15.
83  Mandeville, *Enquiry*, 24.
84  Laqueur, 'Crowds, Carnival and the State in English Executions, 1604–1868', in A.L. Beier et al (eds.) *The First Modern Society* (Cambridge, 1989), 305–55.
85  Beattie, 'Violence and Society', 55. See also A. McKenzie, 'Martyrs in Low Life? Dying "Game" in Augustan England', *Journal of British Studies*, 62 (2003), 197–205, and ead, *Tyburn's Martyrs*, 205–19, which argues that there was increasing intolerance of condemned criminals like Turpin who made a show of bravado at execution and of the excesses of the crowd as polite culture raised expectations of rational sensibility.
86  For the social heterogeneity of execution crowds see Laqueur, 'Crowds, Carnival and the State', 332, 337, 349.
87  Mandeville, *Enquiry*, 10–11.
88  See Zirker, 'General Introduction', to Fielding, *Increase*, lxiv–lxvii.

89 *Increase*, 131–44, 169–71.
90 R. McGowen, '"Making Examples" and the Crisis of Punishment in Mid-Eighteenth-Century England', in D. Lemmings (ed.) *The British and Their Laws in the Eighteenth Century* (Woodbridge, Suffolk, 2005), 182–205; *Ipswich Journal*, 8 Nov., 1783. See also S. Wilf, 'Imagining Justice: Aesthetics and Public Execution in Late Eighteenth-Century England', *Yale Journal of Law and the Humanities*, 5 (1993), 51–78; P. Linebaugh, *The London Hanged: Crime and Civil Society in the Eighteenth Century* (2nd edn., 2003), 363; Gatrell, *Hanging Tree*, 52–4, 602–4.
91 Wilf, 'Imagining Justice', 76. It should be noted that there were counter trends among the Wilkite radicals. For example Wilkes himself was in favour of making the administration of justice more accessible to the reading public, as he demonstrated by moving the City to improve the accuracy and comprehensiveness of the published sessions papers. This may have been a response to architectural changes that rendered the Sessions House at the Old Bailey more imposing. (See S. Devereaux, 'The City and the Sessions Paper: "Public Justice" in London, 1770–1800', *Journal of British Studies*, 35 (1996), 484–8).
92 Beattie, *Crime and the Courts*, 544–6, 614–16; Ignatieff, *Just Measure of Pain*, 90; R. Shoemaker, 'Streets of Shame? The Crowd and Public Punishments in London, 1700–1820', in *Penal Practice and Culture, 1500–1900*, ed. S. Devereaux and P. Griffiths (Basingstoke, 2004), 237–40. See also G.T. Smith, 'Civilised People Don't Want to See that Sort of Thing: The Decline of Physical Punishment in London, 1760–1840', in C. Strange (ed.) *Qualities of Mercy: Justice, Punishment and Discretion* (Vancouver, 1996), esp. 31–41. For an example of two men pilloried at Bristol for 'lewd and unnatural Practises' and treated 'in so cruel a manner as that one of them was near expiring' see Bristol RO, JQS/D/3: Quarter sessions docket book, 12 Sept., 1737. Interestingly, there was a temporary revival of public whipping in Cornwall and in Lancashire during the 1780s and 1790s (P. King, *Crime and Law in England, 1750–1840* (Cambridge, 2006), 270–5; G. Fisher, 'The Birth of the Prison Retold', *Yale Law Journal*, 104 (1995), 1274).
93 Smith, 'Civilised People', 33–6.
94 See McGowen, 'The Body and Punishment', 654–5, 669–70.
95 [W. Eden,] *Principles of Penal Law* (1771), 300.
96 S. Devereaux, 'In Place of Death: Transportation, Penal Practices, and the English State, 1770–1830', in Strange (ed.) *Qualities of Mercy: Justice, Punishment and Discretion*, 57–8. For the progressive alienation of the middle classes from the experience of public execution, see Gatrell, *Hanging Tree*, ch. 9.
97 [S. Romilly,] *Observations on a Late Publication Intituled, Thoughts on Executive Justice* (1786), 31.
98 McGowen, 'Body and Punishment', 670–1, 674–5; Ignatieff, *Just Measure of Pain*, 66–7.
99 [Eden,] *Principles of Penal Law*, 2; [Romilly,] *Observations*, 59–60.
100 See e.g. Blackstone, *Commentaries*, iv. 17–18.
101 [Romilly,] *Observations*, 67.
102 BL, Add. MSS, 34, 416 (Auckland Papers, vol. V), f. 328: Blackstone to William Eden, 25 Apr., 1779.
103 [Romilly,] *Observations*, 60.
104 19 Geo. 3, c. 74. For the complex origins and purposes of the act, which also envisaged the resumption of transportation, see S. Devereaux, 'The Making of the Penitentiary Act, 1775–1779', *Historical Journal*, 42 (1999), 405–33; also W. Prest, *William Blackstone: Law and Letters in the Eighteenth Century* (Oxford, 2008), 296–301.

105 See Ignatieff, *Just Measure of Pain*, 60–2, 66–7.
106 J. Howard, *The State of the Prisons in England and Wales, with Preliminary Observations, and an Account of some Foreign Prisons and Hospitals* (2nd edn., Warrington, 1780), 27, 53 (original emphasis).
107 *Hanging*, 23; Mandeville, *Enquiry*, 37–8.
108 Beattie, *Crime and the Courts*, 569–71; Hanway, *The Defects of Police the Cause of Immorality, and the Continual Robberies committed, particularly in and about the Metropolis* (1775), xii, 3, 212–13, 216, 221, 226–8.
109 *Principles*, ch. 6.
110 *Principles*, 264.
111 For a survey history of houses of correction see J. Innes, 'Prisons for the Poor: English Bridewells, 1555–1800', in F. Snyder and D. Hay (eds.) *Labour, Law, and Crime* (1987), 42–122. For the peculiar case of the City of London Bridewell see also F. Dabhoiwala, 'Summary Justice in Early Modern London', *English Historical Review*, 121 (2006), 796–822.
112 T. Hitchcock, 'Paupers and Preachers: The SPCK and the Parochial Workhouse Movement', in *Stilling the Grumbling Hive*, 145.
113 5 Anne, c. 6, s. 2.
114 Beattie, 'Bloody Code', 57; Corporation of Lond RO, Rep. 110, f. 75v: Sir Charles Hedges to corporation of London, Feb., 1706.
115 See e.g. S. Emlyn, preface to the 1730 edition of the state trials in *A Complete Collection of State Trials*, ed. T.B. Howell (1809–26), i. xxxiii.
116 *A Proposal for Making an Effectual Provision for the Poor* (1753), in *Enquiry*, ed. Zirker, esp. 238, 258, 265–6, 269–71.
117 See Devereaux, 'Making of the Penitentiary Act'.
118 16 Geo. 3, c. 43, preamble; 19 Geo. 3, c. 74, s. 5.
119 Beattie, *Crime and the Courts*, 577–9. The Surrey magistrates seem to have been less persuaded by imprisonment at hard labour, however.
120 [W. Eden,] 'Observations on the Bill to punish by Imprisonment and Hard Labour certain Offenders; and to provide proper Places for their Reception' (1778), in *House of Commons Sessional Papers of the Eighteenth Century*, ed. S. Lambert (Wilmington, Delaware, 1975), xxviii. 337. For the wave of local prison reforms see S. and B. Webb, *English Prisons under Local Government* (1922), 54–62. Overall 45 prisons were built by local authorities in the 1780s and 1790s (Fisher, 'The Birth of the Prison Retold', 1237).
121 24 Geo. 3, c. 56, s. 1.
122 Beattie, *Crime and the Courts*, 601.
123 22 Geo. 3, c. 64.
124 M. De Lacy, *Prison Reform in Lancashire* (Manchester, Chetham Soc., 3rd ser., 33, 1986), chaps. 3–4; Fisher, 'The Birth of the Prison Retold'.
125 24 Geo. 3, c. 54, 55.
126 Ignatieff, *Just Measure of Pain*, 98–108; Moir, *Local Government in Gloucestershire*, 88, 113–15, 147; ead., *The Justice of the Peace*, 111–12; Eastwood, *Governing Rural England*, 247–51; J. Innes, 'Politics and Morals: The Reformation of Manners Movement in Later Eighteenth-Century England', in E. Hellmuth (ed.) *The Transformation of Political Culture: England and Germany in the Late Eighteenth Century* (Oxford, 1990), 94–5; 31 Geo. 3, c. 46.
127 Compare Fisher, 'The Birth of the Prison Retold', 1240–1.
128 Cf. D. Lieberman, *The Province of Legislation Determined* (Cambridge, 1989), pp. 14, 26–8.

129 See e.g. Penitentiary Act, 19 Geo. 3, c. 74; and the Prisons Act, 31 Geo. 3, c. 46.
130 *State of the Prisons*, 31.
131 Igantieff, *Just Measure*, 76–8; Fielding, *Enquiry*, ed. Zirker, 238–9, 253. See also Moir, *Local Government*, 115.
132 A. Atkinson, 'State and Empire and Convict Transportation, 1718–1812', in *New Perspectives*, ed. Bridge, 26, 34–5, 36.
133 Ignatieff, *Just Measure*, 107–9; Fisher, 'The Birth of the Prison Retold', 1238, 1242–3, and *passim*.
134 G.O. Paul, *Considerations on the Defects of Prisons, and their Present System of Regulation* (1784), 50.
135 Beattie, *Crime and the Courts*, 631–2.
136 For the uncertain status of assault and battery see Hawkins, *Pleas of the Crown*, i. 134; Blackstone, *Commentaries*, iii. 120–1.
137 See above, pp. 31–2; W. Paley, *The Law and Practice of Summary Convictions on Penal Statutes by Justices of the Peace* (1814), 73; 18 Geo. 3, c. 19.
138 P. King, 'Punishing Assault: The Transformation of Attitudes in the English Courts', *Journal of Interdisciplinary History* (1996), 43–74; Beattie, *Crime and the Courts*, 75–6, 88–9, 457–8, 609; id, 'Violence and Society', 42, 46–50 (quotation at 49).
139 Gatrell, 'Crime, Authority and the Policeman State', in F.M.L. Thompson (ed.) *The Cambridge Social History of Britain 1750–1950* (Cambridge, 1990), iii. 243–310; also P. O'Brien, 'Crime and Punishment as Historical Problem', *Journal of Social History*, 11 (1978), esp. 517.
140 See, in particular, R. Paley, '"An Imperfect, Inadequate and Wretched System"? Policing London before Peel', in *Criminal Justice History*, 10 (1989), 95–130.
141 Kent, *English Village Constable*, ch. 2.
142 See above, pp. 37–8.
143 See R.D. Storch, 'Policing Rural Southern England Before the Police', in Hay and Snyder (eds.) *Policing and Prosecution*, 211–12, 222–3.
144 13 Edw. 1, stat. 2.
145 Beattie, *Policing and Punishment in London*, ch. 3.
146 In Westminster and Middlesex most of these acts were solicited by and confined to individual parishes, but limited centralizing measures were passed for Westminster in 1756 and 1774. The latter introduced patrols of watchmen to supplement those stationed at particular points. (See E.A. Reynolds, *Before the Bobbies: The Night Watch and Police Reform in Metropolitan London, 1720–1830* (Stanford, Ca., 1998), ch. 4; Radzinowicz, *A History of English Criminal Law and its Administration from 1750*, ii. 185).
147 Reynolds, *Before the Bobbies*, 42, 43.
148 Beattie, *Policing and Punishment in London*, 178–94, 221–5, quotation at 224; Reynolds, *Before the Bobbies*, chs. 2–3.
149 In Newcastle on Tyne, however, householders continued to serve as watchmen into the middle of the eighteenth century (G. Morgan and P. Rushton, *Rogues, Thieves and the Rule of Law* (1998), 27–8).
150 Beattie, *Policing and Punishment in London*, 202–4.
151 Beattie, *Policing and Punishment*, 153–5, 205–6.
152 F.N. Dabhwoila, 'Prostitution and Policing in London, c. 1680–c.1760' (Univ. of Oxford D.Phil. thesis, 1995), *passim*; idem, 'Sex and Societies for Moral Reform, 1688–1800', *Journal of British Studies*, 46 (2007), 303–8. See also J. Innes, 'The Protestant Carpenter – William Payne of Bell Yard (*c.* 1718–82): the Life and Times

153 *Ipswich Journal*, 26 Apr., 1783.
154 Beattie, *Policing and Punishment*, 155–7.
155 *A Treatise on the Police of the Metropolis* (1796), 316–17 (orig. emphasis).
156 S. Johnson, *A Dictionary of the English Language* (1755). A. Smith, *Lectures on Justice, Police, Revenue and Arms*, ed. E. Cannan (New York, 1956), 3, 154; Blackstone, *Commentaries*, iv. 162.
157 *Defects of Police*, 237–8.
158 J. Fielding, *An Account of the Origin and Effects of a Police set on foot by His Grace the Duke of Newcastle in the Year 1753, upon a Plan presented to his Grace by the late Henry Fielding, Esq.* (1758), 15–20, 28–40.
159 *A Treatise on the Police of the Metropolis, explaining the Various Crimes and Misdemeanours which at Present are felt as a Pressure upon the Community, and Suggesting Remedies for their Prevention*.
160 J.H. Langbein, 'Shaping the Eighteenth-Century Criminal Trial: A View from the Ryder Sources', *Univ. of Chicago Law Review*, 50 (1983), 60; id, *The Origins of Adversary Criminal Trial* (Oxford, 2003), 118.
161 Radzinowicz, *History of English Criminal Law and its Administration*, iii. 29–62. See also J.M. Beattie, 'Sir John Fielding and Public Justice: the Bow Street Magistrates' Court, 1754–1780', *Law and History Review*, 25 (2007), 61–100.
162 Beattie, *Crime and the Courts*, 65–6 (describing the Southwark office).
163 *Police of the Metropolis*, 227–8.
164 *Police of the Metropolis*, ch. 9, esp. 228–41.
165 Atkinson, 'State and Empire and Convict Transportation', 29–30.
166 *Parliamentary History*, xxv. 891.
167 Radzinowicz, *History of English Criminal Law and its Administration*, iii. 110–17; Palmer, *Police and Protest*, 90; 'A Bill for the further Prevention of Crimes', in *House of Commons Sessional Papers of the Eighteenth Century*, ed. S. Lambert (Wilmington, Delaware, 1975), xlvi. esp. 519–21.
168 *Parliamentary History*, xxv. 889–90.
169 *Parliamentary History*, xxv. 896, 900–13.
170 Palmer, *Police and Protest*, 81, 92–3, 97–103.
171 *The House of Commons 1790–1820*, ed. R.G. Thorne (1986), iii. 341–3; Radzinowicz, *History of English Criminal Law and its Administration*, iii. 126–30; 32 Geo. 3, c. 53, s. 17.
172 *Parliamentary History*, xxix. 1465, 1469, 1472.
173 See B.P. Smith, 'The Presumption of Guilt and the English Law of Theft, 1750–1850', *Law and History Review*, 23 (2005), 133–71.
174 Id, 'The Emergence of Public Prosecution in London, 1790–1850', *Yale Journal of Law and the Humanities*, 32 (2006), 29–62. See also Beattie, *Policing and Prosecution in London*, 28–9.
175 J. Briggs et al, *Crime and Punishment in England* (1996), 142.
176 Paley, 'Policing London before Peel', 109–11, 118–22; Palmer, *Police and Protest*, 32–3; D. Philips, '"A New Engine of Power and Authority": The Institutionalization of Law-Enforcement in England', in V.A.C. Gatrell et al (eds.) *Crime and the Law: the Social History of Crime in Europe since 1500* (1980), 178–1830, 181–2; Radzinowicz, *History of Criminal Law and its Administration from 1750*, iii. 58–62, 135–7, 293; T. Skyrme, *History of the Justices of the Peace* (Chichester, 1991), ii. 147–8. For an overview of the complex story of policing in this period, see D. Hay and F. Snyder 'Using the Criminal Law: Policing, Private Prosecution and the State', in Hay and Snyder (eds.) *Policing and Prosecution*, ch. 1.

216　*Notes*

177　Philips, 'New Engine', 189.
178　Moir, *Justice of the Peace*, 127; Philips, 'New Engine', 171; 45 Geo. 3, c. 59 (Local and Personal Acts); 53 Geo. 3, c. 72; R. Storch, 'Policing Rural England before the Police', in *Policing and Prosecution*, ed. Hay and Snyder, 216–21; D. Taylor, *The New Police in Nineteenth-Century England* (Manchester, 1997), 24–31; see also Eastwood, *Governing Rural England*, 225–42.
179　Philips, 'New Engine', 156–7.
180　Compare F.M. Dodsworth, '"Civic" Police and the Condition of Liberty: The Rationality of Governance in Eighteenth-Century England', *Social History*, 29 (2004), 199–216, who identifies the defenders of traditional policing with civic humanist ideas.
181　D. Robinson, 'The Local Government of the Metropolis, and other Populous Places', *Blackwood's Edinburgh Magazine*, 29 (1831), 82–104.
182　Beccaria, *Essay* (Edinburgh, 1787), esp. 48–9, 167–8.
183　Blackstone, *Commentaries*, iv. 121, 133; Hawkins, *Treatise of Pleas of the Crown*, i. 125; Mandeville, *Enquiry into the Causes of Frequent Executions*, 1–9; Fielding, *Increase of Robbers*, 154–8.
184　Radzinowicz, i. 366–9; Colquhoun, *Police of the Metropolis*, 249, 253–7.
185　D. Hay, 'Controlling the English Prosecutor', *Osgoode Hall Law Journal*, 21 (1983), 174–6.
186　Beattie, *Crime and the Courts*, 42–8; Philips, 'New Engine', 179.
187　Colquhoun, *Police of the Metropolis*, 219–20.
188　Beattie, *Policing and Punishment*, 378–80, 408–9.
189　*Newcastle Gazette*, 8 and 23 Feb., 1749.
190　Beccaria, *Essay on Crimes and Punishments*, 144–5.
191　For Wild see G. Howson, *Thief-Taker General* (New York, 1970).
192　Langbein, *Adversarial Criminal Trial*, 152–7; id, 'Shaping the Eighteenth-century Criminal Trial', 108–14. See also R. Paley, 'Thief-takers in London in the Age of the McDaniel Gang, c.1745–1754', in Hay and Snyder (eds.) *Policing and Prosecution*, 301–41.
193　Beattie, *Policing*, 85, 131, 233–47, 401–23. For the continued importance of 'entrepreneurial policing' in the Bank of England's campaign against forgery, see also R. McGowen, 'The Bank of England and the Policing of Forgery 1797–1821', *Past and Present*, 186 (2005), 81–116.
194　Fielding, *Enquiry*, ed. Zirker, 154.
195　See Langbein, 'Shaping', 61–76.
196　Hay, 'Controlling the English Prosecutor', 175.
197　Smith, 'The Emergence of Public Prosecution', 60–1.
198　Beattie, *Policing and Punishment*, 105–13; id, 'Sir John Fielding and Public Justice'; Langbein, 'Shaping', 55–84.
199　Beattie, *Policing and Punishment*, 107, 112. Eventually the preliminary hearing was regulated by the statutes 6&7 Wm. 4, c. 114 (1836) and 11&12 Vict. c. 42 (1848).
200　Langbein, 'Shaping', 64 and n., 73–4.
201　2&3 Phil. & Mary, c. 10 (1555).
202　Langbein, 'Albion's Fatal Flaws', 103–4; id, 'Shaping', 81, 84–105.
203　Beattie, *Policing and Punishment*, 103; Langbein, 'Shaping', 92. But see also Beattie, 'Sir John Fielding and Public Justice'.
204　See above, pp. 85, 87.
205　Beattie, *Policing and Punishment*, 384–91.
206　J.H. Langbein, 'The Prosecutorial Origins of Defence Counsel in the Eighteenth Century: The Appearance of Solicitors', *Cambridge Law Journal*, 58 (1999), 314–65; id, *Adversary Criminal Trial*, 111–36. For the prosecution associations see generally

D. Philips, 'Good Men to Associate and Bad Men to Conspire: Associations for the Prosecution of Felons in England 1760–1860', in Hay and Snyder (eds.) *Policing and Prosecution in Britain*, 113–70.
207 Langbein, 'Prosecutorial Origins', 319.
208 Beattie, *Crime and the Courts*, 356–7; id, 'Scales of Justice: Defence Counsel and the English Criminal Trial in the Eighteenth and Nineteenth Centuries', *Law and History Review*, 9 (1991), 226–8; J.H. Langbein, 'The Criminal Trial before the Lawyers', *University of Chicago Law Review*, 45 (1978), 311–14. Lemmings has shown that besides appearing in full trials, during the mid-1750s counsel were also representing defendants in interlocutory hearings relating to motions for the bringing on or deferral of trials (*Professors of the Law*, 209).
209 Langbein, 'Prosecutorial Origins', passim; id, *Adversary Criminal Trial*, 148–77. See also Beattie, *Policing and Punishment*, 395–401.
210 Langbein, *Adversary Criminal Trial*, 196, 242–4. For ideas and speculations about the reasons for the increase in numbers of counsel after 1780 see Lemmings, *Professors*, 214–18; T.P. Gallanis, 'The Mystery of Old Bailey Counsel', *Cambridge Law Journal*, 65 (2006), 159–73.
211 Langbein, *Adversary Criminal Trial*, 258–66; id, 'Shaping', 130–1; Beattie, 'Scales of Justice', 232–6, 248–50; A. May, *The Bar and the Old Bailey, 1750–1850* (Chapel Hill, NC, 2003), 34–5.
212 Langbein, *Adversary Criminal Trial*, 319.
213 Lincoln's Inn Library, Harrowby MSS, doc. 14, pp. 4–6.
214 *Proceedings of the Old Bailey*, Jan., 1790, p. 235 (*R. v. Hayward*). See generally Langbein, *Adversary Criminal Trial*, 277–84; id, 'The Historical Origins of the Privilege against Self-incrimination at Common Law', *Michigan Law Review*, 92 (1993–4), 1066–71.
215 Langbein, *Adversary Criminal Trial*, ch. 5; C. Cottu, *On the Administration of Criminal Justice in England* (1822 [1st edn., 1820]), 33–7, 86–9, 93–4, 105–6; id, 'Criminal Trial before the Lawyers', 273, 307; id, 'Prosecutorial Origins', 328–32.
216 Beattie, 'Scales of Justice', 250–8; 6&7 Wm. 4, c. 114, s. 1. The committal hearing was regulated – and the accused's right to silence enforced – by legislation of 1848 (Langbein, *Adversary Criminal Trial*, 276).
217 Langbein, *Adversary Criminal Trial*, 20–1, 35–6, 48–61.
218 Langbein, *Adversary Criminal Trial*, ch. 1; id, 'Shaping', 41, 131; id, 'Criminal Trial before the Lawyers', 282–3; id, 'Privilege against Self-incrimination', 1047–65.
219 *Proceedings of the Old Bailey*, Oct., 1732, p. 229 (*R. v. Davison*).
220 Langbein, *Adversary Criminal Trial*, 33–4.
221 Beattie, 'Scales of Justice', 254–5.
222 *Treatise*, ii. 400b.
223 Compare Langbein, 'Criminal Trial', 310–11; id, 'Privilege Against Self-incrimination', 1053.
224 See J.M. Mitnick, 'From Neighbour-witness to Judge of Proofs: The Transformation of the English Civil Juror', *American Journal of Legal History*, 32 (1988), 201–9.
225 See Langbein, 'Criminal Trial before the Lawyers', 273–7, 288, 301–6; id, 'Privilege Against Self-incrimination', 1048–66; J. Oldham, *The Mansfield Manuscripts and the Growth of English Law in the Eighteenth Century* (Chapel Hill, NC, 1992), i. 138–9. But compare Langbein, *Adversary Criminal Trial*, 64, describing the early modern trial jury as 'passive triers' compared with their medieval counterparts.
226 Mitnick, 'Transformation of the English Civil Juror', 203–4.
227 Langbein, *Adversary Criminal Trial*, 319.

218  Notes

228  *Proceedings of the Old Bailey*, Oct., 1732, 237 (*R. v. Headly and Chapman*).
229  *Proceedings of the Old Bailey*, Oct., 1732, 244 (*R. v. Headly and Chapman*). See also Langbein, 'Criminal Trial', 288–9, 298n.
230  Langbein, 'Criminal Trial', 291–7.
231  e.g. *Charges to the Grand Jury*, ed. Lamoine, 375–6, 379: charges of 1752 and 1767.
232  Langbein, *Adversary Criminal Trial*, 321–31.
233  Mitnick, 'From Neighbour-witness to Judge of Proofs', 223–6 (discussing *Dormer v. Pankhurst*).
234  A.W.B. Simpson, *Legal Theory and Legal History* (1987), 270, 329–30; J.H. Baker, *An Introduction to English Legal History* (3rd edn., 1990), 398–9.
235  4&5 Wm. & Mary, c. 24, s. 15; 7&8 Wm. 3, c. 32; 3 Geo. 2, c. 25. See D. Hay, 'The Class Composition of the Palladium of Liberty: Trial Jurors in the Eighteenth Century', in J.S. Cockburn and T.A. Green (eds.) *Twelve Good Men and True: the Criminal Trial Jury in England, 1200–1800* (Princeton, NJ, 1988), 310–11, 316–17.
236  J.C. Oldham, 'The Origins of the Special Jury', *University of Chicago Law Review*, 50 (1983), esp. 140, n. 13; 3 Geo. 2, c. 25, ss. 15–17. See also J.C. Oldham, 'Special Juries in England: Nineteenth-century Usage and Reform', in *Journal of Legal History*, 8 (1987), esp. 148–53; id, *Mansfield Manuscripts*, 93–9, 242–4; above, ch. 3, p. 78.
237  S. Landsman, 'One Hundred Years of Rectitude: Medical Witnesses at the Old Bailey, 1717–1817', *Law and History Review*, 16 (1998), 454.
238  M. Gaskill, *Crime and Mentalities in Early Modern England* (Cambridge, 2000), ch. 7, esp. 269–70, 273–5, 279.
239  Of course I am aware that eighteenth-century trial jurors were 'middling sorts', and hardly intimate with the lowest sectors of English society. But I would argue, with Thomas Green, that they were liable to be influenced by the attitudes and preoccupations of those below them in the social scale, especially in the peculiar circumstances of the criminal trial (T.A. Green, 'A Retrospective on the Criminal Trial Jury, 1200–1800', in Cockburn and Green (eds.) *Twelve Good Men and True*, 389–90, 394, 399).
240  B. Shapiro, '"To a Moral Certainty": Theories of Knowledge and Anglo-American Juries 1600–1850', *Hastings Law Journal*, 38 (1986), 153–93; T. Starkie, *A Practical Treatise on the Law of Evidence, and Digest of Proofs, in Civil and Criminal Proceedings* (2nd ed., 1824), i. 514.
241  Langbein, *Adversary Criminal Trial*, 250.

## Chapter 5   Parliament, Legislation and the People: The Idea and Experience of Leviathan

1  J. Hoppit, 'Patterns of Parliamentary Legislation, 1660–1800', *The Historical Journal*, 39 (1996), 109. See also J. Hoppit, J. Innes, and J. Styles, 'Project Report: Towards a History of Parliamentary Legislation', *Parliamentary History*, 13 (1994), 313.
2  P. Langford, *Public Life and the Propertied Englishman* (Oxford, 1991), 165; L. Davison et al (eds.) *Stilling the Grumbling Hive: The Response to Social and Economic Problems in England, 1689–1750* (Stroud, 1992), xli.
3  Holdsworth, *History of English Law*, x. 547–8. See also J. Innes, 'Legislation and Public Participation 1760–1830', in D. Lemmings (ed.) *The British and Their Laws in the Eighteenth Century* (Woodbridge, 2005).

4   See R. Connors, 'The Grand Inquest of the Nation: Parliamentary Committees and Social Policy in Mid-Eighteenth-Century England', *Parliamentary History*, 14 (1995), 296–7. Also generally, E.S. Morgan, *Inventing the People: The Rise of Popular Sovereignty in England and America* (New York, 1988), esp. ch. 2.
5   Langford, *Public Life*, 207, 211, 212.
6   Referring to: (e.g.) the Highways Acts of 1691 and 1696 (3 Wm. & Mary, c. 12; 8 & 9 Wm. 3, c. 16); the increasing numbers and controversial statutory powers of excise officers (for which see Brewer, *Sinews of Power*, 102–5, 113–14; Blackstone, *Commentaries*, i. 308); the Marriage Act of 1753 (26 Geo. 2, c. 33); and the 1751 act for reforming the calendar (24 Geo. 2, c. 23).
7   See ch. 2 above, pp. 32–4. For a balanced account, see also H. Horwitz, 'Liberty, Law, and Property, 1689–1776', in J.R. Jones (ed.) *Liberty Secured? Britain Before and After 1688* (Stanford, Ca., 1992), 281–3.
8   *Principles Upon which the Taking the Oath of Abjuration May be Grounded* (1702), 11–14.
9   BL, Add. 36,115 (Hardwicke MSS), ff. 75v–76: charge to Grand Jury, n.d.
10  P. Langford, *The Excise Crisis* (2002); L.G. Schwoerer, *No Standing Armies: the Antiarmy Ideology in Seventeenth-Century England* (Baltimore, Maryland, 1974), 190–5.
11  See e.g. H.T. Dickinson, *Bolingbroke* (1970), 186–94.
12  Pocock, *Virtue, Commerce and History: Essays on Political Thought and History, chiefly in the Eighteenth Century* (Cambridge, 1985), 48.
13  Langford, *Public Life*, 154–5.
14  *Seasonable and Affecting Observations on the Mutiny-Bill, Articles of War, and Use and Abuse of a Standing Army: in a Letter from a Member of Parliament to a Noble Lord* (1750), 12–14.
15  For the importance of English legal traditionalism in the origins of the American Revolution see generally J.P. Reid, *In Defiance of the Law: The Standing Army Controversy, the Two Constitutions, and the Coming of the American Revolution* (Chapel Hill, NC, 1981).
16  For some pre-Reformation examples of statutory regulation of local communities, see C.W. Brooks, *Law, Politics and Society in Early Modern England* (Cambridge, 2008), 270, 407–16.
17  H.T. Dickinson, 'The Eighteenth-Century Debate on the Sovereignty of Parliament', *Transactions of the Royal Historical Society*, 5th ser., 26 (1976), 191–3.
18  J. Locke, *An Essay Concerning the True Original, Extent and End of Civil Government* (1690), paras. 131, 135, 136, 212, 214, 220, 221–2, 226–7, 242. See also R. Ashcraft, *Revolutionary Politics and Locke's Two Treatises of Government* (Princeton, NJ, 1986), esp. 545–6, 575–7.
19  R. Atkyns, *The Power, Jurisdiction and Priviledge [sic] of Parliament; and the Antiquity of the House of Commons Asserted* (1689), 50–1. Atkyns was lord chief baron of Exchequer 1689–94.
20  Atkyns, *The Power, Jurisdiction and Priviledge of Parliament*, 14, 17–34; G. Petyt, *Lex Parliamentaria: or, A Treatise of the Laws and Customs of the Parliaments of England* (1690), 4–6.
21  J.G.A. Pocock, *The Ancient Constitution and the Fundamental Law* (Cambridge, 2nd edn., 1987), 49–50.
22  Dickinson, 'Sovereignty of Parliament', 197–9, 200–1; J. Carter, 'The Revolution and the Constitution', in G. Holmes (ed.) *Britain after the Glorious Revolution, 1689–1715*, (1969), 40–7.

23 *Jura Populi Anglicani: Or, the Subjects Right of Petitioning Set forth. Occasioned by the Case of the Kentish Petitioners* (1701), 16.
24 See more generally, J.W. Gough, *Fundamental Law in English Constitutional History* (Oxford, 1955), ch. 11; J.C. Holt, *Magna Carta* (Cambridge, 2nd edn., 1992), ch. 1.
25 *Parliamentary History*, vii. 304 (earl of Nottingham), 305, 339; Gough, *Fundamental Law*, 182–3.
26 Gough, *Fundamental Law*, 180, 184–5.
27 N. Rogers, *Crowds, Culture and Politics in Georgian Britain* (Oxford, 1998), 28–44; id, 'Popular Protest in Early Hanoverian London', *Past and Present*, 79 (1978), 70–100; J. Stevenson, *Popular Disturbances in England 1700–1832* (2nd edn., 1992), 27–31.
28 W. Blackstone, *Commentaries on the Laws of England* (Oxford, 1765–9), iv. 142–3.
29 R. Vogler, *Reading the Riot Act: The Magistracy, the Police and the Army in Civil Disorder* (Milton Keynes, 1991), 2; *The Craftsman*, no. 214 (8 Aug., 1730).
30 L. Radzinowicz, *A History of English Criminal Law and its Administration from 1750* (1948–56), i. 77. It was initially enacted for three years, but successively prolonged and made perpetual in 1758.
31 Radzinowicz, *History of English Criminal Law*, i. 51; E.P. Thompson, *Whigs and Hunters: the Origin of the Black Act* (Harmondsworth, 1975).
32 E. Cruickshanks and H. Erskine-Hill, 'The Waltham Black Act and Jacobitism', *Journal of British Studies*, 24 (1985), 358–65.
33 J.M. Beattie, *Policing and Punishment in London 1660–1750* (Oxford, 2001), 431.
34 See above, p. 94.
35 M. Zirker, 'General Introduction', in H. Fielding, *An Enquiry into the Causes of the Late Increase of Robbers and Related Writings*, ed. Zirker (Oxford, 1988), lxiv–lxvii.
36 *Bolingbroke: Political Writings*, ed. D. Armitage (Cambridge, 1997), 82–3, 124–5, 165–6; Dickinson, *Bolingbroke*, 197–206.
37 See Holt, *Magna Carta*, 4, 8–9 (Sir Edward Coke on Magna Carta). Similarly fundamentalist thinking had been applied to develop some current common law principles, as Lord Chief Justice Holt demonstrated, when he argued (in 1701), following Coke in *Bonham's Case* 'if an act of parliament should ordain that the same person should be party and judge, or what is the same thing, judge in his own cause, it would be a void act of parliament' (88 *Eng. Rep.* 1602: *City of London v. Wood*).
38 Q. Skinner, 'The Principles and Practice of Opposition: The Case of Bolingbroke versus Walpole', in N. McKendrick (ed.) *Historical Perspectives: Studies in English Thought and Society* (1974), 92–128; J.G.A. Pocock, *Virtue, Commerce and History* (Cambridge, 1985), 234–6, 239–41.
39 Fielding, 'A True State of the Case of Bosavern Penlez', in *Increase of Robbers*, ed. Zirker, 45.
40 *Seasonable and Affecting Observations on the Mutiny-Bill, Articles of War, and Use and Abuse of a Standing Army: in a Letter from a Member of Parliament to a Noble Lord* (1750), 64; [Augustus Hervey] *A Detection of the Considerations of the Navy-Bill. By a Seaman.* (1749), 12. See also *The Antient and Present State of Military Law in Great Britain Consider'd: With a Review of the Debates of the Army and Navy Bills.* (1749); *A Letter to a Member of Parliament: In Relation to the Bill for Punishing Mutiny and Desertion, &c.* n.d [1749?]; [A. Hervey] *A Letter from a Friend in the Country To a Friend at Will's Coffee-House; in Relation to Three Additional Articles of War* (1749); id, *Objections to the Thirty-Fourth Article of the Navy Bill* (1749); *Considerations on the*

*Bill for the Better Government of the Navy. By a Sea Officer.* (1749); *A Dialogue between a Lieutenant Of a Man of War, and a Captain In the Land Service Upon Half-Pay* (1749). Blackstone condemned the annual mutiny acts for investing 'arbitrary discretion' in the crown (*Commentaries*, i. 402–4).

41 *Parliamentary History*, xv. 6, 13, 72–3, 78. The Royal Marriages Act of 1772 (12 Geo. 3, c. 11) provoked similar arguments (Langford, *Public Life*, 130).
42 J.G.A. Pocock, *Virtue, Commerce and History* (Cambridge, 1985), 236–9, 247, 273–4, 280; above, ch. 4.
43 Dickinson, 'Sovereignty of Parliament', 210; Morgan, *Inventing the People*, 48; Connors, 'Grand Inquest of the Nation', 297–8.
44 Burke, 'Letter to the Sheriffs of Bristol ... on the Affairs of America' (1777), in *The Writings and Speeches of Edmund Burke: Vol. III*, ed. W.M. Elofson and J.A. Woods (Oxford, 1996), 314–15; BL, Add. MSS, 35,353, fos. 222–5: Hardwicke to Hon. Charles Yorke, 8 Sept. 1757 (... this is a Law, which it is impossible to cram down the People's throats by force'). See also P.C. Yorke, *The Life and Correspondence of Philip Yorke Earl of Hardwicke* (Cambridge, 1913), ii. 266–7, iii. 37. The statute in question was 30 Geo. 2, c. 25.
45 'Letter to the Sheriffs of Bristol on the Affairs of America', in *Writings and Speeches*, ed. Elofson and Woods, 319, 320.
46 *Parliamentary History*, xv. 725–34 (24 May, 1756).
47 *Commentaries*, i. 9–10, iv. 4, 239–41, 277–9.
48 *Commentaries*, i. 46, 52, 156.
49 R. Willman, 'Blackstone and the Theoretical Perfection of English Law in the Reign of Charles II', *Historical Journal*, 26 (1983), 42–3, 49–50, 52–3, 56–7, 70.
50 *Commentaries*, i. 70, 122–3, 140–1, 156–7. See also D. Lemmings, 'Blackstone and Law Reform by Education: Preparation for the Bar and Lawyerly Culture in Eighteenth-Century England', *Law and History Review*, 16 (1998), 251–2. And for a fuller account of Blackstone's complex approach to parliamentary sovereignty and legislation, see Lieberman, *Province of Legislation*, chs. 1 and 2.
51 H.G. Koenigsberger, 'Composite States, Representative Institutions and the American Revolution', *Historical Research*, 62 (1989), 150–1.
52 J.P. Reid, *In Defiance of the Law* (Chapel Hill, NC, 1981), 3, 121, and ch. 5 generally.
53 J.P. Greene, 'Competing Authorities: The Debate over Parliamentary Imperial Jurisdiction, 1763–1776', in P. Lawson (ed.) *Parliament and the Atlantic Empire* (Edinburgh, 1995), 59: citing [J. Dickinson,] *An Essay on the Constitutional Power of Great-Britain over the Colonies in America; with the Resolves of the Committee for the Province of Pennsylvania, and their Instructions to their Representatives in Assembly* (Philadelphia, 1774).
54 J.P. Greene, 'The Glorious Revolution and the British Empire 1688–1783', in L.G. Schwoerer (ed.) *The Revolution of 1688–1689: Changing Perspectives* (Cambridge, 1992), 267–8; D. Lemmings, *Professors of the Law* (Oxford, 2000), 239–47.
55 J.P. Reid, *In a Defiant Stance* (University Park, PA, 1977), ch. 16.
56 J.P. Greene, 'From the Perspective of Law: Context and Legitimacy in the Origins of the American Revolution', *South Atlantic Quarterly*, 85 (1986), 69–72.
57 Reid, *In Defiance of the Law*, 107–8, 157, 168.
58 Greene, 'Competing Authorities', 52–3.
59 *Parliamentary History*, xvi. 176.
60 *Parliamentary History*, xvi. 168–71: Lords' debate of 10 Feb., 1766 (my emphasis).

61  L. Namier and J. Brooke, *The House of Commons 1754–1790* (1985), ii. 96–7.
62  P. Langford, 'Old Whigs, Old Tories, and the American Revolution', in P. Marshall and G. Williams (eds.) *The British Atlantic Empire before the American Revolution* (1980), 114–16.
63  G. Sharp, *A Declaration of the People's Natural Right to a Share in the Legislature* (1774), xxix; id, *An Address to the People of England: Being the Protest of a Private Person Against every Suspension of Law that is Liable to injure or endanger Personal Security* (1778), 17–19, 233–9.
64  *Parliamentary History*, xix. 570. See also R. Price, *Observations on the Nature of Civil Liberty, the Principles of Government, and the Justice and Policy of the War with America* (2nd edn., 1776).
65  C. Lofft, *An Argument on the Nature of Party and Faction. In which is considered, the Duty of a Good and Peaceable Citizen at the Present Crisis* (1780), 51.
66  *An Enquiry into the Doctrine, Lately Propogated, Concerning Libels, Warrants, and the Seizure of Papers* (1764), 90. See also J. Brewer, *The Wilkites and the Law, 1763–74: a Study of Radical Notions of Governance*, in J. Brewer and J. Styles (eds.) *An Ungovernable People* (1980), 128–71.
67  C. Macaulay, *An Address to the People of England, Scotland, and Ireland, on the Present Important Crisis of Affairs* (1775), 16–17, 25.
68  Langford, 'Old Whigs, Old Tories', 124–5.
69  K. Wilson, *The Sense of the People: Politics, Culture and Imperialism in England, 1715–1785* (Cambridge, 1995), 440; L. Colley, *Britons: Forging the Nation 1707–1837* (New Haven, CT, 1992), ch. 5.
70  See F. O'Gorman, 'Pitt and the "Tory" Reaction to the French Revolution 1789–1815', in H.T. Dickinson (ed.) *Britain and the French Revolution, 1789–1815* (Basingstoke, 1989), 25–6.
71  34 Geo. 3, c. 54; 36 Geo. 3, c. 7; 36 Geo. 3, c. 8. For contextualization and exegesis of the Treasonable Practices and Seditious Meetings Acts see J. Barrell, *Imagining the King's Death: Figurative Treason, Fantasies of Regicide, 1793–1796* (Oxford, 2000), ch. 16.
72  A.V. Beedell, 'John Reeve's Prosecution for a Seditious Libel, 1795–6: A Study in Political Cynicism', *Historical Journal*, 36 (1993), 799–824.
73  *The Parliamentary Register*, xliii (1795), 322. Another account has Pitt saying 'The power of the law of England, I trust, will be sufficient to defeat the machinations of all who risk such dangerous doctrines, and to punish treason wherever it may be found' (*Parliamentary History*, xxxii. 385: 23 Nov., 1785).
74  *Parliamentary History*, xxxii. 258 (11 Nov., 1795).
75  O'Gorman, 'Pitt and the Tory Reaction', 33. The Treasonable Practices Act was subsequently made permanent.
76  In 1794 the law officers of the crown failed to establish their doctrine of constructive treason sufficiently to secure the conviction of the leading radicals. For an extended narrative, see Barrell, *Imagining the King's Death*, 318–441.
77  See J. Ehrman, *The Younger Pitt: the Years of Acclaim* (1969), esp. ch. 10.
78  Ehrman, *Younger Pitt*, 252; [W. Dent] *The Free-Born Briton or a Perspective of Taxation* (1786) Brit. Museum Catalogue, 6914.
79  Pocock, *Virtue, Commerce and History*, 278.
80  W. Paley, *The Principles of Moral and Political Philosophy* (1785), book 6.
81  Paley, *Principles*, iii–v, 410–11, 423–4, 426–7, 434, 449, 464, 472–3, 488–90. For an interesting argument about the post-1776 emphasis on the benevolence of patrician rule see E. Gould, 'American Independence and Britain's Counter-Revolution', *Past and Present*, 154 (1997), esp. 121–38.

82  E. Burke, *Reflections on the Revolution in France*, ed. C.C. O'Brien (Harmondsworth, 1968), 120, 194–6 (Burke's italics); id, *An Appeal from the New to the Old Whigs* (1791), 39–40, 48–9, 88–90; *Parliamentary History*, xxx. 551, 554–5: 28 Feb., 1793; H.T. Dickinson, *Liberty and Property: Political Ideology in Eighteenth-Century Britain* (1977), 287, 290, 296; See also J.G.A. Pocock, 'Burke and the Ancient Constitution', in id, *Politics, Language and Time* (New York, 1971), 202–32.

83  R. Chambers, *A Course of Lectures on the English Law Delivered at the University of Oxford 1767–1773*, ed. T.M. Curley (Oxford, 1986), 29–39, 140 (Chambers's italics).

84  J. Brewer, 'The Eighteenth-Century British State: Contexts and Issues', in L. Stone (ed.) *An Imperial State at Law: Britain from 1689–1815* (1994), 55–6.

85  [G. Sharp] *An Address to the People of England*, 25–6, 28–9; Blackstone, *Commentaries*, i. 42–3.

86  Blackstone, *Commentaries*, i. 55.

87  *Principles of Penal Law* (1771), ch. 24 (his italics).

88  [S. Romilly,] *Observations on a Late Publication, intituled, Thoughts on Executive Justice* (1786), 2, 15, 36, 38, 43.

89  By comparison with most other species of legislation, 'law and order' measures were more likely to fail (J. Hoppit (ed.) *Failed Legislation 1660–1800* (1997), 9).

90  Lieberman, *Province of Legislation*, 199.

91  [Romilly,] *Observations*, 106–7.

92  See e.g. E.A. Reynolds, *Before the Bobbies: The Night Watch and Police Reform in Metropolitan London, 1720–1830* (Stanford, CA, 1998), 6 and 41–2.

93  Langford, *Public Life*, 156.

94  Adapting a term used by J.G.A. Pocock (*Virtue*, 234).

95  Hoppit, 'Patterns of Parliamentary Legislation', 117–18. Around 27 per cent of all legislation 1689–1800 consisted of general acts.

96  The coincidence between warfare and rising numbers of statutes applying to these areas has been clearly demonstrated for the Revolutionary and Napoleonic wars (P. Harling and P. Mandler, 'From "Fiscal-Military" State to Laissez-faire State, 1760–1850', *Journal of British Studies*, 32 (1993), 50–2).

97  J. Innes, 'Parliament and the Shaping of Eighteenth-Century English Social Policy', *Transactions of the Royal Historical Society*, 5th ser., 40 (1990), 63–93.

98  See S. Biddle, *Bills and Acts: Legislative Procedure in Eighteenth-Century England* (Cambridge, 1971), 71–83.

99  P.G.M. Dickson, *The Financial Revolution in England* (1967), 243; Connors, 'Grand Inquest', 299–312; Rogers, 'Confronting the Crime Wave', 88–92.

100  T.C. Curtis and W.A. Speck, 'The Societies for the Reformation of Manners: A Case Study in the Theory and Practice of Moral Reform', *Literature and History*, 3 (1976), 45–64.; M. Ingram, 'Reformation of Manners in Early Modern England', in P. Griffiths et al (eds.) *The Experience of Authority in Early Modern England* (Basingstoke, 1996), 47–88.

101  Innes, 'Politics and Morals', 83–5, 88, 91, 92–5.

102  R.B. Shoemaker, 'Reforming the City: the Reformation of Manners Campaign in London, 1690–1738', in *Stilling the Grumbling Hive*, ed. Davison et al, 99–120; L. Davison, 'Experiments in the Social Regulation of Industry: Gin Legislation, 1729–1751', in *Stilling the Grumbling Hive*, 25–48; Connors, 'Grand Inquest', 306–7.

103  *Gent. Mag.* xxii (1752), 30–1. The bill became law as 25 Geo. 2, c. 36.

104  *Tory and Whig: the Parliamentary Papers of Edward Harley, 3rd Earl of Oxford, and William Hay, MP for Seaford 1716–1753*, ed. S. Taylor and C. Jones (Woodbridge,

1998), 149: diary of William Hay, MP for Seaford, 3 Feb., 1736/7. See also Davison, 'Gin Legislation', 41; Reid, *In Defiance of the Law*, 121–4. Lord Hardwicke reacted in a similar way (see Yorke, *Hardwicke*, i. 137–40).
105  *Commentaries*, iv. 245–6; for details see Radzinowicz, *History of English Criminal Law*, i. 642–50.
106  See R. McGowen, 'From Pillory to Gallows: the Punishment of Forgery in the Age of the Financial Revolution', *Past and Present*, 165 (1999), esp. 109–10, 114–15, 127–8, 134–7, 139–40. For a broader consideration of forgery legislation see idem, 'Forgery Legislation in Eighteenth-Century England', in N. Landau (ed.) *Law, Crime and English Society 1660–1830* (Cambridge, 2002), 117–38.
107  J.G. Rule, *The Experience of Labour in Eighteenth-century Industry* (1981), 125–34; J. Styles, 'Embezzlement, Industry and the Law in England, 1500–1800', in P. Hudson and M. Sonenscher (eds.) *Manufacture in Town and Country before the Factory* (Cambridge, 1983), 184–7.
108  Douglas Hay has shown that master and servant law generally became harsher for workers in the eighteenth century as a consequence of statutory invention. Besides the particular provisions relating to embezzlement already mentioned, a body of statutes passed between 1720 and 1792 significantly increased the penalties available to magistrates adjudicating masters' complaints against their servants' misdemeanours: terms of imprisonment rose from one to three months and those convicted could be subjected to hard labour or even whipping (D. Hay, 'England, 1562–1875: The Law and its Uses', in D. Hay and P. Craven, *Masters, Servants, and Magistrates in Britain and the Empire, 1562–1955* (Chapel Hill, NC, 2004), 82–91). For the deployment of this law by employers from the mid-eighteenth century see D. Hay, 'Master and Servant in England: using the Law in the Eighteenth and Nineteenth Centuries', in W. Steinmetz (ed.) *Private Law and Social Inequality in the Industrial Age* (Oxford, 2000), 227–64.
109  22 Geo. 2, c. 27. T.S. Ashton, *An Economic History of England: The Eighteenth Century* (1955), 210.
110  Styles, 'Embezzlement, Industry and the Law', 190–1, 196; H. Horwitz, 'Liberty, Law, and Property, 1689–1776', in J.R. Jones (ed.) *Liberty Secured? Britain Before and After 1688* (Stanford, Ca., 1992), 286.
111  Styles, 'Embezzlement, Industry and the Law', sect. III, and app. 3. See esp. 22 Geo. 2, c. 27; 14 Geo. 3, c. 25, and 17 Geo. 3, c. 56.
112  17 Geo. 3, c. 11, 56, 24 Geo. 3, sess. 2, c. 3, 25 Geo. 3, c. 40, 31 Geo. 3, c. 56. See Rule, *Experience of Labour*, 131; Styles, 'Embezzlement, Industry and the Law', 195–6, 209–10.
113  Styles, 'Embezzlement, Industry and the Law', 204.
114  W.R. Cornish and G. de N. Clark, *Law and Society in England 1750–1950* (1989), 291–2; Holdsworth, *History of English Law*, xi. 471–2; 30 Geo. 2, c. 12; 13 Geo. 3, c. 68; 53 Geo. 3, c. 40.
115  T.K. Derry, 'The Repeal of the Apprenticeship Clauses of the Statute of Apprentices [sic]', *Economic History Review*, 3 (1931–2), 67–87; Holdsworth, *History of English Law*, xi. 420–1; 54 Geo. 3, c. 96.
116  For the complex experience of apprenticeship in the eighteenth century see Rule, *Experience of Labour*, ch. 4.
117  *Resolutions of the Master Manufacturers and Tradesmen of the Cities of London and Westminster, and the Vicinity, on the Statute of 5 Eliz. Cap. 4* (1814), 2 (resolution 8). See also M.J. Daunton, *Progress and Poverty: An Economic and Social History of Britain 1700–1850* (Oxford, 1995), 276.

118 E.P. Thompson, *Customs in Common* (Harmondsworth, 1993), chs. 4–5. See also D. Hay and N. Rogers, *Eighteenth-century English Society* (Oxford, 1997), 92–5, 110–13.
119 e.g. *Charges to the Grand Jury 1689–1803*, ed. G. Lamoine (Camden soc., 4th ser., 43, 1992), 313 (Guildford Quarter Sessions, 1745).
120 Thompson, *Customs in Common*, 199–200, citing Kenyon's charge to the Shropshire Grand Jury, 1795; D. Hay, 'Moral Economy, Political Economy and Law', in A. Randall and A. Charlesworth (eds.) *Moral Economy and Popular Protest: Crowds, Conflict and Authority* (Basingstoke, 2000), 93–122; idem, 'The State and the Market in 1800: Lord Kenyon and Mr. Waddington', *Past and Present*, 162 (1999), 101–62.
121 12 Geo. 3, c. 71. See Hay, 'Moral Economy, Political Economy and Law', 97–8.
122 *The Correspondence of Edmund Burke: Vol. IX* (Cambridge, 1970), 361–2; *Parliamentary History*, xxvi. 1169–70 (4 May, 1787).
123 A. Smith, *An Enquiry into the Nature and Causes of the Wealth of Nations*, ed. E. Cannan (repr. Chicago, 1976), 41, 48–9.
124 *Parliamentary History*, xxvi. 1169.
125 See M.E. Turner, *English Parliamentary Enclosure: Its Historical Geography and Economic History* (Folkestone, 1980), 68; also Hoppitt, 'Parliamentary Legislation, 1660–1800', 117, 121. There were over 1,600 more enclosure acts, 1800–19.
126 Turner, *Parliamentary Enclosure*, 135 and ch. 7.
127 J.L. and B. Hammond, *The Village Labourer, 1760–1832: A Study in the Government of England before the Reform Bill* (2nd edn., 1913), 49.
128 Turner, *Parliamentary Enclosure*, 153, 155.
129 *Parliamentary History*, xxii. 59: 30 Mar., 1781.
130 Hoppitt, 'Parliamentary Legislation', 122. Overall, the success rate for enclosure bills was over 75 per cent in the later eighteenth century (Hoppit (ed.) *Failed Legislation*, 9).
131 41 Geo. 3, c. 109.
132 For some examples where counter-petitions caused amendments and delays to enclosure, see M. Turner, 'Economic Protest in Rural Society: Opposition to Parliamentary Enclosure in Buckinghamshire', *Southern History*, 10 (1988), 99–105.
133 J.M. Neeson, *Commoners: Common Right, Enclosure and Social Change in England, 1700–1820* (Cambridge, 1993), 188–207. See also ibid, ch. 8 for evidence that in Northants. generally parliamentary enclosure 'destroyed the old peasant economy'. And for a more sympathetic account of the procedures in parliament, albeit derived from official records only, see Lambert, *Bills and Acts*, ch. 7.
134 Turner, *Parliamentary Enclosure*, 75–6, 93.
135 Turner, *Parliamentary Enclosure*, 157–62.
136 Ibid, 162. Turner rejects the interpretation which sees enclosure as a class struggle, however (Turner 'Opposition to Parliamentary Enclosure in Buckinghamshire', 115).
137 Neeson, *Commoners*, 218, 272–5. Turner notes that in 1800 parliament was actively looking for ways to ease the passage of enclosure bills (Turner, 'Opposition to Parliamentary Enclosure in Buckinghamshire', 98). For several rather selective examples of parliament's partiality in considering enclosure bills see Hammonds, *Village Labourer*, 45–58. And for a more sympathetic but purely institutional account of parliamentary proceedings in enclosure see Biddle, *Bills and Acts*, ch. 7.
138 Neeson, *Commoners*, 207–20; see also Holdsworth, *History of English Law*, xi. 455–6.
139 Hay and Rogers, *Eighteenth-century English Society*, 99–101.

140  E.P. Thompson, *The Making of the English Working Class* (Harmondsworth, 1968), 238–9; id, *Customs in Common* (Harmondsworth, 1993), 136–8; J. Rule, *The Vital Century: England's Developing Economy 1714–1815* (1992), 79; M. Daunton, *Progress and Poverty: An Economic and Social History of Britain 1700–1850* (Oxford, 1995), 107.
141  A. Young, *An Enquiry into the Propriety of Applying Wastes to the Better Maintenance and Support of the Poor* (1801), quoted Hammonds, *Village Labourer*, 83–4.
142  A. Young, *Six Months' Tour through the North of England* (2nd edn., 1771), i. 226.
143  F.W. Maitland, *The Constitutional History of England* (Cambridge, 1965), 382–3; Holdsworth, *History of English Law*, xi. 325–6; Hoppit, 'Parliamentary Legislation', 118, 130–1.
144  D. Lieberman, *The Province of Legislation Determined* (Cambridge, 1989), 23; cf. J.M. Beattie, *Policing and Prosecution in London* (Oxford, 2001), 464.
145  Langford, *Public Life*, 165.
146  Hoppit., 'Parliamentary Legislation', 123. See also R. Sweet, 'Local Identities and a National Parliament, c. 1688–1835', in J. Hoppit (ed.) *Parliaments, Nations and Identities in Britain and Ireland, 1660–1850* (Manchester, 2003), 50–4.
147  Hoppit, 'Parliamentary Legislation', 119, 120–1; *Failed Legislation*, ed. Hoppit, 10.
148  W. Albert, *The Turnpike Road System in England* (Cambridge, 1972), 45.
149  See above, pp. 21, 40, 50.
150  *Commons Journal*, xi. 650; see also 8&9 Wm. 3, c. 15.
151  *Commons Journal*, xxvi. 316 (4 Dec. 1751). See also 25 Geo. 2, c. 21.
152  Holdsworth, *History of English Law*, x. 307–9; E. Pawson, *Transport and Economy: The Turnpike Roads of Eighteenth Century Britain* (1977), 107.
153  The early acts vested these powers in the local JPs, but from 1706 it was usual for the legislation to establish trusts (Albert, *Turnpike Road System*, 22–3).
154  Albert, *Turnpike Road System*, 93.
155  Albert, *Turnpike Road System*, 98–100; Langford, *Public Life*, 250, 253, 258–9, 261. Sir William Blackstone's will shows that he was a heavy investor in turnpike bonds. He was also involved in turnpike schemes as a lawyer and a legislator (W. Prest, *William Blackstone: Law and Letters in the Eighteenth Century* (Oxford, 2008), 105–6, 202, 213, 227, 281).
156  S. and B. Webb, *Statutory Authorities for Special Purposes* (1922), 178–9. See also K. Wilson, *The Sense of the People: Politics, Culture and Imperialism in England, 1715–1785* (Cambridge, 1998), 343, 355. Nefarious practices of this kind seem to have been common in Ireland too: see *The New Circuit Companion; or a Mirror for Grand-Juries* (2nd edn., London, 1769), 26n.
157  See e.g. Reasons why the Bill for amending the High-Ways from Brampton-Bridge, to Welford-Bridge, in the County of Northampton; and also from Morter-Pit Hill in the said County, to Chain-Bridge, leading into Market-Harborough, in the County of Leicester, should not pass into a Law, as it now stands before your Lordships (printed petition to the House of Lords, 1721, at BL pressmark 576.m.17(17)) which included claims that the tolls would raise the price of Birmingham manufactures and increase the cost of travelling between the local markets, and complained specifically about the allegedly high tolls for passage of oxen and sheep.
158  The Kingswood colliers' letter to the Bristol turnpike trust, July 1727, quoted in Albert, *Turnpike Road System*, 28. See also R.W. Malcolmson, 'A Set of Ungovernable People: The Kingswood Colliers in the Eighteenth Century', in *An Ungovernable People*, ed. Brewer and Styles (1980), 95–7.

159 M. Freeman, 'Popular Attitudes to Turnpikes in Early Eighteenth-century England', *Journal of Historical Geography*, 19 (1993), 44. In the 1720s turnpike bills were often passed in six to eight weeks.
160 Freeman, 'Popular Attitudes to Turnpikes', esp. 36–7, 39–40. See also W. Albert, 'Popular Opposition to Turnpike Trusts in Early Eighteenth-Century England', *Journal of Transport History*, new ser., 5 (1979), 12; Rule, *Vital Century*, 247–8.
161 The principal source for my account of these riots is Malcolmson, 'A Set of Ungovernable People', but see also P.D. Jones, 'The Bristol Bridge Riot and its Antecedents: Eighteenth-Century Perception of the Crowd', *Journal of British Studies*, 19 (1980), 76–9 and A. Charlesworth, R. Sheldon, A. Randall and D. Walsh, 'The Jack-A-Lent Riots and Opposition to Turnpikes in the Bristol Region in 1749', in A. Randall and A. Charlesworth (eds.) *Markets, Market Culture and Popular Protest in Eighteenth-Century Britain and Ireland* (Liverpool, 1996), 46–67.
162 Albert, 'Popular Opposition to Turnpike Trusts', 4, 6–7, 10, 12.
163 Malcolmson, 'A Set of Ungovernable People', 107–9; Charlesworth et al, 'The Jack-A-Lent Riots and Opposition to Turnpikes', 49–54.
164 Charlesworth et al, 'The Jack-A-Lent Riots', esp. 55–6.
165 *Hints of Ledbury*, by a native inhabitant (Ledbury, 1831), pp. 126–33 (copy at Herefordshire RO, Hereford, J47/1). See also Thompson, *Whigs and Hunters*, 256–8, who says Reynolds was a collier.
166 Yorke, *Hardwicke*, i. 155–6. See also Malcolmson, 'A Set of Ungovernable People', 113; Charlesworth et al, 'The Jack-A-Lent Riots and Opposition to Turnpikes', 48.
167 Albert, 'Popular Opposition to Turnpike Trusts', 2; Thompson, *Whigs and Hunters*, 190–1.
168 1 Geo. 2, c. 19; 5 Geo. 2, c. 33, 8 Geo. 2, c. 20.
169 See Malcolmson, 'A Set of Ungovernable People', 98, 100–2.
170 Albert, *Turnpike Road System*, 22–3, 58–9.
171 Ibid., 59–60.
172 Albert, *Turnpike Road System*, 58; 13 Geo. 3, c. 84; 3 Geo. 4, c. 126.
173 Langford, *Public Life*, 208–9, 236–8, 239; Pawson, *Transport and Economy*, 174, 177–80.
174 For details of the trusts' administration, albeit with the authors' anachronistic gloss, see Webbs, *Statutory Authorities for Special Purposes* (1922), ch. 3, reprinting much of S. and B. Webb, *The Story of the King's Highway* (1913), ch. 7.
175 See above, pp. 61–2.
176 W. Hutton, *Courts of Requests: their Nature, Utility, and Powers described, with a variety of Cases, Determined in that of Birmingham* (Birmingham, 1787), 24; *Commons Journal*, xxvi. 368–9: Petition of mayor, aldermen, bailiffs & common council of Birmingham, and hamlets thereunto (16 Jan., 1752). For the courts of request generally see W.H. Winder, 'The Courts of Requests', *Law Quarterly Review*, 207 (1936), 369–94.
177 C.W. Brooks, *Lawyers, Litigation and English Society since 1450* (1998), 39–40; Langford, *Public Life*, 158–61.
178 See M. Finn, *The Character of Credit: Personal Debt in English Culture, 1740–1914* (Cambridge, 2003), chs. 5–6.
179 Langford, *Public Life*, 243–8.
180 26 Geo. 3, c. 38. The statutes establishing courts of conscience acts generally included clauses either prohibiting or discouraging removal of process to a higher court (Winder, 'Courts of Requests', 375).
181 See M.E. Fissell, 'Charity Universal? Institutions and Moral Reform in Eighteenth-Century Bristol', in *Stilling the Grumbling Hive*, ed. Davison et al, 121–44.

228  *Notes*

182 The general legislation relating to poor relief was less consistent. Knatchbull's act of 1723 gave parishes the general power to establish workhouses, and signified parliamentary approval of the workhouse test (9 Geo. 1, c. 7). However Gilbert's permissive act of 1782 facilitated relief outside the workhouse (22 Geo. 3, c. 83).

183 See S. and B. Webb, *Statutory Authorities for Special Purposes*, 110–44.

184 Webbs, *Statutory Authorities*, 144–7; F.H. Spencer, *Municipal Origins: An Account of English Private Bill Legislation Relating to Local Government, 1740–1835* (1911), 116–31.

185 Bristol RO, MS. M/BCC/CCP/1/1/8, f. 132: minutes of Common Council, 3 Feb., 1696 (the original proceedings in the establishment of the Bristol Corporation of the Poor). See also Langford, *Public Life*, 156–9, 240–3. There is an account of the parliamentary proceedings in relation to the establishment of the Bury St. Edmunds Corporation of the Poor in R.T. Connors, 'Pelham, Parliament and Public Policy, 1746–1754' (Univ. of Cambridge PhD thesis, 1993), 228–30. It should be noted that this was passed under private bill procedure, *contra* the implication at ibid, 260.

186 Langford, *Public Life*, 248, 251–2, 254–5. For their direct or indirect control over the rates see Spencer, *Municipal Origins*, pp. 125, 301–3.

187 Spencer, *Municipal Origins* 284–6. In the later acts the scope of physical punishment was limited to males.

188 Spencer, *Municipal Origins*, 296–301.

189 Spencer, *Municipal Origins*, 301; Holdsworth, *History of English Law*, x. 214.

190 Quoting the Webbs, commenting on the statutory powers of incorporated guardians (*Statutory Authorities*, 149). Cf. *Tory and Whig*, ed. Taylor and Jones, lxxv–lxxxi; Connors, 'Parliament and Public Policy', ch. 5; *Oxford DNB*, sub. Gilbert, Thomas. See also D. Eastwood, *Governing Rural England* (Oxford, 1994), ch. 5.

191 A. Digby, *Pauper Palaces* (1978), 37–8, 41–5.

192 S. and B. Webb, *English Poor Law History. Part 1: The Old Poor Law* (1927), 141–2 and n; Rule, *Albion's People*, 126–7; Digby, *Pauper Palaces*, 216–17.

193 J. Innes and N. Rogers, 'Politics and Government 1700–1840', in P. Clark (ed.) *The Cambridge Urban History of Britain. Vol. II 1540–1840* (Cambridge, 2000), 536–7; Spencer, *Municipal Origins*, p. 116.

194 For examples see Spencer, *Municipal Origins*, 117, 120.

195 Langford, *Public Life*, 207–8, 221, 267–87; Webbs, *Statutory Authorities*, 243–4.

196 Langford, *Public Life*, 225–7, 229–30.

197 Langford, *Public Life*, 207.

198 Langford, *Public Life*, 249–50.

199 Langford, *Public Life*, 212, 251.

200 Camden Local Studies and Archives Centre, St. Pancras Vestry MS. Minutes 1816–19, p. 51: 30 Jul. 1817. See also Spencer, *Municipal Origins*, 36–7, 118–19, 125.

201 See ch. 2 above; also M. Goldie, 'The Unacknowledged Republic: Officeholding in Early Modern England', in T. Harris (ed.) *The Politics of the Excluded, c.1500–1850* (Basingstoke, 2001), 153–4.

202 *Report of the Committee appointed by a Public Vestry, held on the 30th Day of July, 1817, to investigate the affairs of the Directors of the Poor of the Parish of St. Pancras* (1818), sig. A2.

203 P. Slack, *The English Poor Law, 1531–1782* (Cambridge, 1995), 37–9; Webbs, *Statutory Authorities*, 127–8, 134–5; *Report of the Committee*, 14.

204 *Report of the Committee*, 13–16.

205 For the full story see S. and B. Webb, *The Parish and the County* (1906), 207–11. For contemporary parliamentary opinion, as expressed in the 1817 select committee report on the poor laws and the Stourges Bourne legislation, see D. Eastwood, *Governing Rural England* (Oxford, 1994), 128–31. Around this time many rural parishes were also taking advantage of permissive general legislation to establish their own select vestries and appoint professional assistant overseers to administer poor relief (Eastwood, *Governing Rural England*, 175–8).
206 Baker, *Introduction to English Legal History*, 151.
207 G. Petyt, *Lex Parliamentaria* (1690), 7: quoting Sir Thomas Smith (see Smith, *De Republica Anglorum* (1563) ed. L. Alston (Cambridge, 1906), 49). See also Petyt, *Lex Parliamentaria*, 18–19: an act of parliament is 'the Prince's and the whole Realm's Deed; whereupon justly no man can complain, but must accommodate himself to find it good, and obey it' (also following Smith, *De Republica Anglorum*).
208 Blackstone, *Commentaries*, i. 51.
209 J.H. Plumb, *The Growth of Political Stability in England 1675–1725* (Harmondsworth, 1969), 39–41; G. Holmes, *Politics, Religion and Society in England 1679–1742* (1986), 13–24; F. O'Gorman, *Voters, Patrons, and Parties: The Unreformed Electoral System of Hanoverian England 1734–1832* (Oxford, 1989), 179.
210 O'Gorman, *Voters, Patrons and Parties*, 199–215.
211 J. Cannon, *Aristocratic Century: The Peerage of Eighteenth-century England* (Cambridge, 1984), 104–12.
212 N. Rogers, *Whigs and Cities: Popular Politics in the Age of Walpole and Pitt* (Oxford, 1989), 256–7 and chs. 5, 7, 8, 9; Wilson, *Sense of the People*, chs. 6–8; J. Innes and N. Rogers, 'Politics and Government', in P. Clark (ed.) *The Cambridge Urban History of Britain: Vol. II 1540–1840* (Cambridge, 2000), 558–9; O'Gorman, *Voters, Patrons and Parties*, 109–11, 225–85; H.T. Dickinson, *The Politics of the People in Eighteenth-century Britain* (Basingstoke, 1994), 36–42.
213 O'Gorman, *Voters, Patrons, and Parties*, 13.
214 N. Rogers, 'The City Elections Act (1725) Reconsidered', *English Hist. Rev.*, 100 (1985), 611, 616; id, *Whigs and Cities*, ch. 4. Similar legislation narrowed the civic electorate in Norwich (See Rogers, *Whigs and Cities*, 320–3; Wilson, *Sense of the People*, 390–1).
215 I.G. Doolittle, 'Walpole's City Elections Act (1725)', *English Hist. Rev.*, 97 (1982), 508, 511.
216 M. Knights, *Representation and Misrepresentation in Later Stuart Britain: Partisanship and Political Culture* (Oxford, 2005), 361–75.
217 Langford, *Public Life*, 280–1 (10 Anne, c. 23; 18 Geo., 2, c. 18; 20 Geo. 3, c. 17).
218 Langford, *Public Life*, 283–5.
219 F. O'Gorman, *The Long Eighteenth Century: British Political and Social History 1688–1832* (1997), 141–2. Cf. Langford, *Public Life*, 273–7.
220 J.V. Beckett, *The Aristocracy in England 1660–1914* (Oxford, 1986), 362–9.
221 P. Jenkins, *The Making of a Ruling Class: The Glamorgan Gentry 1640–1790* (Cambridge, 1983), esp. xviii–xix and ch. 9.
222 G. Rudé, *Hanoverian London* (1971), 41–3.
223 F.H.W. Sheppard, *Local Government in St. Marylebone 1688–1835: A Study of the Vestry and a Turnpike Trust* (1958), chs. 8–9; Webbs, *Parish and County*, 205–7.
224 Cf. Langford, *Public Life*, 139–40, 192–5.
225 The following two paragraphs are based principally on J. Innes, 'Legislation and Public Participation', in D. Lemmings (ed.) *The British and their Laws in the Eighteenth Century* (Woodbridge, 2005), 112–30.

230  *Notes*

226 13 Car 2, sess. 1, c. 5. See C.R. Kyle and J. Peacey, '"Under cover of so much coming and going": Public Access to Parliament and the Political Process in Early Modern England', in Kyle and Peacey (eds.) *Parliament at Work: Parliamentary Committees, Political Power and Public Access in Early Modern England* (Woodbridge, 2002), 12.

227 36 Geo. 3, c. 8; 60 Geo. 3 & 1 Geo. 4, c. 6. The former statute was in force for three years only.

228 For the 1780 petitions against the Catholic Relief Act see C. Haydon, *Anti-Catholicism in Eighteenth-century England: A Social and Political* Study (Manchester, 1993), 208–9; Wilson, *Sense of the People*, 366. For some examples of petitioning campaigns on general bills in the early eighteenth century see Hoppit, *Failed Legislation*, 19–20. And for the resurgence of political petitioning see P. Fraser, 'Public Petitioning and Parliament before 1832', *History*, 46 (1961), 201–2.

229 J.A. Phillips, 'Popular Politics in Unreformed England', *Journal of Modern History*, 52 (1980), 599–625.

230 See e.g. P. Jupp, *British Politics on the Eve of Reform: The Duke of Wellington's Administration, 1828–30* (Basingstoke, 1998), 219–25, 368–75.

231 Derry, 'Repeal of the Apprenticeship Clauses of the Statute of Apprentices', 84–7.

232 P.D.G. Thomas, *The House of Commons in the Eighteenth Century* (Oxford, 1971), 68–71.

233 Fraser, 'Public Petitioning', 210. See also C. Leys, 'Petitioning in the Nineteenth and Twentieth Centuries', *Political Studies*, 3 (1955), 47–53.

234 Jupp, *British Politics*, 221–5, 368.

235 For the further growth of popular petitioning during the Chartist agitation see P. Pickering, '"And your Petitioners &c": Chartist Petitioning in Popular Politics 1838–48', *English Historical Review*, 116 (2001), 368–88.

236 D. Dean, *Law-Making and Society in Late Elizabethan England: The Parliament of England, 1584–1601* (Cambridge, 1996), 137, 148, 151.

237 See e.g. D.W. Hayton, *The House of Commons 1690–1715* (2002), i. 402 for general committees of enquiry into social and economic matters.

238 See Jupp, *British Politics*, 173, 177, 210–11, 215–16.

239 Innes, 'Legislation and Public Participation', 128.

240 Innes, 'Legislation and Public Participation', 129–30.

241 J.R. Pole, *The Gift of Government: Political Responsibility from the English Restoration to American Independence* (Athens, Ga., 1983), ch. 4.

242 Kyle and Peacey, 'Public Access to Parliament'; Hayton, *House of Commons 1690–1715*, i. 367–70; Thomas, *House of Commons in the Eighteenth Century*, 141.

243 Thomas, *House of Commons in the Eighteenth Century*, 143–7.

244 P.D.G. Thomas, 'The Beginning of Parliamentary Reporting in Newspapers, 1768–1774', *Eng. Hist. Rev.*, 630, 632; see also A. Aspinall, 'The Reporting and Publishing of the House of Commons' Debates, 1771–1834', in R. Pares and A.J.P. Taylor (eds.) *Essays presented to Sir Louis Namier* (1956), 228–31.

245 Pole, *Gift of Government*, 89–90. In 1775 the House of Lords was also forced to tolerate reporting of its debates. For the crucial disputes over press coverage of debates see P.D.G. Thomas, *John Wilkes: A Friend to Liberty* (Oxford, 1996), ch. 8; W.C. Lowe, 'Peers and Printers: The Beginnings of Sustained Press Coverage of the House of Lords in the 1770s', *Parliamentary History*, vii (1988), 241–56.

246 A. Stephens, *Memoirs of John Horne Tooke* (1813), i. 344.

247 See Aspinall, 'House of Commons Debates', 237–8, 241–5, 247. For the increasingly serious treatment of parliamentary affairs in the newspapers during the early nineteenth century see Jupp, *British Politics*, 343–6, 355.

248  S. Lambert 'Printing for the House of Commons in the Eighteenth Century', *The Library*, 5th ser., 23 (1968), 25–30, 35–6, 38, 40–3.
249  Lambert, 'Printing for the House of Commons', 30–3. See also S. Lambert, *House of Commons Sessional Papers of the Eighteenth Century: Introduction and List* (Wilmington, Del., 1975), 49–53.
250  Innes, 'Legislation and Public Participation', 109–11; Jupp, *British Politics*, 343.
251  Holdsworth, *History of English Law*, iv. 307–13, vi. 312–13, xi. 290, 301–8.
252  See Lambert, *Bills and Acts*, ch. 9; Holdsworth, *History of English Law*, xi. 292–8 for the manifold confusions in classifying the statutes.
253  *The Newcastle Intelligencer*, 30 Nov., 1757. The author went on to complain 'it is difficult for the most cautious Man, who leads an active Life, to avoid offending innocently against some penal Statute; to which perhaps he is as great a Stranger as he may be to the Laws of the Koran'.
254  S. Devereaux, 'The Promulgation of the Statutes in Late Hanoverian Britain', in Lemmings, ed. *The British and Their Laws*, ch. 4.
255  See O'Gorman, *Voters, Patrons and Parties*, 292–300.
256  Fraser, 'Public Petitioning', 196–8; Jupp, *British Politics*, 330.
257  Holdsworth, *History of English Law*, x. 533–8, xi. 320.
258  For the application of private bill procedure see Lambert, *Bills and Acts*, 84–5, 150. It should be noted that the bills subjected to private bill procedure were not necessarily passed and promulgated as private acts.
259  Thomas, *House of Commons in the Eighteenth Century*, 57–60.
260  Above, n. 129. See also J.M. Martin, 'Members of Parliament and Enclosure: A Reconsideration', *Agric. Hist. Rev.*, 27 (1979), 101.
261  Holdsworth, *History of English Law*, xi. 329.
262  Lambert, *Bills and Acts*, 132, 134.
263  Neeson, *Commoners*, 273.
264  See above, n. 159.
265  Lambert, *Bills and Acts*, 96–100. See also Spencer, *Municipal Origins*, 57, 59.
266  Holdsworth, *History of English Law*, xi. 299–300, 337–8, 340.
267  Martin, 'Members of Parliament and Enclosure', 108.
268  Holdsworth, *History of English Law*, xi. 335–6. See Brewer, *Sinews of Power*, 239–49 for a more general consideration of parliamentary lobbying.
269  *Parliamentary History*, xxii. 60. The story was related in 1781 by Lord Chancellor Thurlow, and centred upon a stranger 'habited rather meanly' who attended a private bill committee and became extremely agitated. On Savile's enquiry he related how a clause in the bill was liable to ruin him and his family, but he could not fee counsel 'to defend his rights'. Savile reportedly assisted him so that his interests were protected.
270  See N. Rogers, 'Paul Langford's "Age of Improvement"', *Past and Present*, 130 (1991), 205–6.
271  Sheppard, *Local Government in St. Marylebone*, 110–21.
272  See e.g. Hay and Rogers, *Eighteenth-century English Society*, 192.
273  Langford, *Public Life*, 201; O.C. Williams, *The Historical Development of Private Bill Procedure and Standing orders in the House of Commons* (1948–9), i. 35–7; Lambert, *Bills and Acts*, 150–1, 175.
274  S. Handley, 'Local Legislative Initiatives for Economic and Social Development in Lancashire, 1689–1731', *Parliamentary History*, 9 (1990), 29.
275  Langford, *Public Life*, 176–86, 201, 202.

276 Ibid, 187.
277 Cf. Q. Skinner, *Liberty Before Liberalism* (Cambridge, 1998), 42–3.
278 Quoting a 1785 petition against a bill for paving the streets of Reading (Sweet, 'Local Identities', 52, 53–4).
279 Spenser, *Municipal Origins*, 54–5 provides many eighteenth-century examples. See also Lambert, *Bills and Acts*, 97–8.
280 Neeson, *Common Right*, 273, n. 44; Spenser, *Municipal Origins*, 61–2. For examples of interested parties packing committees for and against bills see Langford, *Public Life*, 202–3; Hayton, *House of Commons 1690–1715*, i. 423–4.
281 Martin, 'Members of Parliament and Enclosure'.
282 See Langford, *Public Life*, 202, citing T. Gisborne, *Enquiry into the Duties of Men* (3rd edn., 1797), i. 157.
283 C.R. Kyle, 'Attendance, Apathy and Order? Parliamentary Committees in Early Stuart England', in *Parliament at Work*, ed. Kyle and Peacey, 46; Paley, *Principles*, 498.
284 Hayton, *House of Commons 1690–1715*, i. 361–2.
285 See J.R. Pole, *Political Representation in England and the Origins of the American Republic* (Berkeley, Ca., 1971), 442–57 for the gradual recognition during the later eighteenth century of interest politics as the basis of parliamentary representation.

## Chapter 6  Conclusion: An Imperial State? Governance, People and Law in the Eighteenth Century

1 *The Whitehall Journal*, no. 46, Tues. 2 Apr., 1723, p. 275.
2 See A. Mckenzie, *Tyburn's Martyrs: Execution in England 1675–1775* (2007), esp. ch. 3.
3 J.M. Beattie, *Crime and the Courts in England, 1660–1800* (Oxford, 1986).
4 D. Lemmings, 'Conclusion: Moral Panics, Law and the Transformation of the Public Sphere in Early Modern England', in D. Lemmings and C. Walker (eds.) *Moral Panics, the Media and the Law in Early Modern England* (2009), 264.
5 S. Devereaux, 'From Sessions to Newspaper? Criminal Trial Reporting, the Nature of Crime, and the London Press, 1770–1800', *London Journal*, 32 (2007), 18.
6 See D. Sugarman, 'Anarchism, Marxism, and the Critique of Law', in D. Sugarman (ed.) *Legality, Ideology and the State* (1983), 218.
7 Cf. E.S. Morgan, *Inventing the People: the Rise of Popular Sovereignty in England and America* (New York, 1988), ch. 2.
8 A. Smith, *Lectures on Jurisprudence*, ed. R.L. Meek et al (Oxford, 1978), 208 (lecture of 1763).
9 A. Musson, 'Reconstructing English Labor Laws: A Medieval Perspective', in K. Robertson and M. Uebel (eds.) *The Middle Ages at Work: Practicing Labor in Late Medieval England* (New York, 2004), 117.
10 Cf. J. Harrington, *The Commonwealth of Oceana and A System of Politics*, ed. J.G.A. Pocock, (Cambridge, 1992), pp. 8–9, 20.
11 Cf. G. Stedman Jones, *Languages of Class* (Cambridge, 1983), 184–5.
12 For an argument about the early development of a representative culture of politics and growing consciousness of the state as separate from society see M. Knights, *Representation and Misrepresentation in Later Stuart Britain: Partisanship and Political Culture* (Oxford, 2005), 37–8, 51 and *passim*.
13 J. Vernon, *Politics and the People: A Study in English Political Culture c.1815–1867* (Cambridge, 1993), 301–2.

14 Vernon, *Politics and the People*, 305; I. McCalman, 'Popular Constitutionalism and Revolution in England and Ireland', in I. Woloch (ed.) *Revolution and the Meanings of Freedom in the Nineteenth Century* (Stanford, Ca, 1996), 142, 150–1.
15 D. Philips, 'Policing', in I. McCalman (ed.) *The Oxford Companion to the Romantic Age: British Culture 1776–1832* (Oxford, 1999), 70.
16 V.A.C. Gatrell, 'Crime, Authority and the Policeman-State', in F.M.L. Thompson (ed.) *The Cambridge Social History of Britain 1750–1950. Vol. 3: Social Agencies and Institutions*, ed. (Cambridge, 1990), 244, 254–5.
17 C. Brooks, 'Litigation, Participation, and Agency', in D. Lemmings (ed.) *The British and Their Laws* (Woodbridge, 2005), 178–9.
18 *Charges to the Grand Jury 1689–1803*, ed. G. Lamoine (Camden soc., 4th ser., 43, 1992), 436, 440–1.
19 *Mr. Justice Ashurst's Charge to the Grand Jury for the County of Middlesex* (1793).
20 Lamoine, Charges, 544, 547; see above, p. 138.
21 See above, pp. 8–9; M. Lobban, 'Custom, Nature, and Authority: The Roots of English Legal Positivism', in Lemmings (ed.) *The British and Their Laws*, ch. 2.
22 D. Hay, 'Legislation, Magistrates, and Judges', in *The British and their Laws*, 67–71; id, 'Dread of the Crown Office: the English Magistracy and King's Bench, 1740–1800', in N. Landau (ed.) *Law, Crime and English Society 1660–1830* (Cambridge, 2002), 29–30; D. Lemmings, 'The Independence of the Judiciary in Eighteenth-Century England', in P. Birks (ed.) *The Life of the Law* (1993), 125–49; Lemmings, *Professors of the Law*, 271–92.
23 Lobban, 'Custom, Nature and Authority', in Lemmings (ed.) *The British and their Laws*, 57.
24 Lemmings, *Professors of the Law*, 311–12, 320–1.
25 See above, p. 136; P.D.G. Thomas, 'Pratt, Charles, first Earl Camden', in *Oxford Dictionary of National Biography*.
26 *Parliamentary History*, xxxix. 1408–9.
27 E.P. Thompson, *Whigs and Hunters: the Origins of the Black Act* (Harmondsworth, 1977), 265–6.
28 G. Van Cleve, '*Somerset's Case* and its Antecedents in Imperial Perspective', *Law and History Review*, 24 (2006), 636.
29 Vernon, *Politics and the People*, ch. 8. See however, Nicolas Rogers, who notes the ability of eighteenth-century seamen to utilize a 'rudimentary knowledge' of the law relating to impressment ('Impressment and the Law in Eighteenth-Century Britain', in Landau (ed.) *Law, Crime and English Society*, esp. 93–4).
30 J. Epstein, *Radical Expression: Political Language, Ritual, and Symbol in England, 1790–1850* (New York, 1994), ch. 2, esp. 32.
31 Epstein, *Radical Expression*, 45, 49–50, 61–2.
32 *Cobbett's Weekly Political Register*, no. 21, 23 Nov., 1816, col. 558 (orig. emphasis).
33 M. Krygier and R. van Krieken, 'The Character of the Nation', in R. Manne (ed.) *Whitewash* (Melbourne, 2003), 100–3.
34 *Old England Journal*, 2 Apr., 1743, cited in R. Harris, *A Patriot Press: National Politics and the London Press in the 1740s* (Oxford, 1993), 32.
35 Van Cleve, '*Somerset's Case*', 625, 632.
36 For some interesting speculations on the complex emotional responses to late eighteenth-century newspaper reports, see P. King, 'Newspaper Reporting and Attitudes to Crime and Justice in Late Eighteenth and Early Nineteenth Century London', *Continuity and Change*, 22 (2007), 73–112.

37 L. Stone, *Road to Divorce* (Oxford, 1990), 248–55.
38 See, however, Knights, *Representation and Misrepresentation in Later Stuart Britain*, who argues that 'Conventions of rational politeness ... narrowed the public voice' because of growing pessimism about the rationality of the common people.
39 See Lemmings, 'Conclusion', in Lemmings and Walker (eds.) *Moral Panics, the Media and the Law*, 245–64. Joanna Innes has recently cautioned against exaggerating the extent to which the growth of the public sphere in the eighteenth century 'empowered ordinary people' (J. Innes, *Inferior Politics: Social Problems and Social Policies in Eighteenth-Century Britain* (Oxford, 2009), 5).

# Appendix: List of Statutes Cited

13 Edw. 1, stat. 2 (1285): Statute of Westminster
2&3 Philip and Mary, c.8 (1555): Act for the Mending of Highways
2&3 Phil. & Mary, c. 10 (1555): Act to take Examination of Prisoners suspected of Manslaughter or Felony
39 Eliz. c. 4 (1597): Act for the punishment of Rogues, Vagabonds and Sturdy Beggars
13 Car 2, sess. 1, c. 5 (1661): Act against Tumults and Disorders, upon Pretence of preparing or presenting publick Petitions
3 Wm. & Mary, c. 12 (1691): Act for better repairing and amending the Highways, and for settling the Rates of Carriage of Goods
4&5 William and Mary, c. 24 (1692): Act for reviving, continuing, and explaining several Laws
5 Wm. & Mary, c. 21 (1694): Act for granting Duties upon Vellum, Parchment and Paper
6 & 7 Will. & Mary, c. 2 (1694): Act for the frequent Meeting and Calling of Parliaments
7&8 Wm. 3, c. 32 (1696): Act for the Ease of Jurors, and better Regulating of Juries
8&9 Wm. 3, c. 15 (1697): Act for Repairing the Highway between *Ryegate* in the County of *Surrey*, and *Crawley* in the County of *Sussex*
8 & 9 Wm. 3, c. 16 (1697): Act for enlarging Common Highways
12 & 13 Wm. 3, c. 2 (1701): Act for the further Limitation of the Crown, and better securing the Rights and Liberties of the Subject
2&3 Anne, c. 19 (1703): Act for raising recruits for the Land Forces and Marines
4 Anne, c. 8 (1705): Act for the better Security of her Majesty's Person and Government, and of the Succession to the Crown of *England*, in the Protestant Line
4 Anne, c. 10 (1705): Act for the better recruiting her Majesty's Army and Marines
5 Anne, c. 6 (1706): Act for repealing a Clause in an Act for the better apprehending, prosecuting and punishing Felons
6 Anne, c. 8 (1706): Act for an Union of the two Kingdoms of *England* and *Scotland*
10 Anne, c. 23 (1712): Act for the more effectual preventing of fraudulent Conveyances, in order to multiply Votes for electing Knights of Shires
1 Geo. 1, stat. 2 c. 5 (1714): Act for preventing Tumults and riotous Assemblies, and for the more speedy and effectual punishing the Rioters
1 Geo. 1, stat. 2 c. 38 (1716): Act for enlarging the Time of Continuance of Parliaments
4 Geo. 1, c. 11 (1717): Act for for the further preventing Robbery, Burglary, and other Felonies, and for the more effectual Transportation of Felons, and unlawful Exporters of Wool; and for declaring the Law upon some Points relating to Pirates
6 Geo. 1, c. 5 (1720): Dependency of Ireland on Great Britain Act
6 Geo. 1, c. 23 (1720): Act for the further preventing Robbery, Burglary, and other Felonies, and for the more effectual Transportation of Felons
9 Geo. 1, c. 7 (1723): Act for the relief of the Poor
9 Geo. 1, c. 22 (1723): Act for the more effectual punishing wicked and evil-disposed Persons going armed in Disguise, and doing Injuries and Violences to the Persons and Properties of his Majesty's Subjects, and for the more speedy bringing the Offenders to Justice
11 Geo. 1, c. 18 (1725): Act for regulating Elections within the City of *London*, and for preserving the Peace, good Order and Government of the said City

1 Geo. 2, c. 19 (1727): Act for punishing such Persons as shall willfully and maliciously pull down or destroy Turnpikes for repairing Highways, or Locks or other Works, erected by Authority of Parliament, for making Rivers navigable
2 Geo. 2, c. 23 (1729): Act for Regulation of Attorneys and Solicitors
2 Geo. 2, c. 25 (1729): Act for the more effectual preventing and further Punishment of Forgery, Perjury and Subornation of Perjury, and to make it Felony to steal Bonds, Notes or other Securities for Payment of Money
3 Geo. 2, c. 25 (1730): Act for the better Regulation of Juries
4 Geo. 2, c. 26 (1731): Act that all Proceedings in Courts of Justice shall be in English
5 Geo. 2, c. 33 (1731): Act to explain, amend and render more effectual an Act passed in the first Year of his present Majesty's Reign, intituled, *An Act for punishing such Persons as shall willfully and maliciously pull down or destroy Turnpikes for repairing Highways, or Locks or other Works erected by Authority of Parliament for making Rivers navigable*
8 Geo. 2, c. 20 (1734): Act for rendering the Laws more effectual for punishing such Persons as shall willfully and maliciously pull down or destroy Turnpikes for repairing Highways, or Locks, or other Works erected by Act of Parliament for making Rivers navigable
9 Geo. 2, c. 36: Act for laying a Duty upon the Retailers of Spirituous Liquors, and for licensing the Retailers thereof
12 Geo. 2, c. 29 (1739): Act for the more easy assessing, collecting and levying of County Rates
17 Geo. 2, c.5, s. 34 (1745): Act to amend and make more effectual the Laws relating to Rogues, Vagabonds and other idle and disorderly Persons, and to Houses of Correction
18 Geo., 2, c. 18 (1745): Act to explain and amend the Laws touching the Elections of Knights of the Shire
19 Geo. 2, c. 21 (1746): Act to prevent profane Cursing and Swearing
22 Geo, 2, c. 27 (1749): Act for the more effectual preventing of Frauds and Abuses committed by Persons employed in the Manufacture of Hats, and in the Woollen, Linnen, Fustian, Cotton, Iron, Leather, Furr, Hemp, Flax, Mohair and Silk Manufactures
24 Geo. 2, c. 23 (1751): Act for regulating the Commencement of the Year; and for correcting the Calendar now in Use
25 Geo. 2, c. 21 (1751): Act for repairing the Roads from *Wallingford* in the County of *Berks* to *Wantage* , and from thence to *Faringdon* , and also from *Wantage* to *Idson* in the said County
25 Geo. 2, c. 36 (1752): Act for the better preventing Thefts and Robberies, and for regulating Places of Publick Entertainment
26 Geo. 2, c. 33 (1753): Act for the better preventing of clandestine Marriages
30 Geo. 2, c. 12 (1757): Act to amend an Act intituled, An Act to render more effectual an Act passed in the twelfth Year of the Reign of his late Majesty King George, to prevent unlawful Combinations of Workmen employed in the Woollen Manufactures, and for better Payment of their Wages
30 Geo. 2, c. 25 (1757): Act for the better ordering of the Militia Forces
5 Geo. 3, c. 12 (1765): Act for granting and supplying certain Stamp Duties, and other Duties, in the *British* Colonies and Plantations in *America*
6 Geo. 3, c. 12 (1766): Act for the better securing the Dependency of his Majesty's Dominions in *America* upon the Crown and Parliament of *Great Britain*
10 Geo. 3, c. 19 (1770): Act for the better Preservation of the Game
10 Geo. 3, c. 39 (1770): Act for registering the Prices at which Corn is sold
12 Geo. 3, c. 11 (1772): Act for the better regulating the future Marriages of the Royal Family

Appendix: List of Statutes Cited    237

12 Geo. 3, c. 71 (1772): Act for repealing several Laws therein mentioned against Badgers, Engrossers, Forestallers, and Regrators

13 Geo. 3, c. 68 (1773): An Act to impower the Magistrates therein mentioned to settle and regulate the Wages of Persons employed in the Silk Manufacture within their respective Jurisdictions

13 Geo.3, c. 78 (1773): Act for the Amendment and Preservation of Publick Highways

13 Geo. 3, c. 84 (1773): Act to explain, amend, and reduce into One Act of Parliament, the general Laws now in being for regulating the Turnpike Roads in that Part of *Great Britain* called *England*

14 Geo. 3, c. 25 (1774): Act for the more effectual preventing Frauds and Embezzlements, by Persons employed in the Woolen Manufactory

16 Geo. 3, c. 43 (1776): Act for the Punishment by Hard Labour of Offenders

17 Geo. 3, c. 11 (1777): Act for preventing Frauds and Abuses committed by Persons employed in the Manufactures of Combing Wool, Worsted Yarn, and Goods made from Worsted

17 Geo. 3, c. 56 (1777): Act for amending and rendering more effectual Laws for the preventing of Frauds and Abuses by Persons employed in the Manufacture of Hats [etc]

18 Geo. 3, c. 19 (1778): Act for the Payment of Cost to Parties, on Complaints determined before Justices of the Peace out of Sessions

18 Geo. 3, c. 60: Act for relieving his Majesty's Subjects professing the Popish Religion from certain Penalties and Disabilities imposed on them

19 Geo. 3, c. 74 (1779): Act to explain and amend the Laws relating to Transportation, Imprisonment, and other Punishment of certain Offenders

20 Geo. 3, c. 17 (1780): Act to remove certain Difficulties relative to Voters at County Elections

22 Geo. 3, c. 64 (1782): Act for amending the Laws relative to Houses of Correction

22 Geo. 3, c. 83 (1782): Act for the better Relief and Employment of the Poor

24 Geo. 3, c. 55 (1784): Act to explain and amend an Act relative to Houses of Correction

24 Geo. 3, c. 56 (1784): Act for the effectual Transportation of Felons

24 Geo. 3, sess. 2, c. 3 (1784): Act for the more effectually preventing Frauds and Abuses committed by Persons employed in the Manufactures of combing Wool, Worsted Yarn, and Goods made from Worsted, in the County of Suffolk

25 Geo. 3, c. 40 (1785): Act for the more effectually preventing Frauds and Abuses committed by Persons employed in the Manufactures of combing Wool, Worsted Yarn, and Goods made from Worsted, in the Counties of Bedford, Huntingdon, Northampton, Leicester, Rutland, and Lincoln, and the Isle of Ely

26 Geo. 3, c. 38 (1786): Act for regulating the Time of the Imprisonment of Debtors imprisoned by Process from Courts instituted for the Recovery of Small Debts

31 Geo. 3, c. 30 (1791): Act for regulating the Importation and Exportation of Corn

31 Geo. 3, c. 46 (1791): Act for regulating Gaols

31 Geo. 3, c. 56 (1791): Act more effectually to prevent Abuses and Frauds committed by Persons employed in the Manufactures of combing Wool and Worsted Yarn, in the County of Norfolk, and City of Norwich and County of the said City

32 Geo. 3, c. 53 (1792): Act for the more effectual Administration of the Office of a Justice of the Peace in some Parts of Middlesex and Surrey

34 Geo. 3, c. 54 (1794): Act to empower his Majesty to secure and detain such Persons as his Majesty shall suspect are conspiring against his Person and Government

35 Geo. 3, c. 3 (1795): Act to continue, for a limited Time, an Act to empower his Majesty to secure and detain such Persons as his Majesty shall suspect are conspiring against his Person and Government

## Appendix: List of Statutes Cited

36 Geo. 3, c. 8 (1795): Act for the more effectually preventing Seditious Meetings and Assemblies

41 Geo. 3, c. 109 (1801): Act for consolidating in one Act certain Provisions usually inserted in Acts of Inclosure; and for facilitating the Mode of proving the several Facts usually required on the passing of such Acts

48 Geo. 3, c. 96 (1808): Act for the better Care and Maintenance of Lunatics

53 Geo. 3, c. 40 (1813): Act to repeal so much of several Acts passed in *England* and *Scotland* respectively, as empowers Justices of the Peace to rate Wages, or set Prices of Work, for Artificers, Labourers or Craftsmen

54 Geo. 3, c. 96 (1814): Act to amend an Act, passed in the Fifth Year of Queen *Elizabeth*, intituled *An Act containing divers Orders for Artificers Labourers, Servants of Husbandry and Apprentices*

60 Geo. 3 & 1 Geo. 4, c. 6 (1819): Act for more effectually preventing Seditious Meetings and Assemblies

3 Geo. 4, c. 126 (1822): Act to amend the general Laws now in being for regulating Turnpike Roads in that Part of *Great Britain* called *England*

7&8 Geo. 4, c. 38 (1827): Act for discontinuing certain Presentments by Constables

10 Geo. 4, c. 44 (1829): Act for improving the Police in and near the Metropolis

2&3 Wm. 4, c. 45 (1832): Act to amend the Representation of the People in *England* and *Wales*

4&5 Wm. 4, c. 76 (1834): Act for the Amendment and better Administration of the Laws relating to the Poor in *England* and *Wales*

6&7 Wm. 4, c. 114 (1836): Act for enabling Persons indicted of Felony to make their Defence by Counsel or Attorney

11&12 Vict. c. 42 (1848): Act to facilitate the Performance of the Duties of Justices of the Peace out of Sessions with respect to Persons charged with indictable Offences

# Bibliography

## 1. Manuscripts

### Camden Local Studies and Archives Centre
St. Pancras Vestry MS. Minutes

### Bristol Record Office
MSS. JQS/D: Bristol Quarter Sessions
MS. M/BCC/CCP/1/1/8: Minutes of Common Council

### British Library, London
Add. MSS., 34,416 (William Eden, Lord Auckland)
Add. MSS., 35,353 (Hon. Philip Yorke)
Add. MSS., 36,115 (Lord Harwicke)

### Centre for Buckinghamshire Studies, Aylesbury
MS. DC 18/39/5: Diary of Edmund Waller

### Cheshire Record Office, Chester
MSS. QJB 3 (Recognizances, orders, indictments and presentments)
Microfilmed as part of *Justice and Authority in England: County Quarter Sessions and Related Records. Series One: Cheshire* (Brighton, 1985)

### Cornwall County Record Office, Truro
MS. FS2/76 (Penzance)

### Essex Record Office, Chelmsford
MSS. Q/SR 271 (Essex Sessions Rolls)

### Herefordshire Record Office, Hereford
MS. BB88/1 (Dr. Henry Yate)

### Hertfordshire County Record Office, Hertford
Panshanger, MSS (Earl Cowper)

### Lincoln's Inn, London
Harrowby MSS (Sir Dudley Ryder)

### London Metropolitan Archives
MSS. DL/C 149, DL/C 39, DL/C 52, DL/C 172, DL/ C 329 (Consistory Court of London)

240  Bibliography

## Corporation of London Record Office, Guildhall, London
MSS. Col/CA/01/01 (Repertories of Court of Aldermen, formerly REP)

## The National Archives, Kew, London
KB101/1/6 (King's Bench affidavits)

## Wiltshire and Swindon Archives, Chippenham
MS. A1260 (summary convictions, 1698–1820)
MS. 383/955 (Sir Richard Colt Hoare)

## 2. Printed Primary Sources

(The place of publication is London, unless given otherwise.)
*The Antient and Present State of Military Law in Great Britain Consider'd: With a Review of the Debates of the Army and Navy Bills* (1749)
Ashurst, W., *Mr. Justice Ashurst's Charge to the Grand Jury for the County of Middlesex* (1793)
Atkyns, R., *The Power, Jurisdiction and Priviledge [sic] of Parliament; and the Antiquity of the House of Commons Asserted* (1689)
Beccaria, C., *An Essay on Crimes and Punishments* (Edinburgh, 1787)
Blackstone, W., *Commentaries on the Laws of England* (Oxford, 1765–9)
Bohun, E., *The Justice of Peace, his Calling and Qualifications* (1693)
*Bolingbroke: Political Writings*, ed. D. Armitage (Cambridge, 1997)
Brereton, C.D., *The Subordinate Magistracy and Parish System Considered in their Connexion with the Causes and Remedies of Modern Pauperism* (Norwich, n.d. [1827?])
*County of Buckingham: Calendar to the Sessions Records. Volume II. 1694–1705*, ed. W. Le Hardy and G. Ll. Reckitt (Aylesbury, 1936)
Bulstrode, W., *The Charge of Whitlocke Bulstrode, Esq; to the Grand Jury, and other Juries, of the County of Middlesex. At the General Quarter Sessions of the Peace, held, April 21$^{st}$, 1718* (1718)
—— *The Second Charge of Whitlocke Bulstrode, Esq* (1718) in *Charges to the Grand Jury 1689–1803*, ed. G. Lamoine (Camden Soc., 4$^{th}$ ser., 43 (1992)
Burke, E., *Thoughts on the Present Discontents* (1770), in *The Writings and Speeches of Edmund Burke*, ed. P. Langford (Oxford, 1981)
—— 'Speech to the Electors of Bristol' (1774), in *Edmund Burke on Government Politics and Society*, ed. B.W. Hill (1975)
—— 'Letter to the Sheriffs of Bristol ... on the Affairs of America' (1777), in *The Writings and Speeches of Edmund Burke: Vol. III*, ed. W.M. Elofson and J.A. Woods (Oxford, 1996)
—— *Reflections on the Revolution in France* (1790), ed. C.C. O'Brien (Harmondsworth, 1968)
—— *An Appeal from the New to the Old Whigs* (1791)
*The Correspondence of Edmund Burke* (Cambridge, 1958–78)
Burn, R., *The Justice of the Peace and Parish Officer* (1755)
—— *The Justice of the Peace and Parish Officer* (2$^{nd}$ edn., 1756)
Chambers, R., *A Course of Lectures on the English Law Delivered at the University of Oxford 1767–1773*, ed. T.M. Curley (Oxford, 1986)
*Charges to the Grand Jury*, ed. G. Lamoine (Camden Soc., 4$^{th}$ ser., 43, 1992)

*Quarter Sessions Records with other Records of the Justices of the Peace for the County Palatine of Chester 1559–1760*, ed. J.H.E. Bennett and J.C. Dewhurst (Lancashire and Cheshire Rec. Soc., 94, 1940)
*The Claims of the People of England, Essayed. In a Letter from the Country* (1701)
*Cobbett's Weekly Political Register* (1802–35)
Coke, E., *The Fourth Part of the Institutes of the Laws of England* (1644)
*The Blecheley Diary of the Rev. William Cole*, ed. F.G. Stokes (1931)
Colquhoun, P., *A Treatise on the Police of the Metropolis* (1796)
*Considerations on the Bill for the Better Government of the Navy. By a Sea Officer* (1749)
Cooper, S., *Erroneous opinions concerning providence refuted, – the true notion stated, – and illustrated by the events which have lately happened to this nation: in a sermon, preached in the parish church of Great Yarmouth, on Friday February the 8th, 1782* (1782)
Cottu, C., *On the Administration of Criminal Justice in England* (1822)
Cox, J.C., *Three Centuries of Derbyshire Annals, as illustrated by the Records of the Quarter Sessions of the County of Derby from Queen Elizabeth to Queen Victoria* (1890)
Danvers, C., *The Second Part of an Argument against Excises; in Answer to the Objections of Several Writers* (1733)
Day, T., *A Dialogue between a Justice of the Peace and a Farmer* (1785)
*A Dialogue between a Lieutenant Of a Man of War, and a Captain In the Land Service Upon Half-Pay* (1749)
Dowdell, E.G., *A Hundred Years of Quarter Sessions: The Government of Middlesex from 1660–1760* (Cambridge, 1932)
Eden, W., *Principles of Penal Law* (1771)
—— 'Observations on the Bill to punish by Imprisonment and Hard Labour certain Offenders; and to provide proper Places for their Reception' (1778), in *House of Commons Sessional Papers of the Eighteenth Century*, ed. S. Lambert (Wilmington, Delaware, 1975)
*English Liberty in some Cases worse than French Slavery, Exemplified by Animadversions upon the Tyrannical and anti-Constitutional Power of the Justices of the Peace, Commissioners of Excise, Customs, and Land-Tax, &c.* (1748)
*The English Reports* (Edinburgh and London, 1900–32)
*An Enquiry into the Doctrine, Lately Propagated, Concerning Libels, Warrants, and the Seizure of Papers* (1764)
Fiennes, C., *The Journeys of Celia Fiennes*, ed. C. Morris (1947)
Fielding, H., *A True State of the Case of Bosavern Penlez* (1749), in *An Enquiry into the Late Increase of Robbers* (1751), ed. M.R. Zirker (Oxford, 1988)
—— *An Enquiry into the Late Increase of Robbers* (1751), ed. M.R. Zirker (Oxford, 1988)
—— *A Proposal for Making an Effectual Provision for the Poor* (1753), in *An Enquiry into the Late Increase of Robbers*, ed. M.R. Zirker (Oxford, 1988)
—— *Amelia*, ed. M.C. Battestin (Oxford, 1983)
—— *The History of Tom Jones*, ed. R.P.C. Mutter (Harmondsworth, 1985)
Fielding, J., *An Account of the Origin and Effects of a Police set on foot by His Grace the Duke of Newcastle in the Year 1753, upon a Plan presented to his Grace by the late Henry Fielding, Esq* (1758)
*The Gentleman's Magazine: and Historical Chronicle* (1731–1833)
Gibson, E., *Remarks on a Bill Now Depending in Parliament for the Better Regulating the Proceedings of the Ecclesiastical Courts. By a Right Reverend Prelate* (1733)
—— *An Admonition against Prophane and Common Swearing* (7th edn., 1745)
Gisborne, T., *An Enquiry into the Duties of Men in the Higher and Middle Classes of Society in Great Britain* (1795)

*Justice in Eighteenth-Century Hackney: The Justicing Notebook of Henry Norris and the Hackney Petty Sessions Book*, ed. R. Paley (London Record Soc., 28, 1991)

*Hanging, Not Punishment Enough* (1701)

Hanway, J., *The Defects of Police the Cause of Immorality, and the Continual Robberies Committed, particularly in and around the Metropolis* (1775)

Harrington, J., *The Commonwealth of Oceana and A System of Politics*, ed. J.G.A. Pocock (Cambridge, 1992)

Hawkins, W., *Treatise of the Pleas of the Crown* (1721)

Hay, W., *Remarks on the Laws Relating to the Poor* (1735)

*Hertfordshire County Records: Calendar to the Sessions Books*, ed. W. Le Hardy and G.L. Reckitt (Hertford, 1930–1939)

Hervey, A., *A Detection of the Considerations of the Navy-Bill. By a Seaman* (1749)

—— *A Letter from a Friend in the Country To a Friend at Will's Coffee-House; in Relation to Three Additional Articles of War* (1749)

—— *Objections to the Thirty-Fourth Article of the Navy Bill* (1749)

*Hints of Ledbury*, by a native inhabitant (Ledbury, 1831)

*The History of the Late Great Revolution in England and Scotland* (1690)

Howard, J., *The State of the Prisons in England and Wales, with Preliminary Observations, and an Account of some Foreign Prisons and Hospitals* (2nd edn., Warrington, 1780)

*The Justicing Notebook of William Hunt 1744–1749*, ed. E. Crittall (Wiltshire Rec. Soc., 37, 1981)

Hutton., W., *Courts of Requests: their Nature, Utility, and Powers described, with a variety of Cases, Determined in that of Birmingham* (Birmingham, 1787)

—— *A Dissertation on Juries; with a Description of the Hundred Court: as an Appendix to the Court of Requests* (Birmingham, 1789)

Johnson, S., *A Dictionary of the English Language* (1755)

*Jura Populi Anglicani: Or, the Subjects Right of Petitioning Set forth. Occasioned by the Case of the Kentish Petitioners* (1701)

Lambarde, W., *Eirenarcha* (1581)

*The Law-Suit: or the Farmer and Fisherman* (London, 1738)

*A Letter to a Member of Parliament: In Relation to the Bill for Punishing Mutiny and Desertion, &c.* (n.d [1749?])

Locke, J., *An Essay Concerning the True Original, Extent and End of Civil Government* (1690)

Lofft, C., *An Argument on the Nature of Party and Faction. In which is considered, the Duty of a Good and Peaceable Citizen at the Present Crisis* (1780)

Macaulay, C., *An Address to the People of England, Scotland, and Ireland, on the Present Important Crisis of Affairs* (1775)

Madan, M., *Thoughts on Executive Justice* (1785)

Mandeville, B., *An Enquiry into the Causes of the Frequent Executions at Tyburn* (1725)

—— *The Fable of the Bees* (Harmondsworth, 1970)

*The Modern Justice, in Imitation of the Man of Taste* (1755)

*The New Circuit Companion; or a Mirror for Grand-Juries* (2nd edn., 1769)

*The Tryal between Henry Duke of Norfolk, plaintiff, and John Jermaine defendant: in an Action of Trespass on the Case at the Court of Kings-Bench at Westminster, on the 24th of November, 1692* (1692)

North, R., *A Discourse of the Poor* (1753)

*The North Riding Record Society for the Publication of Original Documents relating to the North Riding of the County of York. Vol. VII: Quarter Sessions Records* (North Riding Record Soc., 1889)

*The Proceedings of the Old Bailey* (http://www.oldbaileyonline.org)

Ollyffe, G., *An Essay Humbly offer'd, for an Act of Parliament to prevent Capital Crimes, and the Loss of so many Lives; and to Promote a desirable Improvement and Blessing in the Nation* (2nd edn., 1731)
*The Parliamentary History of England* (1806–20)
*The Parliamentary Register; or History of the Proceedings and Debates of the House of Commons* (1781–96)
Paley, W., *The Principles of Moral and Political Philosophy* (1785)
Paley, W., *The Law and Practice of Summary Convictions on Penal Statutes by Justices of the Peace* (1814)
Paul, G.O., *Considerations on the Defects of Prisons, and their Present System of Regulation* (1784)
Petyt, G., *Lex Parliamentaria: or, A Treatise of the Laws and Customs of the Parliaments of England* (1690)
Price, R., *Observations on the Nature of Civil Liberty, the Principles of Government, and the Justice and Policy of the War with America* (2nd edn., 1776)
*Principles Upon which the Taking the Oath of Abjuration May be Grounded* (1702)
*Proposals Humbly Offer'd to the Parliament, for Remedying the Great charge and Delay of Suits at Law, and in Equity* (3rd edn., 1724)
Pye, H.J., *Summary of the duties of a Justice of the Peace out of Sessions* (4th edn., 1827)
Ramsay, A., *Observations upon the Riot Act* (1781)
*Reflections or Hints Founded upon Experience and Facts, touching the Law* (1759)
*Report of the Committee appointed by a Public Vestry, held on the 30th Day of July, 1817, to investigate the affairs of the Directors of the Poor of the Parish of St. Pancras* (1818)
*Resolutions of the Master Manufacturers and Tradesmen of the Cities of London and Westminster, and the Vicinity, on the Statute of 5 Eliz. Cap. 4* (1814)
Robinson, D., 'The Local Government of the Metropolis, and other Populous Places', *Blackwood's Edinburgh Magazine*, 29 (1831), 82–104
Romilly, S., *Observations on a Late Publication Intituled, Thoughts on Executive Justice* (1786)
Ruggles, T., *The Barrister* (2nd edn., 1818 [first published 1791])
de Saussere, C., *A Foreign View of the Reigns of George I and George II: The Letters of Monsieur César de Saussere to his Family*, ed. Madame Van Muyden (1902)
*Seasonable and Affecting Observations on the Mutiny-Bill, Articles of War, and Use and Abuse of a Standing Army: in a Letter from a Member of Parliament to a Noble Lord* (1750)
Shakespeare, W., *Henry IV*, part 2 (1600)
Sharp, G., *A Declaration of the People's Natural Right to a Share in the Legislature* (1774)
—— *An Address to the People of England: Being the Protest of a Private Person Against every Suspension of Law that is Liable to injure or endanger Personal Security* (1778)
Shelton, M., *A Charge Given to the Grand-Jury, at the General Quarter-Sessions of the Peace, holden at St. Edmund's-Bury for the Liberty thereof, in the County of Suffolk: on the 19th of January, An. Dom. 1729/30* (1730)
Smith, A., *Lectures on Justice, Police, Revenue and Arms*, ed. E. Cannan (New York, 1956)
—— *An Enquiry into the Nature and Causes of the Wealth of Nations*, ed. E. Cannan (repr. Chicago, 1976)
—— *Lectures on Jurisprudence*, ed. R.L. Meek, D.D. Raphael and P.G. Stein (Oxford, 1978)
Smith, T., *De Republica Anglorum* (1563) ed. L. Alston (Cambridge, 1906)
Smollett, T., *The Life and Adventures of Sir Launcelot Greaves* (Harmondsworth, 1988)
Starkie, T., *A Practical Treatise on the Law of Evidence, and Digest of Proofs, in Civil and Criminal Proceedings* (2nd edn., 1824)
*A Complete Collection of State Trials*, ed. T.B. Howell (1809–26)

Stephens, A., *Memoirs of John Horne Tooke* (1813)
Stubbs, W. and Talmash, G., *The Crown Circuit Companion* (2nd edn., 1749)
*County of Surrey. Quarter Sessions Records with other Records of the Justices of the Peace for the County of Surrey. Vol. 5* (Surrey Rec. Soc., 32, 1931)
*The Justicing Notebook (1750–64) of Edmund Tew, Rector of Boldon* (Surtees Soc., 205, 2000)
*Tory and Whig: the Parliamentary Papers of Edward Harley, 3rd Earl of Oxford, and William Hay, MP for Seaford 1716–1753*, ed. S. Taylor and C. Jones (Woodbridge, 1998)
*The Diary of Thomas Turner 1754–1765*, ed. D. Vaisey (Oxford, 1985)
*Wiltshire Quarter Sessions and Assizes, 1736*, ed. J.P.M. Fowle (Wiltshire Archaeological and Natural History Soc., 11, Devizes, 1955)
*Deposition Book of Richard Wyatt, JP, 1767–1776*, ed. E. Silverthorne (Guidford, Surrey Rec. Soc., 30, 1978)
Young, A., *Six Months' Tour through the North of England* (2nd edn., 1771)
—— *An Enquiry into the Propriety of Applying Wastes to the Better Maintenance and Support of the Poor* (1801)

## 3. Newspapers

*The Craftsman*
*The Guardian Weekly*
*The Ipswich Journal*
*The London Journal*
*The London Magazine*
*The Newcastle Gazette*
*The Newcastle Intelligencer*
*The Newcastle Journal*
*The Old England Journal*
*The Whitehall Journal*

## 4. Parliamentary Papers

### Commons Journals

*House of Commons Sessional Papers of the Eighteenth Century*, ed. S. Lambert (Wilmington, Delaware, 1975)

### Lords Journals

*Report of the Lords Commissioners appointed to make a survey of the different courts in England, Wales, and Berwick-upon Tweed, – as to the Court of Chancery: Dated 8 November 1740. Parliamentary Papers (House of Commons), 1814–15*, vol. XI, pp. 5–152

## 5. Secondary Sources

(The place of publication is London, unless given otherwise.)
Albert, W., *The Turnpike Road System in England* (Cambridge, 1972)
—— 'Popular Opposition to Turnpike Trusts in Early Eighteenth-Century England', *Journal of Transport History*, new ser., 5 (1979), 1–17
Allan, T.R.S., Law, *Liberty and Justice: The Legal Foundations of British Constitutionalism* (Oxford, 1993)

Amory, H., 'Henry Fielding and the Criminal Legislation of 1751–2', *Philological Quarterly*, l (1971), 175–92
Amussen, S., *An Ordered Society: Gender and Class in Early Modern England* (Oxford, 1988)
Andrew, D.T. and McGowen, R., *The Perreaus and Mrs. Rudd: Forgery and Betrayal in Eighteenth-Century London* (Berkeley, CA, 2001)
Ashcraft, R., *Revolutionary Politics and Locke's Two Treatises of Government* (Princeton, NJ, 1986)
Ashton, T.S., *An Economic History of England: The Eighteenth Century* (1955)
Aspinall, A., 'The Reporting and Publishing of the House of Commons' Debates, 1771–1834', in R. Pares and A.J.P. Taylor (eds.) *Essays presented to Sir Louis Namier* (1956)
Aston, M., 'Segregation in Church', in W.J. Shiels and D. Wood (eds.) *Women in the Church* (Oxford, 1990)
Atkinson, A., 'State and Empire and Convict Transportation, 1718–1812', in C. Bridge (ed.) *New Perspectives in Australian History* (1990)
Bailey, J., 'Voices in Court: Lawyers' or Litigants?', *Historical Research*, 74 (2001), 392–408
—— *Unquiet Lives: Marriage and Marriage Breakdown in England, 1660–1800* (Cambridge, 2003)
Baker, J.H., 'The Changing Concept of a Court', in idem, *The Legal Profession and the Common Law* (1986)
—— *An Introduction to English Legal History* (3rd edn., 1990)
—— *The Common Law Tradition: Lawyers, Books and the Law* (2000)
—— *An Introduction to English Legal History* (4th edn., 2002)
—— (ed.) *The Oxford History of the Laws of England* (Oxford, 2003–)
Barnes, T.G., 'Star Chamber Litigants and Their Counsel, 1596–1641', in J.H. Baker (ed.) *Legal Records and the Historian* (1978)
Barrell, J., *Imagining the King's Death: Figurative Treason, Fantasies of Regicide, 1793–1796* (Oxford, 2000)
Beattie, J.M., 'Violence and Society in Early Modern England', in A.N. Doob and E.L. Greenspan (eds.) *Perspectives in Criminal Law* (Aurora, Ontario, 1985)
—— *Crime and the Courts in England, 1660–1800* (Oxford, 1986)
—— 'Scales of Justice: Defence Counsel and the English Criminal Trial in the Eighteenth and Nineteenth Centuries', *Law and History Review*, 9 (1991), 221–67
—— 'London Crime and the Making of the "Bloody Code", 1689–1718', in L. Davison et al (eds.) *Stilling the Grumbling Hive: The Response to Social and Economic Problems in England, 1689–1750* (Stroud, 1992)
—— *Policing and Punishment in London 1660–1750* (Oxford, 2001)
—— 'Sir John Fielding and Public Justice: the Bow Street Magistrates' Court, 1754–1780', *Law and History Review*, 25 (2007), 61–100.
Beckett, J.V., *The Aristocracy in England 1660–1914* (Oxford, 1986)
Beedell, A.V., 'John Reeve's Prosecution for a Seditious Libel, 1795–6: A Study in Political Cynicism', *Historical Journal*, 36 (1993), 799–824
Bennett, G.V., 'Jacobitism and the Rise of Walpole', in N. McKendrick (ed.) *Historical Perspectives* (1974)
—— *The Tory Crisis in Church and State, 1688–1730: The Career of Francis Atterbury, Bishop of Rochester* (Oxford, 1975)
Biddle, S., *Bills and Acts: Legislative Procedure in Eighteenth-Century England* (Cambridge, 1971)
Black, J., *The English Press in the Eighteenth Century* (Philadelphia, 1987)
Borsay, P., *The English Urban Renaissance: Culture and Society in the English Town, 1660–1760* (Oxford, 1989)

Braddick, M.J., 'Discussion: State Formation and Social Change in Early Modern England: A Problem Stated and Approach Suggested' *Social History*, 16 (1991), 1–17
—— *State Formation in Early Modern England, c. 1550–1700* (Cambridge, 2000)
Brewer, J., 'The Wilkites and the Law, 1763–74: A Study of Radical Notions of Governance', in J. Brewer and J. Styles (eds.) *An Ungovernable People* (1980)
—— *The Sinews of Power: War, Money and the English State, 1688–1783* (1989)
—— 'The Eighteenth-Century British State: Contexts and Issues', in L. Stone (ed.), *An Imperial State at War: Britain from 1689 to 1815* (1994)
—— *The Pleasures of the Imagination: English Culture in the Eighteenth Century* (1997)
Brewer, J. and Styles, J., 'Introduction', in J. Brewer and J. Styles (eds.) *An Ungovernable People: The English and their Law in the Seventeenth and Eighteenth Centuries* (1980)
Brewer, J. and Porter, R. (eds.) *Consumption and the World of Goods* (1993)
Briggs, J. et al, *Crime and Punishment in England* (1996)
Brooks, C.W., *Pettyfoggers and Vipers of the Commonwealth: the 'Lower Branch' of the Legal Profession in Early Modern England* (Cambridge, 1986)
—— 'Professions, Ideology and the Middling Sort in the Late Sixteenth and Early Seventeenth Centuries', in J. Barry and C. Brooks (eds.) *The Middling Sort of People: Culture, Society and Politics in England, 1550–1800* (Basingstoke, 1994)
—— 'Law, Lawyers and the Social History of England', in id., *Lawyers, Litigation and English Society Since 1450* (1998)
—— *Lawyers, Litigation and English Society since 1450* (1998)
—— 'Litigation, Participation, and Agency', in D. Lemmings (ed.) *The British and Their Laws in the Eighteenth Century* (Woodbridge, 2005)
—— *Law, Politics and Society in Early Modern England* (Cambridge, 2008)
Butler, S.M., 'Degrees of Culpability: Suicide Verdicts, Mercy, and the Jury in Medieval England', *Journal of Medieval and Early Modern Studies*, 36 (2006), 263–90
Cannon, J., *Aristocratic Century: The Peerage of Eighteenth-century England* (Cambridge, 1984)
Carter, J., 'The Revolution and the Constitution', in G. Holmes (ed.), *Britain after the Glorious Revolution, 1689–1715* (1969)
—— 'Law, Courts and Constitution', in J.R. Jones (ed.) *The Restored Monarchy* (1979)
Champion, W.A., 'Litigation in the Boroughs: the Shrewsbury *Curia Parva* 1480–1730', *Journal of Legal History*, 15 (1994), 201–22
—— 'Recourse to the Law and the Meaning of the Great Litigation Decline, 1650–1750: Some Clues from the Shrewsbury Local Courts', in C.W. Brooks and M. Lobban (eds.) *Communities and Courts in Britain 1150–1900* (1997)
Charlesworth, A., Sheldon, R., Randall, A. and Walsh, D., 'The Jack-A-Lent Riots and Opposition to Turnpikes in the Bristol Region in 1749', in A. Randall and A. Charlesworth (eds.) *Markets, Market Culture and Popular Protest in Eighteenth-Century Britain and Ireland* (Liverpool, 1996)
Churches, C., 'False Friends, Spiteful Enemies: A Community at Law in Early Modern England', *Historical Research*, 71 (1998), 52–74
—— 'Business at Law: Retrieving Commercial Disputes from Eighteenth-century Chancery', *Historical Journal*, 43 (2000), 937–54
Clark, P., *British Clubs and Societies 1580–1800: The Origins of an Associational World* (Oxford, 2000)
Cleve, G. Van, '*Somerset's Case* and its Antecedents in Imperial Perspective', *Law and History Review*, 24 (2006)
Cockburn, J.S., *A History of English Assizes 1558–1714* (Cambridge, 1972)

Cohen, S. and Young, J., *The Manufacture of News: Social Problems, Deviance and the Mass Media* (1973)

Colley, L., *Britons: Forging the Nation 1707–1837* (New Haven, CT, 1992)

Connors, R., '"The Grand Inquest of the Nation": Parliamentary Committees and Social Policy in Mid-Eighteenth-Century England', *Parliamentary History*, 14 (1995), 285–313

Cornish, W.R. and Clark, G. de N., *Law and Society in England 1750–1950* (1989)

Cranfield, G.A., *The Development of the Provincial Newspaper* (Oxford, 1962)

Cruickshanks, E. and Erskine-Hill, H., 'The Waltham Black Act and Jacobitism', *Journal of British Studies*, 24 (1985), 358–65

Curtis, T., 'Quarter Sessions Appearances and their Background: A Seventeenth-Century Regional Study', in J.S. Cockburn (ed.) *Crime in England 1550–1800* (1977)

Curtis, T.C. and Speck, W.A., 'The Societies for the Reformation of Manners: A Case Study in the Theory and Practice of Moral Reform', *Literature and History*, 3 (1976), 45–64

Dabhoiwala, F., 'Summary Justice in Early Modern London', *English Historical Review*, 121 (2006), 796–822

—— 'Sex and Societies for Moral Reform, 1688–1800', *Journal of British Studies*, 46 (2007), 290–319

Daunton, M.J., *Progress and Poverty: An Economic and Social History of Britain 1700–1850* (Oxford, 1995)

Davey, B.J., *Rural Crime in the Eighteenth Century: North Lincolnshire 1740–80* (Hull, 1994)

Davison, L. et al (eds.) *Stilling the Grumbling Hive: The Response to Social and Economic Problems in England, 1689–1750* (Stroud, 1992)

—— 'Experiments in the Social Regulation of Industry: Gin Legislation, 1729–1751', in *Stilling the Grumbling Hive* (Stroud, 1992)

Dawson, J.P., *A History of Lay Judges* (Cambridge, MA, 1960)

Dean, D., *Law-Making and Society in Late Elizabethan England: The Parliament of England, 1584–1601* (Cambridge, 1996)

Derby, H.C. (ed.) *A New Historical Geography of England* (Cambridge, 1973)

Derry, T.K., 'The Repeal of the Apprenticeship Clauses of the Statute of Apprentices', *Econ. HR*, 3 (1931–2), 67–87

Devereaux, S., 'In Place of Death: Transportation, Penal Practices, and the English State, 1770–1830', in C. Strange (ed.) *Qualities of Mercy: Justice, Punishment and Discretion* (Vancouver, 1996)

—— 'The City and the Sessions Paper: "Public Justice" in London, 1770–1800', *Journal of British Studies*, 35 (1996), 466–503

—— 'The Making of the Penitentiary Act, 1775–1779', *Historical Journal*, 42 (1999), 405–33

—— 'The Promulgation of the Statutes in Late Hanoverian Britain', in D. Lemmings (ed.) *The British and their Laws in the Eighteenth Century* (Woodbridge, 2005)

—— 'From Sessions to Newspaper? Criminal Trial Reporting, the Nature of Crime, and the London Press, 1770–1800', *London Journal*, 32 (2007), 1–27

Dickson, P.G.M., *The Financial Revolution in England* (1967)

Dickinson, H.T., *Bolingbroke* (1970)

—— 'The Eighteenth-Century Debate on the Sovereignty of Parliament', *Transactions of the Royal Historical Society*, 5th ser., 26 (1976), 189–210

—— *Liberty and Property: Political Ideology in Eighteenth-Century Britain* (1977)

—— *The Politics of the People in Eighteenth-century Britain* (Basingstoke, 1994)

Digby, A., *Pauper Palaces* (1978)

Dodsworth, F.M., '"Civic" Police and the Condition of Liberty: The Rationality of Governance in Eighteenth-Century England', *Social History*, 29 (2004), 199–216

Dworkin, R.M. (ed.) *The Philosophy of Law* (Oxford, 1977)

Doolittle, I.G., 'Walpole's City Elections Act (1725)', *English Hist. Rev.*, 97 (1982), 504–29

Eastwood, D., '"Amplifying the Province of the Legislature": The Flow of Information and the English State in the Early Nineteenth Century', *Historical Research*, 62 (1989), 276–94

—— *Governing Rural England: Tradition and Transformation in Local Government 1780–1840* (Oxford, 1994)

—— *Government and Community in the English Provinces, 1700–1870* (Basingstoke, 1997)

—— 'Parliament and Locality: Representation and Responsibility in Late-Hanoverian England', in D. Dean and C. Jones (eds.) *Parliament and Locality 1660–1939* (Edinburgh, 1998)

Elias, N., *The Civilizing Process: Sociogenetic and Psychogenetic Investigation*, trans. E. Jephcott, revd. edn., ed. E. Dunning, Johan Gousblom and S. Mennell (Oxford, 2000)

Epstein, J., *Radical Expression: Political Language, Ritual, and Symbol in England 1790–1850* (New York, 1994)

Ehrman, J., *The Younger Pitt: The Years of Acclaim* (1969)

Erickson, A.L., *Women and Property in Early Modern England* (1993)

Evans, E.J., 'Some Reasons for the Growth of English Rural Anti-Clericalism, c.1750–c.1830', *Past and Present*, 66 (1975), 84–109

Finn, M., *The Character of Credit: Personal Debt in English Culture, 1740–1914* (Cambridge, 2003)

Fisher, G., 'The Birth of the Prison Retold', *Yale Law Journal*, 104 (1995), 1235–324

Fissell, M.E., 'Charity Universal? Institutions and Moral Reform in Eighteenth-Century Bristol', in L. Davison et al (eds.) *Stilling the Grumbling Hive: The Response to Social and Economic Problems in England, 1689–1750* (Stroud, 1992)

Fitzpatrick, P., *The Mythology of Modern Law* (1992)

Fletcher, A., *Reform in the Provinces: The Government of Stuart England* (New Haven, CT, 1986)

Fletcher, A.J. and Stevenson, J., 'Introduction', in A.J. Fletcher and J. Stevenson (eds.) *Order and Disorder in Early Modern England* (Cambridge, 1985)

Fraser, 'P., Public Petitioning and Parliament before 1832', *History*, 46 (1961), 195–211

Freeman, M., 'Popular Attitudes to Turnpikes in Early Eighteenth-century England', *Journal of Historical Geography*, 19 (1993), 33–47

Friedman, L., 'Lawyers in Cross-cultural Perspective', in R.L. Abel and P.S.C Lewis (eds.) *Lawyers in Society, Vol. 3: Comparative Theories* (Berkeley, CA, 1989)

Furley, J.S., *Quarter Sessions Government in Hampshire in the Seventeenth Century* (Winchester, n.d. [1937])

Gallanis, T.P., 'The Mystery of Old Bailey Counsel', *Cambridge Law Journal*, 65 (2006), 159–73

Gaskill, M., *Crime and Mentalities in Early Modern England* (Cambridge, 2000)

Gatrell, V.A.C., 'Crime, Authority and the Policeman State', in F.M.L. Thompson (ed.) *The Cambridge Social History of Britain 1750–1950* (Cambridge, 1990)

—— *The Hanging Tree: Execution and the English People 1770–1868* (Oxford, 1994)

Glassey, L., 'Local Government', in C. Jones (ed.) *Britain in the First Age of Party: Essays Presented to Geoffrey Holmes* (1987)

Goldie, M., 'The Unacknowledged Republic', in T. Harris (ed.) *The Politics of the Excluded, c.1500–1850* (Basingstoke, 2001)

Gough, J.W., *Fundamental Law in English Constitutional History* (Oxford, 1955)
Gould, E., 'American Independence and Britain's Counter-Revolution', *Past and Present*, 154 (1997), 107–41
Gowing, L., 'Language, Power and the Law: Women's Slander Litigation in Early Modern London', in J. Kermode and G. Walker (eds.) *Women, Crime and the Courts in Early Modern England* (1994)
—— *Domestic Dangers: Women, Words, and Sex in Early Modern London* (Oxford, 1996)
Green, T.A., 'A Retrospective on the Criminal Trial Jury, 1200–1800', in J.S. Cockburn and T. A. Green (eds.) *Twelve Good Men and True: The Criminal Trial Jury in England, 1200–1800* (Princeton, NJ, 1988)
Greene, J.P., 'From the Perspective of Law: Context and Legitimacy in the Origins of the American Revolution', *South Atlantic Quarterly* 85 (1986), 56–77
—— 'The Glorious Revolution and the British Empire 1688–1783', in L.G. Schwoerer (ed.) *The Revolution of 1688–1689: Changing Perspectives* (Cambridge, 1992)
—— 'Competing Authorities: The Debate over Parliamentary Imperial Jurisdiction, 1763–1776', in P. Lawson (ed.) *Parliament and the Atlantic Empire* (Edinburgh, 1995)
Habbakuk, J., *Marriage, Debt, and the Estates System* (Oxford, 1994)
Habermas, J., *The Structural Transformation of the Public Sphere*, trans. T. Burger (Cambridge, 1989)
Haigh, C. and Wall, A., 'Clergy JPs in England and Wales, 1590–1640', *Historical Journal*, 47 (2004), 233–59
Hall, S. et al, *Policing the Crisis: Mugging, the State, and Law and Order* (New York, 1978)
Halliday, P.D., review of S. Hindle, *The State and Social Change in Early Modern England*, in *Law and History Review*, 20 (2002), 647–9
Hammond, J.L. and B., *The Village Labourer, 1760–1832: A Study in the Government of England before the Reform Bill* (2$^{nd}$ edn., 1913)
Handley, S., 'Local Legislative Initiatives for Economic and Social Development in Lancashire, 1689–1731', *Parliamentary History*, 9 (1990), 14–37
Hanly, C., 'The Decline of the Civil Jury Trial in Nineteenth-Century England', *Journal of Legal History*, 26 (2005), 253–78
Harding, A., *A Social History of English Law* (Harmondsworth, 1966)
Harling, P. and Mandler, P., 'From "Fiscal-Military" State to Laissez-faire State, 1760–1850', *Journal of British Studies*, 32 (1993), 44–70
Harris, M., *London Newspapers in the Age of Walpole* (Cranbury, NJ, 1987)
Harris, R., *A Patriot Press: National Politics and the London Press in the 1740s* (Oxford, 1993)
Harris, T., 'The People, the Law, and the Constitution in Scotland and England: A Comparative Approach to the Glorious Revolution', *Journal of British Studies*, 38 (1999), 28–58
Harrison, C., 'Manor Courts and the Governance of Tudor England', in C.W. Brooks and M. Lobban (eds.) *Communities and Courts in Britain 1150–1900* (1997)
Hay, D., 'Property, Authority and the Criminal Law', in D. Hay et al (eds.) *Albion's Fatal Tree: Crime and Society in Eighteenth-Century England* (Harmondsworth, 1975)
—— 'Controlling the English Prosecutor', *Osgoode Hall Law Journal*, 21 (1983), 165–86
—— 'The Class Composition of the Palladium of Liberty: Trial Jurors in the Eighteenth Century', in J.S. Cockburn and T.A. Green (eds.) *Twelve Good Men and True: The Criminal Trial Jury in England, 1200–1800* (Princeton, NJ, 1988)
—— 'The State and the Market in 1800: Lord Kenyon and Mr. Waddington', *Past and Present*, 162 (1999), 101–62

—— 'Moral Economy, Political Economy and Law', in A. Randall and A. Charlesworth (eds.) *Moral Economy and Popular Protest: Crowds, Conflict and Authority* (Basingstoke, 2000)

—— 'Master and Servant in England: Using the Law in the Eighteenth and Nineteenth Centuries', in W. Steinmetz (ed.) *Private Law and Social Inequality in the Industrial Age* (Oxford, 2000)

—— 'Dread of the Crown Office: The English Magistracy and King's Bench, 1740–1800', in N. Landau (ed.) *Law, Crime and English Society 1660–1830* (Cambridge, 2002)

—— 'Kenyon, Lloyd, First Baron Kenyon', *Oxford Dictionary of National Biography* (Oxford, 2004)

—— 'England, 1562–1875: The Law and its Uses', in D. Hay and P. Craven, *Masters, Servants, and Magistrates in Britain and the Empire, 1562–1955* (Chapel Hill, NC, 2004)

—— 'Legislation, Magistrates, and Judges: High Law and Low Law in England and the Empire', in D. Lemmings (ed.) *The British and their Laws in the Eighteenth Century* (Woodbridge, 2005)

Hay, D. and Rogers, N., *Eighteenth-century English Society* (Oxford, 1997)

Hay, D. and Snyder, F., 'Using the Criminal Law, 1750–1850: Policing, Private Prosecution, and the State', in D. Hay and F. Snyder (eds.) *Policing and Prosecution in Britain 1750–1850* (Oxford, 1989)

Haydon, C., *Anti-Catholicism in Eighteenth-century England: A Social and Political Study* (Manchester, 1993)

Hayton, D.W., *The House of Commons 1690–1715* (2002)

Hayek, F.A., *Law, Legislation and Liberty* (1982)

Herrup, C.B., *The Common Peace: Participation and the Criminal Law in Seventeenth-Century England* (Cambridge, 1987)

Hindle, S., 'The Keeping of the Public Peace', in P. Griffiths, A. Fox and S. Hindle, *The Experience of Authority in Early Modern England* (Basingstoke, 1996)

—— *The State and Social Change in Early Modern England* (Basingstoke, 2000)

Hitchcock, T., 'Paupers and Preachers: The SPCK and the Parochial Workhouse Movement', in L. Davison et al (eds.) *Stilling the Grumbling Hive: The Response to Social and Economic Problems in England, 1689–1750* (Stroud, 1992)

Holdsworth, W., *A History of English Law* (1922–72)

Holmes, C., 'Popular Culture', in S.L. Kaplan (ed.) *Understanding Popular Culture: Europe from the Middle Ages to the Nineteenth Century* (Berlin, 1984)

—— 'Drainers and Fenmen: The Problem of Popular Consciousness in the Seventeenth Century', in A. Fletcher and J. Stevenson (eds.) *Order and Disorder in Early Modern England* (Cambridge, 1985)

—— 'The Legal Instruments of Power and the State in Early Modern England', in A. Padoa-Schioppa (ed.) *Legislation and Justice* (Oxford, 1997)

Holmes, G., 'The Sacheverell Riots: The Crowd and the Church in Early Eighteenth-Century London', *Past and Present*, 72 (1976), 55–85

—— *Politics, Religion and Society in England 1679–1742* (1986)

Holt, J.C., *Magna Carta* (Cambridge, 2nd edn., 1992)

Hoppit, J., 'Patterns of Parliamentary Legislation 1660–1800', *Historical Journal*, 39 (1996), 109–31

—— (ed.) *Failed Legislation 1660–1800* (1997)

Hoppit, J., Innes, J. and Styles, J., 'Project Report: Towards a History of Parliamentary Legislation', *Parliamentary History*, 13 (1994), 312–21

Horwitz, H., 'Liberty, Law, and Property, 1689–1776', in J.R. Jones (ed.) *Liberty Secured? Britain Before and After 1688* (Stanford, Ca., 1992)

—— *Chancery Equity Records and Proceedings 1600–1800: A Guide to Documents in the Public Record Office* (PRO Handbook 27, 1995)
—— '"Chancery's "Younger Sister": The Court of Exchequer and its Equity Jurisdiction, 1649–1841', *Historical Research*, 72 (1999), 160–82
Horwitz, H. and Polden, P., 'Continuity or Change in the Court of Chancery in the Seventeenth and Eighteenth Centuries?', *Journal of British Studies*, 35 (1996), 24–57
Howson, G., *Thief-Taker General* (New York, 1970)
Humphreys, S., 'Law as Discourse', *History and Anthropology*, 1 (1985), 241–64
Hunt, A., *Explorations in Law and Society: Towards a Constitutive Theory of Law* (1993)
Hunt, M.R., 'Wives and Marital "Rights" in the Court of Exchequer in the Early Eighteenth Century', in P. Griffiths and M.S.R. Jenner, *Londinopolis: Essays in the Cultural and Social History of Early Modern London* (Manchester, 2000)
Ignatieff, M., *A Just Measure of Pain: The Penitentiary in the Industrial Revolution 1750–1850* (Harmondsworth, 1989)
Ingram, M., 'Communities and Courts: Law and Disorder in Early-Seventeenth-Century Wiltshire', in J.S. Cockburn (ed.) *Crime in England 1550–1800* (1977)
—— *Church Courts, Sex and Marriage in England, 1570–1640* (Cambridge, 1987)
—— '"Scolding Women Cucked or Washed": A Crisis in Gender Relations in Early Modern England', in J. Kermode and G. Walker (eds.) *Women, Crime and the Courts in Early Modern England* (1994)
—— 'Reformation of Manners in Early Modern England', in *The Experience of Authority in Early Modern England*, ed. P. Griffiths et al (Basingstoke, 1996)
Innes, J., 'The Crime Wave: Recent Writing on Crime and Criminal Justice in Eighteenth-Century England', *Journal of British Studies*, 25 (1986), 380–435
—— 'Prisons for the Poor: English Bridewells, 1555–1800', in F. Snyder and D. Hay (eds.) *Labour, Law, and Crime* (1987)
—— 'Parliament and the Shaping of Eighteenth-Century English Social Policy', *Transactions of the Royal Historical Soc.*, 5th ser., 40 (1990), 63–92
—— 'The Role of Transportation in Seventeenth and Eighteenth-Century Penal Practice', in C. Bridge (ed.) *New Perspectives in Australian History* (1990)
—— 'Politics and Morals: The Reformation of Manners Movement in Later Eighteenth-Century England', in E. Hellmuth (ed.) *The Transformation of Political Culture: England and Germany in the Late Eighteenth Century* (Oxford, 1990)
—— 'Politics, Property and the Middle Class', *Parliamentary History*, 11 (1992), 286–92
—— 'The Domestic Face of the Military-Fiscal State: Government and Society in Eighteenth-Century Britain', in L. Stone (ed.) *An Imperial State at War: Britain from 1689 to 1815* (1994)
—— 'The Local Acts of a National Parliament: Parliament's Role in Sanctioning Local Action in Eighteenth-Century Britain', in D. Dean and C. Jones (eds.) *Parliament and Locality 1660–1939* (Edinburgh, 1998)
—— 'Legislation and Public Participation 1760–1830', in D. Lemmings (ed.) *The British and Their Laws in the Eighteenth Century* (Woodbridge, 2005)
—— 'The Protestant Carpenter – William Payne of Bell Yard (c. 1718–82): The Life and Times of a London Informing Constable', in eadem, *Inferior Politics: Social Problems and Social Policies in Eighteenth-Century Britain* (Oxford, 2009)
—— *Inferior Politics: Social Problems and Social Policies in Eighteenth-Century Britain* (Oxford, 2009)
Innes, J. and Rogers, N., 'Politics and Government 1700–1840', in P. Clark (ed.), *The Cambridge Urban History of Britain. Vol. II 1540–1840* (Cambridge, 2000)
Isaac, R., *The Transformation of Virginia* (Chapel Hill, NC, 1982)

Isaacs, T., 'The Anglican Hierarchy and the Reformation of Manners', *J. of Ecclesiastical History*, 33 (1982), 391–411

Jenkins, P., *The Making of a Ruling Class: The Glamorgan Gentry 1640–1790* (Cambridge, 1983)

Jones, P.D., 'The Bristol Bridge Riot and its Antecedents: Eighteenth-Century Perception of the Crowd', *Journal of British Studies*, 19 (1980), 74–92

Jones, W.R.D., *The Tudor Commonwealth 1529–1559* (1970)

Jupp, P., *British Politics on the Eve of Reform: The Duke of Wellington's Administration, 1828–30* (1998)

Keith-Lucas, B., *The Unreformed Local Government System* (1980)

Kelch, R.A., *Newcastle: A Duke without Money* (1974)

Kent, J., 'The English Village Constable, 1580–1642: The Nature and Dilemmas of the Office', *Journal of British Studies* 20 (1981), 26–49

—— *The English Village Constable 1580-1642: A Social and Administrative Study* (Oxford, 1986)

King, P., 'Newspaper Reporting, Prosecution Practice and Perceptions of Urban Crime: The Colchester Crime Wave of 1765', *Continuity and Change*, 2 (1987), 423–54

—— 'Prosecution Associations and their Impact in Eighteenth-Century Essex', in D. Hay and F. Snyder (eds.) *Policing and Prosecution in Britain 1750–1850* (Oxford, 1989)

—— 'Punishing Assault: The Transformation of Attitudes in the English Courts', *Journal of Interdisciplinary History*, 27 (1996), 43–74

—— *Crime, Justice and Discretion in England 1740–1820* (Oxford, 2000)

—— 'The Summary Courts and Social Relations in Eighteenth-Century England', *Past and Present*, 183 (2004), 125–69

—— *Crime and Law in England, 1750–1840* (Cambridge, 2006)

—— 'Newspaper Reporting and Attitudes to Crime and Justice in Late Eighteenth and Early Nineteenth Century London', *Continuity and Change*, 22 (2007), 73–112

King, W.J., 'Untapped Resources for Social Historians: Court Leet Records', *Journal of Social History*, 15 (1982), 699–705

Klein, L.E., *Shaftesbury and the Culture of Politeness: Moral Discourse and Cultural Politics in Early Eighteenth-Century England* (Cambridge, 1994)

—— 'Politeness and the Interpretation of the British Eighteenth Century', *Historical Journal*, 45 (2002), 869–98

Knights, M., *Representation and Misrepresentation in Later Stuart Britain: Partisanship and Political Culture* (Oxford, 2005)

Koenigsberger, H.G., 'Composite States, Representative Institutions and the American Revolution', *Historical Research*, 62 (1989), 135–53

Kyle, C.R., 'Attendance, Apathy and Order? Parliamentary Committees in Early Stuart England', in C.R. Kyle and J. Peacey, *Parliament at Work: Parliamentary Committees, Political Power and Public Access in Early Modern England* (Woodbridge, 2002)

Kyle, C.R. and Peacey, J., '"Under cover of so much coming and going": Public Access to Parliament and the Political Process in Early Modern England', in C.R. Kyle and J. Peacey, *Parliament at Work: Parliamentary Committees, Political Power and Public Access in Early Modern England* (Woodbridge, 2002)

Krygier, M. and Van Krieken, R., 'The Character of the Nation', in R. Manne (ed.), *Whitewash* (Melbourne, 2003)

Lacy, M. De, *Prison Reform in Lancashire* (Manchester, Chetham Soc., 3rd ser., 33, 1986)

Lambert, S., 'Printing for the House of Commons in the Eighteenth Century', *The Library*, 5th ser., 23 (1968), 25–46

Landau, N., *The Justices of the Peace, 1679–1760* (Berkeley, CA, 1984)

—— 'The Regulation of Immigration, Economic Structures and Definition of the Poor in Eighteenth-Century England', *Historical Journal*, 33 (1990), 541–71
—— 'Appearances at the Quarter Sessions of Eighteenth-Century Middlesex', *The London Journal*, 23 (1998), 30–52
—— 'Indictment for Fun and Profit: A Prosecutor's Reward at Eighteenth-Century Quarter Sessions', *Law and History Review*, 17 (1999), 507–36
—— 'The Trading Justice's Trade', in N. Landau (ed.) *Law, Crime and English Society 1660–1830* (Cambridge, 2002)
Lander, J.R., *English Justices of the Peace 1461–1509* (Gloucester, 1989)
Landsman, S., 'One Hundred Years of Rectitude: Medical Witnesses at the Old Bailey, 1717–1817', *Law and History Review*, 16 (1998), 445–94
Langbein, J.R., The Criminal Trial before the Lawyers', *University of Chicago Law Review*, 45 (1978), 263–316
—— 'Albion's Fatal Flaws', *Past and Present*, 68 (1983), 96–120
—— 'Shaping the Eighteenth-Century Criminal Trial: A View from the Ryder Sources', *Univ. of Chicago Law Review*, 50 (1983), 263–316
—— 'The Historical Origins of the Privilege against Self-incrimination at Common Law', *Michigan Law Review*, 92 (1993–4), 1047–85
—— 'The Prosecutorial Origins of Defence Counsel in the Eighteenth Century: The Appearance of Solicitors', *Cambridge Law Journal*, 58 (1999), 314–65
—— *The Origins of Adversary Criminal Trial* (Oxford, 2003)
Langelüddecke, H., 'Law and Order in Seventeenth-century England: The Organization of Local Administration during the Personal Rule of Charles I', *Law and History Review*, 15 (1997), 49–76
—— '"Patchy and Spasmodic": The Response of Justices of the Peace to Charles I's Book of Orders', *English Historical Review*, 113 (1998), 1231–48
Langford, P., *The Excise Crisis* (1975)
—— 'Old Whigs, Old Tories, and the American Revolution', in P. Marshall and G. Williams (eds.) *The British Atlantic Empire before the American Revolution* (1980)
—— *A Polite and Commercial People: England, 1727–1783* (Oxford, 1989)
—— *Public Life and the Propertied Englishman* (Oxford, 1991)
—— 'Manners and the Eighteenth-Century State', in J. Brewer and E. Helmuth (eds.) *Rethinking Leviathan* (Oxford, 1999)
Laqueur, T., 'Crowds, Carnival and the State in English Executions, 1604–1868', in A.L. Beier et al (eds.) *The First Modern Society* (Cambridge, 1989)
Lemmings, D., 'The Independence of the Judiciary in Eighteenth-Century England', in P. Birks (ed.) *The Life of the Law* (1993)
—— 'Blackstone and Law Reform by Education: Preparation for the Bar and Lawyerly Culture in Eighteenth-Century England', *Law and History Review*, 16 (1998), 211–55
—— *Professors of the Law: Barristers and English Legal Culture in the Eighteenth Century* (Oxford, 2000)
—— 'Women's Property, Popular Cultures, and the Consistory Court of London in the Eighteenth Century', in M. Ferguson, N. Wright and A. Buck (eds.) *Women and Property in Early Modern England* (Toronto, 2004)
—— 'Introduction', in D. Lemmings (ed.) *The British and Their Laws in the Eighteenth Century* (Woodbridge, 2005)
—— 'Conclusion: Moral Panics, Law and the Transformation of the Public Sphere in Early Modern England', in D. Lemmings and C. Walker (eds.) *Moral Panics, the Media and the Law in Early Modern England* (2009)

Lemmings, D. and Walker, C. (eds.) *Moral Panics, the Media and the Law in Early Modern England* (Basingstoke, 2009)

Leys, C., 'Petitioning in the Nineteenth and Twentieth Centuries', *Political Studies*, 3 (1955), 45–64

Lieberman, D., *The Province of Legislation Determined* (Cambridge, 1989)

Llewellyn, N., 'Honour in Life, Death and in the Memory: Funeral Monuments in Early Modern England', *Transactions of the Royal Historical Society*, 6th ser. 6 (1996), 179–200

Linebaugh, P., 'The Tyburn Riot against the Surgeons', in D. Hay et al (eds.) *Albion's Fatal Tree: Crime and Society in Eighteenth-Century England* (Harmondsworth, 1975)

—— *The London Hanged: Crime and Civil Society in the Eighteenth Century* (2nd edn., 2003)

Lobban, M., Preparing for Fusion: Reforming the Nineteenth-Century Court of Chancery, Part 1', *Law and History Review*, 22 (2004), 389–427

—— 'Custom, Nature, and Authority: The Roots of English Legal Positivism', in D. Lemmings (ed.) *The British and Their Laws in the Eighteenth Century* (Woodbridge, 2005)

Lowe, W.C., 'Peers and Printers: The Beginnings of Sustained Press Coverage of the House of Lords in the 1770s', *Parliamentary History*, 7 (1988), 241–56

Macaulay, T.B., *The History of England from the Accession of James II* (1906)

McCalman, I., 'Popular Constitutionalism and Revolution in England and Ireland', in I. Woloch (ed.) *Revolution and the Meanings of Freedom in the Nineteenth Century* (Stanford, CA, 1996)

McGowen, R., 'The Body and Punishment in Eighteenth-Century England', *Journal of Modern History*, 59 (1987), 651–79

—— 'From Pillory to Gallows: The Punishment of Forgery in the Age of the Financial Revolution', *Past and Present*, 165 (1999), 107–40

—— 'Forgery Legislation in Eighteenth-Century England', in N. Landau (ed.) *Law, Crime and English Society 1660–1830* (Cambridge, 2002)

—— '"Making Examples" and the Crisis of Punishment in Mid-Eighteenth-Century England', in D. Lemmings (ed.) *The British and their Laws in the Eighteenth Century* (Woodbridge, Suffolk, 2005)

—— 'The Bank of England and the Policing of Forgery 1797–1821', *Past and Present*, 186 (2005), 81–116

McKenrick, N., Brewer, J. and Plumb, J.H. (eds.) *The Birth of a Consumer Society: The Commercialization of Eighteenth-Century England* (1982)

McKenzie, A., 'Martyrs in Low Life? Dying "Game" in Augustan England', *Journal of British Studies*, 62 (2003), 167–205

—— 'From True Confessions to True Reporting? The Decline and Fall of the Ordinary's Account', *London Journal* 30 (2005), 55–70

—— *Tyburn's Martyrs: Execution in England 1675–1775* (2007)

Maitland, F., *Collected Papers*, ed. H.A.L. Fisher (Cambridge, 1911)

—— *The Constitutional History of England* (Cambridge, 1965)

Malcolmson, R.W., 'A Set of Ungovernable People: The Kingswood Colliers in the Eighteenth Century', in J. Brewer and J. Styles (eds.) *An Ungovernable People: The English and their Law in the Seventeenth and Eighteenth Centuries* (1980)

Mann, M., *The Sources of Social Power: Volume 1. A History of Power from the Beginning to A.D. 1760* (Cambridge, 1986)

Marchant, R.A., *The Church under the Law: Justice, Administration and Discipline in the Diocese of York 1560–1640* (Cambridge, 1969)

Martin, J.M., 'Members of Parliament and Enclosure: A Reconsideration', *Agricultural History Review*, 27 (1979), 101–9

May, A., *The Bar and the Old Bailey, 1750–1850* (Chapel Hill, NC, 2003)
Meldrum, T., 'A Women's Court in London: Defamation at the Bishop of London's Consistory Court, 1700–1745', *London Journal*, 19 (1994), 1–20
Mitnick, J.M., 'From Neighbour-witness to Judge of Proofs: The Transformation of the English Civil Juror', *American Journal of Legal History*, 32 (1988), 201–35
Moir, E., *Local Government in Gloucestershire 1775–1800* (Gloucester, 1969)
—— *The Justice of the Peace* (Harmondsworth, 1969)
Morgan, E.S., *Inventing the People: The Rise of Popular Sovereignty in England and America* (New York, 1988)
Morgan, G. and Rushton, P., *Rogues, Thieves and the Rule of Law* (1998)
—— and —— 'The Magistrate, the Community and Maintenance of an Orderly Society in Eighteenth-Century England', *Historical Research*, 86 (2003), 54–77
Morrill, J.S., *Cheshire 1630–1660: County Government and Society during the English Revolution* (Oxford, 1974)
—— *The Cheshire Grand Jury, 1625–1659* (Leicester, 1976)
Muldrew, C., 'Credit and the Courts: Debt Litigation in a Seventeenth-century Urban Community', *Economic History Review*, 46 (1993), 23–38
—— 'The Culture of Reconciliation: Community and the Settlement of Economic Disputes in Early Modern England', *Historical Journal*, 39 (1996), 915–42
—— 'Rural Credit, Market Areas and Legal Institutions in the Countryside in England, 1550–1700', in C.W. Brooks and M. Lobban (eds.) *Communities and Courts in Britain 1150–1900* (1997)
—— *The Economy of Obligation: The Culture of Credit and Social Relations in Early Modern England* (1998)
Munsche, P.B., *Gentlemen and Poachers: the English Game Laws, 1671–1831* (Cambridge, 1971)
Musson, A., 'Reconstructing English Labor Laws: A Medieval Perspective', in K. Robertson and M. Uebel (eds.) *The Middle Ages at Work: Practicing Labor in Late Medieval England* (New York, 2004)
Namier, L. and Brooke, J., *The House of Commons 1754–1790* (1985)
Neeson, J.M., *Commoners: Common Right, Enclosure and Social Change in England, 1700–1820* (Cambridge, 1993)
Nenner, H., *By Colour of Law: Legal Culture and Constitutional Politics in England, 1660–1689* (Chicago, 1977)
O'Brien, P., 'Crime and Punishment as Historical Problem', *Journal of Social History*, 11 (1978), 508–20
O'Gorman, F., 'Pitt and the "Tory" Reaction to the French Revolution 1789–1815', in H.T. Dickinson (ed.) *Britain and the French Revolution, 1789–1815* (Basingstoke, 1989)
—— *Voters, Patrons, and Parties: The Unreformed Electoral System of Hanoverian England 1734–1832* (Oxford, 1989)
—— *The Long Eighteenth Century: British Political and Social History 1688–1832* (1997)
Oldham, J., 'The Origins of the Special Jury', *Univ. of Chicago Law Rev.*, 100 (1983), 137–221
—— 'Special Juries in England: Nineteenth Century Usage and Reform', *Journal of Legal History*, 8 (1987), 148–66
—— *The Mansfield Manuscripts and the Growth of English Law in the Eighteenth Century* (Chapel Hill, NC, 1992)
Outhwaite, R.B., *The Rise and Fall of the English Ecclesiastical Courts, 1500–1860* (Cambridge, 2006)
*Oxford Dictionary of National Biography* (Oxford, 2004–)

Paley, R., '"An Imperfect, Inadequate and Wretched System"? Policing London before Peel', in *Criminal Justice History*, 10 (1989), 95–130
—— 'Thief-takers in London in the Age of the McDaniel Gang, c.1745–1754', in D. Hay and F. Snyder (eds.) *Policing and Prosecution in Britain 1750–1850* (Oxford, 1989)
Palmer, S.H., *Police and Protest in England and Ireland, 1780–1850* (Cambridge, 1988)
Pawson, E., *Transport and Economy: the Turnpike Roads of Eighteenth Century Britain* (1977)
Phillips, C.B. and Smith, J.H., *Lancashire and Cheshire from AD 1540* (1994)
Philips, D., 'A New Engine of Power and Authority: the Institutionalization of Law-Enforcement in England', in V.A.C. Gatrell et al, *Crime and the Law: The Social History of Crime in Europe Since 1500* (1980)
—— 'Good Men to Associate and Bad Men to Conspire: Associations for the Prosecution of Felons in England 1760–1860', in D. Hay and F. Snyder (eds.) *Policing and Prosecution in Britain 1750–1850* (Oxford, 1989)
—— 'Policing', in I. McCalman (ed.) *The Oxford Companion to the Romantic Age: British Culture 1776–1832* (Oxford, 1999)
Phillips, J.A., 'Popular Politics in Unreformed England', *Journal of Modern History*, 52 (1980), 599–625
Pickering, P., '"And your Petitioners &c": Chartist Petitioning in Popular Politics 1838–48', *English Historical Review*, 116 (2001), 368–88
Plumb, J.H., *The Growth of Political Stability in England 1675–1725* (Harmondsworth, 1969)
Pocock, J.G.A., 'Burke and the Ancient Constitution', in id., *Politics, Language and Time* (New York, 1971)
—— *Virtue, Commerce and History: Essays on Political Thought and History, Chiefly in the Eighteenth Century* (Cambridge, 1985)
—— *The Ancient Constitution and the Feudal Law: A Study of English Historical Thought in the Seventeenth Century* (Cambridge, 2nd edn., 1987)
Polden, P., 'Judicial Selkirks: The County Court Judges and the Press, 1847–80', in C.W. Brooks and M. Lobban (eds.) *Communities and Courts in Britain 1150–1900* (1997)
—— *A History of the County Court, 1846–1971* (Cambridge, 1999)
Pole, J.R., *Political Representation in England and the Origins of the American Republic* (Berkeley, Ca., 1971)
—— *The Gift of Government: Political Responsibility from the English Restoration to American Independence* (Athens, Ga., 1983)
Porter, R., *Enlightenment: Britain and the Creation of the Modern World* (Harmondsworth, 2000)
Postema, G.J., *Bentham and the Common Law Tradition* (Oxford, 1986)
Prest, W.R., 'Law and Women's Rights in Early Modern England', *The Seventeenth Century*, 6 (1991), 169–87
—— 'The Experience of Litigation', in D. Lemmings (ed.) *The British and Their Laws in the Eighteenth Century* (Woodbridge, 2005)
—— *William Blackstone: Law and Letters in the Eighteenth Century* (Oxford, 2008)
Radzinowicz, L., *A History of Criminal Law and its Administration from 1750* (1948–56)
Rawls, J., *A Theory of Justice* (Cambridge, MA, 1971)
Reid, J.P., *In a Defiant Stance: The Conditions of Law in Massachusetts Bay, the Irish Comparison; and the Coming of the American Revolution* (University Park, PA, 1977)
—— *In Defiance of the Law: The Standing Army Controversy, the Two Constitutions, and the Coming of the American Revolution* (Chapel Hill, NC, 1981)
Reynolds, E.A., *Before the Bobbies: The Night Watch and Police Reform in Metropolitan London, 1720–1830* (Stanford, CA., 1998)

Rogers, N., *Whigs and Cities: Popular Politics in the Age of Walpole and Pitt* (Oxford, 1989)
—— 'Popular Protest in Early Hanoverian London', *Past and Present*, 79 (1978), 70–100
—— 'The City Elections Act (1725) Reconsidered', *English Hist. Rev.*, 100 (1985), 604–17
—— 'Paul Langford's "Age of Improvement"', *Past and Present*, 130 (1991), 205–6
—— 'Confronting the Crime Wave. The Debate over Social Reform and Regulation, 1749–1753', in L. Davison et al (eds.) *Stilling the Grumbling Hive: The Response to Social and Economic Problems in England, 1689–1750* (Stroud, 1992)
—— *Crowds, Culture and Politics in Georgian Britain* (Oxford, 1998)
—— 'Impressment and the Law in Eighteenth-Century Britain', in N. Landau (ed.) *Law, Crime and English Society 1660–1830* (Cambridge, 2002)
Rosenheim, J.R., 'County Governance and Elite Withdrawal in Norfolk, 1660–1720', in A.L. Beier et al (eds.) *The First Modern Society: Essays in English History in Honour of Lawrence Stone* (Cambridge, 1989)
Rubin, G.R., 'Law, Poverty and Imprisonment for Debt, 1869–1914', in G.R. Rubin and D. Sugarman (eds.) *Law, Economy and Society, 1750–1914: Essays in the History of English Law* (1984)
Rubin, G.R. and Sugarman, D., 'Towards a New History of Law and Material Society in England 1750–1914', in G.R. Rubin and D. Sugarman (eds.) *Law, Economy and Society, 1750–1914: Essays in the History of English Law* (Abingdon, 1984)
Rudé, G., *Paris and London in the Eighteenth Century* (1952)
—— *Hanoverian London* (1971)
Rule, J., *The Experience of Labour in Eighteenth-century Industry* (1981)
—— *The Vital Century: England's Developing Economy 1714–1815* (1992)
Russell, C., *Parliaments and English Politics, 1621–1629* (Oxford, 1979)
Schwoerer, L.G., *No Standing Armies: The Antiarmy Ideology in Seventeenth-Century England* (Baltimore, Maryland, 1974)
Shapiro, B., '"To a Moral Certainty": Theories of Knowledge and Anglo-American Juries 1600–1850', *Hastings Law Journal*, 38 (1986), 153–93
Sharpe, J.A., *Defamation and Sexual Slander in Early Modern England: The Church Courts at York* (York, Borthwick Papers, no. 58, 1980)
—— '"Such Disagreement between Neighbours": Litigation and Human Relations in Early Modern England', in J. Bossy (ed.), *Disputes and Settlements: Law and Human Relations in the West* (Cambridge, 1983)
—— 'The People and the Law', in B. Reay (ed.), *Popular Culture in Seventeenth-Century England* (1985)
—— *Crime and the Law in English Satirical Prints 1600–1832* (Cambridge, 1986)
—— *Crime in Early Modern England 1550–1750* (2nd edn., 1999)
Shepard, A., 'Litigation and Locality: The Cambridge University Courts, 1560–1640', *Urban History*, 31 (2004), 5–28
Sheppard, F.H.W., *Local Government in St. Marylebone 1688–1835: A Study of the Vestry and a Turnpike Trust* (1958)
Shoemaker, R., *Prosecution and Punishment: Petty Crime and the Law in London and Rural Middlesex, c.1660–1725* (Cambridge, 1991)
—— 'Reforming the City: The Reformation of Manners Campaign in London, 1690–1738', in L. Davison et al (eds.) *Stilling the Grumbling Hive: the Response to Social and Economic Problems in England, 1689–1750*, (Stroud, 1992)
—— 'The Decline of the Public Insult in London 1660–1800', *Past and Present*, 169 (2000), 97–131
—— *The London Mob: Violence and Disorder in Eighteenth-Century England* (2004)

—— 'Streets of Shame? The Crowd and Public Punishments in London, 1700–1820', in S. Devereaux and P. Griffiths (eds.) *Penal Practice and Culture, 1500–1900* (Basingstoke, 2004)
Silver, A., 'The Demand for Order in Civil Society: A Review of Some Themes in the History of Urban Crime, Police, and Riot', in D.J. Bordua (ed.) *The Police: Six Sociological Essays* (New York, 1967)
Simpson, A.W.B., *Legal Theory and Legal History* (1987)
Skinner, Q., 'The Principles and Practice of Opposition: The Case of Bolingbroke versus Walpole', in N. McKendrick (ed.), *Historical Perspectives: Studies in English Thought and Society* (1974)
—— *Liberty before Liberalism* (Cambridge, 1998)
Skyrme, T., *History of the Justices of the Peace* (Chichester, 1991)
Slack, P., *The English Poor Law 1531–1782* (1990)
Smith, B.P., 'The Presumption of Guilt and the English Law of Theft, 1750–1850', *Law and History Review*, 23 (2005), 133–71
—— 'The Emergence of Public Prosecution in London, 1790–1850', *Yale Journal of Law and the Humanities*, 32 (2006), 29–62
Smith, G.T., 'Civilised People Don't Want to See that Sort of Thing: The Decline of Physical Punishment in London, 1760–1840', in C. Strange (ed.) *Qualities of Mercy: Justice, Punishment and Discretion* (Vancouver, 1996)
Snell, E., 'Discourses of Criminality in the Eighteenth-Century Press: The Presentation of Crime in *The Kentish Post*, 1717–1768', *Continuity and Change*, 22 (2007), 13–47
Spencer, F.H., *Municipal Origins: An Account of English Private Bill Legislation Relating to Local Government, 1740–1835* (1911)
Spring, E., *Law, Land, and Family: Aristocratic Inheritance in England, 1300 to 1800* (Chapel Hill, NC, 1993)
Staves, S., *Married Women's Separate Property in England, 1660–1833* (Cambridge, MA, 1990)
Stedman Jones, G., *Languages of Class* (Cambridge, 1983)
Stein, P., *Legal Evolution: The Story of an Idea* (Cambridge, 1980)
Stevenson, J., *Popular Disturbances in England 1700–1832* (2nd edn., 1992)
Stone, L., *The Family, Sex and Marriage in England 1500–1800* (1977)
—— 'Interpersonal Violence in English Society 1300–1980', *Past and Present*, 51 (1983), 22–33
—— *Road to Divorce: England 1530–1987* (Oxford, 1990)
Storch, R.D., 'Policing Rural Southern England Before the Police', in D. Hay and F. Snyder (eds.), *Policing and Prosecution in Britain 1750–1850* (Oxford, 1989)
Stretton, T., *Women Waging Law in Elizabethan England* (Cambridge, 1998)
Styles, J., 'Embezzlement, Industry and the Law in England, 1500–1800', in P. Hudson and M. Sonenscher (eds.) *Manufacture in Town and Country before the Factory* (Cambridge, 1983)
Sugarman, D., 'Anarchism, Marxism, and the Critique of Law', in D. Sugarman (ed.) *Legality, Ideology and the State* (1983)
Sweet, R., 'Local Identities and a National Parliament, *c.* 1688–1835', in J. Hoppit (ed.) *Parliaments, Nations and Identities in Britain and Ireland, 1660–1850* (Manchester, 2003)
Sykes, E., *Edmund Gibson, Bishop of London, 1669–1748: A Study in Politics and Religion in the Eighteenth Century* (Oxford, 1926)
—— *From Sheldon to Secker: Aspects of English Church History, 1660–1768* (Cambridge, 1958)
Taylor, D., *The New Police in Nineteenth-Century England* (Manchester, 1997)

Thomas, P.D.G., 'The Beginning of Parliamentary Reporting in Newspapers, 1768–1774', *English Historical Review*, 74 (1959), 623–36
—— *The House of Commons in the Eighteenth Century* (Oxford, 1971)
—— *John Wilkes: A Friend to Liberty* (Oxford, 1996)
—— 'Pratt, Charles, First Earl Camden', in *Oxford Dictionary of National Biography* (Oxford, 2004)
Thompson, E.P., *The Making of the English Working Class* (Harmondsworth, 1968)
—— *Whigs and Hunters* (Harmondsworth, 1975)
—— *Customs in Common* (Harmondsworth, 1993)
Thorne, R.G., *The House of Commons 1790–1820* (1986)
Trevelyan, G.M., *The English Revolution 1688–1689* (1938)
Turner, M.E., *English Parliamentary Enclosure: Its Historical Geography and Economic History* (Folkestone, 1980)
—— 'Economic Protest in Rural Society: Opposition to Parliamentary Enclosure in Buckinghamshire', *Southern History*, 10 (1988), 94–128
Twiss, H., *The Public and Private Life of Lord Chancellor Eldon* (1844)
Vernon, J., *Politics and the People: A Study in English Political Culture c.1815–1867* (Cambridge, 1993)
Vogler, R., *Reading the Riot Act: The Magistracy, the Police and the Army in Civil Disorder* (Milton Keynes, 1991)
Waddams, S.M., *Law, Politics and the Church of England: The Career of Stephen Lushington 1782–1873* (Cambridge, 1992)
—— *Sexual Slander in Nineteenth-Century England* (Toronto, 2000)
Walker, G., *Crime, Gender and Social Order in Early Modern England* (Cambridge, 2003)
Wall, A., *Power and Protest in England 1525–1640* (2000)
Webb, S. and Webb, B., *The Manor and the Borough* (1908)
—— *The Parish and the County* (1906)
—— *The Story of the King's Highway* (1913)
—— *English Prisons under Local Government* (1922)
—— *Statutory Authorities for Special Purposes* (1922)
—— *English Poor Law History. Part 1: The Old Poor Law* (1927)
Welby, G., 'Rulers of the Countryside: The Justice of the Peace in Nottinghamshire, 1775–1800', *Transactions of the Thoroton Society*, 78 (1974), 75–87
Wiles, R.M., *Freshest Advices* (Ohio, 1965)
Wilf, S., 'Imagining Justice: Aesthetics and Public Execution in Late Eighteenth-Century England', *Yale Journal of Law and the Humanities*, 5 (1993), 51–78
Willman, R., 'Blackstone and the Theoretical Perfection of English Law in the Reign of Charles II', *Historical Journal*, 26 (1983), 39–70
Williams, O.C., *The Historical Development of Private Bill Procedure and Standing Orders in the House of Commons* (1948–9)
Williams, P. and Dickinson, J., 'Fear of Crime: Read All about It? The Relationship between Newspaper Crime Reporting and Fear of Crime', *British Journal of Criminology*, 33 (1993), 33–56
Wilson, K., *The Sense of the People: Politics, Culture and Imperialism in England, 1715–1785* (Cambridge, 1995)
Winder, W.H., 'The Courts of Requests', *Law Quarterly Review*, 207 (1936), 369–94
Wood, A., 'Custom, Identity and Resistance: English Free Miners and Their Law, c.1550–1800', in P. Griffiths, A. Fox and S. Hindle (eds.) *The Experience of Authority in Early Modern England* (Basingstoke, 1996)
—— *The Politics of Social Conflict: the Peak Country 1520–1770* (Cambridge, 1999)

Wrightson, K., 'Two Concepts of Order: Justices, Constables and Jurymen in Seventeenth-Century England', in J. Brewer and J. Styles (ed.) *An Ungovernable People: The English and Their Law in the Seventeenth and Eighteenth Centuries* (1980)
—— 'The Politics of the Parish in Early Modern England', in P. Griffiths, A. Fox and S. Hindle (eds.) *The Experience of Authority in Early Modern England* (Basingstoke, 1996)
—— and Levine, D., *Poverty and Piety in an English Village: Terling, 1525–1700* (Oxford, 1995)
Zirker, M., 'General Introduction', in H. Fielding, *An Enquiry into the Causes of the Late Increase of Robbers and Related Writings*, ed. M. Zirker (Oxford, 1988)
Yorke, P.C., *The Life and Correspondence of Philip Yorke Earl of Hardwicke* (Cambridge, 1913)

## 6. Unpublished Printed Material

Connors, R.T., 'Pelham, Parliament and Public Policy, 1746–1754' (University of Cambridge PhD thesis, 1993)
Dabhwoila, F.N., 'Prostitution and Policing in London, c. 1680–c.1760' (University of Oxford D.Phil. thesis, 1995)
Morris, P., 'Defamation and Sexual Reputation in Somerset, 1733–1850' (University of Warwick, PhD. thesis, 1985)
Reasons why the Bill for amending the High-Ways from Brampton-Bridge, to Welford-Bridge, in the County of Northampton; and also from Morter-Pit Hill in the said County, to Chain-Bridge, leading into Market-Harborough, in the County of Leicester, should not pass into a Law, as it now stands before your Lordships (printed petition to the House of Lords, 1721, at BL pressmark 576.m.17(17))

# Index

absolutism, 9, 129
Act of Settlement of 1700, 141
Act of Union of 1707, 126, 130, 131
Anglo-Saxons
  frankpledge system, 98
  society, 133
Anne, Queen, 102, 131
anti-turnpike riots of 1749, 152, 153
Ashurst, Sir W., 182
assizes, 2, 11, 17, 18, 28, 57, 82, 92, 163, 187n18
  of Clarendon, 20
  Hertford, 67
  Surrey, 119
Astle, Edward, case of, 41, 44
Atkyns, Sir R., 130
Atterbury Plot, 176
attorneys, 59, 119
  registration of, 75
  see also lawyers, legal professions

Baker, J.H., 126
barristers, 9, 59, 75, 78, 119, 120, 124, 169, 174, 182, 183, 198n137
Bayley, T.B., 103–4, 195n94
Beattie, J., 86, 177
Beccaria, C., 114, 115, 177
Bentham, J., 14, 105, 115
Bill of Rights, 4, 184
Black Act of 1723, 132, 144, 152, 153
Blackstone, Sir W., 8, 9, 13, 14, 35, 36, 62, 135, 137, 139, 140, 144, 18, 190n82, 195n85
  on disuse of trial by jury, 41
  investment in turnpike bonds, 226n155
  Penitentiary Act of 1779, 100, 102
  on punishment, 100
Bloody Code, 98, 99, 132, 141
Blue Books, 166
Bohun, E., 3
Bolingbroke, Lord, 133
borough courts, 18–20, 26, 56, 57, 59–62, 75, 175
  see also courts

Bow Street, 111, 113
  proto-police, 117
  stipendiary magistrates and paid constables, establishment of, 112
Brereton, C.D., 18, 195n85, 195n87
Brewer, J., 7–8
Brooks, C., 59
Bulstrode, W., 76
Burke, E., 1, 10, 134, 139–40, 147
Burn, R., 35–6, 48, 53

Camden, Lord, 136, 183
carceral regime, 103
Catholic Relief Act of 1778, 230n228
central-local relations, 15, 54–5
*certiorari*, writ of, 35, 51, 195–6n96
Chambers, R., 140
church courts, 62–3, 77, 175
  see also courts
citizenship, 15, 178, 181, 183
City Elections Act of 1725, 161, 229n214, 229n215
Cobbett, W., 50, 184
Coke, Sir E., 4, 131, 135, 139, 170, 220n37
*Colchester Chronicle*
  crime reporting, 90
Colquhoun, P., 109–11, 115
common law, 2, 7–11
  challenges to parliamentary absolutism, 128–42, 178–9
  courts, 13, 34, 136, 154
  private prosecution, 115
  rule against defense counsel, 122
  see also law
communal courts, 57
  see also courts
communal participation
  impact on indictment and presentment, 21–4
complaint
  declining access to courts, 72–80
confinement
  institutional, 101
  solitary, 100, 101, 104, 156
  see also punishment

261

consent (to government), 2, 5–6, 11, 15–16, 54, 72, 94, 97, 99, 105, 115, 129, 130, 134, 136, 137, 159, 168, 176, 177, 178, 179, 180, 181, 183
conservatives, 8, 181
Consistory Court of London, 62–3, 64, 71, 75–8, 175, 197*n*119
  defamation cases at, decline of, 76–7, 78
  *see also* courts
constables, 107, 113, 197*n*125
  distinguished from watchmen, 109
  JPs, as paid special constables, 173
  *see also* policing
contract, freedom of, 145
*Cook v. Keep*, 66–7
Cooper, S., 172
corporal punishment, 98
  *see also* punishment
corruption
  church courts', 77
  in gaols, 100, 104–5
  JPs', 47
  moral, 84, 101
  pecuniary, 35
  political, 84, 128–9, 133, 137
  thief-takers', 116
County Rates Act of 1739, 51–3, 174, 196*n*98
courts, 154–5
  appreciation of, 57–8
  borough, 18–20, 26, 56, 57, 59–62, 75, 175
  church, 62–3, 77, 175
  common law, 13, 34, 136, 154
  communal, 57
  complaints about declining access to, 72–80
  Consistory Court of London, 62–3, 64, 71, 75–8, 175, 197*n*119
  distrusted by radicals, 184
  ecclesiastical, 57, 62, 70, 75–6, 143
  guildhall, 58
  manorial, 18, 19, 58
  mayor's, 57
  *nisi prius*, 57, 66, 69, 73
  of quarter sessions *see* quarter sessions
  small-debt, 61–2, 154–5, 175
  of the University of Cambridge, 203*n*22
  Westminster, 57

Coxwell, C., 194*n*69
crime, 81–125
  poverty and, 83–4
  religious context of, 88
  reporting, 85–92, 176–7
    commodification of, 82
    *Ipswich Journal*, 89–92
    *London Journal*, 84–9
  as social problem, 83–94
  violent, 89–91
  *see also* offences; violence
'criminal conversation', 69, 78, 185
criminal law, administration of, 106–25

death sentence, 87, 96
  *see also* punishment
Declaratory Act of 1766, 137
demurrers, 75
de Veil, Sir T., 111, 117, 121
Devereaux, S., 166
Devlin, Lord, 1
Dicey, A.V., 131
Directors Act, 158
divorce *a mensa et thoro*, 75
Duckinfield, Sir C., 49
due process, 137

ecclesiastical courts, 57, 62, 70, 75–6, 143
  *see also* courts
Eden, W., 32–3, 99–103, 140–1
  and Penitentiary Act of 1779, 102–3
  on solutions to punishing crime, 101–2
Eldon, Lord Chancellor, 79
election controversy of 1769 (Middlesex), 137
enclosure, 147–50, 153, 157, 168, 170, 225*nn*130, 133, 136, 137
enclosure commissions, 149, 179
English society
  and rule of law, relationship between, 3–7
  and state, relationship between, 7–11
Enlightenment, 11–16, 82, 99, 105, 125, 179
execution, public, 97–8, 99, 212*n*96
  *see also* punishment
expression, freedom of, 13

Fielding, H., 34, 88, 94, 96, 99, 115, 117, 132–3
  on solution to punishing crime, 102
Fielding, Sir J., 111, 113, 118
Forgery Act of 1729, 144–5
Fox, C.J., 112–13, 165
frankpledge system, 98
freedom, 2, 8, 24, 51, 83, 128, 136, 156, 181
  of contract, 145
  of expression, 13
  of government, 183
  of press, 13, 184–5
  of trade, 147
French Revolution, 139

Game Act of 1770, 32, 194*n*79
Gaskill, M., 124
Gatrell, V.A.C., 107, 181
General Highway Act of 1773, 200*n*193
*Gentleman's Magazine*, 50, 143
gibbet, 6, 96
  *see also* punishment
Gibson, E., 77
Gilbert, T., 103
Gin Act of 1736, 144
Glorious Revolution of 1688, 4
Glorious Revolution of 1689, 126, 130, 136
Gordon riots of 1780, 111
Gough, J.W., 131
Gowing, L., 70, 77
*Grant v. Russell*, 64–6, 70
Great Reform Act of 1832, 181
Grose, Sir N., 182
guildhall court, 58
  *see also* courts

Hale, Sir M., 139
halter, 6
  *see also* punishment
Hanoverian regime, 115, 118
Hanway, J., 81, 101, 110
hard labour, 95, 100–2, 106, 213*n*119, 213*n*120, 224*n*108
  *see also* punishment
Hardwicke, Lord Chancellor, 9, 126, 128, 134, 135, 153, 182, 224*n*104
Harrison, C., 56
Hawkins, Sir J., 181–2, 196*n*107

Hawkins, W., 122–3
Hay, D., 182, 224*n*108
Hay, W., 144, 149
hearing, 18, 25, 32, 33, 44, 56–8, 164, 192*n*38, 216*n*199, 217*n*208
  pre-trial committal, 117–23, 178, 217*n*216
  prosecutions, magistrates' responsibility for, 8
Highways Act of 1691, 47, 219*n*6
Highways Act of 1696, 219*n*6
history, Whig, 4, 129–30
Hoare, R.C., 33
Hobbes, T., 140, 167
Holdsworth, Sir W., 15, 126, 167
Home Office, 111
Hoppit, J., 150
House of Commons, 9, 10, 22, 129, 131, 134–5, 137, 146, 149, 160–8, 170
  bill for punishing buyers and receivers of stolen goods, 89
  as 'the Common Council of the Realm', 165
  standing order of 1774, 168
  votes and proceedings of, 165–6
House of Lords, 9, 131, 135, 230*n*245
  proceedings, publishing and disseminating, 166
Howard, J., 105
  on prison reform and penitentiary movement, 100–1
Hunt, W., 32, 47
Hutton, W., 62, 154, 155

immorality, 30, 92, 93, 105
  *see also* morality
imperialism, administrative, 173–5
imprisonment, 30, 103, 112, 121, 224*n*108
  for debt, 142, 155
  with hard labour, 95, 100, 101–2, 106, 213*n*119, 213*n*120
  oppressive use of, 155
  *see also* punishment
improvement commissions, 157, 158–9, 179
indictments, 28–30, 38, 71, 82, 118, 173
Innes, J., 142, 164, 166
institutional confinement, 101
  *see also* confinement; punishment
insubordination, 88, 93, 96, 105

264 *Index*

intervention, 83, 94, 94, 95, 105, 106, 117, 134, 155, 165, 178
  administrative, 38, 41, 55, 118–19, 174
  of jury, 33
  magisterial, 150
  statutory, 178–9
*Ipswich Journal*
  crime reporting, 89–92, 93
Irish Dependency Act of 1720, 136
Isaac, R., 17

Jacobites, 84, 87
Jenkins, P., 162
Johnson, S., 140
judges, judiciary, 2, 62, 66–7
  agents of government, 11, 18
  and assizes, 18
  concerned about common law, 9
  independence of, 153, 180, 182–3
  and juries, 123–5
  and law reform, 14
  and moral panic, 89
  and popular opinion, 68–9
  and professionalization of trials, 119–20, 178
  protection of JPs, 35
  reviewing legislation 9, 135, 142
  social prejudice of, 76–7, 78–9, 106, 175–6
  and sentencing, 96, 102–3, 121
  supervision of gaols, 104
  and Transportation Act, 95
'judicialized' pre-trial committal process, development of, 117–23, 178
jurisprudence, 14, 69
jurors, 23, 24, 28, 187n18, 218n239
  active, 123–5
  and participation, 1, 5, 17, 24
  passive, 121, 123
jury, juries
  and consent, 2
  'dethronement' of, 121, 124–5
  grand, 21–2, 27, 28, 29, 36, 39, 40, 41, 51–2, 53, 89, 181, 182
  hundred, 22
  inconvenience of, 18
  petty, 21, 27
  of presentment, 20–1
  special, 78, 124
jury trial, 21, 27, 123, 173, 178, 195n85, 205n69
  discretion in, 68–9
  and misogyny, 66
  'pious perjury', 68
  restriction of, 8, 32–3, 41, 62, 128
justice, 3, 5–7, 15
  access to, 37, 57, 59, 62, 72–7, 173, 175–6
  at the discretion of a local magistrate, 33, 173
  class-bias of, 34
  and legislative process, 167–71, 179
  public, 48
  and standing army, 129
  vernacular, 30, 37, 41, 123, 124, 173
justice, administration of, 3, 52, 56
  and communal obligation, 22
  corrective mission of, 99–104, 105–6, 125, 177, 181
  'de-communalization' of, 83
  demand for, 7
  discretion in, 82
  equality in, 3–4
  and experience of authority, 5
  and legislation, 9, 94–6, 135, 141, 142, 153, 178–9
  moral synchronization of, 88
  and newspaper reporting, 87–8, 89–90, 92–3
  and participation, 11, 17, 24, 72, 77–80, 98–9, 105, 173, 176–7, 183, 184–5
  and popular culture, 5–7
  the principal part of government, 2, 9
  professionalization of, 14, 74–5, 80, 82–3, 95, 107–14, 116–21, 124–5, 177–8
  and radicals, 183–4
  reform of, 133
  and rights, 128
justices of the peace (JPs)
  administration of local government under, 24–6
  autonomy of, 33–6
  'basket-justices', 195n91
  Charles Coxwell, 194n69
  clerical, 35, 37, 49, 155, 194n69
  commission of, 20
  communal participation, impact of, 21–4
  eighteenth century, 26–41
  as courts, 19–20
  decisions over appeals on orders of removal, 44–5
  Edmund Tew as, 31

Henry Fielding as, 34
Justice Gobble, 34
Justice Swallow, 195n91
Justice Thrasher, 34
paid special constables, 173
as prefect-type administrators, 20
in quarter sessions, activities of, 173–4
  before 1680, 19–26
responsibilities of, 20
right to award costs, 32
as royal officers, 20
statutory authority of, 41, 44–55
summary conviction by, 32–5
Thomas Phipps as, 33
Thomas Stringer as, 33
trading, 34
William Hunt as, 32, 47
work, in the eighteenth century, 26–41

Kenyon, Lord Chief Justice, 78, 146–7
King, P., 90
*Knowlys v. Castleton*, 69

Lambert, S., 168
Landau, N., 31, 46, 199n160
Langbein, J., 84, 118, 119, 121
Langford, P., 1, 10, 157
  on access to status of politeness, 13
Laqueur, T., 97
law, 1–16
  artificial reason of, 139
  common, 2, 5, 8–9, 10, 11, 13, 14, 15, 19, 20, 21, 27, 32, 34, 35, 37, 41, 44, 54, 55, 58, 66, 68, 77, 94, 106, 115, 122, 125, 127, 128, 129, 132, 133, 134, 135, 136, 138, 139, 145, 146–7, 151, 153, 155, 156, 158, 171, 174, 178, 179, 183, 187n21, 220n37
  'empire of', 180–5
  imperial state at, 7–11
  labour, 180
  and moral reform, relations between, 143
  poor, 25, 44–5, 46, 47, 88, 102, 103, 133, 144, 155–9, 174, 179
  rule of, 3–7, 67, 175, 181–4
  of settlement, 44
lawyers, legal professions
  American, 136
  and ancient constitution, 130
  and committal process, 117
  and elite interests, 78–9
  government, 144
  independence of, 182–3
  and lay participation in justice, 13–14, 69, 124–5
  and legalization of courts, 74–5, 83, 178
  and legislation, 4, 8–9, 135, 166
  and parliamentary sovereignty, 137
  maximizing returns, 75, 175
  progressive, 99–100
  and prosecution of felony, 118–19
  and radicals, 79, 184
  representing felony defendants, 119–20
  in settlement cases, 45, 174
  and transformation of criminal trial, 120–1, 124, 178
  unscrupulous, 73
  and vernacular justice, 76–7
legislation, 7–11
  making, 159–71
  omnipotence, 129
  politics of, 128–42
  substance of, 142–59
legitimacy, 3–7
*levari facias*, writ of, 40
Leviathan, 22, 94, 128, 138, 140, 170
liberty, 2–4, 88, 110, 128, 133, 135, 181
Lieberman, D., 14, 150
litigants, 57, 59–61, 63, 65–8, 71–5
litigation, 56–80, 175
  complaints about declining access to courts, 72–80
  motives and meanings of, 64–72
  patterns of, 57–64
  recession in, 175–6
Lobban, M., 56, 182, 183
Locke, J., 13, 125, 130, 135
Lofft, C., 1
*London Journal*
  crime reporting, 84–9
Lowther, Sir J., 64, 65–6, 68, 73
Luttrell, T., 165

Macdonald, Sir A., 111
Madan, M., 96
magistrates
  police, 112, 113
  responsibility for hearing prosecutions, 8
  Speenhamland, 174
  stipendiary, 114, 177
  in summary proceedings, virtual autonomy of, 182

Magna Carta, 131, 133, 184
Maitland, F., 17
Mandeville, B., 64, 83–4, 96, 101, 115
manorial courts, 18, 19, 58
  see also courts
Mansfield, Lord, 35, 78, 79, 89, 124, 136, 183
Marriage Act of 1753, 134, 144, 219n6
*Marshall, Richard, R. v., et al*, 123
mayor's court, 57
  see also courts
Metropolitan Police Act of 1829, 113–14
middle-class
  consciousness, 12, 94–106
  public opinion and identity, 91
Middlesex Justice Act of 1792, 112, 113, 177
Militia Act of 1757, 134
moral panics, 185
  and crime, 83–92, 178
morality, 103, 139, 141
  see also immorality
motions, 46, 75, 78, 115, 175, 198n137, 217n208
Musson, A., 180
Mutiny Act of 1705, 188n34
Mutiny Acts, 132, 136
Mutiny Bill, 129

Neeson, J.M., 148
Nevill, H., 130
'new police, the', 107
  see also policing
newspapers
  crime reporting, 84–92, 176–7
*nisi prius*, 57, 66, 69, 73
  see also courts
North, R., 83, 126

offences
  community discretion of, 82
  private prosecution of, 82–3
  see also crime
offenders
  apprehension and conviction of, rewards for, 116–17
office of justice of the peace, 19
*Old England Journal*, 184–5
oligarchy, 66, 161
Ollyffe, G., 81, 94, 96
Onslow, Speaker, 163, 167

Paley, W., 139, 170–1
parish officers, 5, 20, 23, 38, 44, 46, 158, 159, 174, 179, 191n30, 191n96
parliament
  attack on the customs of trades, 145–7
  committees of inquiry, 164
  constitutional controversies, 130–1
  debates, reporting and publication of, 164–5
  enclosure, 147–9
  imperial, 142
  law-making, power of, 128–42, 178–9
  legislation, making, 159–71
  Leviathan, 22, 94, 128, 138, 140, 170
  newspaper reporters, admission of, 165
  papers and records of proceedings, publishing and disseminating, 165–7, 179
  petitioning, 162–4, 179
  poor law corporations, establishment of, 155–9
  private enclosure bills, 149–54, 167–8, 169
  Reformation Parliament, 129
  right to resistance, 129
  social welfare measures, 142
  sovereignty, 4, 10, 129, 130, 134–8, 140, 159, 178, 221n50
  supremacy of, 130
paternalism, 32, 78, 162
Paul, Sir G.O., 104
Payment of Costs Act of 1778, 196n98
Peel, Sir R., 113, 181
penitentiary(ies), 94–106, 125, 177
Penitentiary Act of 1779, 100, 102–3, 104, 105, 214n129
Penitentiary Houses, 100
petition(ing), 162–5, 167, 179
  campaigns, 163
  against money bills, 163
  for redress of grievances, 163
petty sessions, 18, 23, 32–3, 35, 39, 41, 45–7, 54, 173, 174, 194n73, 198n140, 198n149, 199n151, 199n160
Petyt, G., 159
Philips, D., 114
Phillips, J., 163
Phipps, T., 33
pillory, 6, 99, 212n92
  see also punishment
Pitt, N., 139
Pitt, W., 138, 182, 222n73

pleading
  repleadings, 75
  special, 75
Pocock, J.G.A., 129
Pole, J.R., 164–5
police(ing), 177–8
  constables, 107, 109, 173, 197n125
  everyday, 107–9
  initiation of prosecution proceedings, 117
  magistrates' forces, 112, 113
  Metropolitan Police, 107, 110–13
  municipal regulations or prevention/suspension of crimes, 109–10
  'new police, the', 107
  preventive, 107, 112, 114
  professional policing, development of, 106–25
  surveillance of, 114
  thief-takers, 116, 117, 119
  see also watchmen
politeness, 12–14, 176
Poor Law Amendment Act of 1834, 155
poor law corporations, 155–9
poverty and crime, 83–4
presentments, 28, 29, 38, 39–40, 50, 197nn124–6
press, freedom of, 13, 184–5
Prisoner's Counsel Act of 1836, 121
prisons
  inspection committees, 104
  new prisons, establishment of, 105–6
  reform of, 55, 100–6
Prisons Act of 1791, 104, 214n129
private enclosure bills, 149–52, 167–8, 169
privilege, 19, 65, 112, 131, 149, 167, 171
  against self-incrimination, 120
Privy Council, 11, 23, 55, 83, 146
Proclamation Society, 143
professionalization, 11, 13–14, 37–8, 52–3, 54, 74–5, 82–3, 95, 105, 107–14, 116–21, 124–5, 126, 158–9, 169, 173, 174, 175–6, 177–8, 179
prosecution
  private, 82–3, 115
    apprehension and conviction of capital offenders, rewards for, 116–17
    legal costs to prosecutors, reimbursement of, 115
  solutions, 106–25

*Public Advertiser*, 111
public opinion *see* public sphere
public sphere, 12, 13
  bourgeois, 82
  degeneracy of the common people, 83–94, 107
  growth of, 185, 234n39
punishment
  capital, 95, 96, 99, 144, 211n73
    Tyburn, 96–7, 98, 152
  confinement
    institutional, 101
    solitary, 100, 101, 104, 156
  corporal, 98
  death sentence, 87, 96
  gibbet, 6, 96
  halter, 6
  imprisonment, 30, 103, 112, 121, 224n108
    for debt, 142, 155
    with hard labour, 95, 100, 101–2, 106, 213n119, 213n120
    oppressive use of, 155
  non-capital, 103
  pillory, 6, 99, 212n92
  and popular consent, 97
  scientific, 114
  solutions, 94–106
  transportation, 89, 95, 101–3, 105, 121, 132
  as treatment, 100
  whipping, 6, 32, 33, 98–9, 102, 156, 212n92, 224

quarter sessions, 173, 175–6
  Cheshire (1678–1818), 26–41, 46, 48–52, 107, 197n125, 198n135, 200n195
    administrative business, 42–3, 49
    indictments, 28–30, 38, 173
    poaching, 32
    presentments, 28, 29, 38, 39–40, 50
    recognizances, 29, 30–2, 40, 192n37, 192n38, 198n137
  at the discretion of a local magistrate, 173
  Essex, 106
  Gloucestershire, 47
  Hampshire, 50
  Hertfordshire, 45, 50, 193n58
  JPs, activities of, 19–26
  Kent, 31
  Lincolnshire, 27, 30, 40–1

quarter sessions – *continued*
  Middlesex, 45, 76
  Nether Knutsford, 39
  Northumberland, 200*n*183
  Salford, 193*n*60
  Surrey, 106
  Wiltshire, 197

Ramsay, A., 172
Raymond, Sir R., 131
recognizances, 29, 30–2, 40, 192*n*37, 192*n*38, 198*n*137
Reeves, J., 138
Reformation Parliament, 129
  *see also* parliament
Regency Act of 1706, 130
Revolution of 1688, 135
Reynolds, T., 152, 153
right to resistance, 129
Riot Act of 1714, 132, 133, 172
riots, rioters, 6–7, 25, 28, 29, 88, 92, 93, 96, 100, 109, 111, 118, 131–2, 134, 144, 146, 148, 152–3, 156, 188*n*30
Robinson, D., 172
Rogers, N., 88, 149
Romilly, S., 99–100, 141
Royal Marriage Bill, 165
Royal Marriages Act of 1772, 221*n*41
Ryder, Sir D., 66, 67, 120

Savile, Sir G., 169, 231*n*269
Scarman, Lord, 1
Septennial Act of 1716, 131–2, 160, 161
Shaftesbury, earl of, 12–13
Shapiro, B., 125
Sharp, G., 137
Sharpe, J., 5
Shoemaker, R., 6
Sidney, A., 130
small-debt courts, 61–2, 155, 175
  commissioners, 155, 179
  *see also* courts
Smith, A., 14, 139, 145, 147, 180
Smith, B., 33, 113
Societies for the Reformation of Manners, 143
solicitor, 118–19
solitary confinement, 100, 101, 104, 156
  *see also* confinement; punishment
Somerset case (1771), 183, 185
South Sea Bubble, 84
sovereignty, 4, 10, 14, 129, 130, 134–8, 140, 159, 178, 221*n*50

Speenhamland, Berks., 50
Spitalfields Act of 1773, 145
Stamp Act of 1765, 136, 137, 143, 163
stamp duty, 75
Starkie, T., 125
state, 7–11
  development of, 7–8
  imperial, 172–85
  post-Revolution, 95
statutory commissions: *see under* enclosure commissions; improvement commissions; small-debt courts, commissioners; turnpike trusts; poor law corporations
Stone, L., 185
Stringer, T., 33
summary conviction, 8–9, 19, 20, 32–5, 36, 37, 43, 46, 47, 54, 105, 112–13, 117, 128, 141, 145, 156, 173, 182, 188*n*39, 194*n*78, 194*n*81, 195*n*85, 195*n*96, 196*n*105

taxation, 7, 51, 54, 163
Tew, E., 31–2, 37
thief-takers, 116, 117, 119
  *see also* policing
Thompson, E., 146
Thurlow, Lord Chancellor, 148, 168, 231*n*269
Tory(ies), 128, 130, 138, 181
trade, freedom of, 147
transportation, 89, 95, 101–3, 105, 121, 132
  *see also* punishment
Transportation Act of 1717, 95, 102, 132, 144
Transportation Act of 1720, 95, 132
Treasonable Practices Act of 1795, 138, 222*n*75
trial by jury, 8, 32, 41, 123, 128, 173, 178, 195*n*85, 205*n*69
  *see also* jury(ies)
Triennial Act of 1694, 131
Turner, M.E., 147–8
turnpike bills, 150–4, 168
turnpike trusts, 151, 153–4, 179
Tyburn, 96–7, 98, 152
  abolition of procession to, 98

Vagrancy Act of 1745, 196*n*98
violence, 24, 28, 76, 86, 89–91, 93, 99, 106, 118, 125
  *see also* crime

Walker, G., 5
Walpole, Sir R., 129, 132, 138, 161
  City Elections Act of 1725, 229*n*215
  Excise Bill, 163
Warburton, Sir G., 170
watchmen, 108, 109, 113
  distinguished from constables, 109
Whigs, 128, 129, 138, 181
whipping, 6, 32, 33, 98–9, 102, 156, 212*n*92, 224
  *see also* punishment

Wilberforce, W., 143
Wild, J., 87, 116, 118
witnessing, 164
Woodcock, E., 120
Wooler, T., 184
writ
  of *certiorari*, 35
  of *levari facias*, 40

Young, A., 149

Printed in Great Britain
by Amazon